MIND ASSOCIATION OCCASIONAL SERIES

IMPRESSIONS OF HUME

MIND ASSOCIATION OCCASIONAL SERIES

This series consists of occasional volumes of original papers on predefined themes. The Mind Association nominates an editor or editors for each collection, and may cooperate with other bodies in promoting conferences or other scholarly activities in connection with the preparation of particular volumes.

Publications Officer: M. A. Stewart
Secretary: B. W. Hooker

Also published in the series:

Perspectives on Thomas Hobbes
Edited by G. A. J. Rogers and A. Ryan

Reality, Representation, and Projection
Edited by J. Haldane and C. Wright

Machines and Thought
The Legacy of Alan Turing, Volume I
Edited by P. J. R. Millican and A. Clark

Connectionism, Concepts, and Folk Psychology
The Legacy of Alan Turing, Volume II
Edited by A. Clark and P. J. R. Millican

Appearance versus Reality
New Essays on the Philosophy of F. H. Bradley
Edited by Guy Stock

Knowing Our Own Minds
Edited by Crispin Wright, Barry C. Smith,
and Cynthia Macdonald

Transcendental Arguments
Problems and Prospects
Edited by Robert Stern

Reason and Nature
Essays in the Theory of Rationality
Edited by José Luis Bermúdez
and Alan Millar

Impressions of Hume

Edited by

M. FRASCA-SPADA and P. J. E. KAIL

CLARENDON PRESS · OXFORD

OXFORD

UNIVERSITY PRESS

Great Clarendon Street, Oxford OX2 6DP

Oxford University Press is a department of the University of Oxford.
It furthers the University's objective of excellence in research, scholarship,
and education by publishing worldwide in

Oxford New York

Auckland Cape Town Dar es Salaam Hong Kong Karachi
Kuala Lumpur Madrid Melbourne Mexico City Nairobi
New Delhi Shanghai Taipei Toronto

With offices in

Argentina Austria Brazil Chile Czech Republic France Greece
Guatemala Hungary Italy Japan Poland Portugal Singapore
South Korea Switzerland Thailand Turkey Ukraine Vietnam

Oxford is a registered trade mark of Oxford University Press
in the UK and in certain other countries

Published in the United States
by Oxford University Press Inc., New York

British Library Cataloguing in Publication Data

Data available

Library of Congress Cataloging in Publication Data

Data available

Typeset by Newgen Imaging Systems (P) Ltd., Chennai, India
Printed in Great Britain
on acid-free paper by
Biddles Ltd., King's Lynn, Norfolk

ISBN 0–19–925652–7   978–0–19–925652–5

1 3 5 7 9 10 8 6 4 2

PREFACE

The original occasion for most of the papers contained in this volume was the editors' wish to establish a forum where Hume scholars of various provenances and convictions could meet and discuss all matters Humean. This wish materialized in an interdisciplinary workshop, 'Hume Studies in Britain', held in Cambridge in September 2000. That first workshop was then followed by 'Hume Studies in Britain II' (Edinburgh, 2002) and III (Oxford, 2004).

The editors are grateful to all the participants in the 'Hume Studies in Britain' workshops and to the contributors to this volume. We also thank the Mind Association, the British Society for the History of Philosophy, and the International Society of Intellectual History for sponsoring our group; the Department of History and Philosophy of Science, University of Cambridge, for hosting the first meeting; Peter Momtchiloff, Jacqueline Baker, Rebecca Bryant, Rupert Cousens, and Oxford University Press for their interest and support; and Jean von Altena, who copy-edited the volume, for her invaluable assistance and insight.

The cartoon with Hume and the billiard balls is from N. Ubaldo, *Altlante illustrato di filosofia dalle origini all'era moderna*, Firenze: Giunti Gruppo Editoriale, 2002, p. 294. The editors wish to thank the Giunti Gruppo Editoriale for their kind permission to reproduce it.

The editors worked together at the planning and preparation of this volume, which has no senior editor.

CONTENTS

NOTES ON CONTRIBUTORS

MARTIN BELL is Professor of Philosophy at the Department of Politics and Philosophy at the Manchester Metropolitan University. His publications include: 'The relation between philosophical content and literary form in Hume's *Dialogues concerning Natural Religion*', *Hume Studies*, 27/2 (2001); 'Belief and instinct in Hume's First *Enquiry*', in P. J. R. Millican (ed.), *Reading Hume on Human Understanding* (Oxford, 2002); 'Hume, Hutcheson e le due specie di filosofia', in A. Santucci (ed.), *Filosofia e cultura nel Settecento britannico* (Bologna, 2000); 'Sceptical doubts concerning Hume's causal realism', in R. Read and K. Richman (eds.), *The New Hume Debate* (London, 2000); 'Relations between Deleuze, Hume and Kant', in A. Rehberg and R. Jones (eds.), *The Matter of Critique: Readings in Kant's Philosophy* (Manchester, 2000); 'Hume on superstition', in D. Z. Phillips and T. Tessin (eds.), *Philosophy of Religion and Hume's Legacy* (Basingstoke, 1999); 'Hume on causal powers: the influences of Malebranche and Newton', *British Journal for the History of Philosophy*, 5/1 (1997).

MARINA FRASCA-SPADA is an Affiliated Lecturer of the Department of History and Philosophy of Science and a Fellow of St Catharine's College, Cambridge (UK). Her publications include *Space and the Self in Hume's Treatise* (Cambridge, 1998; pbk edn. 2002) and a number of articles on various aspects of Hume's philosophy. She co-edited *Books and the Sciences in History* (with N. Jardine, Cambridge, 2000), and is co-editor of *Studies in History and Philosophy of Science*.

JAMES A. HARRIS is a Lecturer in Philosophy at the University of St Andrews. He is the author of *Of Liberty and Necessity: The Free Will Debate in Eighteenth-Century British Philosophy* (Oxford, forthcoming); and the editor of Lord Kames's *Sketches of the History of Man* (Indianapolis, forthcoming). He is currently at work on a new intellectual biography of Hume, to be published by Cambridge University Press.

SUSAN JAMES is Professor of Philosophy at Birkbeck College, University of London. Her work on early-modern philosophy includes *Passion and Action: The Emotions in Seventeenth-Century Philosophy* (Oxford, 1997) and a forthcoming book on the political philosophy of Spinoza. Her contribution to this volume is part of a larger project on the relationship between moral psychology and politics in the eighteenth century.

P. J. E. KAIL is Lecturer in Philosophy at the University of Edinburgh, and was previously a British Academy post-doctoral Research Fellow with the

Faculty of Philosophy, Cambridge, UK. His publications include *Projection and Realism in Hume* (Oxford, forthcoming), and a number of articles on Hume and on early modern philosophy.

PETER LIPTON is the Rausing Professor in History and Philosophy of Science at the Department of History and Philosophy of Science, University of Cambridge (UK). His publications include *Inference to the Best Explanation* (London, 1991; 2nd edn. 2004), and 'The epistemology of testimony', *Studies in History and Philosophy of Science*, 29/1 (1998).

SUSAN MANNING is Grierson Professor of English Literature and Director of the Institute for Advanced Studies at the University of Edinburgh. Her primary research interests lie in the fields of the Scottish Enlightenment and Scottish-American literary relations, the subjects of her books *The Puritan-Provincial Vision* (Cambridge, 1990), and the transatlantic study *Fragments of Union* (Basingstoke, 2002). She has edited the works of Henry Mackenzie, including a new edition of *Julia de Roubigné* (East Linton, 1999), Walter Scott's *Quentin Durward*, Washington Irving's *The Sketch-Book of Geoffrey Crayon, Gent.*, and Hector St. John de Crèvecoeur's *Letters from an American Farmer*. Her edition of Nathaniel Hawthorne's *The Marble Faun* for Oxford University Press was published in 2001. She is a Board Member and past President of the Eighteenth-Century Scottish Studies Society; with Dr Nicholas Phillipson, she is currently conducting a three-year research project on 'The science of man in Scotland', funded by the Leverhulme Trust.

EMILIO MAZZA teaches History of Ideas at the Libera Università di Lingue e Comunicazione IULM in Milan, where he has a research grant on 'David Hume: scepticism and modern philosophy'. He has published numerous articles on Hume and an edition and translation into Italian of Hume's *Dialogues concerning Natural Religion* (Genoa, 1996). He has edited the collections *Spinoza secondo Fénelon, Bayle, Chambers e Hume* (Milan, 1997); *Fantasmi della notte alla luce del mattino: scetticismo e filosofia moderna dall'* Art de Penser *a Hume* (Milan, 1999); and *Falsi e cortesi: pregiudizi, stereotipi e caratteri nazionali in Montesquieu, Hume e Algarotti* (Milan, 2002).

SARAH M. S. PEARSALL is a member of the Department of Modern History, University of St Andrews. Previous publications include 'Gender', in David R. Armitage and Michael Braddick, (eds.), *The British Atlantic, 1500–1800* (Basingstoke, 2002), and ' "The late flagrant instance of depravity in my family": the story of an Anglo-Jamaican cuckold', *William and Mary Quarterly*, 60 (2003). She is currently working on a book entitled *Tyranny and Sympathy: Transatlantic Family Correspondence in the Age of Revolution*.

R. M. SAINSBURY teaches at the Department of Philosophy of the University of Texas at Austin. He was Susan Stebbing Professor of Philosophy at King's College London and, from 1990 to 2000, editor of *Mind*. He has published books with the titles *Russell* (London, 1979); *Paradoxes* (Cambridge, 1988; 2nd edn. 1995); *Logical Forms* (Oxford, 1991; 2nd edn. 2000); *Departing from Frege* (London, 2002); and *Reference without Referents* (Oxford, 2004). Previous publications on Hume include 'Hume's idea of necessary connection', *Manuscrito*, 20 (1997); 'Il naturalismo di Hume', in Evandro Agazzi and Nicola Vassallo (eds.), *Introduzione al naturalismo filosofico contemporaneo* (Milan, 1998), and 'Projections and relations', in Barry Smith and Peter Menzies (eds.), *Secondary Qualities Generalized* (*The Monist*, 1998).

RICHARD SERJEANTSON is a Fellow of Trinity College, Cambridge, and is the author of a number of studies in the history of the natural and human sciences in the early modern period. He has also edited *Generall Learning: A Seventeenth-Century Treatise on the Formation of the General Scholar* by Meric Casaubon (Cambridge, 1999), a work that helps to illuminate Hume's comment in 'My own life' that he spent his early years pursuing 'philosophy and general learning'.

M. A. STEWART is Honorary Research Professor in the History of Philosophy at the Universities of Lancaster and Aberdeen, and Senior Research Fellow at Harris Manchester College, Oxford. He has published extensively on English philosophy in the seventeenth century, on Scottish and Irish intellectual history of the seventeenth and eighteenth centuries, and on philosophy in the Dissenting tradition. He is general editor of the Clarendon Locke Edition and co-editor of the Clarendon Hume. In Spring 1995 he delivered the Gifford Lectures at Aberdeen, on ' "New light" and Enlightenment'. His edited collections include *Studies in the Philosophy of the Scottish Enlightenment* (Oxford, 1990) and, with John P. Wright, *Hume and Hume's Connexions* (Edinburgh, 1994).

Introduction

MARINA FRASCA-SPADA AND P. J. E. KAIL

———•———

Hume's thought and works have made different impressions in the different areas of literacy, historical, and philosophical investigation represented in this volume. Thus his writings can be taken as transparent vehicles for philosophical intuitions, problems, and arguments that are still at the centre of philosophical reflection today. On the other hand, there are readings that try to locate Hume's views against the background of concerns, debates, and discussions of his own time. And this is not all. Hume's texts may be read as highly sophisticated literary-cum-philosophical creations: in such cases, the reader's attention tends to be directed at issues of genre and persuasive strategies rather than philosophical questions and arguments. Or they may be regarded as moments in the construction of the ideology of modernity, and as contributions to the legitimation of a given social order. As the true classics that they are, Hume's works are typical 'open texts', in which readers keep finding an ever new and varied bounty of inspirations. It is the editors' conviction that the borders between these approaches are far from neat; and that as much trespassing as possible is to be promoted. The volume that we present here offers a range of such approaches and interests.

We start with M. A. Stewart's article, which is a biographical and intellectual reconstruction of Hume's career, from his entering the College of Edinburgh at the age of 10 to the completion of his main philosophical writings thirty years later. Much of the emphasis is on the hitherto under-researched earlier part of this period; and the result challenges much of the present literature both on Hume's biography and on the relative weight we should assign to his different philosophical writings. In the first two sections, this article offers a detailed picture of the intellectual scene which would have met a young student starting to attend the College. It then moves on to examine the documentary traces of the young Hume's presence at Edinburgh, assessing them against remarks which Hume scattered throughout his work, to tease out what exactly and how he is likely to have been taught. There follows a fresh look at Hume's correspondence and early writing, and an assessment of his likely range of readings and conversations, philosophical or otherwise, with friends and correspondents. The article concludes with a discussion of the projects Hume was entertaining around the time of the publication of the *Treatise*, and of how he revised his plans and adjusted his interests in the post-*Treatise* period. Throughout Stewart emphasizes the need for caution in weighing the evidence, including that supplied by Hume himself. His 'thick descriptions' establish a seamless continuity between life and thought, and restore to us the author of the *Treatise* as a compellingly concrete intellectual and human presence.

But there are other ways in which Hume is a lively presence for us. Peter Lipton's contribution is a good expression of how questions that emerge from Hume's writings and, in turn, Hume's own position are taken up by those who are first and foremost concerned with philosophical problems rather than the history of philosophy. Hume was an original source for Lipton's own interest in the subject. What is interesting here is to see a philosopher reflect again on his forebear. Lipton offers a hypothesis about why Hume was the first major thinker to formulate the famous problem of induction. Certainly, according to Lipton, induction had attracted some sceptical attention, but this was due mainly to a general sceptical thesis: namely, the underdetermination of theory by data. Hume's contribution, says Lipton, was to shift the focus from the deliverances of induction to the methods and presuppositions themselves. Part, but only part, of this shift has to do with Hume's abandonment of an epistemology which gives demonstration pre-eminence, and with his rejection of the view that the con-nection between cause and effect is intelligible to us. But Hume's scepticism is ultimately located in his naturalism about the mind and in what Lipton calls the 'ubiquity' of induction: namely, in Hume's idea that the only source for any unobserved 'matter of fact' is inductive inference.

What Lipton reflects on, Mark Sainsbury exhibits: his paper shows how Hume's thoughts about cause and effect continue to play a central role in contemporary metaphysical discussions. Sainsbury starts with what is known as Hume's 'second definition', and finds in it a definition not of causation *per se*, but of causal belief. Sainsbury then distinguishes between implicit and explicit causal beliefs, where, roughly, the former can be possessed by creatures who lack the concept of causation (allowing, as Hume does, for animals to have causal beliefs), and a more sophisticated way of having the belief which does involve possession of the concept. Thinking of the second definition as a definition of causal belief allows us to combine a reductionism about the metaphysics of causation (roughly, singular causal relations are particular events subsumed under a regularity, in the spirit of Hume's first definition) with a projectivist account of the modal aspect of causal belief. What Hume's second definition captures is a *mode* of belief in a constant conjunction. There is not here a distinct modal *content* to causal belief, but instead a difference in the way in which the constant conjunction is viewed. This proposal, which bears affinities to the views of Frank Ramsey and, more recently, Simon Blackburn, is then given more detailed investigation. Concentrating on the mode of belief distinctive of causal generalizations, rather than of singular causal transactions, Sainsbury considers how the contrast between causal and accidental generalizations can be drawn in terms of a difference not in content or in the kind of facts affirmed, but in the mode of belief. To believe in causal mode is to be in the 'grip' of the regularity, but this is not so for the accidental mode of believing. Sainsbury's investigations are at once hopeful and negative: the prospects for drawing the distinction in terms of Hume's second definition look bleak, but the general project seems more promising if we think in terms of modes of belief having different degrees of modal resilience. The brilliance of Hume's second definition is therefore, as Sainsbury concludes, in its being the (brilliant, if incorrect) answer to a brilliant new question.

In different ways, both Lipton and Sainsbury attend strictly to philosophical content, examining Hume's ideas from the perspective of current philosophical concerns. The philosophical substance of Hume's work is also the focus of Martin Bell's study, which takes Deleuze's critique of Hume as an occasion to reflect on the relation between philosophy and its history. Kant's view of empiricism, according to Deleuze, fails to capture a distinctly Humean thought: namely, that in addition to mere experience, association of ideas is required for thought, and centrally for beliefs about the external world and the self, and so in some sense there must be 'synthesis' as well as mere 'experience' for Hume as well as for Kant. Bell considers Deleuze's own characterization of what makes Hume an empiricist, which rests on Hume's treatment of *relations*. Deleuze says that any theory is 'non-empiricist' in so far as it holds that '*in one way or another*, relations are derived from the nature of things'. Hume is an empiricist in so far as for him relations are not derived from the nature of things. Here the principles of association make their appearance, determining 'natural relations' among ideas. These relations do not depend on the 'qualities of the ideas themselves', but are 'the effects of the principles of human nature'. More provocatively, even the four philosophical relations which depend 'solely on the ideas' (resemblance, proportion in quantity and number, degrees in quality, and contrariety) are not 'derived from the nature of things'. Although these relations are said to be discovered by comparison, they are also said to 'arise merely from the comparison' itself. This is a crucial move: 'discovered' sounds epistemic, of ideas standing in relations that are 'there anyway'; but even these relations are imposed on inchoate experience, a view that sounds quite Kantian. A related form of empiricism makes its presence felt in Hume's emphasis on passion and affect, and Bell connects this briefly with Hume's distinction between personal identity 'as it regards our thought and imagination' and 'as it regards our passions'. Viewed as the former, there is nothing but distinct perceptions, and any relation is 'external'; but viewed as the latter, there is activity and concern. In the final section of the paper, he turns to

Deleuze's 'transcendental empiricism'—an apparent oxymoron. But this stance concerns the source of relations holding among experiences, and for Deleuze's Kant the issue turns on whether the relations are empirical or non-empirical in Deleuze's sense. For this Kant, the twist is that relations among experiences derive from the 'nature of things' in a sense that the ultimate source is the transcendental subject. This rethinking of Kant, suggests Bell, both offers a different perspective on Hume and the relation of his thought to Kant's and widens our view of Hume's legacy to philosophy beyond the analytic tradition.

Two contributions, Susan James's and Peter Kail's, discuss aspects of Hume's thought in light of his reading of Nicolas Malebranche. The importance of Malebranche's writings as background to Hume's reflection is increasingly acknowledged in philosophical and historical-philosophical studies of Hume. James adds further evidence for this by comparing aspects of Malebranche's treatment of the passions, in particular of esteem and contempt, with Hume's own views expressed in Book II of the *Treatise*. She discusses Malebranche's complex theory of the passions, and shows how it is taken up and modified by Hume. Some of Hume's alterations are, James suggests, markers for the different political structures that each account of the passions serves to legitimate. In Malebranche's account, pride and esteem work so as to be subservient to hierarchical societies, thus reflecting the absolutism that marks seventeenth-century France. For Hume, by contrast, pride, admiration, and contempt are checked by the operation of sympathy. In this way love and compassion come to play a more prominent role in the Humean psychological economy, which leads to an investment in common good fortune.

Kail devotes his paper to a fascinating and ambiguous page of Hume, the conclusion of Book I of the *Treatise*, and reads it as a point-by-point response to Malebranche. His purpose is to foreground once more the primacy of ethical concerns in Hume's philosophical work. Here Kail considers not only Malebranche's major and best-kown work, *De la Recherche de la vérité*, but also his *Traité de morale*. Malebranche is, together with Pascal, the ideal representative of that Christian ethic which regards as the purpose of human life the enhancement of man's similarity to God. To this purpose, it sets human rationality against human nature, and preaches the promotion of the former by means of the mortification and denial of the latter. Famously inspired by Malebranchean analyses of perception and of the ideas of cause and effect, Hume is, however, repelled by this ethic, against which he reacts very strongly. The conclusion of Book I is an expression of that reaction. The philosophy 'in a careless manner' which Hume advocates, apparently shallowly, is in fact, if read against Malebranche's ethical theory, the outcome of Hume's firm ethical commitment to human nature and to the defence of a humane moral philosophy against the artificiality of 'monkish' virtues. So Malebranche embarks on his search after truth because he follows St Augustine in identifying truth with God himself. And Hume reflexively puts forward a typically down-to-earth and naturalistic alternative: we search after truth because we draw pleasure from hunting that particular sort of quarry. The unexpected conclusion of this close textual reading is the identification of a parallel between Hume's discussion of curiosity and the love of truth in terms of the pleasures of hunting, and the Nietzschean condemnation of the 'ascetic ideal'.

A reassessment of Hume and religion is also at the centre of James Harris's contextual study. A popular understanding of Hume on religion is that he argues for an enlightened atheism by showing that there can be no rational grounds for the existence of God. In its simplest version, this reading faces some textual and contextual obstacles. Hume was no doubt familiar with strains of religious thinking, such as fideism and Calvinism, which quite readily admit, and even embrace, reason's impotence in religious matters. Reason is one thing, faith quite another. This contextual fact needs to be borne in mind when considering the textual facts. For there are a number of places where Hume seems to suggest that faith has the upper hand, and that scepticism is 'the first and most essential step towards being a sound, believing Christian'. Such remarks are most often read as heavy-handed irony. Harris articulates a more interesting hypothesis. He takes the Calvinist rhetoric in the First *Enquiry* as his focus and, building on work by M. A. Stewart, locates its place in Hume's response to his rejection for the Chair at Edinburgh. It is now known that the main opposition to Hume came not from the old guard, but from the more moderate thinkers, Hutcheson among them; and the First *Enquiry* should be seen in part as a response to them. Harris thinks that Hume's talk of faith is an element of that response. For the moderates, the traditional doctrines of Calvinism, that human reason had been ruined by the Fall, and that faith, and faith alone, is the route to salvation, needed to be superseded by a natural theology and a more optimistic view of reason's scope. Hume's sceptical philosophy sets itself against the optimism of the kind of natural religion which seeks to prove that this is the best of all possible worlds. In offering Calvinist rhetoric in conjunction with his own sceptical broadsides, Hume presents his philosophy as more amenable to Christianity than that of his opponents, and inserts himself into the eighteenth-century debate between the moderate and orthodox wings of the Church of Scotland. None of this means that Hume actually endorses Calvinism, as Harris is very careful to emphasize— indeed, the article closes with a caution against trying to determine what Hume's personal attitude to religion really was.

Marina Frasca-Spada's contribution considers in tandem Hume's *Treatise* and Charlotte Lennox's *The Female Quixote*, a novel of 1752, whose central character, Arabella, has a view of the world derived solely from seventeenth-century French heroic romances. As a consequence, she is unaware of any difference between real life and romantic fiction. Reading the *Treatise* in the company of *The Female Quixote* situates Hume's notorious discussion of belief and its relation to vivacity and 'feeling' against the background of the eighteenth-century culture of sentiment. Hume's reflections on the different feelings and judgements involved in reading history and fiction are thus illumined by, and of a piece with, his remarks on female readers and with contemporary authors' reflections on the impact of books on their different readerships. One of the interesting issues to emerge from this concerns Hume's use of idea as mental object and idea as act of the mind. Enthralling romances may produce very vivid ideas, but not the attitudes associated with beliefs; beliefs are, in the first instance, accounted for in terms of 'manners of conception' or acts of the mind. However, further complications and causes can enter here, and it is not so easy to distinguish true belief from mere liveliness of content—as Frasca-Spada's discussion of the solution of Arabella's case then goes on to illustrate—when 'folly', 'madness', and Quixotic confusion need to be corrected by resorting to 'general rules' and sociability.

Hume's remarks on 'general rules' and his pragmatics of the understanding have recently become the object of increasing attention in Hume scholarship. R. Serjeantson considers them against the background of a dissatisfaction with regard to human nature and human understanding which characterizes philosophy in the seventeenth century. This is the dissatisfaction—variously expressed from Bacon and Descartes to the Port-Royalists and Malebranche to Leibniz and Locke—with the traditional discipline of logic in the face of contemporary developments in the investigations of nature. Within this frame of reference, Hume's rules belong with the attempts to give a less 'artificial' account of the reasoning process, more in tune with the intellectual character of the recent 'experimental natural philosophy'. Hume's approach does, however, have its own distinctive features. The most characteristic is his denial of a clear-cut distinction between the rules which obtain in natural philosophy and those appropriate for the study of human nature and human society. The continuity between the two realms means that the investigation of natural phenomena is guided by the same kind of mental (logical) processes as that of moral and political phenomena. As a result of Serjeantson's reconstruction, Hume's general rules turn out to be crucial to define the distinctive nature and tasks of philosophy. Indeed, it is in the very ability to unify our inevitably fragmented experience by extracting rules from it that Hume singles out the difference between the philosopher—natural and moral—and the 'vulgar'. Moreover, these rules, which turn out to be of such fundamental theoretical importance in the abstract reasonings of the *Treatise*, reappear again, in applied forms, in Hume's political essays, in his historical writing, and in his essays in criticism. The historian of ideas is thus able to identify a deeper unity in Hume's varied intellectual enterprises.

Serjeantson locates Hume's views of general rules within a fascinating history of ideas developed over two centuries across many countries. Emilio Mazza's essay considers Hume's approach to religion and to the general task of philosophy in light of his philosophical temperament, his scepticism and its mitigations, and does so from a very specific and individual standpoint by exploring in close and colourful detail an episode in the reception of Hume. The main character of Mazza's series of Humean vignettes is Alessandro Verri, a young and lively Italian traveller to Paris and London in 1766–8, who was later to become one of the major figures of the Enlightenment in eighteenth-century Milan. In the course of his journeys Alessandro described, in his frequent letters to his older brother Pietro, his curiosities, excitement, and discoveries—in particular, Mazza highlights for us his disillusion with Paris and the French thinkers and his subsequent love affair with London and the English. In Alessandro Verri's letters the irritation with the more extreme and flamboyant attitudes of the Parisian *philosophes* on matters of politics and religion is combined with frustration at the quarrels and rivalries within his own cultural milieu. In this way Hume's dispute with Rousseau became, to Alessandro's eyes, a counterpart, or even a kind of amplification, of his own row with Cesare Beccaria. It is in this context that he ended up developing his own interpretation of Hume's mitigated scepticism as a mild, indeed as he put it as a 'meek', alternative to what he perceived as the intellectual pushiness and aggression of the French. According to Mazza, Alessandro's reading of Hume's views on religion and on the manner in which such matters as religion should be discussed casts a new light on Hume's famous denial of ever having met an atheist, on his underlying attitude to religious belief, and indeed, on his philosophy itself as a style of life and thought. It is also telling about the ways in which that philosophy is apt to be appropriated—by philosophers and historians of philosophy today as it was, yesterday, by the French *philosophes* and by such Enlightened Milanese as the Verri brothers.

Susan Manning's essay is devoted to uncovering ideological elements in Hume's theorizing by means of analysis of his language in the *Treatise*. She starts from his view of the self as a 'bundle' or 'heap' of unconnected perceptions. In the *Treatise* Hume famously used the classical image of a 'republic' as a metaphor for the self: in both cases the changes in personnel/ perceptions are smooth enough to allow our imagination to construct the notion of an underlying continuity. And this accounts for our tendency to think of each of them as a union above and beyond all turn-over in the elements constituting them. This metaphor is revealing of the more comprehensive presence in the *Treatise* of a reflection on notions of unity, divisibility, and fragmentation. It also alerts us to the frequent presence in Hume's philosophical prose of political language and images hidden or disguised under a psychological and epistemological veneer. In this sense Hume's philosophy is to be regarded as a crucial genealogical moment of the ideological reflection on union and connection which is characteristic of eighteenth- and nineteenth-century Scottish and American literary texts as well as in contemporary political rhetoric. And in this respect the *Treatise* itself is, in Manning's view, a particularly powerful expression of the concern with those ideas of integration and disintegration with regard to crucial matters of selfhood and nationhood, but expressed in the abstract and apparently neutral language of metaphysical elaboration on the nature and composition of the physical world. It is also Hume's unified, systematic presentation of his philosophical thought, and expresses the individualism and solitariness of his analytic phase—Hume's Shandean phase, so to speak. That thought was subsequently fragmented by Hume when it was presented in the socialized and 'conversable' form of communication of the essays; and in his *History* the unifying mode is clearly prevalent. The *Treatise*'s legacy of anxieties in the face of the risk of disintegration can still be traced, however, both in the opposition it aroused in the Common Sense philo-sophers, and in the literary production of Enlightenment Scotland and in Scottish Romanticism.

Sarah Pearsall's article is concerned with a fundamental stage in the construction of views of marriage, gender, and authority: the passage from marriage viewed as a contract to marriage as an intimate mutual friendship. The theme is how the moral-philosophical language of sympathy, sensibility, and sentiment was used and altered in the course of concrete negotiations in cases of marital disagreement. A concrete individual life story is set along-side contemporary theoretical elaborations: the transatlantic correspon-dence of an American couple discussing, after the Revolution, plans for their common future—where should they settle? The ways in which the two spouses negotiate their different views and aspirations are examined along-side Locke's political treatises, Hutcheson's moral writings, and Hume's essay 'On marriage', casting light on the theories' impact on contemporary lives, and thus throwing their features and their limitations into particularly sharp relief. Pearsall bridges the gap between the views of Hume *qua* moral philosopher and the concrete problems and life experiences of his contemporaries.

Our agenda was to assemble a cornucopia of varied Humean traces and 'impressions' of Hume. Yet, as is probably already evident from this introduction, it is easy to identify some recurrent themes. For example, in their different ways the essays by Serjeantson, Frasca-Spada, and Kail all involve attention to the issue of 'general rules' and the pragmatics of belief, which is also central to Sainsbury's analysis. Stewart and Serjeantson go in different, but complementary, directions from a common interest in Hume's early philosophical training; and both, together with Lipton, discuss Hume's reaction to traditional logic. Hume's attitude to religion attracts new approaches in the papers by Mazza and Harris. Several papers share a preoccupation with the task which Hume attributed to philosophical reflection—for instance Kail, Serjeantson, and Mazza. Many of them concentrate on the more abstruse and challenging text of the *Treatise*, even though most of them refer often to Hume's other philosophical and historical works for comparison or confirmation—witness Stewart, Bell, Manning, and James. The ideological import of Hume's work and figure runs through the papers by Manning, Pearsall, and James. Most of the papers combine the attention to a fine-grained location of Hume's work against the culture of his time and place with the provision of a better understanding or further appreciation of its philosophical significance. And taken as a whole, they show the endless fascination of Hume's writing and thought.

Hume's Intellectual Development, 1711–1752

M. A. STEWART

―――――•――――

I

1. The human mind is endowed by its creator with such extensive faculties that, if it would use the same aright, it could both know and delight in God himself. So that it may indeed attain this felicity that consists in the enjoyment of the creator, it has very many gifts vouchsafed to it, natural and supernatural alike, by which it may recognize its duty and learn to persist in a right course.

2. *Supernatural gifts* are the light of revelation delineated on the sacred page, and the inward aid of divine grace through which we are directed and assisted in understanding external revelation and observing its precepts. They are the foundation of *theology* properly speaking; for theology is the knowledge contended for by the light of revelation, that leads to felicity.

3. *Natural gifts* are the powers and faculties that humans are born with, along with diverse works, as much of creation as of divine providence, by which almighty God makes manifest in some degree to human minds the knowledge of himself and of human duty.

4. Such, in truth, are the faculties of human beings, and such the works of God, that when these have been duly reflected upon and properly attended to, more things about God and about the duty of humans towards God, self, and other humans come to be known without any positive and external revelation; and the knowledge acquired by these helps is called *philosophy*. Philosophy is the certain and evident knowledge of matters both divine and human that can be procured by a human being through the light of nature.

If this is converted back into the undistinguished Latin of which it is an approximate translation, we probably have here the first words of philosophy that Hume would have heard as a student at the College of Edinburgh.[1] In the first hour on the first day of his first philosophy class it would have

<hr/>

[1] 'Institutiones Logicae a Domino Collino Drummond Dictitatae. Anno. 1723': National Library of Scotland (hereafter NLS), MS 3938, pp. 1–3. This is a fair copy of dictates taken in the session 1722–3; I am grateful to Alexander Broadie for comments on my translation. Charles Echelbarger's discussion of the same document in 'Hume and the logicians', in P. A. Easton (ed.), *Logic and the Workings of the Mind* (Atascadero, Calif.: Ridgeview, 1997), 137–51, came to my notice when I was revising this chapter for publication. It is useful, if not entirely reliable.

been drummed into him that our mental faculties are there to bring us to the knowledge of God and our duty. We have a set of dictates recorded by Alexander Boswell, father of James Boswell the diarist, a year before Hume attended. Boswell senior was at this time neither a good note-taker nor a good Latinist, although he was to acquire textual skills later.[2] Five years older than Hume, he had repeated the first two years of study. We can, however, confirm his account from another document of uncertain provenance and date from the same course, which records slightly more of the syllabus than survives in Boswell's transcription. It does so in question-and-answer instead of narrative form.[3] This doubtless reflects the way in which students would subsequently be tested on the content of the dictations, but it is stated to have been 'composed' by their 'most learned' professor, who is called its 'author'. It may therefore have been circulated for them to copy and memorize. When one sees the questions and answers on the page, the memorizable structure is striking—not least, a tendency for a topic to divide, and divide again, until it has been explored through all its parts. The testing proceeds almost phrase by phrase, regardless of banality.

The mission of education in Hume's day was to train students for virtuous living in a society regulated by religious observance.[4] This had long been the case, although the political and theological conceptions associated with the mission changed over time. The student would take the professor's *Prooemium* in his stride, because it involved little more than the initial moves of the Single Catechism that he would know by heart. The end of man, he would already have learnt, 'is to glorifie God, and to enjoy him for ever'. The Scriptures 'teach what man is to believe concerning God, and what duty God requires of man'. God 'executeth his decrees in the works of Creation and Providence'. The work of creation is 'Gods making all things of nothing, by the Word of his Power, in the space of six days, and all very Good', and the works of providence are 'his most holy, wise, and powerful preserving, and governing all his creatures, and all their actions'.[5] Moving on, at college if not before, to the full Westminster Confession, he would learn that the light of nature affords some further degree of revelation.

---

[2] James Boswell, *Journal of a Tour to the Hebrides with Samuel Johnson, LL.D.* (London, 1785), at 2 Nov. 1773, recalling his father's studies at Leiden.

[3] 'Compendium logicae Authore Domino Drummond': Edinburgh University Library (hereafter EUL), MS 2651.

[4] Richard B. Sher, 'Professors of virtue: the social history of the Edinburgh moral philosophy chair in the eighteenth century', in M. A. Stewart (ed.), *Studies in the Philosophy of the Scottish Enlightenment* (Oxford: Clarendon Press, 1990), 87–126.

[5] *The Confession of Faith, together with the Larger and Shorter Catechisms* (1648), 5th edn. (London, 1717), 282, 284. In a letter to James Edmonstoune in 1757, Hume spoke flippantly of targeting 'the Lord's Prayer & the Ten Commandments & the Single Cat' which were commonly issued together as the ordinary parishioner's moral vade-mecum: see Raymond Klibansky and Ernest C. Mossner (eds.), *New Letters of David Hume* (Oxford: Clarendon Press, 1954) (hereafter *New Letters*), 43, with erroneous annotation. The 'Single' Catechism was the Shorter Catechism issued without biblical notes.

It may still surprise us that what I have provided was the preface to the *logic* course, as taught by the Professor of Logic and Metaphysics, Colin Drummond. In fact, virtually any eighteenth-century college course might in principle be promoted for its supposed relevance to our eternal good.[6] Having distinguished those gifts that come to us by direct revelation from those that do not—while still emphasizing the religious relevance of those that do not—Drummond proceeded to stress our limitations for the philosophical enterprise in a way that continues the moral message:

The imperfection and blindness of fallen humanity are so great that, no less in the understanding of the principles themselves than in the deducing of propositions from them, they too often sink in error.[7]

This becomes the justification for the teacher–pupil relationship and a pitch for students' fees:

The talented in every age have derived payment for their pains in transmitting certain rules and precepts by which deficiencies in knowledge, and errors in the knowledge of things, may be uncovered and thereby avoided and corrected.

The course continued with an account of logic as the 'system' of these rules and precepts, reached through a study of the 'operations of the mind' employed in the attainment of truth. Anyone hoping to detect here the glimmerings of a Humean philosophy in the making will, however, be disappointed. The professor meant by the operations of the mind only the three traditional functions of apprehension, judgement, and *discursus*—'discourse' in the old sense of the act of being discursive or thinking sequentially—that Hume would later contest in discussing the nature of belief in the *Treatise*.[8] Discourse is defined and illustrated through a religious example: from judging that 'that which is best is to be loved above all' and that 'God is best', we infer that 'God is to be loved above all'. Drummond's account is almost entirely scholastic: almost, because he does allow that others employ, and he himself occasionally employs, the post-scholastic term 'idea' as an alternative to 'apprehension' and 'notion'. He is, however, critical of the usage, arguing that while all ideas are apprehensions, not all apprehensions are ideas. He rejects, in effect, Locke's category of ideas of reflection, arguing that the mind's acts are known to itself directly just by being internal or 'intimate' to it, without need of any 'vicarious' representation that he believes is the distinctive function of ideas.[9] Nor does he pursue the theory of ideas as far

---

[6] The same volume that contains the question-and-answer version of Drummond's course includes, in the same hand, transcriptions of both logic and mathematics lectures from Marischal College, Aberdeen, dated 1725. Colin MacLaurin addressed his mathematics students at Aberdeen in terms similar to those I have just quoted.   [7] 'Institutiones', p. 3.

[8] Hume, *A Treatise of Human Nature* (1739–40), I. iii. 7 (footnote), a passage that would attract the criticism of Thomas Reid, e.g. *Essays on the Intellectual Powers of Man*, ed. Derek Brookes and Knud Haakonssen (Edinburgh: Edinburgh University Press, 2002), 24–7, 290–3.

[9] 'Institutiones', pp. 6–7. Cf. John Locke, *An Essay Concerning Human Understanding* (1690), II. i. 4; II. vi–vii.

as someone would who had taken on board the main lines of the Cartesian revolution, for he equally rejects that there is a fourth study: namely, 'method'. There is nothing to the much-vaunted method, he argues (and here we must switch to the other transcription to complete the picture), other than apprehension, judgement, and discourse. Of course, we could argue with hindsight that Drummond's distancing himself from the way of ideas was a sign of discernment rather than reaction, but Hume at least would not have come to think so.

With the preliminaries in place, Hume's studies settled to a conservative routine of scholastic logic and semantics. An aura of sanctity, or sanctimony, still hung over the class. The theory of simple apprehension is extended to a theory of signs, illustrated by the sign function of baptism and communion, the two sacraments recognized by Protestants. Singular terms are illustrated by the names of the Apostles, and the predicables (genus, species, differentia, etc.) by the attributes of the Apostles. Whether we suppose that the long tradition of building logic-book examples round the names of Peter, Paul, James, and John is to direct young minds to simple Bible history, or to cash in on their already existing knowledge, it clearly has the function of reinforcing biblical instruction. In the theory of judgement, the nature of propositions is illustrated with improving sentiments such as 'It is not wealth but virtue that renders a person blessed'. In the protracted explanation of syllogism, the necessary relationship of conclusion to premises is extolled, and there is an enunciation of both narrative and mnemonic rules. But the presentation also follows tradition in being peppered with examples of which a fair number point some redeeming lesson in the spirit of the times:

> Every evil is to be avoided.
> Every vice is evil.
> Therefore every vice is to be avoided.

> No sins are permitted.
> Some actions are permitted.
> Therefore some actions are not sins.

> No spirit is mortal.
> Every soul is a spirit.
> Therefore no soul is mortal.

> Every body is extended.
> No spirit is extended.
> Therefore no spirit is a body.

Within flexible limits, each professor determined the details of his own syllabus. We should not, therefore, infer too hastily from one person's syllabus to a contemporary's without evidence; more importantly, we should not do it across generations or across institutions. There is little sign that Hume's teacher introduced any significant post-scholastic elements into his teaching.[10] One piece of evidence is, however, ambiguous: an autobiographical retrospect on his education set down by Alexander Boswell's younger brother, John, in 1733.[11] John Boswell had followed Drummond's course three years after Hume. The professor still taught his own 'small Compend of Logics', which seems to be an allusion to the manuscript manual ascribed to him under that title. Boswell also testifies, however, that Drummond made use of Jean le Clerc's *Logica* in his class. Assuming that this was in use three years earlier—a reasonable assumption, since few teachers changed their routines, and Drummond lacked any pioneering spirit—it would probably be the most up-to-date thing that Hume encountered on the course. It was a post-Cartesian text of a kind, offering a Protestant counterweight to Port-Royal's *L'Art de penser*. There has been no adequate study of Le Clerc's work, the first edition of which (Amsterdam, 1692) was dedicated to Robert Boyle, to whom Le Clerc appears to owe his concept of 'sensible qualities'. After Boyle's death it was re-dedicated to their common friend, Locke. Locke's *Essay* is commended in the preface, but this seems to be based on Le Clerc's acquaintance with the abstract that he himself published in *Bibliothèque universelle et historique* in 1688. Where Le Clerc goes beyond Port-Royal, his main debt is to Malebranche; only in the fairly free-floating opening chapter on 'ideas' does he owe much to Locke—but equally much, one might argue, to Port-Royal.[12]

The likeliest explanation for the appearance of Le Clerc's text on Drummond's syllabus is that it served as a foil to his own instruction, given that both versions of the class dictates are geared to resisting Cartesian and post-Cartesian innovation. Drummond was a ruling elder in the Kirk, and Robert Wodrow recorded his reputation for 'gravity'.[13] Le Clerc's Remonstrant theology always bothered the orthodox: at one point he illustrates the power of demonstration by claiming to prove that on a pre-destinarian theory God must be unjust.[14] Drummond would not have been alone in his opposition. John Loudon, a more progressive teacher who taught a logic of 'ideas' at Glasgow, had condemned 'what Le Clerk teacheth De Scientiâ, Fide & Opinione inter se collatis', citing this to illustrate

---

[10] This was recognized by Alexander Grant, *The Story of the University of Edinburgh during its First Three Hundred Years*, 2 vols. (London: Longmans, Green, 1884), ii. 328. Later attempts to credit Drummond with a more advanced syllabus appeal to the fact that all the philosophy professors six years later subscribed to Pemberton's epitome of Newton. That only shows the success of an effective subscription agent operating in the College.

[11] Joy Pitman, 'The journal of John Boswell: Part I', *Proceedings of the Royal College of Physicians of Edinburgh*, 20 (1990): 67–77, at p. 69. A photocopy of the manuscript is held in the RCPE library, Boswell Family Papers, box 1, folder 4. I amend Pitman's transcriptions where necessary.

[12] For another recent perspective on Le Clerc, see Paul Schuurman, 'The empiricist logic of ideas of Jean le Clerc', in W. van Bunge (ed.), *The Early Enlightenment in the Dutch Republic, 1650–1750* (Leiden: Brill, 2003), 137–53.

[13] Robert Wodrow, *Analecta*, 4 vols. (Edinburgh: Maitland Club, 1842–3), iii. 515.

[14] Joannes Clericus, *Logica, ontologia, et pneumatologia*, 4th edn. (Cambridge, 1704), IV. vi. 13.

recent logics 'industriously stuff'd with doctrines of a very dangerous tendency . . . & examples apt enough to make a bad impression on the minds of Youth'.[15] Nevertheless, if we compare Drummond's dictates with others, the contrast is striking. A different Edinburgh teacher, William Law, more than twenty years earlier had presented a more Cartesian logic and had extended the theory of ideas to embrace some Lockean concepts, including the language of primary and secondary qualities.[16] But only after Hume's attendance did Locke formally enter the curriculum under Drummond's successor.

As for the metaphysics section of the syllabus, John Boswell tells us that the *Ontologia* of Gerhard de Vries was Drummond's textbook, rather than the continuation of Le Clerc. That means he taught the conventional metaphysics of the day, built round the traditional concepts of being and substance, essence and existence, individual and universal, quality and relation, as presented by 'the hammer of the Cartesians'. This is compatible with the anti-Cartesian tenor of the logic teaching. Boswell recorded that the subject in Drummond's hands was 'a pedantic insipid thing' and that 'there were but few or none' who were attracted to it. A degenerate form of disputation was still part of the routine.

Mr Drummond did not manage them with spirit enough, we had no public impunging (*sic*) of Theses save only in our own Class where there was so little Care taken that the students often gott one-another's Thesese's to read.

The love of Drummond's life was not logic but Greek, and when the Greek chair fell vacant in 1729, he transferred to it.

II

We must now put this into context. Although details of the Edinburgh curriculum and Hume's presumed attendance are patchy, what we have cannot be ignored if we are to dispel some prevalent misunderstandings in the secondary literature. Hume signed the matriculation register, as an earnest of serious intentions, on 27 February 1723, aged 11.[17] Such signing is not to be confused with his arrival. Edinburgh students lived in the city, and often

[15] Glasgow University Archives 43228. For an example of a Glasgow student who published a dissertation critical of Le Clerc close to this time, see William Smith, *Dissertatio philosophica inauguralis de natura spirituum* (Glasgow, 1714). Smith was a friend of Francis Hutcheson, went into the book trade, moved from Dublin to Amsterdam, and would figure in Hume's correspondence in 1740. Hume's *Treatise* and *Abstract* were sent to him to secure a review in the *Bibliothèque raisonnée* facilitated by Hutcheson. See J. Y. T. Greig (ed.), *The Letters of David Hume*, 2 vols. (Oxford: Clarendon Press, 1932) (hereafter *Letters*), i. 37, with erroneous annotation.

[16] 'Systema philosophiae, a Gulielmo Law Philosophiae professore in Academia Edinburgena', transcribed by Daniel Campbell (1699): NLS, MS 183.

[17] Matriculation register, 1704–62: EUL, shelfmark Da, p. 62. The Scottish year began on 1 January of the Julian calendar. The Gregorian calendar was adopted from January 1752.

their families with them, throughout the winter; Hume's family conformed to this pattern in his post-college years and would have had even more reason to do so while he was such a young student. The students signed the register in one of several formal ceremonies relatively late in the session, but Hume would have been *attending* the class in question since the previous November. It was the Greek class and, with a precision that some matriculants showed and others did not, he recorded that he was now in his *second* year of attendance; two years later we find him in the final (fourth) year class, so he was following the regular sequence.[18] Signing the register normally went hand in hand with subscribing £1 10s. (Scots) to the library's book fund, a formality that brought borrowing instead of merely reading rights.[19]

Thus Hume had *entered* the College in the session 1721–2, aged 10. This would probably not have happened if his brother, John, aged 12, were not attending too, and we should think of Hume's college contemporaries as those of his brother's generation; but the fact that Hume was able to accompany him shows that he had developed linguistic and reading skills ahead of his age.[20] Not that we should underestimate the elder brother's competence either: Hume's letters to him in the 1740s assume that John would still read Latin and French at sight and pick up literary allusions, and James Boswell in 1762 would record that he was 'a sensible good man, who reads more than usual'.[21]

Chirnside had a parish library which was periodically inspected by the local presbytery, but we do not know what was in it. It also had a parish school where the brothers could have received the basics of reading, writing, and religious instruction, but the family's divided domicile between village

[18] Michael Barfoot, 'Hume and the culture of science in the early eighteenth century', in Stewart (ed.), *Studies*, 151–90, p. 151 n. 2. No record survives of matriculations in the first-year class the previous year, but this is not particularly material. An analysis of the overlap between the matriculation list for the Greek class in 1722–3 and the subscription list for the class library in the natural philosophy class in 1724–5 shows Hume as part of a consistent cohort of students following the standard curriculum together: see *The Physiological Library, Begun by Mr. Steuart, and some of the Students of Natural Philosophy in the University of Edinburgh, April 2. 1724: and Augmented by some Gentlemen; and the Students of Natural Philosophy, December 1724* (Edinburgh, 1725). The main exceptions to this matching of the lists are a small group of students admitted as *supervenientes* directly to the third-year logic class in the intervening year. It is similarly possible to trace the consistent progress of the preceding year's cohort through their several class registrations up to the natural philosophy class in 1723–4. My thanks to Michael Barfoot for alerting me to these facts.

[19] For Hume's and his brother's library subscriptions, see EUL, Da 1. 37, fos. 17^v–18^r.

[20] 'From my earliest Infancy,' he would later say with some temporal licence, 'I found alwise a strong Inclination to Books & Letters': *Letters*, i. 13. 'Infancy' in Hume's idiolect is a relative rather than absolute period. The wider family context may well have helped the development of this literary culture, since several prominent members of the Hume families in the region in Hume's childhood have left literary remains, including the redoubtable Lady Grizel Baillie. James Thomson, the poet, was a relation.

[21] *Private Papers from Malahide Castle*, ed. G. Scott *et al.*, 18 vols. (New York: privately published, 1928–34), xv. 109.

and city would have impeded consistent schooling. Hume at least was too young to have gone through grammar school, and the fact that he needed to attend Latin at college is confirmation that he had not done so.[22] He would, even so, have needed to arrive with sufficient rudiments of Latin and arithmetic. It is likely, therefore, that both brothers had a private teacher and, since the family was not wealthy, that they were taught together.[23] After basic grammar and vocabulary, they would already have studied a Latin catechism, probably devotional aids such as George Buchanan's Latin metrical Psalms, and elementary texts like the *Disticha* ascribed to Dionysius Cato, and perhaps the fables of Phaedrus. Hume would later recall 'the Latin classics, whom we peruse in our infancy', identifying himself with those bound for college from an early age. The message of such classics, which he seems to have read at least as far as Sallust's *Catiline War*, had been that Rome reached greatness through the 'virtue and public spirit' of its people and was brought to ruin by Eastern 'arts and riches'.[24] Renaissance moralists were also in common use for beginners, and included Corderius, Sulpitius, and Erasmus.

James Boswell, in the rambling account of his final meeting with Hume, recorded that Hume was 'religious when he was young' and would examine himself by *The Whole Duty of Man* 'to try if, notwithstanding his excelling his schoolfellows, he had no pride or vanity'. He had made an abstract of the 'Brief Heads of Self-Examination' appended to this family manual; but 'youth', then as now, was an indeterminate age, and the comparison is as likely to be with Hume's college as his pre-college contemporaries.[25]

---

[22] John Boswell began Latin under a tutor at the age of 8 and went to the High School at 12. When he entered the College at 15 he went straight to the Greek class (Pitman, 'Journal', 67).

[23] Their mother, as tutrix under the terms of her deceased husband's will, appears to have had full control over the children's upbringing as well as the daily conduct of the estate after the other legal tutors named by the father delegated their responsibilities to her. See National Archives of Scotland, RH15/15/11, a packet of family papers that contains an unsigned copy, endorsed 1715, of a deed transferring responsibilities to the mother. The father had died in 1713 when Hume was 2.

[24] 'Of luxury', later retitled 'Of refinement in the arts', in E. F. Miller (ed.), *Essays Moral, Political and Literary* (Indianapolis: Liberty Classics, 1985) (hereafter *Essays*), 275. On instructional books available at this date, see M. L. Clarke, *Classical Education in Britain 1500–1900* (Cambridge: Cambridge University Press, 1959), ch. 10; Alexander Law, *Education in Edinburgh in the Eighteenth Century* (London: University of London Press, 1965), ch. 6. Teaching materials are to be distinguished from primary sources, which, if studied to any extent, would exempt the young student from comparable studies at college; into the latter category would come much of the High School curriculum (Law, *Education in Edinburgh*, 74–81). For another reference in Hume to Sallust's portrayal of Roman virtue see *Treatise*, III. iii. 4, para. 2.

[25] James Boswell, 'An account of my last interview with David Hume, Esq.', in *Private Papers*, xii. 227–32, at pp. 227–8. Hume refers to the same section of *The Whole Duty of Man* in an early letter to Hutcheson (*Letters*, i. 34), and in a note added to the final appendix of the Second *Enquiry* from 1764. It is called the 'Catalogue of vices' in the Boswell interview, and is rejected as a source for a 'Catalogue of Virtues' in the letter to Hutcheson. The notion of a 'catalogue' of virtues or vices is found also in the *Treatise* (III. iii. 4, para. 2) and in the Second *Enquiry* (III, para. 3; IX, paras. 3, 12; cf. also VI, para. 21 and appendix IV, para. 1).

Who in a Calvinist culture would have openly recommended a work of seventeenth-century Anglican piety to Hume is unclear. Strict Calvinists considered the virtues and vices to be comprehensively defined by the Decalogue,[26] and when the Presbyterians recovered control of the Church of Scotland at the Revolution, *The Whole Duty of Man* had joined the episcopalian catechism in being 'much spoken against, and severely condemn'd as erroneous'.[27] Hume's copy was probably handed down from an older generation: his maternal grandfather, Sir David Falconer, had held high judicial office under the episcopalian administration.

For those who did not have exemption, the first year at the College of Edinburgh consisted in 'humanity'; that is, Latin language and culture—it was not our modern 'humanities'. Latin was the foundational study for other subjects, even for the teaching of Greek. The only known instruction in English in Hume's time was in experimental philosophy.[28] The humanity class was largely over before any of the students paid a library subscription; Hume, as we have noted, did not seek that privilege until a year later, and some students never sought it at all. The second year was Greek, which students could again evade, particularly if their previous schooling had not provided the permitted rudiments of it.[29] Those unequipped for Greek or excused from it were classed as *supervenientes*, but neither Hume nor his brother came into this—generally inferior, not superior—category. That Hume was in the correct sequence and went through the regular course of the first and second years shows two things: his Latin had not been unduly strong, or his Greek impossibly weak, on entry.

Laurence Dundas, the long-serving Professor of Humanity, gave them a good deal of poetry. Three sets of prose translations from the Latin poets, in which Horace is the dominant author, survive in student transcriptions.[30]

---

[26] Thomas Hog, *Some Missives Written to a Gentleman* (Edinburgh, 1718), 6.

[27] [John Cockburn], *An Historical Relation of the late General Assembly, held at Edinburgh, from Octob. 16 to Nov. 13. In the Year 1690* (1691), 12. Cf. p. 11: 'Mr. *Johnstone* of *Salin* was accused for being too much affected to the Episcopal Government, and for recommending superstitious and erroneous Books to the people, as they were pleased to call the *Whole Duty of Man*, which was expresly mentioned.' If, as is likely, the minister of Chirnside, Hume's uncle George Home, took an interest in his fatherless nephew's upbringing, it is possible that there was dissension in the family about suitable religious reading, and that this had some effect on Hume's later attitude to the subject; but this is speculative. (My thanks to Annette Baier for broaching this issue.)

[28] Barfoot, 'Hume and the culture of science', 163. Mathematics as late as 1720 was still being taught in Latin. Colin MacLaurin's mathematical lectures at Aberdeen (cited, n. 6 above) were in English, although some of the exercises were in Latin; but MacLaurin did not move to Edinburgh until Hume—if he studied mathematics—had completed his course.

[29] M. A. Stewart, 'The origins of the Scottish Greek chairs', in Elizabeth M. Craik (ed.), *'Owls to Athens': Essays on Classical Subjects Presented to Sir Kenneth Dover* (Oxford: Clarendon Press, 1990), 391–400. Schools were barred from teaching college-level Greek, but there was no consistent policy between the College and Edinburgh town council over attendance at the Greek class.   [30] EUL, Dc 7. 54; La. III. 459, 759.

Where they are versions of the same originals, they are all different, showing at least that Dundas engaged in extempore translation and did not repeat a prepared text to his classes. A notice of the Edinburgh curriculum that originated in *Magnae Britanniae notitia* in 1708 calls him 'Professor of Humanity, Roman History and Oratory'.[31] This London-based compendium of official information, which continued to carry the name of John Chamberlayne, FRS, long after Chamberlayne's death in 1723, was poorly compiled, particularly in Scottish matters; its reliability is greatest with respect to the year in which any information is first recorded. On that understanding, it would appear that Dundas taught Roman history earlier in his career, so quite likely taught it in Hume's day. The 1708 *Notitia* describes the curriculum as it existed before the establishment of the professorial system in philosophy in that year, but the Latinist had been in post since 1690 and was not affected by this reform. The signed copy of Justin's epitome of ancient history which belonged to the Hume brothers early in their studies may therefore indicate a historical element in the Latin course, possibly in a private class.[32] The reference to 'oratory' is a sign that students were trained in oral composition.

The Greek professor whom Hume attended in 1722–3 was William Scot. Wodrow was agitated over reports of Scot's theological deviancy, but there is no evidence that the allegations caused any concern in Edinburgh, where he was a popular figure among both staff and students.[33] Some notes on *Iliad* A and B, transcribed from the professor's circulating manuscript, are preserved in a copy once again by Alexander Boswell, where the instruction is more linguistic than literary.[34] It looks uninspiring now, but to John Boswell this was entering into the deep character of the language; he indicates that the balance was in any case redressed over the course as a whole, and that Lucian and Aesop were also read, as well as the Greek Testament. The emphasis on moral instruction here is evident. However, they studied drama (Euripides' *Medea*) in Buchanan's Latin translation, and we should remember that most Greek classics were published with facing Latin versions. In keeping up the tradition from the age of the regents, when the same instructor would have continued the earlier year's Greek instruction into the following year, Colin Drummond gave warm-up classes in Greek at the start

[31] John Chamberlayne, *Magnae Britanniae notitia* (London, 1708), 544.

[32] EUL, JA 3285. John recorded his ownership in March 1721, David two years later. At the first date, John may still have been under a tutor; at the second, David would have already attended the public humanity class at the College. However, if they were studying the subject together, the formal change in ownership may be immaterial. Hume does not appear to have made any explicit reference to Justin in his published writing until 'Of the Populousness of Ancient Nations' (1752).

[33] Wodrow, *Analecta*, iii. 515; Pitman, 'Journal', 68–9; Colin MacLaurin to Charles Mackie, 13 Aug. 1735: EUL, La. II. 236.

[34] 'Annotata In Libros A et B Homeri Iliados Autore D. Gulielmo Scot' (1720): EUL, MS 2671.

of the third year while waiting for straggling students to arrive from the country for their logic. He continued Scot's classes on Homer and the Greek Testament and added Herodian; that is, Roman imperial history of the age of Aurelius.[35] Drummond does not appear to have lectured on the classical literary theory favoured by his successor, John Stevenson. Late in life, Hume admitted he 'too much neglected' his Greek at this stage, but it seems at least to have kindled some affection for Lucian that stayed with him.[36]

The third year (for Hume, 1723–4) was predominantly logic and metaphysics, and the fourth (1724–5) natural philosophy. Although every year was defined by one of these principal studies, there was room for other things. Most professors offered advanced or 'private' classes as well as the staple fare—the Greek professor offered French and published a serviceable textbook—and mathematics was commonly taken, in the third or fourth year, to assist the study of natural philosophy. Mathematics was not yet compulsory, and how much of it Hume was able to study is uncertain, since by this time the professor, the Newtonian James Gregory, was an invalid, and substitutes carried his teaching. Our strongest reason for thinking that Hume did study mathematics is that it appears to have given him a grounding upon which to try to study more after leaving college. His transcription survives of a course or textbook, in English, on the theory of fluxions by the extramural lecturer George Campbell in 1726.[37] This was a year or more after we now know he attended Robert Steuart's natural philosophy class, when he subscribed to the class library.

Although we cannot deduce from the catalogue of the Physiological Library what particular titles, if any, Hume or any other student actually read, Michael Barfoot's reconstruction of the character of the syllabus from this and other fragmentary evidence has been confirmed by John Boswell's rediscovered testimony.[38] Boswell would study John Keill's *Introduction to Natural Philosophy*, David Gregory's *Elements of Catoptrics and Dioptrics*, Steuart's own presentation of hydrostatics, and Keill's *Introduction to the*

---

[35] Pitman, 'Journal', 69.

[36] 'My own Life', *Letters*, i. 2. When Hume 'recovered' his knowledge of Greek in the 1740s, Lucian—on the evidence of the First *Enquiry*—was one of the sources to which he turned. Hume's greatest use of Greek sources was in his *Political Discourses* (1752), particularly in 'Of the Populousness of Ancient Nations'. For this he claimed to have 'read over almost all the Classics both Greek and Latin' (*Letters*, i. 152), but his grasp of Greek material was queried by George Ensor, *An Enquiry concerning the Population of Nations: Containing a Refutation of Mr. Malthus's Essay on Population* (London: Wilson, 1818), 57–60.

[37] George Campbell, 'A Treatise of Fluxions': NLS, Acc. 11333 (photocopy). Cf. Stewart (ed.), *Studies*, 8–9; Barfoot, 'Hume and the culture of science', 190 n. 76. Hume's is a fair copy transcribed from another copy, rather than from dictation, and we cannot be sure if he was rewriting his own notes or copying a manuscript that was circulating. Of the relatively few corrections he made, most are deletions of repetitions that have arisen by accidentally shifting back to a verbal similarity a few lines previously. Where they involve the recopying of technical formulae, Hume is not consistent in his transcriptions, so was perhaps not following all the detail of what he was transcribing. [38] Barfoot, 'Hume and the culture of science'; Pitman, 'Journal'.

True Astronomy. While the theoretical part of Steuart's instruction was in Latin, Boswell gives English short titles of the printed works, and it may just be relevant that by this time these technical works all had English translations. Steuart, like Drummond, was a prominent church elder, and Wodrow noted that he and Law were 'notticed for their gravity and recommending religion'.[39] A copy of his dictates on hydrostatics and on the planetary part of astronomy survives, dated 1724, again in the hand of Alexander Boswell. The segment of the astronomy lectures is primarily concerned with calculations of the size and distance of the planets and the evidence provided by telescopes for the number of the stars; the last four pages extol with a combination of rhetoric and poetry the power, wisdom, and perfection of the divine being capable of such an achievement.[40] Boswell's brother, on the other hand, while admitting that Steuart 'took his head much up about Church affairs, & was said to have been truly a Pious man', particularly remembered his tobacco chewing, his 'facetious' temper, and that 'He was att more pains to make you Laugh than to teach you N. Phyl.'[41]

As part of the 1708 settlement which established the professorial system at Edinburgh, the Professor of Natural Philosophy had a formal brief also to teach ethics—that is, to provide elementary moral instruction, probably under the cover of natural theology. There is no reason to think he did— there is no mention of it in the 1710 *Notitia*, the first edition to list the appointments—and on John Boswell's evidence the regulation was a dead letter at least by the mid-1720s. Boswell appears to have completed his course without any instruction in that part of the discipline that was central to college studies elsewhere in Scotland. With the introduction of the professoriate at Edinburgh in 1708 and the fixing of the first two years to Latin and Greek, the traditional three years of philosophical instruction had been telescoped into two by making moral philosophy optional and increasing the relevant professor's salary to compensate him for loss of fees; and so it was to remain for thirty years.[42] William Law, the Professor of Moral Philosophy, was empowered to lecture on any branches of his subject that the professors of Logic and Natural Philosophy omitted, but that may well have been all of it. Earlier in his career, when Law was a regent and was not even theoretically required to defer to anyone else's teaching, his moral

[39] Wodrow, *Analecta*, iii. 515.

[40] 'Principia Hydrostaticae ac Astronomiae Authore D.D. Roberto Stewart' (1724): Mitchell Library, Glasgow, MS S.R. 171. Appended to Latin notes on algebra and geometry taken down by Alexander Cuninghame (later Sir Alexander Dick) in 1720 are some 'Excerptions from Mr Stewarts Colledge of Experimentall Philosophy begun Febry 6th 1724' (Glasgow University Library, in MS Murray 273). They are mostly on hydrostatic experiments, but also include some Boylean 'Experiments concerning the Air'. Cuninghame, who graduated with an MD at Leiden in 1725 after three years' study there, appears to have returned briefly to Edinburgh to complete his studies in natural philosophy in spring 1724.   [41] Pitman, 'Journal', 69.

[42] When the subject was restored to the requirements at the insistence of John Pringle in 1737, no additional year was provided for its study.

philosophy syllabus had consisted in lectures on the end of man and the principles of human action, on law and the law of nature, on the passions, and on virtue and the virtues.[43] He does not appear to have lectured in his public class, as some teachers did, on any specific classic text such as Grotius or Pufendorf; but on human action and on the passions, the surviving dictates make a number of references to Descartes.

It is quite possible that this syllabus continued largely unchanged when Law was awarded the chair. The 1710 edition of the *Notitia*, the first to carry information on the new professorial structure, indicates that the fourth professor, after those assigned to Greek, logic and metaphysics, and natural philosophy, 'has no fix'd Class, but reads Publick Lectures' on the full range of 'Pneumaticks' (pneumatology—the theory of mind or spirits),[44] together with moral philosophy and natural religion, 'to all that please to come and hear him'. Whether Hume pleased to do so remains unknown. If he did, the likeliest thing to have had some impact on him is pneumatology as it relates to the theory of action and the passions, since that is the earliest documented interest in philosophy that he went on to develop after college; but we cannot extrapolate from that development to insist that the spark must have been kindled this early. Other study options were provided by the recently created Professor of History, Charles Mackie. Since this professor kept a class register, and Hume is not on it, we cannot say that he attended classes there either, and it is unlikely that he did.[45] Hume later claimed that in writing on the Stewarts in his *History of England*, 'I conquer'd some of the Prejudices of my Education'; this is tantalizing, but need be no more than a reference to childhood acculturation (*Letters*, i. 221–2).[46] There had,

---

[43] 'Ethica ab Illustrissimo eruditissimoque Domino Magistro Gullielmo Law Dictata', transcribed by John Smith: EUL, in Dc 8. 53.

[44] Through three editions, 1710–18, the moral philosophy professor was credited with lecturing on 'Incumaticks' in addition to moral philosophy and natural religion. There is no such word: unfamiliar with the term 'Pneumaticks', the London printer must have misread a written 'P' as 'I' and 'e' as 'c'. When, over a decade later, they realized there was no such word, the publishers changed it to 'Mathematicks', which there is no reason to think was ever part of the moral philosophy brief. Chamberlayne failed to remove the conflicting information on the regent system (correct in 1708) when he introduced updated information on specialist chairs (correct in 1710), and the conflict in the account remained for decades.

[45] EUL, Dc 5. 24²; L. W. Sharpe, 'Charles Mackie, the first Professor of History at Edinburgh University', *Scottish Historical Review*, 41 (1962): 23–45. Mackie records a David Home, son of 'Clerk Home of Edinburgh' (George Home, formerly conjunct town clerk), as attending his classes in universal history in 1725 and 1726. He drew up his consolidated list in the summer of 1746, with later updates and annotations on his students' careers. By that time Hume the philosopher had begun to make his name, and it was only a year since the furore over his candidacy for the moral philosophy chair. Given the intimate relationship between the College and the town, and Mackie's close connections with the legal community, it is unlikely that he could have confused the newly notorious 'son of Ninewells' with the son of a civic officer he would almost certainly have known.

[46] On education, cf. *Treatise*, I. iii. 9; *Natural History of Religion*, XI, XII, XV. In allowing a role to education in the development of moral sentiments, however, Hume means more than acculturation: it is a nurturing of prior instincts that can only be effective when there is a conscious recognition of the convergence of public and private interest: *Treatise*, III. ii. 2.

after all, been recent Jacobite activity in the neighbourhood, and different branches of the Hume family had had different loyalties.

No doubt Hume was a bright lad, and his brightness helped him get to college at age 10. We do not have to suppose that it also lay in his attending, at an earlier age than other students, all the further courses that many other students did not attend.[47] It is important to take seriously his own retrospect on his college studies ten years later. Ten years is a long time, and perceptions can become discoloured in less, but it is the safest piece of autobiographical evidence we have. He recalled them as dominated by 'the Languages', so philosophy and other studies left less of a mark, and if we are looking for an optional class that he might have added to the basic diet, we may better to consider French. In the letter that he drafted to an unknown physician in 1734, he wrote that 'our College Education in Scotland, extending little further than the Languages, ends commonly when we are about 14 or 15 Years of Age' (*Letters*, i. 13).[48] It may seem curious that he needed to say this to a fellow Scot; but to say that their education commonly ended at 14 or 15 was a way of discreetly tailoring the facts to his own case. Relatively few started and finished quite as young as Hume.[49] It is a fair inference that, like John Boswell, he gained little from the logic class, and that the teaching that it typified is the target of his unsympathetic remarks in the *Treatise* (I. iii. 15, para. 11):

Our scholastic head-pieces and logicians show no such superiority above the mere vulgar in their reason and ability, as to give us any inclination to imitate them in delivering a long system of rules and precepts to direct our judgment, in philosophy. All the rules of this nature are very easy in their invention, but extremely

[47] Without taking their classes Hume could have heard occasional public orations by members of the professoriate. Four of Mackie's survive from over a twenty-year period (EUL, La. II. 37, items 1, 2, 6, 7), but Mackie indicates that they occurred irregularly, with a frequency less than annual.

[48] Much of the medical description seems to be consciously modelled on George Cheyne's *The English Malady* (London and Bath, 1733) which had appeared the previous year: see John H. Burton, *Life and Correspondence of David Hume*, 2 vols. (Edinburgh: William Tait, 1846), i. 42–7. It is uncertain if what survives is more than a draft or copy, and uncertain if the text was ever despatched. The extant version has no opening salutation, and there are other awkwardnesses. Though seeking a reply, it is neither signed nor provided with a return address. If sent and returned, it must have been conveyed through a third party, known to both Hume and the addressee. Even if the letter was merely intended to be sent, some such mechanism must have been envisaged unless Hume was even more mixed up than he made out. Burton guessed that it was intended for Cheyne himself, and certainly Cheyne's book shows that he conducted a significant part of his practice through correspondence. The mechanism would then have had to include provision for delivery of the letter to Bath while Hume was in London or in transit to Bristol. Mossner conjectured that it was intended for Cheyne's friend and critic, John Arbuthnot, the ailing author of works on diet and respiration, but offered no evidence that Arbuthnot had or was known for the relevant specialism. Neither case is conclusive, but for a significant reappraisal of the debate, see John P. Wright, 'Dr George Cheyne, Chevalier Ramsay, and Hume's letter to a physician', *Hume Studies*, 29 (2003): 125–41.

[49] Hume later, in 1763, described his nephew Joseph as too young for college at 11, even though he had had advanced tuition in Latin (*Letters*, i. 412).

difficult in their application; and even experimental philosophy, which seems the most natural and simple of any, requires the utmost stretch of human judgment.

The pretended superiority of the professionals, 'our scholastic head-pieces and logicians', and their 'long system of rules and precepts to direct our judgment', were matters on which Drummond had prided himself, while his lectures on De Vries would have provided first-hand experience of the 'school metaphysics' that Hume thought fit only for the flames at the end of the First *Enquiry*. Hume's more indeterminate references to 'school' and 'schools' throughout his writing tend to be derogatory references to traditional logic or metaphysics.

The one course where he seems to have learnt something is the natural philosophy class, even if it 'stretched' his 'judgment' by requiring rather more than a simple application of rules. Certain influences are traceable in his later writing, as Barfoot has illustrated. But his overall picture of philosophy at this time, as described in the letter to the physician, was that 'Every one, who is acquainted either with the Philosophers or Critics, knows that there is nothing yet establisht in either of these two Sciences, & that they contain little more than endless Disputes, even in the most fundamental Articles'. Even the disputes had been conducted perfunctorily. In an unrelated letter a year later, Hume was even more outspoken. Writing from France to a young Bristol friend, Jemmy Birch, he told the aspiring young scholar not to waste time going to college:

There is nothing to be learnt from a Professor, which is not to be met with in Books, & there is nothing requir'd in order to reap all possible Advantages from them, but an Order & Choice in reading them; in which, besides the small Assistance I can give you, your own Judgement wou'd alone be sufficient; I see no reason why we shou'd either go to an University, more than to any other place, or ever trouble ourselves about the Learning or Capacity of the Professors.[50]

The evidence is plainly incomplete but, such as it is, it gives no grounds to think that Hume caught the philosophical bug at college—and he was still very young. Whatever tuition he had is likely to have consisted in the inculcation more of drills than skills. At the end of one of his early essays, 'Of Eloquence', he remarked that 'a man cannot escape ridicule, who repeats a discourse as a school-boy does his lesson, and takes no notice of any thing that has been advanced in the course of the debate' (*Essays*, 109). The age reference is ambiguous, but debating was a college activity, and Hume himself allowed the use of the term 'boy' for what he also calls a 'student'.[51]

[50] Hume to James Birch, 18 May 1735, in E. C. Mossner, 'Hume at La Flèche, 1735: an unpublished letter', *University of Texas Studies in English*, 37 (1958): 30–3, at p. 32 (corrected).

[51] Commenting to Joseph Spence some years later on Thomas Blacklock's unsuitability 'for managing boys or teaching a school' because 'he would retain no authority', Hume observed that this had barred Blacklock from being considered for a university Greek chair (*Letters*, i. 203). Wodrow spoke of 'lads' and 'boys' at the College of Edinburgh (*Analecta*, iii. 515).

III

Hume indicates that he followed the 'common' college course (*Letters*, i. 1, 13). This brings him to 1725, just turned 14, and, like many of his peers, he did not graduate. He returned home, under no pressure to do anything immediately, or in particular, and his bookish interests took over. Free from the constraints of the curriculum, 'I was after that left to my own Choice in my Reading, & found it encline me almost equally to Books of Reasoning & Philosophy, & to Poetry & the polite Authors' (ibid. 13). This is not to say that he never exercised such choice previously; but he does seem to imply that it was by being able to pick his own reading, rather than by engaging in what he elsewhere calls 'task-reading', that he began to develop an enthusiasm both for philosophy and for literature, whereas at college his studies had revolved too much round 'endless Disputes'. For the next few years, the correspondence with Michael Ramsay and the letter to the physician are crucial documents, more crucial than anything Hume would subsequently write in longer-term retrospect, although that cannot be ignored. But historical recollection is not a constant: it changes as memories merge and the motives for the recollection change, so that the further one moves from the events, the greater the likelihood of rationalization and reinvention. Even the letter to the physician is likely to be influenced by Hume's beliefs about the intended recipient's expectations. Hume's testimony is the best we have, but it is not exempt from the kind of scrutiny that he himself applied to historical sources.

At some stage between 1725 and 1729—between the ages of 14 and 18— he first began, and later abandoned, training for the law: it was, he seems to imply, expected of him. What the training was we do not know for sure, but it is likely to have been training as an advocate, the family profession, rather than as a 'writer' or solicitor. Edinburgh had a Professor of Scots Law and a Professor of Civil Law. A sinecure chair of the Law of Nature and Nations—in effect, of the philosophy of law—was held by Charles Areskine, later Lord Tinwald, who befriended Hume in the 1740s, but he did not teach. The fact that Hume's training included the Latin texts of the Dutch jurists Voet and Vinnius[52] suggests that he enrolled in the law school, but does not prove it, since there were also private teachers of law.

Hume had probably been attempting to pursue his legal studies in 1727, for in the summer of that year, during what would be the legal vacation, he is doing what he can to escape 'task-reading'. Now 16, he is cooped up

---

[52] 'My own Life', *Letters*, i. 1. Although Johann Voet's *Compendium juris juxta seriem Pandectarum* survived in the family library and is no doubt the right title, the actual copy was dated 1731: see David Fate Norton and Mary Norton, *The David Hume Library* (Edinburgh: Edinburgh Bibliographical Society, 1996), entry 1312 and p. 22. Hume appears to have abandoned law by then; if so, this was his nephew's copy.

amidst his books, but it appears to be from choice (*Letters*, i. 9). He misses the conversation with Ramsay that he had earlier in the year—he would have been in the city studying over the winter before returning to Ninewells in the spring. Both appear to be spending the summer reading with a view to writing, but not necessarily on the same things: Hume fears that he will be a 'trouble' to Ramsay if he talks too much 'like a Philosopher'. Ramsay has sent down some books Hume needed, which suggests that Hume had not fully planned his reading at the time he left Edinburgh, unless he was simply purchasing some newly published titles. The correspondence shows that Ramsay had legal connections, and he may have had the services of friends to borrow sometimes from the Advocates' Library. Like Hume, he had subscribed to the College library as a student, and might still therefore have had borrowing rights there. Literature he could probably obtain from Allan Ramsay's lending library (no direct relation). But in the case of a Milton volume, he sent his own. 'I read some of Longinus already', comments Hume (ibid. 11), in terms that suggest something that has recently come into his hands, either brought from Edinburgh or sent by Ramsay: it had just what Hume wanted to stimulate his interest in the 'rules' of writing, as if this too was a new, burgeoning interest. 'Longinus' (not his real name) wrote in Greek, but Hume probably read him in Latin.

Although these interests would come to displace his interests in law, it should not be assumed that he embarked on them in the hope or expectation that they would. It is as likely that he considered literary accomplishments as an essential part of the life of a professional person. This is certainly how he would portray it in the last year of his life, when writing to his nephew David, whom he was supporting through law school; the advice is tempered by his own early experience, but there is no reason to think he is trying to wean the nephew off the law:

You will now enter on a Course of Summer Reading, and Exercise, which you will intermingle properly together. I cou'd wish to see you mix the Volumes of Taste and Imagination with more serious Reading; and that sometimes Terence, and Virgil and Cicero, together with Xenophon, Demosthenes, Homer and Lucian (for you must not forget your Greek) shoud occupy your Leizure together with Voet, Vinnius, and Grotius. I did not observe you to be very fond of the Poets, and surely one may pass through Life, though not so agreeably, without such Companions: But the Familiarity with them gives Taste to prose Reading and Compositions; and one wou'd not allow so agreeable a Vein to dry up entirely for Want of Exercise.[53]

---

[53] Hume to David Hume the younger, 20 May 1776, Library of the Princes Czartoryski, National Museum, Cracow. See Tadeusz Kozanecki, 'Dawida Hume'a nieznane listy w zbiorach Muzeum Czartoryskich (Polska)', *Archiwum Historii Filozofii i Mysli Spolecznej*, 9 (1963): 127–41, at p. 138 (corrected).

The most interesting part of Hume's 1727 letter describes the balance he is striking between literature and philosophy:

I diversify them at my Pleasure; sometimes a Philosopher, sometimes a Poet; which change is not unpleasant nor disservicable neither; for what will more surely engrave upon my mind a Tusculan Dispute of Cicero's de aegritudine lenienda than an Eclogue or Georgick of Virgils; the Philosophers Wiseman, & the Poets husbandman agree in peace of mind, in a Liberty & Independancy on Fortune, & Contempt of Riches, Power & Glory. Every thing is placid & quiet in both; nothing perturbd or disorderd. (*Letters*, i. 10)

Hume cites here the same authors, Cicero and Virgil, whom he would cite nearly half a century later when recalling the same consolations (ibid. 1). The letter therefore seems to capture precisely the period when he is becoming unsettled about his career. It shows him already interested in two related topics that he would never abandon—the 'phenomena' of the mind and the passions—although he has not yet written anything coherent on them. He is keeping loose notes:

Would you have me send in my loose, uncorrect thoughts? Were such worth the transcribing? All the progress that I made is but drawing the Outlines, in loose bits of Paper; here a hint of a passion, there a Phenomenon in the mind accounted for, in another the alteration of these accounts; sometimes a remark upon an Author I have been reading, And none of them worth to any Body & I believe scarce to my self. (Ibid. 9)[54]

On the other hand, his *approach* to these topics is different from what it would be later: it is introspective and Stoical, even if the Stoicism is controlled. He is seeking to cultivate, through study and contemplation, the tranquillity to eschew riches and face 'humane Accidents'. At present he is more at home on the literary side, but the literature is drawing him towards philosophy as a subject that now at least has the potential to go beyond 'endless Disputes':

Virgils Life is more the Subject of my Ambition, being what I can apprehend to be more within my power. For the perfectly Wise man that outbraves Fortune is surely greater than the Husbandman who slips by her; And indeed this pastoral & Saturnian happyness I have in a great measure come at, just now; I live like a King pretty much by my self; Neither full of Action nor perturbation, Molles somnos. This State however I can forsee is not to be rely'd on; My peace of Mind is no sufficiently confirmd by Philosophy to withstand the Blows of Fortune; This Greatness & Elevation of Soul is to be found only in Study & contemplation, this can alone teach us to look down upon[55] humane Accidents. You must allow ⟨me⟩ to talk thus like a Philosopher; tis a Subject I think much on & could talk all day long off, B⟨ut⟩ I know I must not trouble you. (*Letters*, i. 10)

[54] It is reading too much into this communication to infer with certainty that Hume had *already* resolved on a life of letters.   [55] 'upon' *repeated*.

This reads like the excitement of new departures rather than something that was under way when Ramsay and Hume last talked together. The sense of his solitariness is quite striking. It marks the period, referred to in the letter to the physician, when Hume was beginning to react to his reading with a sense of intellectual independence and discovery, as he sought 'some new Medium, by which Truth might be establisht' (ibid. 13). Although it is drawing him away from the *content* of *The Whole Duty of Man*, there is a degree of continuity in concern and method with that earlier reflective phase; and reading that had begun with Cicero—whose Stoicism was part of a broader eclecticism—extended to other ancient moralists:

[H]aving read many Books of Morality, such as Cicero, Seneca & Plutarch, & being smit with their beautiful Representations of Virtue & Philosophy, I undertook the Improvement of my Temper & Will, along with my Reason & Understanding. (Ibid. 14)

Although he was seeking his own independence of mind, there is no evidence that Hume had yet abandoned the ancients' conception of the philosophical enterprise when, around his eighteenth birthday (April 1729), he was confronted with 'a new Scene of Thought'.[56] A new scene, he said, 'seem'd' to be opened to him, and the force of this qualified remark is unclear. We do not know, in spite of intense speculation, whether the prospect was short-lived or long-lived, or what it was. Hume describes it in terms of Shaftesburian rhapsody. It 'transported me beyond Measure, & made me, with an Ardor natural to young men, throw up every other Pleasure or Business to apply entirely to it': it 'raised' his mind to a 'pitch' that gave 'excessive Pleasure' (*Letters*, i. 13). What he did abandon at this point—around the end of the law session 1728–9—was the law, believing that his search for a 'new Medium' was going somewhere. Professionally, the die was cast, but it is unclear whether he yet had a philosophy, or a sustainable method. For when, six months later, everything fell apart, it was still the Stoic regime that took the blame: 'I was continually fortifying myself with Reflections against Death, & Poverty, & Shame, & Pain, & all the other Calamities of Life.' The self-regulation he was still seeking was the thing he most conspicuously failed to achieve. He came to realize too late that contemplative studies

no doubt are exceeding useful, when join'd with an active Life; because the Occasion being presented along with the Reflection, works it into the Soul, & makes it take a deep Impression, but in Solitude they serve to little other Purpose, than to waste the Spirits, the Force of the Mind meeting with no Resistance, but wasting itself in the Air, like our Arm when it misses its Aim. (*Letters*, i. 14)

[56] This point is well made in one of the best analyses so far of the letter to the physician: Reinhard Brandt's 'The beginnings of Hume's philosophy', in George Morice (ed.), *David Hume: Bicentenary Papers* (Edinburgh: Edinburgh University Press, 1977), 117–27.

The result was a psychosomatic illness which shattered his concentration:

[A]ll my Ardor seem'd in a moment to be extinguisht, & I cou'd no longer raise my Mind to that pitch, which formerly gave me such excessive Pleasure. I felt no Uneasyness or Want of Spirits, when I laid aside my Book;[57] & therefore never imagind there was any bodily Distemper in the Case, but that my Coldness proceeded from a Laziness of Temper, which must be overcome by redoubling my Application. (*Letters*, i. 13)

The crisis precipitated by these studies was at its peak over nine months, from the beginning of September 1729 through and beyond the winter 1729–30. He consulted 'a very knowing Physician' in Edinburgh about signs of scurvy, and did not listen when he was diagnosed with 'the Vapours'. Only after a second consultation did he reluctantly come to accept that his problems had a different physical basis.

There is probably something else in the background here: a religious crisis. We know from the letter to the physician that Hume had been reading 'the Writings of the French Mysticks' and those of 'our Fanatics here' (*Letters*, i. 17). This suggests the deeply introspective period, when he too was trying to give himself 'a History of the Situation of [his] Soul', and when he faced the ensuing crisis he looked back for parallels in their writings; but it is difficult to date it relative to his reading in the ancient moralists. Several fervent divines had described and warned against the turmoil induced by letting the tempting light of reason into their faith, the best known being Thomas Halyburton. Hume appears to have felt this temptation, but to have yielded to reason to resolve it. Writing to Gilbert Elliot about the manuscript of his *Dialogues* in March 1751, he recalled recently destroying a religious notebook he had compiled over a period, and before he was 20—that is, before April 1731. It

contain'd, Page after Page, the gradual Progress of my Thoughts on that head. It begun with an anxious Search after Arguments, to confirm the common Opinion: Doubts stole in, dissipated, return'd, were again dissipated, return'd again; and it was a perpetual Struggle of a restless Imagination against Inclination, perhaps against Reason. (*Letters*, i. 154)[58]

---

[57] That is, his reading of the moment; or, possibly, a book *in* which he was writing. He has said nothing to suggest to the physician that he was at this time 'writing a book'. The context (Hume's account of his reading) favours the first interpretation, as does his usage in *Letters*, ii. 188: 'Had I been born to a small Estate . . . I shoud have remaind at home all my Life, planted and improvd my Fields, read my Book, and wrote Philosophy.'

[58] The doubts he represents to Elliot are continued, constructively, into the whole *Treatise* project, as Hume describes this elsewhere in the same letter: 'If in order to answer the Doubts started, new Principles of Philosophy must be laid; are not these Doubts themselves very useful? Are they not preferable to blind, & ignorant Assent? . . . At some Times one is happier in his Researches & Enquiries than at others. Still I have Recourse to the *si quid novisti rectius*. Not in order to pay you a Compliment, but from a real philosophical Doubt & Curiosity' (ibid. i. 156).

In context, this appears to be referring to the design argument rather than to theistic reasoning in general. If so, one has to wonder how it relates to James Boswell's report of the deathbed interview: 'He said he never had entertained any beleif in Religion since he began to read Locke and Clarke.'[59] It was the cosmological argument in different forms, not the argument from design, that was central to the theistic defences of both Locke and Clarke, but it would be surprising if Hume was not aware of their work by the time he was compiling his notebook, since John Simson's support at Glasgow for the full Clarkean theology had been a Scottish *cause célèbre* at just that time.[60] One could try arguing that the references are to different occasions— that at one time Hume was engaged in a 'perpetual Struggle' but did not lose his faith over it, and at a later period finally gave up after reading the defences of Locke and Clarke. One could even suggest that the second reference need not be to their theistic arguments at all, but to their controversial analyses of Christian theology—Locke's *Reasonableness of Christianity* and Clarke's *Scripture-Doctrine of the Trinity*. Neither line looks very convincing. The letter to Elliot does not rule out that Hume was wrestling with more than one body of literature, and the simplistic picture presented by Boswell, in which Hume removes the sense of struggle and projects a carefully controlled image of cool reflection, has the marks of a stage-managed account. Piecing the information together, therefore, we have, on the one hand, a picture of Hume pursuing his studies until hit by a crisis at the age of 18, his recovery starting to take effect a year later but being more marked at 20, and, on the other hand, periods of reading in the 'Fanatics' and in the rational divinity of the period, leading to a mental struggle that went on till he was about 19 and then reached a resolution. What this suggests is that he had been attempting to place his early self-appraisal and philosophical reflection within a conventional theistic framework which it cost him some pains to abandon.

Hume responded to the nervous crisis by changing his study habits and taking up exercise.

I now began to take some Indulgence to myself; studied moderately, & only when I found my Spirits at their highest Pitch, leaving off before I was weary, & trifling away the rest of my Time in the best manner I could. In this way, I liv'd with Satisfaction enough; and on my return to Town next Winter found my Spirits very much recruited, so that, tho they sunk under me in the higher Flights of Genius, yet I was able to make considerable Progress in my former Designs. (*Letters*, i. 14)

[59] Boswell, 'An account', 227. There is no reason to put back this reading to Hume's student days.
[60] Anne Skoczylas, *Mr Simson's Knotty Case* (Montreal: McGill–Queen's University Press, 2001). Norton and Norton, *David Hume Library*, 61, note some avowedly tenuous evidence that a pamphlet on the Simson case may have been in Hume's library.

The temporal reference here appears to be to the winter of 1730–1, when he was 19. The initial recovery was probably more limited than he suggests, since the letter to Ramsay of March 1732, written closer to the event, shows him to be altogether much better a year later (ibid. 11). More significantly, however, he rethought his whole programme of study. Older and wiser, he would now be cautious of the ancient moralists for the rest of his career.

I found that the moral Philosophy transmitted to us by Antiquity, labor'd under the same Inconvenience that has been found in their natural Philosophy, of being entirely Hypothetical, & depending more upon Invention than Experience. (Ibid. 16)[61]

In erecting 'Schemes of Virtue & of Happiness', we must 'regard human Nature, upon which every moral Conclusion must depend'. He is enunciating this clearly cardinal principle in 1734, and it is important to see that it represents a still recent conversion: its application to moral subjects comes to him *after and as a result of the nervous crisis*, 'having now Time & Leizure to cool my inflam'd Imaginations' (ibid.).[62] It is not to be equated, as many commentators have supposed, with the 'new Scene of Thought' which preceded the crisis. Prior to 1730–1, Hume may have been—indeed, clearly was—considering schemes of virtue and happiness ('my former Designs'); and he learnt a technique of self-discipline that stayed with him for the rest of his life. But only after the shock of his illness did the particular approach he would adopt to these subjects begin to take clear shape. This fits with his later statement to Gilbert Elliot in March or April 1751, that 'so vast an Undertaking' as the *Treatise* was 'plan'd before I was one and twenty'—that is, before 1732 (ibid. 158). By an independent route I have him there at 20, but struggling, as he continues to do throughout the period documented in the letter to the physician.

In July of 1730 or 1731, Hume asks Ramsay to bring or send 'Pelisson's History, & the last Volume of Rapin', one or other of which was to replace a private copy borrowed from James Home, a near neighbour and relation (*Letters*, ii. 337).[63] So he is dabbling at that time both in French literary

[61] Cf. M. A. Stewart, 'The Stoic legacy in the early Scottish Enlightenment', in M. J. Osler (ed.), *Atoms, 'Pneuma', and Tranquillity* (Cambridge: Cambridge University Press, 1991), 273–96; *idem*, 'Two species of philosophy: the historical significance of the first *Enquiry*', in P. Millican (ed.), *Reading Hume on Human Understanding* (Oxford: Clarendon Press, 2001), 67–95. Hume's four popular essays on 'philosophical sects' constitute a kind of retrospect on this period. Of the three approaches he repudiated (the Epicurean, the Stoic, and the Platonist), the Stoic has the fullest coverage. His Sceptic, from the standpoint of the modern philosophy, studies life as it is, accepts 'the maxims of common prudence, and discretion' (*Essays*, 161), and believes that, up to a point, habits can be trained; beyond that, the maxims cultivated by the ancients are contrary to nature. 'A man may as well pretend to cure himself of love, by viewing his mistress through the *artificial* medium of a microscope or prospect, and beholding there the coarseness of her skin, and monstrous disproportion of her features, as hope to excite or moderate any passion by the *artificial* arguments of a SENECA or an EPICTETUS' (ibid. 172).   [62] Cf. Brandt, 'Beginnings of Hume's philosophy'.

[63] On James (later Sir James) Home of Blackadder, with whom Hume would at some time discuss the family history, see *Letters*, i. 275–6. The year of the letter to Ramsay is not stated, and a reference to Hume's poor health leaves the options open. The paper is from the same stock as Hume was using in the early 1730s.

history (and so, one would expect, in some of the literature itself) and in British political history. Paul Pellisson-Fontanier's *Histoire de l'Académie françoise* (1653) had been newly updated by the abbé d'Olivet in an edition of 1729. Paul de Rapin-Thoyras had, at the time of his death in 1725, published his *Histoire d'Angleterre* up to the reign of Charles I, but left a continuation to 1689 in manuscript. This was published with a 'Dissertation sur les Whigs et les Torys' in 1727, and is likely to be what Hume was referring to. An English translation reached the same point in 1731. This period of history was still topical in Hume's youth: his older relatives had lived through the 1688 Revolution, and Hume himself was born four years after the controversial Act of Union and four years before the Jacobite army marched across the Border counties in 1715. It is not surprising that he would be interested in the origins and legitimacy of the modern political system.

Depending on how we construe the date, this French reading may have been part of the diversion, or part of the recovery. If we are plotting the origins of his philosophy, it will look like a diversion, but Hume will still have seen his territory as the combined field of philosophy and literature. Over 'these three Years'—the length of time Hume himself cites for the period between the revolution in his approach and his departure for London and Bristol—he read voraciously, taking in 'most of the celebrated Books in Latin, French & English, & acquiring the Italian', and 'scribled many a Quire of Paper' (*Letters*, i. 16). The momentum set off by the 'new Scene of Thought' has been recovered to the point where Hume is working once again on literary plans, if somewhat changed ones. 'Most of the celebrated Books' may be hyperbole, and in any case it is not a description from which we can infer that he has actually read any title in particular, since the list would have to be relative to the state of Hume's knowledge of what the celebrated books were.

Once again, however, things are not working out:

my Disease was a cruel Incumbrance on me. I found that I was not able to follow out any Train of Thought, by one continued Stretch of View, but by repeated Interruptions, & by refreshing my Eye from Time to Time upon other Objects. Yet with this Inconvenience I have collected the rude Materials for many Volumes; but in reducing these to Words, when one must bring the Idea he comprehended in gross, nearer to him, so as to contemplate its minutest Parts, & keep it steddily in his Eye, so as to copy these Parts in Order, this I found impracticable for me, nor were my Spirits equal to so severe an Employment. (*Letters*, i. 16)

It is interesting that in the letter to the physician, Hume has already discovered the image of mental 'anatomy' that he would reuse in his debates with Hutcheson in the 1740s, but what he will believe he has achieved by the latter date is still in the future in 1734. The 'many Volumes' are at this point a dream. The distraction of too many subjects, which he portrays here as a form of relief, may also have contributed to the problem.

To this period belongs the earliest piece of original writing to survive, Hume's essay on chivalry, of which the ending is now lost.[64] This can be dated to the early 1730s, when the crisis has passed its peak. The essay starts from the conventional wisdom about the decline of ancient Rome, from virtue to luxury, that Hume had imbibed in his youth, but it places the degeneration firmly in the imperial period. Superimposed on this conventional picture are certain speculative hypotheses about human nature: that where such degeneration appears, the arts of 'common Life' will survive the loss of virtue; that the luxury of the Romans would naturally attract the envy of aggressors, and the ensuing conflict create a 'Conformity' between the customs of both; the conquerors, ignorant of the cultural roots of the new ideas they met with, would create a fanciful framework for them based upon 'a new set of Passions, Affections, Desires, Objects'; and the conquered, being equally ignorant, would be attracted by the extravagance of the new conceptions. ''Twas thus that that Monster of Romantick Chivalry or Knight-Errantry, by the necessary Operation of the Principles of Human Nature, was brought into the World', a proposition illustrated by an analogy with the way the Gothic people uncomprehendingly added 'a wild Profusion of Ornaments' to the simple beauties of classical architecture: in the same way they took the courage and heroism extolled in antiquity and turned it into something fantastic—an ability to conquer giants and monsters, in the defence of chastity and the pursuit of love.[65] Hume has mistakenly conflated pre-Norman Gothic civilization and the post-Norman architecture castigated as 'Gothic' by Renaissance critics of both.

Some recognizably Humean themes are here in embryo: notably the role of the passions and the imagination in forming irrational conceptions. What is also noticeable is that the themes are there before the evidence for them. They are also there before Hume has developed the mental mechanisms to explain them.[66] Though billed as a 'historical essay' it is a 'natural history' in the sense that *The Natural History of Religion* will be, a study in which the line between empirical history and conceptual thinking is not clearly drawn. It does, nevertheless, belong centrally in the period when Hume *believes* he has abandoned the hypothetical methods of antiquity:

Tis observable of the human Mind, that when it is smit with any Idea of Merit or Perfection, beyond what its Faculties can attain, & in the pursuit of which, it uses

[64] 'An Historical Essay on Chivalry and modern Honour': NLS, MS 23159, item 4. On the dating, see M. A. Stewart, 'The dating of Hume's manuscripts', in P. Wood (ed.), *The Scottish Enlightenment: Essays in Reinterpretation*, (Rochester, NY: University of Rochester Press, 2000), 267–314. A small residue from Hume's essay survives in the Roman–Norman volume of his *History of England*, particularly at the end of the second appendix. This becomes vol. 1 in the numeration established in 1762.   [65] Quoted phrases from 'An Historical Essay', fos. 1–4.

[66] John Wright, in unpublished researches, has explored the likely influence on Hume of Mandeville's *An Enquiry into the Origin of Honour* (1732). If his hypothesis is correct, we can assign Hume's essay a less tentative date than handwriting tests alone can provide.

not Reason & Experience for its Guide, it knows no Mean, but as it gives the Rein & even adds the Spur to every florid Conceit or Fancy, runs in a moment quite wide of Nature.... The same thing is observable in Philosophy, which tho it cannot produce a different World in which we may wander, makes us act in this as if we were different Beings from the rest of Mankind; at least makes us frame to ourselves, tho' we cannot execute them, Rules of Conduct different from these which are set to us by Nature. No Engine can supply the place of Wings, & make us fly, tho' the Imagination of such a one may make us stretch & strain & elevate our selves upon our Tip-toes. And in this case of an imagin'd Merit, the farther our Chimera's hurry us from Nature, & the Practice of the World, the better pleas'd we are, as valuing ourselves upon the Singularity of our Notions, & thinking we depart from the rest of mankind only by flying above them.[67]

In March 1732, Hume thanks Ramsay for his 'trouble about Baile', perhaps trouble in borrowing and despatching a volume for him to consult, perhaps simply a matter of looking something up for him (*Letters*, i. 12). The Bayle background that is acknowledged in Hume's earliest writing is the *Dictionnaire*, not the *Œuvres diverses*, but the latter had just come out as a collection over the period 1727–31; certainly at some date it found its way into the Hume library, and would be an influence later in Hume's career. Neither compilation exactly counts as 'a Book' ('I hope it is a Book you will yourself find Diversion & Improvement in', Hume says to Ramsay), and the reference may be to one of Bayle's shorter individual writings.

Hume agreed—he was probably pushed—to seek a more active life. Being a trader's clerk did not suit him, and yet after this we hear no more about psychological problems. It looks as if, fond though he was of his home, Hume was ill at ease in the home environment and was finding it difficult to reconcile the direction of his thoughts with the expectations of the family circle.[68] He had left Scotland for London, probably direct from the family's winter quarters in Edinburgh, by about the end of February,[69] so he would have arrived by early March. He probably had enough introductions to enable him briefly to explore the southern capital; but if he had a job to go to, he cannot have stayed in London for long. The next firm date we have for him is 12 September (1 September in the Scottish and English calendar), by which time he has been and gone from Bristol, crossed to France, received the hospitality of the Chevalier Ramsay in Paris, moved to Reims, and observed enough of the customs and courtesies of the French of all ranks to be able to send Michael Ramsay an intelligent analysis of national differences in social conventions (*Letters*, i. 19–21). There is a puzzle about this.

[67] 'An Historical Essay', fos. 2–3.

[68] A more graphic form of this scenario is offered by J. Y. T. Greig, *David Hume* (London: Cape, 1931), 88.

[69] This date is derived from information in the case of Agnes Galbraith recorded in the minutes of the Chirnside Presbytery, National Archives of Scotland, CH2/16/3, p. 355.

His departure from Bristol, after at most five months, appears to have been quite abrupt—the employment, he says, was 'totally unsuitable' (ibid. 1–2);[70] and the move to France seems to have had its impulsive aspect too—he had taken no steps to acquire a speaking knowledge of the language which hitherto he had only read. On the other hand, he appears to have turned very quickly to philosophical work after making the move. It is difficult to believe that when he settled down to the *Treatise* in earnest, he had nothing before him but a *tabula rasa*. He must have travelled with at least a selection of his books and papers; and therefore even the move to Bristol cannot have been quite the clean break that he made it out to be. His commercial experience looks to have been nothing more than another form of semi-engagement, like his legal experience.

There is no reason to dispute the evidence that when he went to France he had the plan of the *Treatise* in mind and that, particularly after settling at La Flèche, he worked systematically and productively on it without the writing block that had dogged his time at Ninewells. He did not entirely shun company, and he sought scholarly contacts. The Chevalier gave him introductions at Reims, which was a university city, and when he moved on to La Flèche, it is difficult to believe it was exclusively from pecuniary considerations. Hume went where there were scholars and libraries; he is unlikely to have done all his writing without some more reading, and he is unlikely not to have exploited the opportunity to improve his knowledge of French writers.

IV

Hume has not told us the whole story of this period of exploration and resolve; indeed, we have little more than a fragment. We learn relatively little about what he read and when he read it, and even less about those, if any, who guided him and with whom he discussed it. We can guess the type

---

[70] Personal experience may have prompted Hume's remark, in discussing 'the love of fame', that a merchant 'little values the character' of learning (*Treatise*, II. i. 11, para. 13). But we should beware of trying to find autobiography behind the broader picture that Hume presents in that section of 'men of good families, but narrow circumstances' who 'leave their friends and country' and go to live among strangers who know nothing of 'their birth and education'. This is a conventional literary stereotype. Although Hume left friends and country in going to England and later to France, other details do not fit. His employment in Bristol was not 'mechanical', and he did not 'seek a livelihood' at all when he went to France. He carried letters of introduction to Bristol, Paris, and Reims, and was open in communicating his interests to those with whom he could share them (*Letters*, i. 22–3, 361). Nor have we reason to think that he had previously been 'every day expos'd to the contempt' of his 'kindred and countrymen' (*Treatise*, II. i. 11, para. 17). While he does not match the stereotype, there is, of course, a wealth of psychological description in this section of the work from which we can extrapolate what he *would* apply to his own case if he had chosen to make an example of it. Likewise for the later section 'Of the love of relations'. (My thanks to John Wright for first raising the issues here.)

of educational materials he studied, even if not the specific titles; and in the years after he finished college, he is clearly reading a lot in Latin—whether in law, philosophy, or literature. In the letter to the physician, he finds no occasion to mention other languages until he comes to the revolution in his approach to his studies in the period 1731–4. There is then a great broadening in his reading, which outstrips his ability to concentrate his writing.

If Hume has been reading Latin works for a good many years, then for a competent reader of Latin and French it is not going to be a great step to develop a reading acquaintance with Italian: the relevant interests may have been literary, or they may have been moving in a political-historical direction. An apparent intensification of his reading in French and English authors is nevertheless interesting, and consistent with a plan eventually to visit France. It would be natural to think that these works included most or all of the English, and some of the French, authors that later figure as foundational to the *Treatise* project either in the Introduction to that work, or in the 1737 letter to Ramsay,[71] or in the *Abstract*, even if his reading was not exclusively philosophical.

If we go back over the early reading that is firmly identified in the correspondence or other sources, the list is quite meagre: Sallust among the early classics; French mystics and Scots fanatics somewhere in the background; Milton, Virgil, Cicero (*Tusculan Disputations*), and Longinus in 1727; Seneca and Plutarch added before 1729, and probably Locke and Clarke soon after. When illness is still a problem, he asks for Pellisson and Rapin, and when he is improved, there is the unidentified Bayle. Whether fortuitously or not, the explicit French references (Pellisson, Rapin, Bayle) all appear to fall within the 1731–4 period when he is making a great effort to expand his horizons. What more can we add?

In 1726, the year before the letter to Ramsay, Hume acquired his copy of one of the most fashionable pieces of progressive reading favoured by the younger generation: Shaftesbury's *Characteristicks of Men, Manners, Opinions, Times*.[72] Shaftesbury would be one of the precursors whose contributions to the 'science of man' Hume would acknowledge in the Introduction to the *Treatise*, and some of his discussion of moral character as well as of moral appraisal no doubt left its impression on Hume's later work, contributing to the tradition within which he would make his own mark.[73] We do not know when Hume started to study it, but the effects of

---

[71] Hume to Ramsay, 31 Aug. 1737, in Kozanecki, 'Dawida Hume'a nieznane listy', 133–4.

[72] Hume's dated set of the 3rd (1723) edn. is in the University of Nebraska Library, SPEC 108n Sh1c, v.1–v.3. Members of Edinburgh's Rankenian Club, like George Turnbull and William Wishart, had already been greatly influenced by reading Shaftesbury, as had the poet Thomson and other contributors to *The Edinburgh Miscellany* (Edinburgh, 1720).

[73] The best discussion of this is by Isabel Rivers, *Reason, Grace and Sentiment: A Study of the Language of Religion and Ethics in England 1660–1780*, 2 vols. (Cambridge: Cambridge University Press, 1991, 2000), ii. esp. ch. 4.

doing so seem fairly clear in the later 1720s and continue through to his work as a professional essayist; in particular, it has a direct bearing on Hume's 'new Medium'. *Characteristicks* is a difficult book, with deliberately disorienting changes of style. At its heart is a dual attempt, by dialogue and by narrative, to engage the reader in the study and practice of virtue. Preceding that are studies in literary form and other matters dealing with the promotion of a message to a reluctant or estranged public; and following it, a literary and philosophical commentary on what has been presented. The metaphysical analysis never goes very deep. It has a theistic base, but freed from the shackles of any particular theology. The reader is urged to go back to the ancient moralists and rediscover in human nature the springs of personal and civic virtue, abstracted from the corrupting influences of religious institutions and from the inculcation of a catechism. 'For this to be achieved', as Isabel Rivers expresses it in a valuable summary, 'the novice must come to understand the relation of the inward anatomy or architecture or economy, as he variously calls it, to the outward, of the parts to the whole. The essential first step to this knowledge is self-examination, meditation, or soliloquy.'[74] For this purpose, written exercise is encouraged, but only as a means to meditation. It is not for publication, and is not to be confused with the literary technique which Shaftesbury discusses for arresting the attention of his readership. As the exercise proceeds, the examination extends to one's relationship with others and with the rest of the cosmos, something that is essential to personal development. The primary purpose of the self-examination is to inform one's practice. Philosophy is not a matter of speculation, but of virtuous living in society, something for which we all have an instinct awaiting recognition and development.[75]

It is this introspective technique recommended by Shaftesbury that Hume appears to have set himself to follow in his late teens, with reading concentrated on the primary sources of classical Stoicism. If Shaftesbury was indeed part of the inspiration, however, then Hume had failed to incorporate the second half of the regimen that Shaftesbury recommended. His self-searching was to be balanced by an *active* life, a life that involved at a minimum active communication with his peers, but for Shaftesbury also a participation in the business of the community.

Shaftesbury is the most striking example of reading that we can identify on circumstantial grounds, but some other possibilities are suggested by a chronological analysis of the Nortons' catalogue of the Hume library.[76] It is

[74] Isabel Rivers, 'Shaftesburian enthusiasm and the evangelical revival', in J. Garnett and C. Matthew (eds.), *Revival and Religion since 1700: Essays for John Walsh* (London: Hambledon, 1993), 21–39, at pp. 27–8.

[75] This theme would later be picked up by Francis Hutcheson at the end of the introduction for students prefixed to the 2nd edn. of his *Philosophiae moralis institutio compendiaria* (Glasgow, 1745), translated posthumously as *A Short Introduction to Moral Philosophy* (Glasgow, 1747).

[76] Norton and Norton, *David Hume Library*.

a version of the catalogue of Baron Hume's (the nephew's) library after his death, the baron having eventually inherited much of Hume's own and other books from the Ninewells estate—and also having disposed of a fair amount of it. Books that pre-date Hume's death cannot, except in rare cases, be definitively shown to have been Hume's own, or even to have been in the library in his lifetime, and many of the legal books will not have been his; but some of the evidence is nevertheless suggestive of what was accessible to him.

Thus, if we see what books survive from the sixteenth century, many of which are likely to have been family heirlooms that Hume would have had access to, there are a small number of classical texts, including an Aldine Demosthenes, the agricultural writer Columella, and (not in the catalogue, but surviving with the David Hume book-plate) an edition of Martial. There is rather more in the way of Italian and Spanish literature, including Ariosto's *Orlando furioso*. The seventeenth-century holdings are more extensive. Classical texts include Aristophanes, Arrian, Claudian, Lysias, Velleius Paterculus, Plautus, Polybius, Seneca's tragedies, and Theophrastus; and although not in the catalogue, seventeenth-century editions of Anacreon, Apuleius, and Sallust have survived with the Hume book-plate.[77] There is a Grotius, Bacon's moral and political works in Latin, Locke's *Two Treatises* (1690), and Molesworth's *Account of Denmark* (1694). Relevant to college studies in natural philosophy are Boyle's *Experiments Physico-Mechanical, Touching the Spring of the Air* (1682) and his *Physiological Essays* (1661). John Graunt's *Natural and Political Observations Made upon the Bills of Mortality* (1665) is of interest because this was a subject that Hume himself refers to in the early fragment on the problem of evil.[78] Works more centrally germane to his interests include Perrault's *Paralelle des anciens et des modernes, en ce qui regarde les arts, et les sciences* (1693), Temple's *Memoirs of What Passed in Christendom from 1672 to 1679* (1692), and Wotton's *Reflections upon Ancient and Modern Learning* (1694). Italian authors include Bentivoglio and Tasso, and there are some French volumes, including a complete Rabelais and the letters of Balzac. A three-volume set of Malebranche's *De la Recherche de la vérité* (Lyon, 1684), which is not in the catalogue, survives with the Hume book-plate.[79]

[77] Brian Hillyard and David Fate Norton, 'The David Hume bookplate: a cautionary note', *The Book Collector*, 40 (1991): 539–44, observe that there are two engravings of the book-plate. The Sallust volume (EUL, JA 3821) has it in an apparently later form, where the paper employed is of a kind that was not manufactured before the late 1750s, and in this form it is sometimes affixed to volumes published or bound after Hume's death within the lifetime of his nephew David. That does not lessen the likelihood that this is the Ninewells copy that Hume 'perused in his infancy'. It is an old edition of a study text, bearing his brother John's signature, and abounds in marginal and interlinear marks that reflect heavy use. The brothers for the most part shared the same home until 1751, when Hume's philosophical output was all but complete.

[78] M. A. Stewart, 'An early fragment on evil', in M. A. Stewart and J. P. Wright (eds.), *Hume and Hume's Connexions* (Edinburgh: Edinburgh University Press, 1994), 160–70, at p. 167.

[79] EUL, Df. 4. 74–75*. All three volumes carry an early signature of ownership, erased and now indecipherable, but not Hume's, on the title-page.

Moving into the eighteenth century, we may be coming closer to works that bear directly on Hume's own studies, whether at college or later. They were not necessarily all acquired—by Hume or another of his family—in the same decade as they were published, but a fair amount of the literature starts to show up in the *Essays* and *Enquiries*.

Classical editions from the first decade of the century include Marcus Aurelius, Cornelius Nepos (a relatively easy Latin historian and a potential class text), and Menander. Also of interest is Berkeley's *New Theory of Vision* (1709), although that is not a work with which Hume was as familiar as he should have been.[80] From the second decade there is a higher proportion of French works, including Bellegarde's *Reflexions sur l'elegance et la politesse du stile* (1715) and La Motte's *Reflexions sur la critique* (1715). There are the works of Corneille and an English translation of the works of St Evremond. From the 1720s, the 1722 edition of Buchanan's Euripides seems plainly to have been bought as a course text, although a 1724 edition of Herodian seems to have missed the relevant course by a few months. Other classical works include a Lucretius of 1725. Buffier's *Grammaire françoise* in an edition of 1723 looks like a purchase for practical use within the coming decade, as does a French guide to Italian grammar, Antonini's *Traité de la grammaire italienne* (1726). French editions originating in the 1720s include Bayle's *Œuvres diverses*, as previously noted, and works of Boileau and La Fontaine. Possibly significant are Houssaye's *Reflexions, sentences et maximes morales* (1725) and Leibniz's *Essais de theodicée* (1720).[81] Italian editions originating from the same decade include Ariosto's comedies, Boccaccio—and Machiavelli. English works include Addison and a set of *The Spectator*. There is also a set of *The Guardian* and a second edition of Hutcheson's *Inquiry* (1726). Titles from the 1730s include some that Hume had undoubtedly studied previously in other editions, so they are of no special significance, and may not even have been his—for example, a 1732 Virgil and 1733 Longinus. Titles of some potential interest are 1730 editions of Olivet's *Histoire de l'Académie françoise depuis 1652 jusqu'à 1700* and Montesquieu's *Lettres persanes*, a 1732 Dante and a 1732 edition of Dubos's *Reflexions critiques*, a 1736 (first or second) edition of Butler's *Analogy*, and a 1738 Guicciardini. A fair number of French titles probably reflect Hume's purchases abroad in this decade, although some were published in the Netherlands. These may include Brumoy's *Le Théâtre des grecs* in three volumes (1730), Cardinal de Retz's *Mémoires* in four volumes (1731), a six-volume Molière (1734), and the Abbé Trublet's *Essais sur divers sujets de littérature et de morale* in two volumes (1735). Of English works, only Hume amongst his family is likely to have acquired Thomas Morgan's laborious deistic tract *The Moral Philosopher* in three volumes (1737–40).

---

[80] Barfoot, 'Hume and the culture of science', 169–70.
[81] Hume discusses Boileau in a 1739 letter to Henry Home (*New Letters*, 6) and cites Leibniz's view of logic from the preliminary dissertation to *Theodicée* in the *Abstract* of the *Treatise* (1740).

All I have done here has been to present a sample of what is on offer, and interested readers will be able to do more for themselves, including seeking out occasional but significant volumes of history. Little weight attaches to any particular title, because of the history of the collection, but rather more can be placed on the general picture that is conveyed. In addition to trying to eke out the record of Hume's likely reading, however, we must also consider one further body of circumstantial evidence relating to his development: the identity of his closest contacts in his formative years. Hume seems always to have been a gregarious person, but also something of an intellectual loner, particularly on his home patch. There is no evidence that in later years he contributed to the active debate in the professional societies to which he belonged, with the exception of the Glasgow Literary Society, where he seems to have transmitted his communications by post.[82] The correspondence suggests that he could in fact discuss his mature views comfortably with educated friends like Gilbert Elliot, William Mure, and Adam Smith, and it shows too that he would discuss them with select correspondents. He would discuss literature with Hugh Blair and history with William Robertson, but it is doubtful that he would discuss philosophy, or at least his own philosophy, with most of his Edinburgh literary circle. In his early period he is not likely to have been any more forthcoming, but three names suggest themselves as persons who were in his confidence. It should be kept in mind, nevertheless, that as late as 1737 they were still in the dark as to the true nature of the *Treatise* project, and it is not known if any of them saw anything of it before publication: Hume in his correspondence always takes sole blame for its failure and never suggests that he got bad advice or that he foolishly disregarded good advice.

The first is Henry Home of Kames, a Berwickshire neighbour and distant relation fifteen years his senior. Correspondence from 1737 and again in the 1740s demonstrates Hume's regard for his older kinsman and his willingness to share ideas with 'the best Friend, in every respect, I ever possest'.[83] Henry had qualified as an advocate when David was still a young student in the Greek class. At that period, he was involved in a philosophical correspondence on at least two fronts: with Samuel Clarke on the nature of God's necessary existence, the compatibility of human liberty with divine foreknowledge, and the source of the human duty to do good; and with Andrew Baxter on Clarke's moral system and on the communication of motion in a continually changing universe.[84] At the same time he was galvanized and disturbed by reading Locke's account of 'power'. Less easy to place is a

[82] Hume to David Hume the younger, 21 Jan. 1776, in Kozanecki, 'Dawida Hume'a nieznane listy', 137. The specific reference here is probably to Hume's essay on Ossian.

[83] *New Letters*, 17.

[84] Ian Simpson Ross, *Lord Kames and the Scotland of his Day* (Oxford: Clarendon Press, 1972), 60–6. Remnants of the correspondence are in the National Archives of Scotland, GD24/1/547–548.

report that Home and two other young advocates, or advocates in training, 'went into' one of the Edinburgh clubs 'to puzzle and make mischief, and they succeeded but too well with many, making them Deists. My Lord had to speak to them to be decent.'[85] This leaves it unclear whether Home himself for a time espoused deism, a movement that attained local notoriety in the Borders in the 1730s through the activity of William Dudgeon. If he did, that makes sense of Hume's willingness to trust him with a copy of his manuscript on miracles, and it is at least noteworthy that both of them went through phases of struggling with the ideas of Locke and Clarke. Boswell additionally notes that Home would later call on Joseph Butler in London and converse on Butler's answers to the deists.[86] Henry Home's simultaneous pursuit of legal and philosophical studies in the early 1720s very likely served as a model for Hume after the latter left college, and Home will in any case have been one of the influences helping to open up Hume's reading when he embarked on similar studies.

There are two others who were for a time part of Henry Home's social circle, which may or may not have been what caused them to be part of Hume's as well. The two overlapped as students at Edinburgh, where they preceded Hume by several years. One was William Hamilton of Bangour, one of the leading personalities on the Edinburgh literary scene until he ran into difficulties by too publicly associating himself with the Jacobite cause. He is the one person, other than Henry Home, whom Hume is known to have authorized to read the narrative on miracles that he suppressed from the *Treatise* (*Letters*, i. 24). The other, more interesting but elusive, is Michael Ramsay, the recipient of much of the important early correspondence.

Ramsay was born in 1702 and was closer in age to Home than to Hume.[87] His father, and later Ramsay himself, was laird of Mungal, an area that became seriously degraded in the nineteenth century by being absorbed after Ramsay's son's death into the territory of the Carron Iron Works founded by a later friend of Hume's, John Roebuck. Ramsay entered the

[85] Boswell, *Private Papers*, xv. 284. Boswell interviewed Home (Lord Kames) on the subject in 1780, but his record is affected by the confusions of another elderly informant, Alexander Dick (pp. 314–15): either Dick or his amanuensis conflated two distinct clubs (Ross, *Lord Kames*, 71). Boswell understood Kames to be recalling the Rankenian Club, frequented by young professionals, particularly jurists and theologians, although Kames does not appear to have been a regular or long-term member of that club. Another anecdotal writer, John Ramsay of Ochtertyre, in *Scotland and Scotsmen in the Eighteenth Century*, 2 vols. (Edinburgh: Blackwood, 1888), i. 196 n., thought he was not a member at all.

[86] Boswell, *Private Papers*, xv. 292–3. After Home had paid two calls, they continued a correspondence, now lost.

[87] Ramsay's baptismal record is in the Falkirk parish register at the date 1 Sept. 1702 (microfilm, Falkirk public library). I am grateful to David Raynor for collateral family information that confirmed the identity of Ramsay's parents. See the genealogy of the family of Burn-Callander of Preston Hall, *Burke's Landed Gentry of Great Britain*, 19th edn., i (2001), 132–4, at p. 133.

College of Edinburgh in 1717–18 with enough Latin to proceed straight to the logic class, and had probably completed such studies as he pursued there by 1719, two years and a summer before Hume attended. He went into tutoring, and later served for a time in the family of the Earl of Home, but in the short term he may have been studying law. A reference in one of Hume's letters shows him securing legal advice for Hume's mother; a later one suggests that he may have contemplated entering the Anglican Church (*Letters*, i. 11, 28). There has to be a possibility, but no more, that he was Hume's private tutor in the period immediately before and even during Hume's attendance at college. The intimate character of Hume's letters shows that by 1727 they considered themselves equals, and a later surviving letter of Ramsay's suggests something of an attitude of awe.[88] Given the age gap, it is quite likely that Ramsay, in his (lost) side of the early correspondence, was trying to nurture Hume's talents rather than contribute on equal terms to the dialogue. Much has been made of the letter to Ramsay in 1737 in which Hume appears to be taking up an offer from him to read the manuscript of the *Treatise*, but too little attention has been given to its wording. He always welcomes Ramsay's advice, Hume seems to be saying, and this includes advice on his 'Conduct & Behaviour', but this is immediately tempered with a qualification that seems to put Ramsay on a wrong foot: health and other reasons prevented Ramsay from ever being 'a regular Student', and he has never applied himself 'to any part of Learning in a methodical manner'. Yes, to be sure, he can read and comment, but he needs to prepare himself by first reading right through Malebranche's *Recherche*, Berkeley's *Principles*, Descartes's *Meditations*, and 'some of the more metaphysical Articles' (unspecified) in Bayle. The implication is that this is unfamiliar territory to Ramsay; and if it is not, and not intended as, a tactful deterrent, it is difficult to know what would be.[89]

V

We have three clues as to where Hume intended to go after the *Treatise*, and we have them because he began to go there. One was a move into a kind of philosophical journalism; one was into writing on politics and 'criticism', that is, critical writing on literature and the arts; and one was into topics relating to religion. Once he was set on a literary career, he would have to have some sort of forward plan (and so by the late 1740s, for example, we find signals that he is hoping to move more single-mindedly into history) and would take such opportunities as offered to lay the foundations for future work.

---

[88] Ramsay to Hume, 5 June 1764: NLS, MS 23156, item 105.
[89] Kozanecki, 'Dawida Hume'a nieznane listy', 133.

Hume thought it a mistake to try to attract the sophisticated and the unsophisticated reader in the same works: their needs and tolerances are different. But he also thought it possible to write at a popular level in a way calculated to help untrained readers enlarge their minds. So we find him planning a series of pieces, probably of graduated degrees of difficulty, which might feature in a literary periodical with philosophical overtones on the model of the London periodicals of the recent past. In casting himself as a latter-day Addison or Steele, he no doubt intended to avoid the sense of conventional piety that had characterized their productions. His ambitions are recalled in the 'Advertisement' to the 1741 *Essays*, but by then the project has been abandoned in favour of issuing a collection in book form. The 1741 and 1742 *Essays* contain specimens of the popular genre, some of them distinctly ephemeral and soon to be dropped, but also specimens of a more challenging type of political essay. Of the two, the first volume is higher in serious content and was a sufficient success to justify a speedy second edition; and Hume and his publisher cashed in on the popularity of the first volume by issuing a second within a year. Some of these are serious pieces too, which survive into the permanent canon, but Hume released also the more lightweight pieces in his bottom drawer to eke out the volume.

At least four essays were already drafted by the summer of 1739, as shown by his correspondence with Henry Home in June and July of that year.[90] Hume himself considers them to be of mixed quality: he thinks one 'will be found very cold' and another 'be esteem'd somewhat sophystical'. That he abandoned the journal project may be due in part to the failure of the *Treatise* and the need he felt to reconsider his literary strategy and find a new medium for his serious thought. It is noteworthy that Hume was working on these essays *between* the publication of the first two books of the *Treatise* and the submission of the third, but noteworthy too that he says to Home that his heart is not in it, 'having received news from London of the success of my Philosophy, which is but indifferent'. If, however, the projected periodical was all along a collaborative project, then the reason it did not materialize may be more prosaic: the collaboration may simply have failed.

Evidence that it was collaborative is only circumstantial. A 'Manuscript' with which Henry Home reciprocated the 'Papers' that Hume sent to him in 1739 could have been a legal narrative rather than other essays; and Hume's attributing lack of news of Home's 'Friends' over 'the last Vacation' to their 'laziness' points to a writing coterie only if its members were in professions that gave them vacations for leisure. Most weight attaches to the episode in

---

[90] *New Letters*, 5–7. The essays already drafted included 'Of Moral Prejudices' and 'Of Love and Marriage'. It is sometimes said that Hume and Henry Home were in the journal project together. There is probably no hard evidence for this, but the last sentence of the 1 July letter may point to the existence of a literary club or network.

1762 when Home, by then Lord Kames, encouraged James Boswell to think of writing 'lively periodical papers' and recalled that he himself 'once had a scheme for the Publication of a Work of that kind at Edinburgh' and had still 'a couple of dozen of Essays which he intended for that purpose'.[91] If this is the same project as Hume describes, they had different perceptions of why it failed. Kames, after supposedly sitting on two dozen still unpublished essays for twenty-three years, recalled the abandonment as his initiative, due to 'a want of witty and humourous writers'. Hume, on the other hand, claimed to have 'dropt that Undertaking, partly from Laziness, partly from Want of Leisure', but in the same breath falsely represented the collected volume as his first literary venture.[92] Both were probably economical with the truth.

Secondly, Hume intended to follow the first two books of the *Treatise*, according to his initial 'Advertisement', with further volumes devoted to 'Morals, Politics and Criticism' if the public was sufficiently responsive. It was not, but the volume on morals was already sufficiently far advanced, and Hume saw it through with a change of publisher. He would experience the challenge of Hutcheson's opposition to his psychologically founded natural jurisprudence and had probably misread Hutcheson's self-proclaimed allegiance to Shaftesbury as adhesion to a naturalistic ethic. He had not bargained for the forcefulness of his antagonist's challenge, much of which was theologically motivated, and thought it sufficiently misdirected to warrant addressing. As for politics and criticism, these interests survived in his more serious essays, but relatively little of what he wrote is in a form that still reflects the ambitions of the *Treatise* project. The political essays, for example, notwithstanding the theoretical content, have a topical relevance to which the *Treatise* never pretended, and reflect a critical attitude to the use and abuse of liberties under the British constitution that aligns Hume with the opposition to the Walpole government.[93] The use of principles of association in section iii of the lifetime editions of the First *Enquiry* to explain the distinctive unity achieved in different literary genres is the closest Hume comes to applying his detailed psychology to literary analysis, although other aspects of Humean psychology are retained in his aesthetic essays.

Politics is the study of the nature and forms of communal order and the processes of their development. In Hume's hands it is a continuation of the study of human nature and motivation, but the data are as much social and

[91] Boswell, *Private Papers*, i. 101.

[92] Hume, *Essays Moral and Political* (1741), 'Advertisement'. Late in life, Hume referred to some of his withdrawn essays as 'bad Imitations of the agreeable *Trifling* of Addison' (*Letters*, ii. 257).

[93] M. M. Goldsmith, 'Faction detected: ideological consequences of Robert Walpole's decline and fall', in P. J. Korshin (ed.), *The American Revolution and Eighteenth-Century Culture* (New York: AMS Press, 1986), 1–30.

historical as experiential and mental. If he is redirecting his political project to conform to the new literary mould, there is probably a separate reason why he did not take the subject much further than the first volumes of essays (1741–8). His reading for it is opening up new interests. Several of the early political essays are starting to show an economic spin. In 'That Politics may be Reduced to a Science' he notes the effects of the legislators' power exercised through taxation and the control of wealth, based on classical examples; and in 'Whether the British Government inclines more to Absolute Monarchy or to a Republic', he starts to wonder about the relationship between power and personal wealth in the light of both classical and Renaissance examples. In 'Of the Independency of Parliament' he is beginning to note the relationship between parliamentary power and the control of the money supply, and in 'Of Parties in General' he is thinking about the relationship between the landed and commercial interests in England. But among the early essays, it is the essay 'Of Civil Liberty' that contains the main foray into economic matters, based on both classical and modern examples of the practical consequences of taxation and of public debt. Such themes are consistently interwoven with Hume's more political thoughts on the relationship between liberty and the forms of government. This meshes well with the evidence of his surviving reading notes, the so-called 'memoranda', which show his substantive interests in the post-*Treatise* period beginning to move on from pure politics towards political economy. That he mostly writes in broad terms in the early essays, without the detailed statistics that we find in some of the memoranda, is immaterial. This is in keeping with his present literary conceptions, but the essays nevertheless give the same evidence as the memoranda that he has been reading *authors* where greater information lies.

Thirdly, we have the evidence of the fragment on evil that Hume is engaged at a relatively early date on a critique of natural theology, an interest that is also manifest in the memoranda. This interest was in a sense coeval with the origins of the *Treatise*, if the foregoing reconstruction of events is true; but the relationship of the manuscript to that work is unclear, because of the imprecision of the date. It may, like the discussion of miracles, have been withdrawn from the *Treatise*; it may be part of a lost narrative work that he was planning as a sequel.[94] Since it is written on English, not French, paper, it seems to belong to the period of Hume's return from France, and after looking further at the writing and watermark evidence I am now prepared to countenance a third possibility: that it was part of Hume's abortive plans for a second, revised edition of the *Treatise*. But it remains true that, at around the time of the publication of the *Treatise*, Hume had sketched out a significant part of the argument that would eventually

[94] Stewart, 'An early fragment on evil'.

be presented through the character of Philo in the *Dialogues*. He was simply seeking a form and an occasion for its expression.

All these projects were derailed by the failure of the *Treatise*. Instead, Hume reconsidered his plans for the essay genre, and adapted it to the redevelopment of certain elements of his *Treatise* philosophy, both past and projected. More work has still to be done to relate the memoranda to the deferred development of his views on political economy and religion, but since the publication of my argument for placing the memoranda after Hume's return from France and in the period of his development as an essayist, new evidence has come to light. There are more overt matches than I was aware of between the untitled section of the memoranda and Hume's 1741-2 and 1748 *Essays* collections, and more matches between the Philosophy section and Hume's writings on religion.[95] The most important evidence is that presented in a so far unpublished paper by Tatsuya Sakamoto, showing that there are up to six matches between the memoranda and the three editions of the *Essays* in the 1740s, and that some of these take the form of parallels with erroneous 1741 or 1742 wording which is amended in the 1748 edition.[96]

VI

By 1752, when Hume is appointed Keeper of the Advocates' Library, his philosophical *œuvre* is virtually complete. The rest, to coin a phrase, is *History*—a generalization that will withstand the clearly true qualification that Hume's *History* is in important respects philosophical and that his philosophy is informed both by history and by the philosophy of history from an early stage. Still to come, certainly, are *Four Dissertations* (1757) and some revisions, including additions and subtractions, to the now established corpus. We do not know when the individual dissertations were written, except that 'Of the Standard of Taste' was a late makeweight.[97]

---

[95] For recent discussion of the relevance of the memoranda both to Hume's *Dialogues* and to *The Natural History of Religion*, see F. A. Bahr, 'Pierre Bayle en los "Early Memoranda" de Hume', *Revista latinoamericana de filosofía*, 25 (1999): 7–38, and Lothar Kreimendahl, 'Humes frühe religionsphilosophische Interessen im Lichte seiner "Early Memoranda"', *Zeitschrift für philosophische Forschung*, 53 (1999): 553–68. For the dating, see Stewart, 'Dating of Hume's manuscripts', 276–88.

[96] Tatsuya Sakamoto, 'Hume's "Early Memoranda" and the Shaping of his Political Economy', presented at the Conference on David Hume's Political Economy, Barnard College, 9–10 May 2003. The evidence there cited seems to me conclusive for a date *c.*1740 for a significant part of the untitled memoranda, although Sakamoto seeks to evade this inference. I am grateful to Professor Sakamoto for letting me read and comment on a revised draft of his paper.

[97] The roots of 'The Natural History of Religion' lie in Hume's preparation for the 1741 essay 'Of Superstition and Enthusiasm'. Even if the finished work reflects his greater access to a historical library after 1752, some at least of his documentation has been traced to the period of the

Two further political essays were added to the *Essays* collection in 1760 ('Of the Jealousy of Trade' and 'Of the Coalition of Parties'), and a third ('Of the Origin of Government') was completed only in 1774 and was published posthumously. Hume's letter to William Strahan in which he describes the completion of the last essay throws light on one quite worldly motive he had for periodically revising his works: although the legal situation was in dispute, Hume believed that by providing new matter, he confirmed his publishers in a new fourteen-year copyright and prevented the emergence of pirated editions (*Letters*, i. 287, 288).[98] But the fact remains that, barring some significant revisions, the two *Enquiries* had been published by 1751, the *Dialogues* were already in draft, and the *Political Discourses* were out by January 1752. A few months earlier Hume had left the family home for good, and was embarking on a new life in more than one sense.

The extent and significance of the substantive changes in his thinking between the *Treatise* and the *Enquiries* are contested matters which there is no space to consider fully here. In the run-up to publication of the *Treatise* and beyond, Hume had been bothered in case his exposition lacked the lucidity necessary to compensate for the novelty and abstruseness of the subject.[99] When initial sales were slight, he tried to console himself that abstract reasoning does not sell, and that a study whose 'Principles' would tend to 'a total Alteration in Philosophy' must necessarily face considerable public inertia. Authors, like lovers, are 'besotted with a blind Fondness of their Object'. 'My Fondness for what I imagin'd new Discoveries made me overlook all common Rules of Prudence.'[100] So he vacillates over whether the failing lay with the presentation, the content, or the subject. By the time of the *Abstract*, the potential technical failings are identified as a combination of length and abstractness: 'those who are not accustomed to abstract reasoning, are apt to lose the thread of argument, where it is drawn out to a great length, and each part fortified with all the arguments, guarded against all the objections, and illustrated with all the views, which occur to a writer in the diligent survey of his subject.'[101] The letter to John Coutts which was adapted by Henry Home to form half of *A Letter from a Gentleman* in 1745 contains the clear admission that in the *Treatise* Hume got some things wrong—but not his 'Principles'. He was by now beginning the task of reinventing himself through the preparation of the *Enquiry*: 'I am indeed of

memoranda. 'Of the Passions', derived from Book II of the *Treatise*, contains no new substance, but it is important for demonstrating Hume's continuing and whole-hearted commitment to the associationist psychology. 'Of Tragedy' and 'Of the Standard of Taste' reflect an old familiarity with the work of Dubos.

[98] My thanks to M. A. Box for alerting me to this context.

[99] *New Letters*, 1; *Letters*, i. 29.   [100] *New Letters*, 3, 5.

[101] *An Abstract of a Book lately Published; entituled, A Treatise of Human Nature, &c.* (1740), preface.

Opinion, that the Author had better delayed the publishing of that Book [the *Treatise*]; not on account of any dangerous Principles contained in it, but because on more mature Consideration he might have rendered it much less imperfect by further Corrections and Revisals.'[102]

In the early months of 1751, when Hume has sent Gilbert Elliot all or part of the manuscript of the *Dialogues* for comment, Elliot presses him on aspects of his philosophy. From the context, the topics appear to be causal reasoning and the detection of the causal relation. Hume cautions against getting bogged down in this subject: 'I am sorry our Correspondence shou'd lead us into these abstract Speculations.' On the other hand, he defends himself as a philosopher for having pursued them: 'If in order to answer the Doubts started, new Principles of Philosophy must be laid; are not these Doubts themselves very useful? Are they not preferable to blind, & ignorant Assent?' (*Letters*, i. 156). Elliot is dissatisfied and feels he should get to the bottom of Hume's argument in the *Treatise*. Hume redirects him to the *Enquiry*:

I believe the philosophical Essays contain every thing of Consequence relating to the Understanding, which you woud meet with in the Treatise; & I give you my advice against reading the latter. By shortening and simplifying the Questions, I really render them much more complete. *Addo dum minuo.* The philosophical Principles are the same in both: But I was carry'd away by the Heat of Youth & Invention to publish too precipitately. (Ibid. 158)

His early comments have now become routine, to the effect that there was nothing wrong with the philosophical principles of the *Treatise*, but the fault was in the presentation. It should have been shorter and simpler, but he was young and impetuous.

The same topics dog Hume in his correspondence with John Stewart three years later:

But allow me to tell you, that I never asserted so absurd a Proposition as *that any thing might arise without a Cause*: I only maintain'd, that our certainty of the Falshood of that Proposition proceeded neither from Intuition nor Demonstration; but from another Source. *That Caesar existed, that there is such an Island as Sicily*; for these Propositions, I affirm, we have no demonstrative nor intuitive Proof. (Ibid. 187)

Though he finds, still, nothing wrong in his argument, Hume does admit 'a very great Mistake in Conduct, viz my publishing at all the Treatise of human Nature, a Book, which pretended to innovate in all the sublimest Parts of Philosophy'. Indeed, he has become neurotic about it. 'Above all, the positive Air, which prevails in that Book, & which may be imputed to

---

[102] *A Letter from a Gentleman to his Friend in Edinburgh* (1745), 33.

the Ardor of Youth, so much displeases me, that I have not Patience to review it. But what Success the same Doctrines, better illustrated & exprest, may meet with, *Ad huc sub judice lis est.*' And yet, within a few months of this, Hume would be despatching his *Dissertation on the Passions* to the printer, with only minimal changes to a text derived directly from the *Treatise*.

Years later, galled by the success of James Beattie's *Essay on the Nature and Immutability of Truth*, Hume was to send Strahan in 1775 the 'compleat Answer' to Reid and Beattie that was to be prefixed as an 'Advertisement' to all remaining and future copies of the volumes containing his *Enquiries* and the *Dissertation on the Passions* (*Letters*, ii. 301). As an attempt to draw attention away from the *Treatise*, it is long on rhetoric and short on substance. Hume had eschewed most of the substance when, in the early 1760s, he had the chance to answer Reid (as he answered Campbell of Aberdeen) in private correspondence. He now belabours those who 'have taken care to direct all their batteries against that juvenile work, which the Author never acknowledged', when almost from the outset he had been 'sensible of his error in going to the press too early'. To 'have affected to triumph in any advantages, which, they imagined, they had obtained' over a work born in such circumstances was a kind of moral cowardice, a 'strong instance of those polemical artifices, which a bigotted zeal thinks itself authorized to employ'. Admitting that 'most of the principles, and reasonings' of the *Enquiries* and the *Dissertation* were first published in the *Treatise*, and conceding no more than 'some negligences in his former reasoning and more in the expression', he asks that his later works 'may alone be regarded as containing his philosophical sentiments and principles'.[103]

This combination of the moral high ground with the admission only of 'some negligences' in the matters of substance falls short of the disavowal or repudiation it is often made out to be;[104] indeed it is less strong on that score than the letter to Stewart. But it is curious on several grounds. Reid, who unlike Beattie recognized the *Treatise* as a major achievement, had been scrupulous in print in not picking on Hume by name, but in targeting the

---

[103] 'Advertisement', in *Essays and Treatises on Several Subjects*, 2 vols. (1777), ii. sig. A2^r. Although the Advertisement was sent to Strahan in 1775, there was a fire at the warehouse soon after, and it became generally known only through the version that appeared in the posthumous 1777 edition. This is reproduced before the text of the First *Enquiry* in the edition of *Enquiries concerning Human Understanding and concerning the Principles of Morals* revised by P. H. Nidditch (Oxford: Clarendon Press, 1975), 2, and in the critical edition of *An Enquiry concerning Human Understanding* edited by Tom L. Beauchamp (Oxford: Clarendon Press, 2000), 1. One of the costs of later curricular developments and publishing strategies has been that Hume's acceptance into the canon has led to the fragmentation of an *œuvre* that he and his publisher sought to integrate.

[104] The idea that Hume 'disowned' the *Treatise* was popularized in the modern literature by Greig (*David Hume*, 107, 391; *Letters*, ii. 301 n. 2), from whom it was taken up by Kemp Smith.

anonymous work by title alone;[105] it was only *after* the acknowledgement implied in the 'Advertisement' that Reid in later publications identified the doctrines of the *Treatise* as Hume's, so the 'Advertisement' was counter-productive. Furthermore, although Reid missed his target in a number of criticisms, his searching critique of what he called the 'ideal theory' had a lasting impact that Hume was powerless to prevent. Beattie was the one who, intermittently, named Hume in his lifetime, but in doing so even he was careful to state that the 'principal doctrines' of the *Treatise* 'he hath since republished again and again, under the title of, *Essays Moral and Political*, &c.'—a wrong title, but making the point that Hume had already sought to make to Elliot and Stewart and now repeats in the 'Advertisement'.[106] Hume was either ironic or naive, or was assuming Strahan's ignorance, in suggesting that the *Enquiries* could do anything to deflect Beattie's critique, since that was premised on the conviction that Hume's philosophy was an unmitigated threat to religious belief, a conviction that the First *Enquiry* seemed only to confirm. Hume's comment that he 'cast the whole' of the *Treatise* 'anew' in the *Enquiries* and the *Dissertation* goes beyond the more careful earlier claims that his principles have not changed. There are some significant divergences in the topics covered, some that even Hume had found unsatisfactory being dropped and new ones put in their place, and there are sufficient differences of balance and emphasis to change one's sense of the targets and topicality of the message. His final comment, in 'My own Life', continues to minimize these differences: once again we are told that the failure of the *Treatise* was due more to the manner than the matter, and he therefore cast 'the first part' anew in the First *Enquiry* and 'another part' in the Second. This is certainly an over-simplification of the relationship, and one may want to claim that it is a misrepresentation.

The First *Enquiry* is more an overview of his whole philosophy, and it includes forays into morals, religion, and other subjects throughout; but it became convenient to think of it more narrowly as the sequels to it evolved. At the time when he was working on it in 1745 (a time of crisis in his own career), Hume had written to Henry Home, 'I intend to continue these philo-sophical & moral Essays, which I mention'd to you'.[107] 'Philosophical' sounds, with hindsight, like the First *Enquiry*, so Klibansky and Mossner proposed that the 'moral' essays would be the Second *Enquiry*. That would not explain Hume's distinction between two genres, since both *Enquiries* fall

---

[105] In the chapter 'Of Seeing', in *An Inquiry into the Human Mind on the Principles of Common Sense* (1764), VI. vi, Reid makes unspecific references to Hume by name without identifying any work.

[106] James Beattie, *An Essay on the Nature and Immutability of Truth* (Edinburgh, 1770), 9–10.

[107] *New Letters*, 18. On Hume's changing view of his literary products as he attempted to redefine his market in the 1740s, see Stewart, 'Two species of philosophy'.

squarely in the category of 'philosophical'; he may therefore not yet have had a clear plan for the second as a distinct work. There is a broad use of the genre term 'moral essays' which would apply to Hume's volumes of *Essays, Moral and Political*, and he did indeed work on additional pieces which were three years later added to that collection; but they are partly coloured by political events immediately subsequent to Hume's letter and not anticipated in it. So with regard to both of his declared projects he would have been adjusting his intentions as events evolved, and we should not try to be over-precise about them simply to accommodate his later retrospect on them.

If we look at the criticisms and questions Hume faced, from early reviews, through the controversies and correspondence of his middle career, and up to the scurrilities of Beattie, we find that they reflect a good deal of misunder-standing and sometimes straight incomprehension on the part of the critics and questioners. Furthermore, the individual misunderstandings are recur-rent. Critics regularly misread the function of his portrayal of the sceptical mind, particularly in the Conclusion to Book I, and fail to see it as a literary artifice out of which a durable position is made to emerge; so they read him as an unreconstructed Pyrrhonian, discount a multitude of statements that are incompatible with that, and credit his position with implications he has not derived from it. They see the limitations he imposes on the scope of reason as the denial of reason and fail to understand the need for other aspects of our psychology both in epistemology and in morals. The limits in experience to our knowledge of the processes of causation are taken to be a denial of those processes; and his reconsideration of the theoretical founda-tions of social institutions is read as undermining those institutions.

It is obvious why this had to be a worry to Hume. He was failing to get across his central tenets. In his more objective moments—for example, in his letters to Coutts and Stewart—he is prepared to spread the blame: if his critics cannot shake off their entrenched preconceptions, he is also at fault for not making himself clearer, or for losing the clarity that was there by an over-elaboration of detail. But the message has worn thin and is becoming con-fused in Hume's last years. He has been finalizing the form in which his writings will be passed to posterity, and for this purpose has had to regard the *Treatise* as a write-off. Other writers of the period, such as Adam Smith, Reid, and Dugald Stewart, would also take considerable pains to control their liter-ary legacies in ways that later intellectual historians have not fully endorsed. But Hume is controlling not only the literary record but also the biographical one. The evidence prepared for publication in the last couple of years of his life is carefully staged, and not without a vein of irony running through it. He is engaged in a deliberate manœuvre to settle some scores and to try to influ-ence the posthumous record, and he did not realize how much of a trail from earlier in his career he was leaving behind and contradicting in the process.

Corresponding with Elliot and Stewart in the early 1750s, Hume had said that the *Treatise* was 'plan'd before I was one and twenty, & compos'd before twenty five' (*Letters*, i. 158; cf. 187). Already there has been some telescoping of the time scale. I saw no reason above to contest the date for his planning of the *Treatise*, which fits well with the information coming out of the letter to the physician. But that he had the whole thing drafted after only two of the three years he spent in France is taking some licence. Uppermost in his mind is Book I, but even that was still being worked on after he returned to London a year later, and Book III was not completed until after he had met and corresponded with Hutcheson in 1739. The chronology is further distorted by the time of the 1775 'Advertisement'. It is creative imagination, if not wilful misrepresentation, to pretend that the *Treatise* was either written or published 'not long after' Hume left college. He left college in 1725, and published the work in 1739–40. (To talk about 'leaving college' is to talk about completing the arts course—as when Hume wrote to the physician that 'our College Education . . . ends commonly when we are about 14 or 15 Years of Age' and that *after* this he started to plan his own programme of study.) Fifteen years after is *not* 'not long after'. And if this is clear falsification, it is misplaced ingenuity to try to salvage the suggestion that Hume had projected *this* work in any meaningful sense 'before he left College'. Whatever philosophical thoughts crossed his mind before he left college, there is no reason to think that he had yet adopted the Stoic model or repudiated the religious framework that were likely factors in his nervous crisis, or that he had learnt to adjust his sights to the proper regard to 'human Nature' that that crisis forced upon him.

Hume is engaged in his last years in damage limitation. If he never goes so far as to disown the *Treatise*, he is distancing himself from it by increasingly 'projecting' the work back into a remote past. In 'My own Life' he is more accurate on the composition of the *Treatise*, but describes the failure of its reception in too black-and-white terms.[108] Sales may have been poor, and the notices tended to be critical, but the press coverage across Europe was exceptional for a work of its kind at the time. Another contemporary working in the same field, George Turnbull, would have been glad of a fraction of Hume's notices. Hume puts an exaggerated distance between the publication of the *Treatise*, backdated to 'the End of 1738', and 'the first part of my Essays', which he defers to 1742. The *Treatise* was actually published at the end of January 1739, as he reported to Henry Home at the time (*New Letters*, 3), and the original volume of the *Essays* in July 1741, as indicated by

---

[108] 'My own Life', *Letters*, i. 2. The early press reception of the *Treatise* has been extensively researched by David Fate Norton and Mary Norton in their forthcoming critical edition for the Clarendon Hume.

contemporary announcements in the Edinburgh press.[109] He is, however, correct to note that the latter work 'was favourably received', which falsifies his later remark that the *Political Discourses* was 'the only work of mine, that was successful on the first Publication'.[110] Hume minimizes the reception accorded to *The Natural History of Religion* 'along with some other small Pieces' in order to answer in kind the abuse he received from Richard Hurd; but within a few weeks of publication he had learnt through the grapevine that his primary critic in the pamphlet attributed to Hurd was actually William Warburton (*Letters*, i. 265). The *Natural History* did attract the reviewers, and the volume as a whole gained a good deal of publicity from common knowledge of the protracted history of its publication and from Hume's controversial dedication to John Home. But all this is suppressed.

In short, Hume is more concerned with projecting a general picture of his career than with precision of detail. He is willing to gloss the details and take some liberties with the facts, and some he has doubtless misremembered. The extravagances of the 'Advertisement', written only a few months earlier, are part of the same promotional machinery, and it is more important to identify its real message. Hume has long since come to see the *Treatise* as a humiliating failure, given his lifelong resolve to be a successful man of letters. If there was a humiliation, however, his own judgement appears to concur with the predominant view of posterity, that it was literary rather than philosophical. He has not overtly retracted any significant body of his philosophy. His 'desire' that the *Enquiries* and the *Dissertation on the Passions* 'may alone be regarded as containing his philosophical sentiments and principles' must be seen in relation to his intended readership. The *Treatise* was suited only to a specialized readership, one whose nature and extent Hume had not fully thought out when he went to press. In the 'Advertisement' to the *Treatise* he addressed himself generally to 'the public'. He does not include what, early in the Introduction, he calls 'the rabble without doors', but he was at least hoping to tempt 'those, who profess themselves scholars'.[111] He quickly came to see that this was over-sanguine in the context of the times. Thus it would be inappropriate for Henry Home to take 'a great many Copys' and 'push the Sale'. '[T]here is so little to be gain'd that way in such Works as these, that I wou'd not have you take the Trouble.' Home would do him a greater service if he could find anyone at all with the skills to give him informed comment,[112] and the result

---

[109] Advance notices gave an imprecise title, *Essays on Various Subjects*, but it is identifiable as Hume's *Essays* from the detailed contents lists. This discovery was first made by Brian Hillyard. It is true that the first part of the *Essays* was not completed until the addition of a second volume in 1742, but Hume did not date the publication of the *Treatise* from the *completion* of volume III in 1740. Nor is it likely that he was seriously dating the first volumes from the old English legal year, a convention that neither he nor his publisher had observed.

[110] 'My own Life', *Letters*, i. 2, 4. For Hume's own more contemporary report on the success of the first collection, see pp. 42–3.   [111] *Treatise*, Introduction, paras. 2, 3.

[112] *New Letters*, 4. Hume also sought informed comment through Des Maizeaux: *Letters*, i. 29–30.

was a contact with Hutcheson that generated benefits as well as frictions. In the *Abstract*, a work possibly composed at Hutcheson's suggestion (since it appears to be patterned on Hutcheson's submission of an abstract of his own *Inquiry* to the *London Journal* of 14 and 21 November 1724), Hume is still uncertain of his audience. He can make no claims on 'the people', yet he is trying to make his work 'more intelligible to ordinary capacities', notwithstanding that they are 'not accustomed to abstract reasoning'. But in the end, he seems to be waiting for the verdict of 'the learned world', 'the FEW' who have thought on these things, notwithstanding the partialities and prejudices they have acquired in the process.[113]

Because of the urgent need to address an uncomprehending public and to clarify his general conclusions, Hume had to be prepared to cut back drastically on the psychological descriptions that had deprived him of a readership. This can create the illusion that the psychological foundations have been abandoned; but this is to read the *Enquiries* out of context. By the end of his career, the *Dissertation on the Passions* is part of the same project as they are, and not only shows the associationist psychology surviving in its full vigour, but embeds it within the wider philosophy to which there is periodic reference. Here it is the technicalities that make the subject; it was a risk to re-launch it, but the work is never presented except as part of a collection with other works. Hume learnt the hard way that 'the FEW' were fewer than he had bargained for. They did not include most of those in the professions who constituted what he perceived as the reading classes. By 1751 they did not include cultured friends like Gilbert Elliot. The *Enquiries* were a conscious attempt to expand his readership beyond the few who were equipped to understand the *Treatise*, to the educated public at large, and it is to this expanded readership that the 'Advertisement' to the *Enquiries* and the *Dissertation* is addressed. There is an irony in his seeing some of the professors of the day as members only of the expanded class, but when did Hume ever feel particularly beholden to professors?

REFERENCES

Manuscript Primary Sources

Anon., transcription of 'Compendium logicae Authore Domino Drummond': Edinburgh University Library, MS 2651.
—— transcriptions of translations of Horace and other Latin poets dictated by Laurence Dundas: Edinburgh University Library, Dc 7. 54; La. III. 459, 759.
Boswell, Alexander, transcription of 'Annotata In Libros A et B Homeri Iliados Autore D. Gulielmo Scot Philosophiae et Linguae Graecae Professore In

---

[113] *An Abstract of a Book lately Published*, Preface.

Academia Edinensi Ingenio Doctrina et Moribus pariter Illustri' (1722): Edinburgh University Library, MS 2671.

—— transcription of 'Institutiones Logicae a Domino Collino Drummond Dictitatae' (1723): National Library of Scotland, MS 3938.

—— transcription of 'Principia Hydrostaticae ac Astronomiae Authore D. D. Roberto Stewart' (1724): Mitchell Library, Glasgow, MS S.R. 171.

Campbell, Daniel, transcription of 'Systema philosophiae a Gulielmo Law, Philosophiae professore in Academia Edinburgena' (1699): National Library of Scotland, MS 183.

Chirnside Presbytery Minutes: National Archives of Scotland, CH2/16/3.

Cuninghame, Alexander, 'Excerptions from Mr Stewarts Colledge of Experimentall Philosophy begun Feb. 6th 1724': Glasgow University Library, in MS Murray 273.

Home, David, transcription of 'A Treatise of Fluxions by George Campbell' (1726): National Library of Scotland, Acc. 11333 (photocopy).

Hume, David, 'An Historical Essay on Chivalry and modern Honour': National Library of Scotland, MS 23159, item 4.

Hume of Ninewells family deposit: National Archives of Scotland, RH15/15/11.

Library accounts, 20 Feb. 1696–1 Feb. 1765: Edinburgh University Library, Da 1. 37.

Mackie, Charles, 'Alphabetical List of those who attended the Prelections on History and Roman Antiquitys. From 1719 to 1744 Inclusive. Collected 1 July, 1746': Edinburgh University Library, Dc 5.24², pp. 203–21.

Matriculation register, 1704–62: Edinburgh University Library, Da.

Smith, John, transcription of 'Ethica ab Illustrissimo eruditissimoque Domino Magistro Gullielmo Law Dictata': Edinburgh University Library, in Dc 8. 53.

Printed Primary Sources

Anon., *The Whole Duty of Man* (London, 1659).

Boswell, James, *Journal of a Tour to the Hebrides with Samuel Johnson, LL.D.* (London, 1785).

—— *Private Papers from Malahide Castle*, ed. G. Scott *et al.*, 18 vols. (New York: privately published, 1928–34).

—— 'An account of my last interview with David Hume, Esq.', in G. Scott *et al.* (eds.), *Private Papers of James Boswell from Malahide Castle*, 18 vols. (New York: privately published, 1928–34), xii. 227–32.

Chamberlayne, John, *Magnae Britanniae notitia* (London, 1708, 1710).

Cheyne, George, *The English Malady* (London and Bath, 1733).

Clericus, Joannes [Jean le Clerc], *Logica, ontologia, et pneumatologia*, 4th edn. (Cambridge, 1704).

The Confession of Faith, together with the Larger and Shorter Catechisms (1648), 5th edn. (London, 1717).

The Edinburgh Miscellany (Edinburgh, 1720).

Greig, J. Y. T. (ed.), *The Letters of David Hume*, 2 vols. (Oxford: Clarendon Press, 1932).

Hog, Thomas, *Some Missives Written to a Gentleman* (Edinburgh, 1718).

Hume, David, *A Treatise of Human Nature* (London, 1739–40).

—— *Essays Moral, Political and Literary*, ed. Eugene F. Miller (Indianapolis: Liberty Classics, 1985).

Hutcheson, Francis, *Philosophiae moralis institutio compendiaria*, 2nd edn. (Glasgow, 1745).

Klibansky, Raymond, and Mossner, Ernest C. (eds.), *New Letters of David Hume* (Oxford: Clarendon Press, 1954).

Kozanecki, Tadeusz, 'Dawida Hume'a nieznane listy w zbiorach Muzeum Czartoryskich (Polska)', *Archiwum Historii Filozofii i Mysli Spolcznej*, 9 (1963): 127–41.

Locke, John, *An Essay Concerning Human Understanding* (London, 1690).

Mossner, Ernest C., 'Hume at La Flèche, 1735: an unpublished letter', *University of Texas Studies in English*, 37 (1958): 30–3.

The Physiological Library, Begun by Mr. Steuart, and some of the Students of Natural Philosophy in the University of Edinburgh, April 2. 1724: and Augmented by some Gentlemen; and the Students of Natural Philosophy, December 1724 (Edinburgh, 1725).

Pitman, Joy, 'The journal of John Boswell: Part I', *Proceedings of the Royal College of Physicians of Edinburgh*, 20 (1990): 67–77.

Reid, Thomas, *Essays on the Intellectual Powers of Man*, ed. Derek Brookes and Knud Haakonssen (Edinburgh: Edinburgh University Press, 2002).

Shaftesbury, Anthony Ashley Cooper, third Earl of, *Characteristics of Men, Manners, Opinions, Times*, 3rd edn. (London, 1723).

Smith, William, *Dissertatio philosophica inauguralis de natura spirituum* (Glasgow, 1714).

Voet, Johann, *Compendium juris juxta seriem Pandectarum* (Leiden, 1731).

Wodrow, Robert, *Analecta*, 4 vols. (Edinburgh: Maitland Club, 1842–3).

Secondary Sources

Bahr, F. A., 'Pierre Bayle en los "Early Memoranda" de Hume', *Revista latinoamericana de filosofia*, 25 (1999): 7–38.

Barfoot, Michael, 'Hume and the culture of science in the early eighteenth century', in M. A. Stewart (ed.), *Studies in the Philosophy of the Scottish Enlightenment* (Oxford: Clarendon Press, 1990), 151–90.

Brandt, Reinhard, 'The beginnings of Hume's philosophy', in George Morice (ed.), *David Hume: Bicentenary Papers* (Edinburgh: Edinburgh University Press, 1977), 117–27.

Burton, John H., *Life and Correspondence of David Hume*, 2 vols. (Edinburgh: William Tait, 1846).

Clarke, M. L., *Classical Education in Britain 1500–1900* (Cambridge: Cambridge University Press, 1959).

Echelbarger, Charles, 'Hume and the logicians', in P. A. Easton (ed.), *Logic and the Workings of the Mind* (Atascadero, Calif.: Ridgeview, 1997), 137–51.

Goldsmith, M. M., 'Faction detected: ideological consequences of Robert Walpole's decline and fall', in P. J. Korshin (ed.), *The American Revolution and Eighteenth-Century Culture* (New York: AMS Press, 1986), 1–30.

Grant, Alexander, *The Story of the University of Edinburgh during its First Three Hundred Years*, 2 vols. (London: Longmans, Green, 1884).

Greig, J. Y. T., *David Hume* (London: Cape, 1931).

Hillyard, Brian, and Norton, David Fate, 'The David Hume bookplate: a cautionary note', *The Book Collector*, 40 (1991): 539–44.

Kreimendahl, Lothar, 'Humes frühe religionsphilosophische Interessen im Lichte seiner "Early Memoranda"', *Zeitschrift für philosophische Forschung*, 53 (1999): 553–68.

Law, Alexander, *Education in Edinburgh in the Eighteenth Century* (London: University of London Press, 1965).

Norton, David Fate, and Norton, Mary, *The David Hume Library* (Edinburgh: Edinburgh Bibliographical Society, 1996).

Rivers, Isabel, 'Shaftesburian enthusiasm and the evangelical revival', in J. Garnett and C. Matthew (eds.), *Revival and Religion since 1700: Essays for John Walsh* (London: Hambledon, 1993), pp. 21–39.

—— *Reason, Grace and Sentiment: A Study of the Language of Religion and Ethics in England 1660–1780*, 2 vols. (Cambridge: Cambridge University Press, 1991, 2000).

Schuurman, Paul, 'The empiricist logic of ideas of Jean le Clerc', in Wiep van Bunge (ed.), *The Early Enlightenment in the Dutch Republic, 1650–1750* (Leiden: Brill, 2003), 137–53.

Sharpe, L. W., 'Charles Mackie, the first Professor of History at Edinburgh University', *Scottish Historical Review*, 41 (1962): 23–45.

Sher, Richard B., 'Professors of virtue: the social history of the Edinburgh moral philosophy chair in the eighteenth century', in M. A. Stewart (ed.), *Studies in the Philosophy of the Scottish Enlightenment* (Oxford: Clarendon Press, 1990), 87–126.

Skoczylas, Anne, *Mr Simson's Knotty Case* (Montreal: McGill–Queen's University Press, 2001).

Stewart, M. A., 'The origins of the Scottish Greek chairs', in Elizabeth M. Craik (ed.), *'Owls to Athens': Essays on Classical Subjects Presented to Sir Kenneth Dover* (Oxford: Clarendon Press, 1990), 391–400.

—— 'The Stoic legacy in the early Scottish Enlightenment', in Margaret J. Osler (ed.), *Atoms, 'Pneuma', and Tranquillity* (Cambridge: Cambridge University Press, 1991), 273–96.

—— 'An early fragment on evil', in M. A. Stewart and J. P. Wright (eds.), *Hume and Hume's Connexions* (Edinburgh: Edinburgh University Press, 1994), 160–70.

—— 'The dating of Hume's manuscripts', in P. Wood (ed.), *The Scottish Enlightenment: Essays in Reinterpretation* (Rochester, NY: University of Rochester Press, 2000), 267–314.

—— 'Two species of philosophy: the historical significance of the first *Enquiry*', in P. Millican (ed.), *Reading Hume on Human Understanding* (Oxford: Clarendon Press, 2001), 67–95.

—— (ed.), *Studies in the Philosophy of the Scottish Enlightenment* (Oxford: Clarendon Press, 1990).

Wright, John P., 'Dr George Cheyne, Chevalier Ramsay, and Hume's letter to a physician', *Hume Studies*, 29 (2003): 125–41.

Waiting for Hume

PETER LIPTON

———•———

It was David Hume's great sceptical argument about non-demonstrative reasoning—the problem of induction—that hooked me on philosophy. I am still wriggling, but in the present essay I will not consider how the Humean challenge to justify our inductive practices might be met; rather, I ask why we had to wait until Hume for the challenge to be raised. The question is a natural one to ask, given the intense interest in scepticism before Hume for as far back as we can see in the history of philosophy, and given that Hume's sceptical argument is so simple and so fundamental. It is not so easy to answer. I am no historian of philosophy, and given the pull that the problem of induction exerts on my own philosophical thinking, I know there is a considerable risk that the historical speculations I consider here will turn out to be worthlessly anachronistic. But I hope not.

Hume's discussion is deeply attractive for a number of reasons. In part it is the scope of Hume's scepticism. Our reliance on induction is ubiquitous, and Hume's argument seems to impugn all of it. But this does not explain why Hume impressed me even more than Descartes, who in his First Meditation questions far more. (I was, however, pretty excited by Descartes too.) The contrast is explained in part by the fact that Hume's argument is in at least two senses more radical than the sceptical arguments that Descartes offers. Descartes intends to argue against the possibility of certainty; but Hume argues against the possibility of any warrant whatever. (In fact, Descartes's arguments may well also yield the stronger conclusion, a point I will return to below.) And whereas Descartes focuses on a problem of moving from one level to another, notably from inner experience to the external world, Hume showed that the most severe sceptical arguments remain even when the inference remains modestly at the same level. Put differently, Hume showed that even if one is granted the existence of whatever one seems to observe, one cannot go any further. Hume's argument is in this sense more severe, because it undermines inferences that are more modest.

I am grateful to the participants at the Impressions of David Hume workshop for their reactions to my presentation there, and to Anjan Chakravartty, Marina Frasca-Spada, Anandi Hattiangadi, Peter Kail, Tim Lewens, and Neil Manson for their helpful comments on a draft of this essay.

In addition to the excitement generated by the depth and breadth of Hume's attack, I was struck by the power and beauty of the central dilemma he constructs.[1] To justify induction, we need a cogent argument for the conclusion that nature is uniform, that the future will be like the past. There are only two kinds of argument: demonstrative and probable. There is no demonstrative argument for the conclusion of uniformity, since demonstrative arguments have premises and conclusions that are necessary truths, and the claim of uniformity is clearly contingent. And there is no cogent probable argument for the uniformity of nature, because all probable arguments assume that uniformity and so would beg the question. So there is no cogent argument. In a more modern version, to justify induction, we need some reason to believe it will be reliable, and reasons are either deductive or inductive. Limiting ourselves to premises that do not themselves rely on induction, we cannot deduce that induction will be reliable, and any inductive argument for induction would be viciously circular. The circularity of any empirical justification of induction hit me particularly hard, since induction's track record had seemed the only good reason to trust induction in future, and this reason was now taken from me.

Another impressive feature of Hume's argument was its curious independence from the details of our inductive practices. One would have thought that the question of just what kind of inferences we make would be prior to the question of how they might be justified, since until we know what our practices are, we do not know what we are being asked to justify. Or so one would have thought. Hume does of course give some description of inductive practices, in terms of habit and mundane extrapolation, but the description seems primitive: it fails to do justice to the richness and complexity of our inductive practices. Yet this weakness of description appears not to undermine Hume's sceptical argument, because the argument is independent of the details of our inductive practices: all that counts is that they are not deductive. (Another famous Humean discussion that exhibits a related independence is his treatment of causation. Hume's case against our ability to conceive of a connection between external cause and effect is developed in the context of his implausibly restrictive copy principle, according to which every idea is a copy of a preceding impression; but the case against our ability to conceive of objects connected, and not just conjoined, is strangely undiminished by the primitiveness of the principle.)

These four features of Hume's sceptical argument—its severity, its scope, the beauty and power of its destructive dilemma, and especially of the circularity argument, and its independence from the details of our inductive practices—are the main reasons why the argument so attracted me and,

[1] David Hume, *A Treatise of Human Nature*, ed. L. A. Selby-Bigge, 2nd edn., rev. P. H. Nidditch (Oxford: Clarendon Press, 1978), 88–90; and *An Enquiry Concerning Human Understanding*, ed. L. A. Selby-Bigge, 3rd edn., rev. P. H. Nidditch (Oxford: Clarendon Press, 1975), 34–6.

I suppose, so many other fledgling philosophers. As impressive as Hume's intellectual achievement here is, however, it remains remarkable that the argument did not appear much earlier in the history of philosophy. Indeed, another reason the argument is so impressive is because, from a certain point of view, it seems so obvious. Certainly none of the aspects of the argument that so impressed me seem to have been conceptually unavailable to earlier philosophers. So why did we have to wait for Hume for the problem of induction?

A FALSE PRESUPPOSITION?

Maybe the answer is simple: we didn't. Certainly there are philosophical discussions of induction before Hume, to which Sextus Empiricus and Francis Bacon were particularly conspicuous contributors.[2] It was widely appreciated that since inductive reasoning is non-demonstrative, it always remains possible that the premisses are true yet the conclusion false. Thus Sextus wrote that 'some of the particulars omitted in the induction may contravene the universal'.[3] Indeed, more than the mere possibility of error was acknowledged for at least some forms of induction, with Bacon calling enumerative induction 'utterly vicious and incompetent', 'gross and stupid', and 'childish'.[4]

To appreciate the range of pre-Humean concern with inductive inference, we must not limit ourselves to enumerative induction, but consider non-demonstrative argument generally. (I use the unqualified term 'induction' in that broader sense.) In particular, we must consider discussions of 'vertical' induction, where the conclusion employs a different vocabulary from that used to describe the evidential premisses, and especially when the inference is from the observed to the unobservable, not just to the unobserved. There is a rich pre-Humean history of discussion, both of the importance of such inductive inferences and of the sceptical threat they raise, especially because of the underdetermination of theory by evidence.[5] The worries often focus on astronomical hypotheses, though the point is general. Thus in the ancient period Epicurus suggests in his 'Letter to Pythocles' that we embrace all the possible explanations of celestial phenomena, since choice between them would be capricious:

In the case of celestial events . . . both the causes of their coming to be and the accounts of their essence are multiple . . . Now in respect of all things which have

---

[2] John R. Milton, 'Induction before Hume', *British Journal for the Philosophy of Science*, 38 (1987): 49–74, provides a particularly helpful account of induction before Hume, on which I have relied for much of my information on the subject.   [3] Ibid. 56.
[4] Ibid. 57.   [5] Larry Laudan, *Science and Hypothesis* (Dordrecht: Reidel, 1981), ch. 6.

a multiplicity of explanations consistent with things evident, complete freedom from trepidation results when someone in the proper way lets stand whatever is plausibly suggested about them. But when someone allows one explanation while rejecting another equally consistent with what is evident, he is clearly abandoning natural philosophy altogether and descending into myth.[6]

In the Middle Ages, Thomas Aquinas expresses a very similar concern:

. . . the assumptions of the astronomers are not necessarily true. Although these hypotheses appear to save the phenomena, one ought not affirm that they are true, for one might be able to explain the apparent motions of the stars in some other way.[7]

Having been sensitized to the breadth of non-demonstrative argument, one can find sceptical worries about induction throughout the history of philosophy. For example, it is natural to gloss the many sceptical arguments about the senses and about belief based on testimony as problems of induction. Neither what we see nor what we hear entails the diverse beliefs we form on these bases, and this has given sceptics the ammunition to raise doubts based on underdetermination considerations. Perhaps the most famous example of this is Descartes's dream argument.[8] As he put it in the Sixth Meditation:

. . . every sensory experience I have ever thought I was having while awake I can also think of myself as sometimes having while asleep; and since I do not believe that what I seem to perceive in sleep comes from things located outside me, I did not see why I should be any more inclined to believe this of what I think I perceive while awake.[9]

This is tantamount to a sceptical argument about inductive inference from the testimony of the senses to claims about the external world. Descartes's doubt about the senses is also a doubt about belief based literally on testimony: that is, doubt about inductive inferences from the fact that someone tells you something to the fact you are told. In his *Conversation with Burman*, Descartes glosses 'from the senses':

i.e. from sight, by which I have perceived colours, shapes, and such like. Leaving aside sight, however, I have acquired, everything else *through the senses*, i.e. through hearing; for this is how I acquired and gleaned what I know from my parents, teachers, and others.[10]

---

[6] A. A. Long, and D. N. Sedley, *The Hellenistic Philosophers*, i (Cambridge: Cambridge University Press, 1987), 91–2.   [7] Quoted in Laudan, *Science and Hypothesis*, 81.
[8] René Descartes, *Meditations on First Philosophy*, in *The Philosophical Writings of Descartes*, ed. and trans. J. Cottingham, R. Stoothoff, and D. Murdoch, ii (Cambridge: Cambridge University Press, 1984), 1–62, at p. 13.   [9] Ibid. 53.
[10] René Descartes, *Descartes' Conversation with Burman*, trans. J. Cottingham (Oxford: Oxford University Press, 1976), 3 (italics in original).

Descartes's sceptical arguments about the senses are sceptical arguments about induction, and they were recognized at the time as already having a long pedigree in the history of philosophy. Thus, in his objections to the *Meditations*, Thomas Hobbes remarks:

But since Plato and other ancient philosophers discussed this uncertainty in the objects of the senses, and since the difficulty of distinguishing the waking state from dreams is commonly pointed out, I am sorry that the author, who is so outstanding in the field of original speculations, should be publishing this ancient material.[11]

Hume was certainly not the first to raise sceptical doubts about induction.

HUME'S CONTRIBUTION

Is there, then, anything left to our question? Does Hume bring anything new to scepticism about induction, anything both striking and obvious enough to make us seriously wonder why nobody thought of it before? As we have seen, there is in particular a long history of sceptical argument based on underdetermination. This is particularly natural in the case of vertical inferences, but it applies also to the most mundane enumerative induction: the observed cases underdetermine the next case. To take a Humean example, in the past bread has nourished me, but that is compatible both with future nourishment and future poisoning. But what does this kind of underdermination that both Hume and his predecessors discuss actually show? In the first instance, only that the inference in question is not deductive, because all it shows is that it is possible for the premises to be true yet the conclusion false. In other words, underdetermination initially shows only that the inference in question is indeed inductive. But this is enough to show that inductive conclusions are invariably uncertain, which gets us to a form of inductive scepticism, whether in Epicurus, Aquinas, Descartes, or Hume.

Nevertheless, there is something new in Hume. Unlike underdetermination arguments, which do their work by highlighting the possibility of alternative conclusions for inductive arguments, Hume's argument focuses on the method of inference itself and the principle of the uniformity of nature that it is supposed to presuppose. As we know, Hume argues that it is impossible to justify this principle, because demonstration cannot establish a contingent claim of this sort, and any non-demonstrative argument would need to assume the principle it was supposed to justify, and so 'must be evidently going in a circle, and taking that for granted, which is the very point in

[11] Thomas Hobbes, 'Third set of objections' in Descartes, *Meditations*, 121.

question' (*Enquiry*, 36). Hume constructs an impossibility proof, and it is this argument, and especially the circularity point it contains, that marks Hume's distinctive and seminal contribution to the induction debate. When we now attempt to answer our original question as to why we had to wait for Hume for the problem of induction, what we ought to be asking primarily is why we had to wait for Hume for this particular dilemma.

Before we begin to consider answers to this question, however, let us consider briefly how much of a sceptical advance the dilemma makes. As I mentioned at the start of this essay, one of the things that particularly impressed me about Hume's argument is that it attacked inferences that are so mundane and modest. In particular, his dilemma shows that scepticism about induction does not depend on supposing that what is inferred is unobservable: presently unobserved is enough. This makes Hume's argument more radical than at least many of the problems of induction that preceded it. Thus, while Descartes certainly worried about the inference from experience to external object, he does not seem much concerned about inference from present to past or future experience. And although his scepticism about the senses includes scepticism about the reliability of testimony, which seems a mundane case, here too the inference is vertical as Descartes conceives it, an inference from the *experience* of testimony to the truth of the claim made, a claim not about experience.

A second respect in which Hume's argument is more radical than what preceded him is that it secured the amplification of sceptical arguments about induction from doubts about certainty to doubts about any warrant whatever. The significance of this amplification is clear. Arguments for doubting the certainty of inductive conclusions can be shrugged off: this is a liveable form of scepticism, since probability is enough for rational choice. But this is not what Hume showed.[12] The dilemma shows that we have no reason at all for preferring one inductive conclusion over any other, no reason for preferring science over animal entrails, so far as reliability of prediction goes. The defect of circular arguments is not that they provide less than conclusive reasons to believe their conclusions, but that they provide no reason whatever. As Hume recognized, his dilemma yields an unliveable scepticism and an incredible position. Underdetermination arguments by themselves show only that the inferences in question are not deductive; Hume's dilemma shows that they are indefensible.

Underdetermination arguments seem capable of supporting these more radical sceptical claims too, however, even if their pre-Humean proponents

---

[12] When my students write 'Hume showed that we can never be absolutely certain about the future', I rebuke them for describing 'Hume the plumber', not Hume the great philosopher. But my students are not alone: for a discussion of non-sceptical readings of Hume on induction, see Don Garrett, *Cognition and Commitment in Hume's Philosophy* (Oxford: Oxford University Press, 1997), ch. 4.

did not exploit the fact. For, as we have seen, it is easy enough to present the most modest enumerative inductions as inferences where the premises underdetermine the conclusions. Moreover, underdetermination arguments also seem to support the radical claim that the conclusions of inductive arguments are not just uncertain but completely unwarranted, since the observation that all the competing hypotheses or predictions are consistent with the data suggests that any preference among them would be arbitrary. But suggesting is not the same as arguing, and the mere fact of consistency with the data does not rule out the possibility that one hypothesis may be much more likely than another. Indeed, many of us who have realist inclinations in the philosophy of science have tried more or less desperately to describe the 'super-empirical virtues'—simplicity, projectibility, prior probability, explanatory power, etc.—that break the tie between empirically equivalent hypotheses. That we actually rely on some such devices seems clear, given that we do make determinate inferences. But what the dilemma shows is that all of these devices are in effect inductive assumptions, and that none of them can be defended without ultimate circularity. This is a distinctive philosophical achievement that easily supports our original question.

HUME'S EXPLANATIONS

Having made my pitch for the claim that Hume's sceptical argument really does take inductive scepticism to new heights (or depths), and having suggested what that new contribution amounts to, I turn now to answering the original question: why did we have to wait until Hume for this? By trying to get into focus just where Hume goes beyond his predecessors, we have sharpened up our original question, but have also made it harder to answer. For while underdetermination by itself is not, I have argued, the same as the problem of induction, underdetermination seems to provide almost all the necessary ingredients. Indeed, it is not at all obvious what the extra ingredients are that Hume had and his predecessors lacked. What was different before Hume that might explain the wait? In this section I consider two answers that are not only natural, but also ones that have in effect been offered by a most eminent authority on these matters: Hume himself. Each appeals to a pre-Humean commitment that Hume was able to abandon: an epistemic commitment to *demonstration* and a metaphysical commitment to causal *connection*. I will argue that both answers are part of the story, but also that they both leave something out.

The first answer is that philosophers before Hume did not care much about induction, in which case it is not so surprising that they did not come up with its problem. And the reason they did not care much about induction, to go one more link down the chain of explanations, is that before Hume the only knowledge thought by philosophers worth having was demonstrative knowledge.[13] And Hume is eager to distinguish himself from his predecessors precisely on the grounds that he, unlike them, does not neglect probabilities. In the anonymously published *Abstract* to the *Treatise*, he writes:

The celebrated *Monsieur Leibnitz* has observed it to be a defect in the common systems of logic, that they are very copious when they explain the operations of the understanding in the forming of demonstrations, but are too concise when they treat of probabilities, and those other measures of evidence on which life and action entirely depend, and which are our guides even in most of our philosophical speculations. In this censure, he comprehends *The Essay Concerning Human Understanding, Le Recherche de la verité*, and *L'Art de penser*. The author of the *Treatise of Human Nature* seems to have been sensible of this defect in these philosophers, and has endeavoured, as much as he can, to supply it.[14]

Or, as he puts it without naming names in the *Enquiry*,

It may, therefore, be a subject worthy of curiosity, to enquire what is the nature of that evidence, which assures us of any real existence and matter of fact, beyond the present testimony of our senses, or the records of our memory. This part of philosophy, it is observable, has been little cultivated, either by the ancients or moderns . . . (p. 26)

Demonstration does appear to have been the pre-eminent model for knowledge for virtually all of the pre-Humean history of philosophy, and the view that non-demonstrative reasoning is too feeble and unimportant to be worth arguing over would certainly help to explain why philosophers did not work on induction before Hume.

A pre-Humean obsession with demonstration may be part of the answer to our question, but it cannot be the whole story. First of all, a desire to privilege demonstration, or rationalism more generally, provides a powerful motive precisely to generate sceptical arguments about induction. And of course this is exactly what we see in Descartes. The celebrated Leibniz provides another example of inductive scepticism prompted by rationalist commitments:

. . . the senses never give anything except examples, that is to say, particular or individual truths. Now all the examples which confirm a general truth, however numerous they be, do not suffice to establish the universal necessity of this

---

[13] Cf. Ian Hacking, *The Emergence of Probability* (Cambridge: Cambridge University Press, 1975), ch. 19; Edward J. Craig, *The Mind of God and the Works of Man* (Oxford: Clarendon Press, 1987), ch. 2.

[14] David Hume, *An Abstract of a Book Lately Published Entitled A Treatise of Human Nature*, in *A Treatise of Human Nature*, 646–7.

same truth; for it does not follow that what has happened will happen in the same way.[15]

Yet, neither Descartes nor Leibniz came up with Hume's distinctive sceptical argument against induction. More generally, the demonstration answer runs the risk of explaining too much, since, as we have seen, plenty of philosophers before Hume did worry about induction. What the demonstration answer does not explain is why *they* did not come up with the dilemma. As is often the case, we can clarify the explanatory situation by bringing contrasts into the question. The neglect or disdain of non-demonstrative reasoning will at best explain why Hume, rather than Plato, discovered the problem of induction in all its glory, but it will not explain why the discovery was made by Hume rather than by Sextus, Epicurus, Aquinas, Bacon, Descartes, or any of the other pre-Humeans who did worry about induction. (The range of contrasts we must address to give a full answer to our original question should make us suspicious that there is any single factor that will explain them all.) It is the latter set of contrasts that particularly interests me here. What did Hume have that others who thought about induction lacked, that brought him to construct his novel dilemma?

The second natural answer to our question, closely related to the demonstration answer, appeals to the metaphysics of causation. If one believes that there is some metaphysical connection between cause and effect, one may hold out the hope that it is possible to deduce effect from cause if only one is clever enough. Hume famously argued that we have no conception of necessary connections between external cause and effect: all we can conceive of out there is a pattern of events or objects (*Enquiry*, sect. 7). According to the connection answer to our question, we had to wait for Hume for the problem of induction because we had to wait for Hume for a decisive denial of any conception of connection between cause and effect. As Ian Hacking puts it,

There is a sceptical problem of induction not because . . . we may be in doubt as to whether we have located the necessary connections that will guide our predictions about the future, but because we now think there are no necessary connections, not even unknown ones.[16]

The denial of necessary connections makes radical scepticism about induction possible, on this view, because it leaves a metaphysical atomism, such that events or objects are all entirely 'loose and separate' from each other, so that information about some is no guide to the others. (Since Hacking wrote, it has become increasingly popular to interpret Hume as denying the conceivability rather than the existence of causal connections

[15] Gottfried W. F. Leibniz, *New Essays on the Understanding*, Preface, in P. P. Wiener (ed.), *Leibniz Selections* (New York: Charles Scribner's Sons, 1951), 369–70.

[16] Hacking, *Emergence of Probability*, 116.

between objects. My comments in what follows are intended to go through on either reading.) As in the case of the appeal to demonstration, the connection answer to our question enjoys a kind of endorsement from Hume himself. In both the *Treatise* (pp. 90–1) and the *Enquiry* (p. 33) Hume writes that the case for inductive scepticism is easier to make in the context of his analysis of causation, because the absence of conceivable necessary connections makes it manifest that the problem of induction cannot be avoided by appeal to objects' 'natural powers'.

Like the demonstration answer, the connection answer is clearly relevant, but it is not the full story either. Hume certainly thinks that inductive inference has a great deal to do with causation. As he puts it in the *Enquiry*, 'When it is asked, *What is the nature of all our reasonings concerning matter of fact?* the proper answer seems to be, that they are founded on the relation of cause and effect.' (p. 32). And had Hume not taken causal inferences to be empirical and inductive, I venture to say that the problem of induction would probably not have arisen for him. Certainly the claim that inferences about unobserved matters of fact rely on experience is a prerequisite for the problem. The connection answer also has an edge over the demonstration answer in that, whereas many pre-Humeans considered non-demonstrative argument, relatively few held Hume's view that we can conceive of no external connection whatever between cause and effect. I would also say that the atomistic picture that Hume's account of causation encourages does at least serve to make the epistemological problem vivid.

Now for the limitations of the connection answer. First of all, it is worth emphasizing that there were some pre-Humeans who denied causal connection between objects (though perhaps affirming it between God and objects). George Berkeley is one such, since for him objects are made up of ideas, and ideas are inert:

. . . the connexion of ideas does not imply the relation of *cause* and *effect*, but only of a mark or *sign* with the thing *signified*. The fire which I see is not the cause of the pain I suffer upon my approaching it, but the mark that forewarns me of it. In like manner, the noise that I hear is not the effect of this or that motion or collision of the ambient bodies, but the sign thereof.[17]

Occasionalists provide further examples of pre-Humean philosophers who deny that objects are connected. According to Nicolas Malebranche,

We should say that the air dries the earth because it stirs and raises with it the water that soaks the earth, and that the air or subtle matter freezes the river because in this season it ceases to communicate enough motion to the parts of which the water is composed to make it fluid. In a word, we must give, if we can, the natural and particular cause of the effects in question. But since the action of

---

[17] George Berkeley, *A Treatise Concerning the Principles of Human Knowledge*, in *Philosophical Works*, ed. M. R. Ayers (London: Dent, 1975), 61–127, para. 65 (italics in original).

these causes consists only in the motor force activating them, and since this motor force is but the will of God, they must not be said to have in themselves any force or power to produce any effects.[18]

The religious commitment of Berkeley and Malebranche may have rendered them sceptic-proof, but they show that a denial of conceivable connections between natural objects or properties is not sufficient to generate the problem of induction.

Nor is it necessary. Hume was far from the first philosopher to acknowledge a role for experience in causal inference. Even Descartes, the exemplary rationalist, allowed in his *Discourse on the Method* that:

The power of nature is so ample and so vast, and my principles so simple and so general, that I notice hardly any particular effect of which I do not know at once that it can be deduced from my principles in many different ways, and my greatest difficulty is usually to discover in which of these ways it depends on them. I know of no other way to discover this than by seeking further observations whose outcomes vary according to which of them provides the correct explanation.[19]

Indeed, all those of Hume's predecessors who acknowledged inductive inference also acknowledged the need for experience to make the inferences. And this is all the problem of induction requires. Denying the conceivability of causal connection may make the problem a bit easier to see, but the problem does not depend on this. Like the demonstration answer, the connection answer does not explain why those before Hume who considered induction did not come up with the dilemma.

Hume himself clearly recognizes that he does not need his own anti-metaphysics of causation to run his sceptical argument. We have indirect evidence for this: Hume's presentation, in both in the *Treatise* and in the *Enquiry*, places the discussion of the idea of necessary connection only after the sceptical argument has already been given in full. But there is also direct evidence, in the passages already cited, where Hume suggests that his case is easier to make in light of his analysis of causation, since the point of these remarks in context is precisely that the assistance is not required. What counts is that we need experience to work out that bread nourishes us, and that the observation that it has nourished us in the past does not entail that it will nourish us in future. And this is compatible with the existence and even the conceivability of strong causal connection. As Hume puts it in the *Enquiry*:

But notwithstanding this ignorance of natural powers and principles, we always presume, when we see like sensible qualities, that they have like secret powers, and

---

[18] Nicolas Malebranche, *The Search after Truth*, ed. and trans. T. M. Lennon and P. J. Olscamp, 6th edn. (Cambridge: Cambridge University Press, 1997), 662.

[19] René Descartes, *Discourse on the Method*, in *The Philosophical Writings of Descartes*, ed. and trans. J. Cottingham, R. Stoothoff, and D. Murdoch, i (Cambridge: Cambridge University Press, 1985), 111–49, at p. 144.

expect that effects, similar to those which we have experienced, will follow from them . . . The bread, which I formerly eat, nourished me; that is, a body of such sensible qualities, was, at that time, endowed with such secret powers: But does it follow, that other bread must also nourish me at another time, and that like sensible qualities must always be attended with like secret powers? (p. 33)

Hume here recognizes that even if every cause has a necessary effect, the same effect type may have different causes on different occasions, and this is enough to support the sceptical argument. Hume held that the problem of induction is neither solved nor avoided by adopting a non-Humean account of causation. I think he is right, so we have more work to do to explain why we had to wait until Hume for the problem of induction.

MOTIVE AND OPPORTUNITY

What can we add to the demonstration and connection answers, to improve the explanation? I think that we can make some advance by thinking as detectives are supposed to think when they solve murder mysteries. We need to consider motive and opportunity. One of the reasons why Hume found an argument for radical inductive scepticism whereas others who considered induction did not may be that he wanted such an argument more than they did. Such an argument would provide powerful support for one of his central philosophical projects: namely, the naturalist programme of showing that our thought is governed by principles of custom or natural instinct rather than by principles of reasoning. As he makes clear in the *Abstract*, what he aims to establish is that ''Tis not, therefore, reason, which is the guide to life, but custom' (p. 652). Hume's aim is to reduce as much mental activity as possible to instinctual principles governing the evolution of ideas, and his preferred means is to show that a cognitive transition cannot be governed by reason:

We have already taken notice of certain relations, which make us pass from one object to another, even tho' there be no reason to determine us to that transition; and this we may establish for a general rule, that wherever the mind constantly and uniformly makes a transition without any reason, it is influenc'd by these relations. (*Treatise*, 92)

We can see Hume as advancing his naturalistic programme by adopting a 'method of doubt'. That is an expression we associate with Descartes, but whereas Descartes's method of doubt was designed to wean us from the senses and attach us to reason, Hume's method is designed to wean us from reason and attach us to custom. Actually, Descartes thinks that we were already using some reason without realizing it (this is the point of the wax argument in the Second Meditation), and Hume is not here aiming primarily to change our cognitive practice; but the method of doubt is meant to get us to see more clearly what our practice really is. So my suggestion is that Hume especially wants a sceptical argument about induction, because he wants to end up with the position that inferences about matters of fact cannot be a matter of reason.

This is a motive to construct a sceptical argument. Moreover, it seems to me that it is a motive to construct an argument that goes beyond the pre-Humean underdetermination considerations, to the great dilemma Hume invents. Merely to observe that observations themselves do not entail predictions will not effectively undermine the thought that induction is a matter of reason. For the possibility remains open that the argument proceeds by means of additional premisses that secure its validity. If these additional premisses are themselves governed by reason, then so can the entire inference be. This is of course precisely the possibility that Hume proceeds to scotch in his discussion of the principle of the uniformity of nature.

Given that Hume seeks to convince us that induction is not a matter of reason, it is, I think, natural that he should wish to show that inductive inferences are completely unjustifiable, not just uncertain. For if they are merely uncertain, then it remains possible that the inferences proceed by reasonable argument, whereas if the argument would be entirely worthless, this would strengthen the case for saying that the cognitive mechanism is not one of argument at all. Moreover, Hume's desire to show this may even favour the specific appeal to circularity that lies at the heart of his argument. For, as he observes, there is a sense in which a circular argument is not just a bad argument, it is no argument at all:

... probability is founded on the presumption of a resemblance betwixt those objects, of which we have had experience, and those, of which we have had none; and therefore 'tis impossible this presumption can arise from probability. The same principle cannot be both the cause and effect of another ... (*Treatise*, 90)

Hume wants to show not just that the presumption of resemblance (a.k.a. the uniformity of nature) is unwarranted, but that it is not part of the inferential mechanism; and the circularity argument is a particularly efficacious way of getting to this conclusion. The only possible source of the presumption required by reason would be itself; but this is impossible, so reason is not the mechanism of inductive inference. Hume's method of doubt clears away the false image of reason, so that the real mechanisms of custom and habit can be exposed.

So Hume has a motive to come up with a certain kind of sceptical argument, in order to wean us from the image of reason. But, as I have already suggested, some pre-Humeans also had a motive to derogate induction, in the cause of demonstration or rationalism. Descartes is the obvious case in point, as he uses his method of doubt to wean us from the senses. Descartes did not, however, need radical inductive scepticism for his purposes, since he had convinced himself that his programme required only that he show that an inference from the senses is non-demonstrative and hence uncertain. And, as we will see, there are other reasons why he might not have seen the radical dilemma, whereas Hume did. But it remains possible that there were pre-Humeans who wished to argue against induction by showing that non-demonstrative arguments are completely indefensible, not just uncertain. If there were such figures, the appeal to motivation will not by itself explain why they did not discover the Humean argument. We need also to say something about opportunity.

Hume had an exceptional opportunity to come up with the problem of induction, because his brand of empiricism left him with an epistemology in which induction is *ubiquitous*, the only route to any beliefs about unobserved matters of fact. Unlike Berkeley and Malebranche, for example, Hume could allow God no epistemic role in induction. And it is the ubiquity of induction that makes the circularity argument so natural. If you think that there are other matters of fact that can be known without induction, including the existence of a benevolent deity, then the circularity need not arise. If induction is required for all unobserved matters of fact, however, there is nothing outside induction to justify it. Ubiquity creates circularity. This ubiquity that Hume perceived also helps to explain why his argument is so maddeningly independent of the description of our inductive practices. As I remarked near the beginning of this essay, Hume's description of these practices seems primitive, yet this does not seem to affect the power of his sceptical argument. In the end, what matters to the argument is not that induction takes a particular form, but simply that it be non-demonstrative and ubiquitous. That is enough to get the circularity going. And while those of Hume's predecessors who considered induction recognized that it is non-demonstrative, they did not appreciate its ubiquity. This, I suggest, is a central reason why they did not come up with the problem of induction.

The ubiquity of induction is the source of the circularity problem that is central to Hume's dilemma, and my proposal is that Hume's appreciation of this ubiquity enabled him to see the circle that others had missed. It seems to me that this appreciation also helped Hume in another way. As we have seen, much of the pre-Humean interest in induction focused on vertical inferences and the underdetermination from which they suffer. But the specific circularity that Hume spots is considerably more transparent in mundane cases of horizontal enumerative induction, cases that Hume's awareness of the ubiquity of induction, along with his interest in everyday inference, naturally lead him to consider. (Indeed, strictly speaking one should probably say that for Hume all induction is inference from and to observables, since for him only what is observable is conceivable.)

One reason why it is easier to see the circularity in the case of horizontal induction is that it is only in the case of inferences to observables that our inductive practices have an observable track record. We have seen that our past predictions about the sun rising were correct; but we never get to see the unobservable entities and processes postulated by our theories. It is this observed track record in the horizontal cases that most of us believe in our hearts supplies a reason to trust induction: we have seen that induction has worked in the past, and that is the reason we give for saying that it will work in future. But it is also this mundane situation that makes the threat of circularity particularly vivid, because here it is obvious that we are trying to use induction to justify induction. For vertical induction, by contrast, there is a sense in which we may not even get as far as seeing the circularity problem, because we do not have the track record to tempt us into it. This is not to say that vertical inferences are not also ultimately susceptible to the Humean argument—they are—but the problem is more immediate in the horizontal case, so a great philosopher who is considering the horizontal case is more likely to discover the problem than one who is considering only our more ambitious vertical inferences.

This way of thinking about the inductive justification of induction—induction has worked in the past, so it is likely to work in future—is perhaps mildly post-Humean, but Hume's own way of seeing the problem makes the same point, I think. As we know, he finds the circularity in 'the presumption of a resemblance betwixt those objects, of which we have had experience, and those, of which we have had none' (*Treatise*, 90). And this is a presumption that applies directly only to horizontal inferences. Not only is this presumption not applicable to vertical inferences, but, as the work on non-demonstrative inference and confirmation of the last century has shown, it is extraordinarily difficult to specify what those presumptions that govern vertical inference actually are. Strangely perhaps, the threat of radical inductive scepticism is easier to see for the more mundane and intuitively more secure inductive inferences. So Hume's awareness of the ubiquity of induction helped him to get to his argument by focusing his attention on mundane horizontal inference, as well as by seeing that there is no way out by appeal to matters of fact that do not themselves depend upon induction.

CONCLUSION

The problem of induction is one of that handful of great sceptical arguments that combine stunning power with striking simplicity. This is what makes the question why it had to wait for Hume both natural to ask and difficult to answer. In my view there are many factors involved: different philosophers failed to see the problem for different reasons. You are unlikely to see the problem of induction if you are interested only in demonstrative argument, and you may find it harder to see if you think that cause and effect have some kind of quasi-logical connection. But I have suggested that there is more to it than that. Hume's strong naturalistic motivations made an argument for radical inductive scepticism particularly desirable, as a way of making the case for a model of cognition that appeals to instinct rather than reason. And his appreciation of the ubiquity of induction enabled him to see the circularity upon which his sceptical argument depends, by helping to focus his attention on horizontal inductions where the circle is most visible, and by revealing the absence of any independent route to matters of fact that would make it possible to break out of the circle. This helps to explain why even those pre-Humeans who took an interest in non-demonstrative reasoning failed to find Hume's dilemma.

How does my appeal to naturalism and ubiquity compare with the answers that appeal to demonstration and to causal connection? Unlike the appeal to demonstration, my answer explains not just why many pre-Humeans did not consider induction at all, but also why those who did still did not discover the sceptical argument. At the same time, the demonstration answer complements my own, since the obsession with demonstration helps to explain why pre-Humeans did not appreciate the ubiquity of induction. What about the connection answer? I have observed, and have observed Hume observing, that the atomistic picture that the denial of a concept of necessary connection leaves does make it easier to see the sceptical problem. Similarly, I have suggested that a focus on simple enumerative induction makes the circularity problem easier to see, and so may have helped Hume to see it. Both factors were heuristic aids, helping to make the problem visible, though ultimately not necessary for the argument. What is essential to the argument is the absence of autonomous matters of fact that might justify inductive inference, and this is what is assured by the ubiquity of induction. Moreover, unlike the connection answer, my appeal to naturalism and ubiquity helps to explain the genesis of the fine structure of Hume's argument. The denial of necessary connection does not take us beyond underdetermination, which we had anyway before Hume; the appeal of naturalism and ubiquity takes us further, helping to explain why it was Hume who found the devastating and original point about circularity.

As Hume describes the course of the *Abstract*, 'Almost all reasoning is there reduced to experience; and the belief, which attends experience, is explained to be nothing but a peculiar sentiment, or lively conception produced by habit' (p. 657). I have suggested that an important part of the explanation of why we had to wait for Hume for the problem of induction is that none of his predecessors both appreciated the ubiquity of induction and wanted as much as he did to reduce reason to natural instinct. By appreciating the ubiquity of induction, Hume was able to see a circularity problem that is especially vivid for the mundane inferences that even many of his predecessors who did worry about induction did not focus upon, and that is unanswerable because of the absence of autonomous knowledge of unobserved matters of fact. And Hume had a particularly strong motive for finding this argument, because of the support it would give to one of his main philosophical projects: the replacement of a model of human cognition as the exercise of reason with one that portrays us as animals whose thought is governed by natural instincts.

REFERENCES

Berkeley, George, *A Treatise Concerning the Principles of Human Knowledge*, in *Philosophical Works*, ed. M. R. Ayers (London: Dent, 1975), 61–127.

Craig, Edward J., *The Mind of God and the Works of Man* (Oxford: Clarendon Press, 1987).

Descartes, René, *Discourse on the Method*, in *The Philosophical Writings of Descartes*, ed. and trans. J. Cottingham, R. Stoothoff, and D. Murdoch, i (Cambridge: Cambridge University Press, 1985), 111–49.

——*Meditations on First Philosophy*, in *The Philosophical Writings of Descartes*, ed. and trans. J. Cottingham, R. Stoothoff, and D. Murdoch, ii (Cambridge: Cambridge University Press, 1984), 1–62.

——*Descartes' Conversation with Burman*, trans. J. Cottingham (Oxford: Oxford University Press, 1976).

Garrett, Don, *Cognition and Commitment in Hume's Philosophy* (Oxford: Oxford University Press, 1997).

Hacking, Ian, *The Emergence of Probability* (Cambridge: Cambridge University Press, 1975).

Hobbes, Thomas, 'Third set of objections', in Descartes, *Meditations on First Philosophy*, 121–37.

Hume, David, *A Treatise of Human Nature*, ed. L. A. Selby-Bigge, 2nd edn., rev. P. H. Nidditch (Oxford: Clarendon Press, 1978).

—— *An Abstract of a Book Lately Published Entitled A Treatise of Human Nature*, in *A Treatise of Human Nature*, 641–62.

—— *An Enquiry Concerning Human Understanding*, ed. L. A. Selby-Bigge, 3rd edn., rev. P. H. Nidditch (Oxford: Clarendon Press, 1975).

Laudan, Larry, *Science and Hypothesis* (Dordrecht: Reidel, 1981).

Leibniz, Gottfried W. F., *New Essays on the Understanding*, Preface, in P. P. Wiener (ed.), *Leibniz Selections* (New York: Charles Scribner's Sons, 1951), 367–94.

Long, A. A., and Sedley, D. N., *The Hellenistic Philosophers*, i (Cambridge: Cambridge University Press, 1987).

Malebranche, Nicolas, *The Search after Truth*, ed. and trans. T. M. Lennon and P. J. Olscamp, 6th edn. (Cambridge: Cambridge University Press, 1997).

Milton, John R., 'Induction before Hume', *British Journal for the Philosophy of Science*, 38 (1987): 49–74.

Meeting the Hare in her Doubles: Causal Belief and General Belief

R. M. SAINSBURY

———•———

I

A CAUSE is an object precedent and contiguous to another, and so united with it, that the idea of the one determines the mind to form the idea of the other, and the impression of the one to form a more lively idea of the other.

This is standardly called Hume's second definition of causation. So construed, it gives rise to familiar problems. As a definition of causation it is circular, for 'determines' is a synonym for 'causes'. Given that Hume himself criticizes using synonyms in attempts to define causation,[1] it would be odd if he were to engage in the practice himself. It is also visibly not equivalent to the first definition, which makes no mention of minds.

These worries disappear if we treat it not as a definition of causation, but rather as a definition of what it is to believe in causation: for short, as a definition of causal belief. One way to make this explicit, guided by Ramsey's phrase 'a habit of singular belief',[2] is as follows:

S implicitly believes that Fs cause Gs iff S is in the grip of an F–G regularity; i.e.

(i) coming to believe an F has occurred causes S to believe that a G will occur nearby and later;

(ii) coming to believe that a G has occurred causes S to believe that an F has occurred nearby and earlier.

Although this is not equivalent to the first definition, equivalence is no longer to be expected, for one would not suppose that causation and causal belief are the same thing; there can be unsuspected causes and false causal

---

[1] 'If a cause be defined, *that which produces any thing*; it is easy to observe, that *producing* is synonymous to *causing*' (David Hume, *Enquiry Concerning Human Understanding*, ed. L. A. Selby-Bigge, 3rd edn., rev. P. H. Nidditch (Oxford: Clarendon Press, 1975), VIII. ii. 96 n.) The context makes it plain that this is regarded as unsatisfactory.

[2] F. Ramsey, 'General propositions and causality', in D. H. Mellor (ed.), *Foundations: Essays in Logic, Mathematics and Economics* (London: Routledge and Kegan Paul, 1978), 133–51, at p. 136. Ramsey applies the phrase to 'variable hypotheticals', sentences like 'All men are mortal'. He argues that laws are special cases of such hypotheticals.

beliefs. Moreover, relative to the ambition of defining causal belief, the definition is not circular, for the concept of causal belief does not occur in it: although the concept of causation is used, it is not used within the belief context. The definition could therefore be useful to someone who understands causation but needs an account of the kind of psychological state a person is in if they believe some causal generalization.

The definition is not the same as Hume's second definition, for I have made no attempt to do justice to Hume's first phrase ('an object precedent and contiguous to another'), which may perhaps be a condensed repetition of the first definition. Perhaps, in this context, 'an object' means 'a kind of object'; and precedence and contiguity between *kinds* of objects are naturally understood as entailing the constant conjunction of all objects falling under the kinds.

On this interpretation of the second definition, the first and second definitions would not only be definitions of different things, they would also differ in another way. Whereas the first definition, in my opinion, defines singular causation (in terms of the particular cause and its effect being subsumed under a regularity), the second definition addresses not belief in singular causation but belief in causal generalization. I will not defend my exegetical claims (which are far from idiosyncratic), for the main theme of the present paper is a question which is of interest even if the exegesis is defective: can a definition of belief in a causal generalization differentiate it from belief in a non-causal generalization? Before approaching this directly, the next section sets some background, including the notion of implicit as opposed to explicit belief.

II

The beauty of the second definition, under this construal, is that it explains causal belief as something not requiring belief in a causal content, and this makes room for various reductive or eliminative options for Humeans (see section III below). It also makes causal belief something that could be possessed by creatures lacking the concept of causation. Let us call a belief concerning the unexperienced 'inductive'. It is beyond doubt that Hume thought it important to point out that non-human animals have inductive beliefs (despite not being capable of argumentation), and that such beliefs normally arise only through the experience of constant conjunction. According to the present account of the second definition, it would follow that any creature with a normally produced inductive belief has a causal belief, that is, implicitly believes something of the form Fs cause Gs. This is indeed what we find Hume claiming:

they [sc. non-human animals] become acquainted with the more obvious properties of external objects, and gradually, from their birth, treasure up a knowledge of the nature of fire, water, earth, stones, heights, depths, &c., and of the effects, which result from their operation. (*Enquiry*, 105)

The final phrase, about 'the effects, which result from their operation', shows that the knowledge of fire, water, and so on includes causal knowledge. In the light of this context, we can read Hume as attributing causal knowledge to the old and canny greyhound who 'meets the hare in her doubles': the dog's 'conjectures' are that being chased one way by the younger dogs will, given the lie of the land, *drive* the hare back this way.

Even those sympathetic with an account of causal belief which would make it correctly attributable to creatures lacking the concept of causation may feel that we should distinguish between that way of having a causal belief and a way of having such a belief available only to a creature who does employ the concept of causation. For example, it might be held that we need to employ the concept if we are going to make use of Hume's 'rules to judge of causes and effects', and so entertain causal generalizations merely hypothetically. This requires an account of a causal generalization being before the mind without being believed. If evidence then leads to belief, this is explicit belief, apparently involving a relation to a causal content. It was in deference to this view that I took the definiendum of the second definition to be *implicit* causal belief. But what is implicit belief?

An explicit belief involves, at least superficially, a relation between a believer and a content. Being in a state of believing a content generally makes a difference to dispositions to act. This enables us to indicate the schema of a definition of implicit belief:

S implicitly believes that p iff S has dispositions characteristic of explicit belief that p.

This is only a schema, for it does not specify the relevant 'characteristic' dispositions. Not all can be involved, as some of these are dispositions to exercise the concept of causation. The schema ensures that explicitly believing that p entails implicitly believing that p, but not vice versa. Those unpersuaded by the explicit–implicit distinction can just set it to one side.

III

If one has a definition of causation, why would one need an additional definition of causal belief? If p is defined as q, then surely the belief that p just is the belief that q?

This assumes that definition induces a relation which permits substitution *salva veritate* even in hyperintensional contexts. It is reasonable to suppose, however, that this is not how Hume thought of his first definition—that is, his definition of causation—for he thought that this deflated the ordinary conception. In causal belief we aspire to believe not just that things are constantly conjoined, but that they are also necessarily connected. Since we tend not to have the right view even of what we are aspiring to in exercising the concept of causation, it would be incorrect merely to equate our causal beliefs with beliefs in constant conjunctions.

The considerations which follow are supposed to apply, with appropriate adjustments, regardless of the precise version of Humeanism adopted. However, the presentation requires a definite version, one which settles, for example, whether causation is to be reduced to constant conjunction, so that it is something real and potentially knowable, or whether it is to be eliminated in favour of constant conjunction, so that there is no intelligible concept of causation, constant conjunction being merely the closest intelligible approximation. The version I will discuss in detail is a form of reductionism: the content of a general causal proposition is the same as that of a proposition affirming constant conjunction among kinds of events, along with priority and contiguity in the pairings of tokens of the kinds. Causation is thus a perfectly genuine, real, and knowable phenomenon, and is so even for Hume, provided that we do not read him as sceptically denying that we possess inductive knowledge. (I think the non-sceptical reading is correct, and it is supported by what I have already quoted of Hume's view of the inductive knowledge which non-human animals possess.) When a generalization involves a causal idiom, however, it can be believed in a different way from the way in which the same proposition, or a proposition of the same kind, can be believed when expressed in a causal-free idiom. This difference in mode of belief is easily confused with a difference in content believed, thus giving rise to the widespread myth that causation is something more than constant conjunction. We generally fail to recognize that a general causal fact is just a fact of constant conjunction (plus priority and contiguity). This is why the second definition is important: it describes the mode of belief, being in the grip of a regularity, which constitutes a special way of believing in a constant conjunction, a way which makes us wrongly think we are believing in some kind of necessity in the world. The projectivist confusion could be expressed as the move from

believing something to be an *F* caused the belief that it is a *G*

to

its being an *F* made it a *G* (by a necessary connection).

The issues on which we are about to embark have an interest beyond the exegesis of Hume. For example, some versions of functionalism, the thesis that each mental state is individuated by its location in a causal network of other states, could use something along the lines of the second definition.

We cannot expect to be able to define what it is implicitly to believe arbitrary kinds of content in the way proposed for causation. For example, the following are dubious:

   (i) S implicitly believes that not-*p* iff it is not the case that S believes that *p*.
  (ii) S implicitly believes that *a* is F iff, concerning *a*, S believes that it is F.
 (iii) S implicitly believes that something is F iff there is something which S believes to be F.
 (iv) S implicitly believes that (*p* or *q*) iff (S believes that *p*) or (S believes that *q*).
  (v) S implicitly believes that (*p* because *q*) iff (S believes that *p*) because (S believes that *q*).

Since we can be agnostic, we can fail to believe *p* without believing not-*p*. Non-conceptual creatures might exemplify the equivalence in (ii), but according to Fregeans a conceptual creature could believe of Hesperus that it is visible in the morning without believing that Hesperus is visible in the morning. Unless intuitionist norms are invariably adhered to, there are cases in which one believes that something is F without believing of anything in particular that it is F; the point carries over to disjunction. The final case, (v), is close to our official target. The most obvious counterexamples are ones which involve causal connections between things neither of which is the cause of the other. For example, I may believe that the toast is done because I believe it is emitting a certain smell, but the proposition 'The toast is done because it is emitting a certain smell', understood as an identification of a cause, is not one which I accept: smell emission does not cause done-ness. In such cases there is a causal connection (the heat that caused the doneness caused the smell), even if it is not one which sustains the application of 'because'. As I will elaborate at the start of section IV, I will not press Hume's account to adapt to the distinction between causal connection and causation.

   A causal belief is a belief with causal content; but on the version of Humeanism adopted here, a belief with causal content is a belief with merely a certain kind of constant conjunction as its content. What makes some such beliefs special is the mode of believing, not the content believed. We can also have beliefs about beliefs: we believe we have beliefs with a content involving not merely causation (that is, on the present formulation, constant conjunction) but also necessary connection, which is unintelligible. These second-order beliefs do have a distinctive content: namely, the special mode of causally believing. The distinction can easily be slid over, and this is just what we find in Hume: the 'idea of necessary connection' is sometimes explained in terms of the determination mentioned in the second definition, and sometimes in terms of awareness of that determination (an awareness not mentioned in the second definition). The present formulation equates what is distinctive in causal belief with the determination, and this may become a distinctive content for a second-order belief, one involving awareness of the determination.

IV

The main questions of the paper can now be expressed as follows: is there a distinctive way of believing a generalization which has this feature: when we believe a generalization in this way, we (wrongly, in Hume's view) take ourselves to be believing something which involves necessity? If so, does *being in the grip of a regularity* constitute that mode of belief? We do not need to raise more familiar questions, like whether there are counterexamples to the reduction of causation to constant conjunction. Counterexamples are likely to be allegedly non-causal constant conjunctions. But it might be that if they are believed in the special way, then they are, wrongly even by the lights of those who allow necessity, treated as necessity-involving. So our present question has some independence from questions about the correctness of Hume's first definition.

In the present formulation, the Humean is committed to the possibility of at least two ways of believing a constant conjunction: a way distinctive of causal belief and some other way. This is because, as I assume, there are generalizations which are merely 'accidental' and are not believed in the causal way and are not supposed to correspond to any causal fact: for example, 'All the coins in my pocket are silver'. This is consistent with the reduction of causation to constant conjunction, for the reduction identifies only a specific kind of generalization with causation: generalizations quantifying over specified kinds of events and affirming priority and contiguity of the pairings of the tokens. However, there are complications in saying in more detail just what a Humean could reasonably take as her aim.

The second definition does not speak directly to the mode of belief distinctive of belief in a singular causal statement. According to the first definition, a singular causal statement is true only if some regularity subsumes it, but because no regularity is entailed, belief in the singular causal statement intuitively requires only belief in the existence of a regularity and does not require believing one; hence it cannot require being in the grip of one. Perhaps belief in the existence of a subsuming regularity can in turn be indirectly explained in terms of grip, possibly as the disposition to fall into the grip of any regularity which appears to subsume any singular case which is believed. But I leave on one side this problem for the Humean, and focus only on belief in causal generalizations. Of these, there are at least two kinds. There is a kind which simply summates a number of singular causes, for example:

All the players on the team make their spouse happy.

These are 'accidental' (or non-projectible) general causal truths. There is nothing (I am assuming) about being a player on the team which promotes making a spouse happy. Given the relation of such generalizations to singular causal statements, it seems no more appropriate to say that belief in them requires being in the grip of a regularity than to say the same of any of the singular causal beliefs they summate. By contrast, there are causal generalizations which we think of as non-accidental: for example, 'Dropping wine glasses makes them break'. In possibly non-Humean terms, the contrast is that in the accidental cases no causal regularity is specified, not even in a vague or incomplete way, whereas in the non-accidental cases there is at least a sketch of a relevant regularity. We can put matters this way only if we have some adequate conception of a kind of regularity not exemplified by the regularity that all the players on the team make their spouses happy. The idea behind the second definition is that Hume can mark the contrast between these kinds of regularity not in terms of difference of content or difference of kind of fact affirmed but merely in terms of difference in mode of belief: to believe in the non-accidental way is to be in the grip of a regularity, but this is not so for belief in accidents, even when these accidental cases contain a causal content. (The accidental causal content's relation to belief can be addressed only after an account of belief in singular causal statements is in place.) The grip mode of belief needs to be what is distinctive of non-accidental generalizations, the other cases involving one or more kinds of non-grip modes of belief. On this Humean position, the contrast between accidental and non-accidental generalizations, which at first appeared to be a contrast of content, is dissolved into a contrast of mode of belief. It is something subjective, in that, with no cognitive error, the same thing may be believed in the grip way by some but not all subjects, even if they coincide in informational state; in this sense the contrast is, as Hume might have put it, 'in the mind'.

The first phase of the argument is to try to discover a mode in which generalizations can be believed which does not amount to grip: a non-grip mode. One could just stipulate some primitive mode, but this would be unenlightening. Since believing that all Fs are Gs does involve a commitment to believing to be G whatever one believes to be F, we need to have as much detail as possible about how being in the grip of a regularity is something more than this. The theme of this section is that the account of the non-grip mode of belief requires successive enrichments to avoid counterexamples, and we end up with the second definition. This is not what was wanted, for it means that the second definition does not, after all, identify a distinctive mode of belief, the grip mode.

A first proposal for a non-grip mode of believing that all Fs are G might be:

(1) For all x, S believes that if x is F, then it is G.[3]

Although universal quantification occurs in both definiens and definition, there is no circularity relative to the aim of defining general belief, for in the definition the quantifier lies outside the belief context. The definition looks quite different from the second definition, so there is a good prospect that the definitions pick out quite different psychological states: the grip mode needs to guarantee the presence of a non-grip mode, but not conversely. However, (1) is not correct, for it is not the case that anyone who believes any generalization is thereby belief-related to every object in the universe and believes a singular conditional concerning it. Even if the domain of the quantifier in the definition is somehow restricted—for example, to just the objects S encounters—it is still highly implausible to suppose that general belief requires having so many singular conditional beliefs about wholly irrelevant objects (non-Fs).

This problem could be addressed by getting the conditional out of the belief context:

(2) For all x, if S believes that x is F, then S believes that x is G.

This might be without counterexample (i.e. there might be no object S believes to be F without also believing it to be G) even when S does not believe that all Fs are Gs, for S believes that there are Fs which are not G. I believe there are white geraniums, and, being consistent in at least this respect, I do not believe that all geraniums are red. But all the geraniums I have come across have been red, so it is true of each thing that if I believe of it that it is a geranium, I believe of it that it is red. (2) can be true even when S does not believe the generalization.[4]

It seems that we need to get some kind of actual or potential transition into the picture. I can think of two (potentially combinable) ways to achieve this: by relying on counterfactuals or by relying on causation. One might improve (2) by modifying it so that the belief that x is F causes the belief that x is G. In the state envisaged in the previous paragraph, it is arguably false

---

[3] 'To believe that all men are mortal—what is it? Partly to say so, partly to believe in regard to any x that turns up that if he is a man he is mortal' (Ramsey, 'General propositions and causality', 136). Ramsey would not approve of the use to which his idea is put here, for he takes 'All men are mortal' to be an example of a non-accidentally true sentence, whereas I use his account in search of a non-grip mode of belief. Another difference is that Ramsey will conclude that 'variable hypotheticals' are not really propositions at all. This is a good route for an eliminativist: if beliefs apparently in a complex content can be reduced to relations between beliefs in a simpler content, one is free to say that the supposed complex content is unintelligible nonsense, and that the question of something satisfying it does not so much as arise.

[4] The example can be made transtemporal by supposing that I never have the good fortune to encounter a white geranium.

that my believing something to be a geranium causes me to believe it to be red; so that counterexample would be avoided. But the price is high: the 'improvement' would lead to something barely distinguishable from the second definition, and so would not be an advisable route to take in the service of finding a distinct, non-grip mode of belief in generalizations.

This is a route that we will, in the end, be forced to take; but let us first try instead to bring counterfactuals to bear:

(3) For all *x*, if *S* were to come to believe that *x* is *F*, then *S* would come to believe that *x* is *G*.[5]

This is not right as it stands, for some ways of coming to believe of an object that it is *F* are ways of coming to believe of it that it is not *G*, and these would typically lead *S* to abandon the generalization rather than to believe that the object in question is *G* (as well as not-*G*). (3) would wrongly represent *S* as not in fact believing that all *F*s are *G*s. For example, it might be true that I believe that all the people in the room speak English, but also true that were a reliable informant to assert something I did not previously believe—namely, that Pierre is a monolingual Frenchman and is in the room—I would come to believe that Pierre is in the room but would not go on to believe that Pierre speaks English. I would change my mind about whether everyone in the room speaks English. But as things are, I do believe that everyone in the room speaks English, even though I am not in the state specified in (3).

Peacocke gestures towards a solution in terms of modes of presentation: (3) should hold for any object presented under a minimal mode of presentation like 'the next one to be encountered'.[6] Relating this to the example just given, the idea is that if Pierre were presented simply as the next person in the room to be encountered, I would go on to believe that he speaks English. Any single suggestion of this kind will be inadequate, since if, for example, one believes that

I'll never encounter an honest politician (where this equals: all honest politicians are things I'll never encounter),

it will not be counterfactually true that were an honest politician presented under the mode 'the next one to be encountered', one would believe that one will never encounter it.

Fixing up (3) will no doubt involve introducing caveats about what other information is acquired in the course of coming to believe of something that it is *F*: ideally, this information should not itself carry reason to believe that the object is not *G*. Such caveats are in any case required by the present

[5] Cf. C. Peacocke, 'Causal modalities and realism', in M. Platts (ed.), *Reference, Truth and Reality* (Henley: Routledge and Kegan Paul, 1980), 41–68.

[6] Ibid. 55; cf. Ramsey, 'General propositions and causality', 136: for 'any *x* that turns up' (cited above in n. 3).

formulation of the second definition. All beliefs are defeasible, even those in the obtaining of generalizations one takes to be non-accidental. One way in which they can be defeated is by finding a counter instance, an F that is not a G. That one would abandon belief in a generalization were one to encounter a counter instance does not show that one does not in fact believe it. So both the second definition and (3) will need to be supplemented by some proviso allowing the possibility of coming to disbelieve a generalization that one in fact believes. One could add something like the following: provided that S does not, in coming to believe of x that it is F, come to believe anything else of x which causes (or would cause) S to believe that x is not G.

We are now in danger of obliterating any substantive difference between the grip mode of belief, as characterized in the second definition, and any other. If we set aside those features of the second definition specially adapted to events, the difference between it and (3) is just that shown in the following skeletons (omitting the envisaged provisos), where p and p' range over singular instances of the generalization in question:

coming to believe that p causes one to come to believe that p';

if one came to believe that p, one would come to believe that p'.

I will suggest that each skeleton needs to add the feature of the other which it lacks: the first skeleton needs to add counterfactual dependence, and the second needs to add causation. Then the skeletons will converge, and the difference will well and truly have been obliterated, and thus Hume's project will have run into the ground.

In the first skeleton, corresponding to the second definition, 'causes' matches 'determines', a semantically somewhat mysterious 'continuous present'. The present tense in the definiendum can be taken as 'Believes (timeless) at t'; but one can believe some generalization at a time without the causal transaction the second definition envisages occurring at *that* time, so we cannot treat the present tense in 'determines' in the same way. If we interpret the definiens as a quantification over all actual acts (by S) of coming to believe that p, past, present, and future, to the effect that each causes an act of coming to believe that p', we fail to allow for the fact that one can believe a generalization today and not tomorrow, in which case one would (today) believe the generalization while not being in the (transtemporal) state that the second definition would require. If we interpret the continuous present (in a way not generally justifiable—but we are trying our best!) as saying that belief in p has caused belief in p' *up to now* (the time of the belief in the generalization), the definition is insufficient, since the believer may have abandoned the belief after the last occasion for the causal transaction. The second skeleton overcomes this difficulty, in that the time associated with belief in the generalization can be linked with the time of the believing in the definiens. Expanding the skeleton a bit: for all times t, one believes a certain generalization at t iff if one came to believe at t that p, one would come to believe at $t + \varepsilon$ that p'. This solution is available because a modal fact can be true at a time when nothing relevant is actually happening. It is hard to find an interpretation of Hume's 'determines', other than the counterfactual one, which gives the second definition any promise of correctness. So let us amend it accordingly, taking the new skeleton of the second definition to be:

(*) if S came to believe that p, this would cause her to come to believe that p'.

The attempt to describe the non-grip mode of belief in a generalization, using the skeleton 'if one came to believe that p, one would come to believe that p'', is inadequate. Believing even an accidental generalization, like 'All the coins in my pocket are silver', requires it to be the case that coming to believe an instance of the antecedent should potentially *produce* belief in the corresponding instance of the consequent. In some actual or counterfactual circumstance in which I come to believe that this is a coin in my pocket, my coming to believe that it is silver does not manifest my belief in the generalization if it arises independently (e.g. by perception); to manifest my belief in the generalization, it should be caused by the belief that it is a coin in my pocket. If we add this causal feature to the earlier counterfactual skeleton, we get:

(**) if S came to believe that p, this would cause her to come to believe that p'.

This is the same as (*), the skeleton we arrived at when trying to improve the second definition towards something acceptable. We have converged from different directions on essentially the same condition. This does not bode well for the attempt to find substantively different accounts of belief in grip mode and belief in non-grip mode. However, the modal notions which have been brought to bear are rich, and it is worthwhile considering other applications of them, without trying to achieve a simple definition.

V

The hypothesis now to be considered is that to believe in grip mode is to believe with a high degree of resilience, and to believe in non-grip mode is to believe with a low degree of resilience. Resilience is a modal notion, and reflects the likelihood of the subject revising his belief (or revising downwards his degree of confidence in it) in the light of potential conflicting information. Resilience is not the same as degree of confidence or credence, which is a this-world matter of strength of belief, and could be measured by betting quotients. High confidence might combine with low resilience. Someone in the motor trade assures me that Ford does not make a magenta car. I believe this with complete confidence (I have no independent information and no reason to doubt the word of someone in a position to know). But I might believe it with low resilience, in that I would abandon it with no struggle were I to see a Ford-shaped magenta car with the Ford logo. A more resilient believer would discount the new evidence, supposing that the Ford-shaped magenta car had been resprayed by an enthusiast or was a Ford look-alike produced by another manufacturer.

Examples lend some initial plausibility to the identification of grip with resilience. Consider two responses available to someone who comes to learn that Mary was at the party, given that the person previously believed both that everyone at the party got drunk and that Mary is a model of sobriety. One option is to abandon the generalization, holding to the belief in Mary's sobriety. Another is to abandon the belief in Mary as a model of sobriety in favour of the generalization about the party. What factors might influence the choice between these revisions? One possible factor is this: if you supposed it was the kind of party which of its nature ensured that the guests became drunk, you would be more likely to think that Mary's sober disposition had been overstretched, and to retain the opinion that everyone at the party got drunk; whereas if you supposed it just an accident that those who got drunk did so, you are more open to the thought that Mary stayed sober, and that the generalization should be qualified or abandoned. In short, if you took the generalization to reflect something non-accidental, you would be less likely to qualify or abandon it were you to be faced by some potentially defeating evidence than if you took it not to reflect anything non-accidental.

A Humean distinguishes 'laws of nature' from 'accidental generalizations' without supposing that there is a difference of content between them. What we call a statement of a law of nature, like 'All animals are mortal', contains no more 'nomic content' than an accidental generalization like 'Everyone in the room speaks English'. The difference is not a difference in content, an implausible view given the invisibility of a relevant semantic difference, but a widespread difference in mode of belief: laws are believed in grip mode, that is, resilient mode; accidental generalizations in non-grip mode, that is, non-resilient mode. If we learn of something we had supposed to be immortal that it is an animal, we will typically revise our belief in its immortality. If we learn of someone we believe to be in the room that she does not speak English, we will typically revise our belief in the generalization that everyone in the room speaks English.

It has been held that the content of a law-statement somehow entails, sustains, or supports a counterfactual, whereas this is not so for the content of an accidental generalization. A difficulty with such views is that it is hard to say in any way at all, let alone a systematic way, what expressions encode the relevant difference of content. A Humean can mark the difference not as a difference in content but as a difference in mode of belief, itself reflected in what resilience counterfactuals are true of typical believers. Strictly, there is no such thing as being a law or non-accidental generalization, but we call something a law if it is believed in grip mode by us, or by us and our friends, or by the experts, or by the majority (the relativization is normally not determinate).

There is some initial plausibility in the identification of grip with resilience; but there are also difficulties. Here are some possible counter-examples. Suppose I believe that every guest at the party got drunk, but I regard this as pure accident: I know of nothing about the party which made it specially conducive to drunkenness. The generalization should be believed in non-grip mode, and let us suppose that it is in fact thus believed. But suppose I came to this accidental belief by having been present (say as a spy rather than a guest, so that I can soberly observe without being a counter instance of the generalization) and having observed every guest get drunk. Were I to learn that Mary, whom I had supposed a model of sobriety, was among the guests, I would revise my belief in Mary's sobriety rather than abandon the generalization. So a belief held in what ought, for a Humean, to be non-grip mode might meet a condition for being resilient—that is, for being held in grip mode. A belief in an accidental generalization may be resilient because of the way in which it is acquired, and may not reflect a view of the generalization as non-accidental.[7] Other examples suggest the converse kind of failure: one may have a non-resilient belief in something one treats as non-accidental; that is, one may regard as non-accidental something one believes in non-resilient mode. For example, a firm has been working on alternative unbreakable drinking vessels for wine. I am convinced of their success, know that they are about to drop their prototype on to concrete, and believe that this occurrence will not be followed by a breaking. I also believe that dropping wine *glasses* (vessels made of glass) is followed by their breaking. This is a causal generalization, and being, arguably, more than just a summation of singular causal facts, it is the kind of generalization that I should, and we will suppose do, believe in grip mode, reflecting my perception of what I believe as something non-accidental. But were I to come to learn that the dropping of the prototype is in fact the dropping of a wine glass (the innovation was to develop unbreakable glass), I would maintain my confidence in the firm, and abandon the belief that all droppings of wine glasses are followed by breakings. On the present account, this lack of resilience means that I am not in the grip of a regularity; but this

---

[7] Hume would not regard generalizations all of whose instances had been observed as even candidates for being believed with grip. For him, the relevant cases involve inductive projection, which is what grip sustains.

is a case of non-accidental belief, and so should be a case of grip. Resilience is almost never total, for almost all beliefs can be defeated by conflicting evidence, so we cannot demand that total resilience is what reflects the grip mode of belief.

Confidence can mimic resilience. In the first counterexample, I am totally confident in the accidental generalization that every guest at the party was drunk because I have observed each guest to be drunk, and am well placed to know that none had escaped my observation. The confidence in this case held in place the counterfactual that I would be inclined to discount, if not the new evidence offered (Mary was at the party), at least its impact on the hypothesis, given previous beliefs. The mechanisms are complex and depend upon both kind and weight of evidence. Hume was concerned only with inductive beliefs, ones believed on grounds which do not include observation of every instance, and inserting this as a restriction of the subject-matter would help protect his approach. But confidence must still be separated from resilience, as shown by the example of the magenta Ford. In the party case, it makes a difference whether the apparent counter evidence takes the envisaged form, or whether it simultaneously provides an explanation of my mistake. For example, if I were to be told that Mary had been hiding in a cupboard, so I hadn't seen her, it is more likely that I would revise my belief in the generalization.

There is a morass of factors at work in the notions now under discussion (degrees of confidence, evidence and its weight, and the probabilities of revision in the light of new information), and it would be of little help to a Humean to be told that he has a clear thesis only once the issues have been sorted out. I think, however, that one can sketch a promising direction by trying to hold as much constant as possible, and by transforming the essentially quantitative notions into qualitative ones. We need to make explicit the implicit relativity of resilience: just about every belief is resilient to some but not other potential new information. To call one belief more resilient than another is a way of saying that one is resilient to 'more' information than another. If the beliefs are different, the comparison will not be straightforward, since new information relevant to one may be irrelevant to the other. Every belief is resilient to irrelevant information, so there is a danger of incorrect measurement of relative degrees of resilience of distinct beliefs. In the promising approach, we consider a single belief and a single set of background beliefs (or a single distribution of subjective probabilities), and for a series of pieces of potential new information, we ask two questions: is there a way of holding the belief such that, given this background, it would be resilient to this information? And is there a way of holding the belief such that, given this background, it would not be resilient to this information? Here '(believing that p) is resilient to (q)' means something like: the probability of the believer revising her belief that p on encountering the information that q is low. Those pieces of information for which the answer to both questions is 'Yes' are the 'sensitive' ones: one might or might not revise in the light of them. Given a psychological state of believing, we can rank its resilience in terms of how many of the sensitive pieces of potential information it is resilient to: the number of pieces of sensitive information, those which *might* cause a revision in belief, which would *not* do so. Finally, we can identify grip mode for that belief with having high resilience, and non-grip mode with having low resilience. (Or we could rework grip as a matter of degree, and so claim yet another illusion in the supposition that there is a difference of kind between the accidental and the non-accidental.)

To show the promise of the approach, I briefly apply it to two of the problematic examples. There are two ways to believe that every guest at the party got drunk: one may think of it as an accident, or one may regard the party as the kind of party which makes drunkenness likely or even inevitable. The first way of believing is less resilient: there is a piece of information, that Mary was at the party, coming to learn which would probably lead one to revise one's belief about the party, given one's background confidence in Mary's sobriety. The second way of believing is more resilient, for coming to learn this would probably cause no revision, but would instead cause a revision in the background belief about Mary's sobriety, even though this was held with the same degree of confidence as in the previous case. There are two ways to believe that glasses break when dropped: I may believe that this just happens to be so, or I may believe that it is held in place by causation. In both cases, the belief is not resilient with respect to the potential information that the firm's unbreakable drinking vessel is made of glass. But there is information to which the latter way of believing is resilient and the former not: for example, seeing a magician drop what appears to be a glass and it not break. In one case there is a fair chance that the evidence will be taken at face value and the generalization revised, in the other a fair chance that it will be discredited and the generalization retained (what appears to be glass is not always glass).

As the examples reveal, resilience will always be hard to assess definitively, for it involves consideration of potential responses to every piece of relevant information. But there is nothing circular about an application of induction here: the fact that this belief is believed with resilience to *these* pieces of sensitive information can give reason to believe that it is also resilient to *other*, or *many more*, or even *all* such pieces of information.

VI

We have come some way from Hume's second definition, and I close by estimating this distance. There were two initial Humean hopes: that causal belief could be distinguished as a mode of belief rather than as belief with a distinctive content, and that this could be achieved by the second definition. The second hope was disappointed, because even belief in an accidental generalization required the relevant kind of causal and counterfactual connection between singular beliefs. Since resilience is defined for beliefs in generalizations, beliefs some of which the second definition was supposed to define, it is not likely that resilience can be used to produce a new definition which would look anything like what Hume offered. With this, many bright consequential hopes have to be abandoned: we can no longer expect the kind of definition of causal belief which will help a functionalist (or not one who takes it that there is a substantial difference between grip and non-grip modes); nor can we expect the kind of definition which will make it straightforward that non-human animals have such beliefs.[8]

Despite this, the first hope remains appealing. Recognizing non-accidental, non-causal beliefs and accidental causal ones, we modified it into the hope that we could single out distinct modes of belief in terms of which to mark the distinction between accidental and non-accidental. Thus far, it seems, we remained more or less within a Humean perspective. But the attempt to mark this distinction in terms of the modal notion of resilience may seem both antithetical to Hume's philosophy and hopelessly circular. It may seem antithetical, because Hume apparently had no truck with this kind of modality, and it may seem circular, because the relevant counterfactual facts themselves involve the concept of the non-accidental.

Hume saw nothing wrong with a kind of necessity and possibility arising from a comparison of ideas and not considered to hold 'between the objects themselves'; this may be approximately equated with a priori necessity and possibility. On this view, the possible is the coherently thinkable, and this notion played a pivotal role in his philosophy. The range of worlds involved in the account of resilience does not exceed the coherently thinkable ones, but we must restrict our attention to a proper subset of them, those in which the subject assigns the same subjective probability to all save the target belief and the newly acquired evidence as to her actual beliefs. Restrictions like this do not involve a new notion of possibility: we can stipulate that these are the worlds to be considered, and a 'comparison of ideas' can check whether, for an arbitrary alternative to the actual world, this restriction has been honoured. The claim that the approach is positively antithetical to Hume (as opposed merely to being not something one could attribute to Hume) would need to be based on something more than that it exploits a modal notion.

---

[8] Though it is not nothing that a development of the second definition will ground an ascription of general beliefs to creatures lacking the concept of universal quantification.

Perhaps we can find the something more in the explanation of the alleged circularity. The allegation is that the concept of counterfactuality involved in the concept of resilience itself involves the concept of the non-accidental. But how does this enter? Not, if the point of the previous paragraph is accepted, with the notion of a non-actual possibility as such. Perhaps it enters with the assessment of the likelihood of belief revision in the light of the envisaged new information. To assess the likelihood, we must bring to bear knowledge of non-accidental matters, laws relating to the subject's dispositions and psychology. Does this not show that the approach is both circular and anti-Humean?

Resilience is just a pairing of worlds with a number, a number which measures the likelihood that the target belief will be abandoned at the paired world. As such, it contains nothing about psychological laws. But even if it did, this would not amount to circularity: what is to be defined is belief in the non-accidental, not the non-accidental as such (though given the character of the former, there is room for a Humean deflation of the latter). The structure here is that of the second definition: causation is used in the definition of causal belief, not in the definition of causation (though, given the character of the former, there is room for a Humean deflation of the element of necessity supposedly contained in the latter).

Perhaps there is circularity in that we need beliefs about psychological laws in order to have *evidence* for which number measures resilience at a world. This is the right content for an accusation of circularity, but it falls in the wrong place. It would be damaging only if this content, belief in the non-accidental, belonged to the concept of resilience. There is nothing wrong if it belongs merely to what is involved in possessing evidence for its application. Similarly, an analysis of perception which uses causation is not rendered circular by the fact that much, or even all, causal knowledge is based upon perception.

Hume's second definition is extraordinary, not only for being a brilliant answer, but also for being an answer to a brilliant question, one which Hume thought, correctly as far as I am aware, had never been asked by any of his predecessors. If the arguments of this paper are accepted, his second definition is not a correct answer, but the underlying idea that we can distinguish a distinctive way of believing a generalization, a way which in some sense puts us in its grip, remains promising, and highly relevant to many currently debated issues in metaphysics and philosophy of mind.

REFERENCES

Hume, David, *Enquiry Concerning Human Understanding*, ed. L. A. Selby-Bigge, 3rd edn., rev. P. H. Nidditch (Oxford: Clarendon Press, 1975).

Peacocke, C., 'Causal modalities and realism', in M. Platts (ed.), *Reference, Truth and Reality* (Henley: Routledge and Kegan Paul, 1980), 41–68.

Ramsey, F., 'General propositions and causality', in D. H. Mellor (ed.), *Foundations: Essays in Logic, Mathematics and Economics* (London: Routledge and Kegan Paul, 1978), 133–51.

Transcendental Empiricism? Deleuze's Reading of Hume

MARTIN BELL

The development of Gilles Deleuze's own philosophy was intertwined with his studies in the history of philosophy. Perhaps it is true that the connection to his reading of Hume, although there to be found, is not so evident in the major works of the 1960s, *Difference and Repetition* (1968) and *The Logic of Sense* (1969), as is the relation to his other studies at this time of great philosophers—the books on Nietzsche (1962), Kant (1963), Bergson (1966), and Spinoza (1970). Yet Deleuze's book on Hume, *Empiricism and Subjectivity* (1953), pre-dates all his other writings on the history of philosophy, and his commitment to a form of empiricism, which persists throughout all his work and which he called 'transcendental empiricism', begins with that study.

Deleuze's approach to writing the history of philosophy was governed by his conception of the nature of philosophy. Philosophy begins from problems or questions, but it does not aim at solutions or answers so much as at the creation of concepts by means of which the problem or question can be explored, in its presuppositions and its consequences. In a sense, philosophers are concerned not with the question 'Is this a good answer or solution?' but with the question 'Is this a good question?':

. . . a philosophical theory is an elaborately developed question, and nothing else; by itself and in itself, it is not the resolution to a problem, but the elaboration, *to the very end*, of the necessary implications of a formulated question. It shows us what things are, or what things should be, on the assumption that the question is good and rigorous.[1]

It is therefore in the elaboration of the question that a philosopher creates, and what is created are concepts; for example, Aristotle's substance, Descartes's cogito, Leibniz's monad, Kant's condition, Schelling's power, Bergson's duration.[2]

---

[1] Gilles Deleuze, *Empiricism and Subjectivity: An Essay on Hume's Theory of Human Nature*, trans. C. V. Boundas (New York: Columbia University Press, 1991), 106.

[2] Gilles Deleuze and Félix Guattari, *What is Philosophy?*, trans. G. Burchell and H. Tomlinson (London and New York: Verso, 1994), 7.

In the preface which Deleuze supplied for the English translation of *Empirisme et Subjectivité* he spoke of a dream of 'a history of philosophy that would list only the new concepts created by a great philosopher'.[3] In the case of Hume, the history would record the creation of such concepts as belief, probability, illusion, the association of ideas, relations, and habit. Furthermore, Deleuze suggested that all of these concepts are created and employed by Hume in relation to what he called 'the problem of the Self': that is, the subjectivity referred to in the title of his book. So the theme of Deleuze's study could be put this way: What is it about the concepts—of belief, probability, relations, and so on—that Hume creates that makes his thought an empiricism? And how is this assemblage of concepts used to elaborate the implications of a question about subjectivity?

It might be said that there is nothing problematic about ascribing empiricism to Hume. Empiricism is usually understood as a thesis about knowledge: that all knowledge not only begins with experience but is derived from experience. It is empiricism so understood that Kant has in mind as a target at the start of the first *Critique*:

> But though all our knowledge begins with experience, it does not follow that it all arises out of experience. For it may well be that even our empirical knowledge is made up of what we receive through impressions and of what our own faculty of knowledge (sensible impressions serving merely as the occasion) supplies from itself (B1).[4]

Deleuze, however, argues that this Kantian notion of empiricism fails as a characterization of Hume's empiricism because it does not fit with what Hume says about experience. If by 'experience' in Hume's writings is meant what Kant describes as 'what we receive through impressions', then Hume does not assert that all knowledge (taking this broadly enough to include empirical beliefs) derives merely from experience. Simple ideas may indeed be repetitions (copies) in the imagination of simple impressions, but 'those complex ideas, which are the common subjects of our thoughts and reasoning', and therefore the common contents of empirical belief or knowledge, are not merely repetitions of sensible impressions, but rather 'effects of [the] union or association of ideas'.[5] Only if the association of ideas itself derived merely from the nature of the ideas themselves (considered as copies of sensible impressions) would it be true that empirical beliefs are derived from 'experience' in the limited sense that Kant used to characterize empiricism. But, argues Deleuze, Hume does not hold that the association of ideas in the imagination derives from the nature of the ideas themselves.

---

[3] Deleuze, *Empiricism and Subjectivity*, p. ix.

[4] Immanuel Kant, *Critique of Pure Reason*, trans. N. Kemp Smith (London: Macmillan, 1929), B1.

[5] David Hume, *A Treatise of Human Nature*, ed. L. A. Selby-Bigge, 2nd edn., rev. P. H. Nidditch, (Oxford: Clarendon Press, 1978), 13.

'Experience' is used in the *Treatise* more commonly to refer to a synthesis in the memory or the imagination of previous encounters with objects:

The nature of experience is this. We remember to have had frequent instances of the existence of one species of objects; and also remember, that the individuals of another species of objects have always attended them, and have existed in a regular order of contiguity and succession with regard to them. (p. 87)

Hume gives this definition in the course of arguing that experience in this sense and by itself is precisely insufficient to account for empirical beliefs. He shows that empirical beliefs, especially causal beliefs, transcend what is given in experience (in Hume's second sense), for experience in itself does not account for the idea of necessity. The idea of necessity 'makes an essential part' of the idea of causation;[6] but it does not derive merely from repetition:

From the mere repetition of any past impression, even to infinity, there never will arise any new original idea, such as that of a necessary connection. (Ibid. 88)

Empirical beliefs can transcend the mere synthesis of past experience and employ a 'new original idea' because, in addition to experience, there is habit. On the side of the objects there is regularity; on the side of the subject there is not only repetition (experience) but also habit and expectation. Experience and habit, then, are both required for empirical beliefs, and they are different:

Experience is a principle, which instructs me in the several conjunctions of objects for the past. Habit is another principle, which determines me to expect the same for the future; and both of them conspiring to operate upon the imagination, make me form certain ideas in a more intense and lively manner, than others, which are not attended with the same advantages. (Ibid. 265)

Whether 'experience' means sensible impressions or whether it means the synthetic repetition of regularity, for Hume empirical beliefs do not derive or 'arise' from experience, although they do 'begin' from it. Hume's empiricism does not fit Kant's definition.

The remainder of this paper is divided into three sections. The first reviews Deleuze's proposal about a better way to identify and characterize what constitutes or, better, manifests Hume's empiricism. Deleuze's exploration of this theme runs right through his book. For the purposes of this essay, however, I concentrate on only one major element, the nature of relations. I initially found it intriguing, even surprising, that Deleuze should put so much weight on Hume's treatment of relations. But it turns out that thought about relations traces a trajectory from Hume through Kant to Deleuze's own transcendental empiricism. The next section turns to subjectivity. Here

---

[6] David Hume, *An Enquiry Concerning Human Understanding*, ed. L. A. Selby-Bigge, 3rd edn., rev. P. H. Nidditch (Oxford: Clarendon Press, 1975), 97.

certainly, part of the picture is the specific issue of Hume's treatment of the idea of the self. But in Deleuze's reading that issue is presented as an aspect, or perhaps an echo, of the question or problem that Hume calls 'human nature' and Deleuze calls 'the question of subjectivity'. The topics of these sections, relations and subjectivity, are not independent. Very roughly, in Deleuze's reading of Hume, relations of perceptions are the effects of principles of human nature. There are two kinds of principles, those of associations and those of the passions, and these, as Hume says, have a great influence on each other. Each needs the other. Association gives structure, but the passions give sense and direction. Human nature, human subjectivity, is to be understood as constituted in history and in action, not only in reflection: 'we must distinguish betwixt personal identity, as it regards our thought or imagination, and as it regards our passions or the concern we take in ourselves' (ibid. 253). The final section offers a few brief remarks about Deleuze's own idea of a 'transcendental empiricism', intended to indicate how this can be seen to have part of its origin in Deleuze's reading of Hume, a reading which, in the end, is an attempt to mobilize some of Hume's conceptual creations in a confrontation with Kant's conception of the transcendental.

ALL RELATIONS ARE EXTERNAL TO THEIR TERMS

As we have seen, Deleuze argues that the Kantian definition of empiricism fails to fit Hume's thought. Yet Hume is, of course, an empiricist, in a sense in which Kant is not; and so we must find a deeper characterization of the differences. In Kantian thought, the subject determines the form of what is given in experience, and this form is specified as so many forms of unity, of sameness—we think of the forms of judgement and the forms of synthesis and of their fundamental identity. By contrast, Deleuze points out, originally and at the start, for Hume what is given is characterized not by sameness but by difference. His most fundamental way of characterizing the perceptions of the mind is as a multiplicity of differences:

We have observ'd, that whatever objects are different are distinguishable, and that whatever objects are distinguishable are separable by the thought and imagination. And we may here add, that these propositions are equally true in the *inverse*, and that whatever objects are separable are also distinguishable, and that whatever objects are distinguishable are also different. (*Treatise*, 18)

So in its original condition the imagination is a flux of different, distinguishable, and separable ideas. No forms of unity, sameness, or relation between distinct ideas are original, given to the mind in the givenness of the ideas. The imagination's initial or 'native situation' is one of 'indifference' (ibid. 125). In this state, the mind has no preferences, tendencies, or dispositions, for it is nothing but a multiplicity. For thought, reason, and belief to be possible, the mind must become determinate: something must determine it. Ideas must become associated. This is the work of the principles of human nature, which establish tendencies and transitions within the imagination. In this way ideas are related, naturally; and an easy transition (Hume describes this as the essence of relation) is set up as a kind of 'vibration of thought', a 'double motion' (ibid. 357) from one term of the relation to the other and back. With the operations of the principles of association, relations are established, and these relations are therefore not qualities of perceptions themselves, given already in the givenness of the perceptions. Relations are external to their terms. This is what Deleuze proposes as a slogan to mark empiricism:

the criterion of empiricism becomes evident. We will call 'nonempiricist' every theory according to which, in one way or another, relations are derived from the nature of things.[7]

Deleuze finds this mark of empiricism in Hume, first in the doctrine of the association of ideas. Because Hume does not explain association as a product of the nature of the terms, the qualities of the ideas themselves, but as the effect of the principles of human nature, relations between perceptions are external to their terms. Relations between perceptions that are effects of the principles of human nature constitute what Hume calls 'natural relations' (*Treatise*, 13, 94, 170). Here the ascription of empiricism in the form of the thesis of the externality of relations seems well grounded. But in the *Treatise* there is another sense of 'relation' in which it designates 'that particular circumstance, in which, even upon the arbitrary union of two ideas in the fancy, we may think proper to compare them' (ibid. 13). A relation in this second sense Hume calls 'philosophical', and he identifies seven general kinds. Furthermore, within these kinds he distinguishes a class of four kinds (relations of resemblance, of proportions in quantity or number, of degrees in a quality, and of contrariety), which are 'such as depend entirely on the ideas, which we compare together', and a class of three kinds (relations of identity, of time and place, and of causation), which are 'such as may be chang'd without any change in the ideas' (ibid. 69). Hume also describes the difference between the two classes by saying that relations in the first class depend 'solely upon ideas', while those in the second class 'depend not upon the idea' (ibid. 70, 73).

At least since Kant,[8] many philosophers have taken this division of relations into two classes to be based on a distinction between analytic

---

[7] Deleuze, *Empiricism and Subjectivity*, 109.

[8] Immanuel Kant, *Prolegomena to Any Future Metaphysics*, trans. P. Carus, rev. J. W. Ellington (Indianapolis: Hackett Publishing Co., 1977), 15–16: 'what [Hume] said was equivalent to this: that pure mathematics contains only analytic, but metaphysics synthetic, a priori judgements. In this, however, he was greatly mistaken.'

judgements on the one hand and synthetic judgements on the other hand.
Deleuze, however, understands Hume's division differently. Certainly relations that depend 'solely upon ideas' are knowable a priori. But when
Hume speaks of how such a priori knowledge is acquired (for example, how
'from the idea of a triangle . . . we discover the relation of equality, which
its three angles bear to two right ones' (*Treatise*, 69) he speaks of an act
of 'comparison', a bringing together of ideas, rather than an act of analysis,
a separation of a complex idea into its components. The latter is what Hume
usually means by 'definition',[9] and he is explicit in rejecting the notion that
mathematical truths are true by definition:

'Tis true, mathematicians pretend they give an exact definition of a right line,
when they say, *it is the shortest way betwixt two points* But in the first place
I observe, that this is more properly the discovery of one of the properties of
a right line, than a just definition of it. For I ask any one, if upon mention of a
right line he thinks not immediately on such a particular appearance, and if 'tis
not by accident only that he considers this property? A right line can be
comprehended alone; but this definition is unintelligible without a comparison
with other lines, which we conceive to be more extended. In common life 'tis
establish'd as a maxim, that the streightest way is also the shortest; which wou'd
be as absurd as to say, the shortest way is always the shortest, if our idea of
a right line was not different from that of the shortest way betwixt two points.
(Ibid. 49–50)

That the shortest way is always the shortest is analytically true. Hume
evidently means to contrast geometrical truths, and mathematical truths in
general, with merely analytic judgements.[10] Humean relations that depend
'solely upon the ideas' are relations discoverable a priori, by comparison
rather than analysis. Deleuze claims that the relation depends upon the
comparison, citing the passage in which, referring to the definition of equality of geometrical figures by their congruity, Hume says, 'In order to judge
of this definition let us consider, that since equality is a relation, it is not,
strictly speaking, a property in the figures themselves, but arises merely from
the comparison, which the mind makes betwixt them' (ibid. 46). He argues
therefore that in the case of those philosophical relations which depend
'solely upon the ideas', Hume still maintains the empiricist thesis that all
relations are external to their terms, because all depend on something other
than the terms themselves. In the case of mathematics, he argues, Hume

---

[9] The idea of cause can be defined because it is complex (*Treatise*, 169), whereas the ideas of
love and hatred cannot be defined because they arise from a simple impression (ibid. 329).
[10] This point is made by Marina Frasca-Spada, *Space and Self in Hume's* Treatise (Cambridge:
Cambridge University Press, 1998), 142. In this section, in which I am going beyond what Deleuze
actually says in his discussion of Hume on the a priori, I am indebted to Frasca-Spada's study in
general, and also to Donald W. Livingston, *Hume's Philosophy of Common Life* (Chicago:
University of Chicago Press, 1984).

regards the relations as dependent on an act of comparison. We recall that Hume says: 'all kinds of reasoning consist in nothing but a *comparison . . .*' (ibid. 73). This is presumably as true for a priori reasoning as for probable reasoning.

Relations are all discovered by comparison, and the difference between the two classes depends on the scope of the comparison. In the case of a priori relations, the comparison is restricted to the ideas in question 'consider'd as such' (ibid. 448), whereas in the case of relations discoverable a posteriori, the scope of the comparison is wider. The relations of causation, identity, and time and place emerge only from comparison of ideas considered, as Deleuze puts it, 'collectively . . . distributively . . . in the determinable collection where their own modes of appearance place them'.[11] *What* other ideas enter the comparison is then a matter of taking ideas not merely 'as such' but as ideas of objects in space and time; and what other ideas of objects in space and time must be compared cannot be known a priori. As Hume says, for instance 'the place [of an object in space] depends on a hundred different accidents, which cannot be foreseen by the mind' (ibid. 69).

Two points have emerged so far in this brief account of Deleuze's reading of Hume. First, he finds in Hume a thesis of the externality of relations which is not based on a contrast between analytic and synthetic judgements, nor on a contrast between a priori and a posteriori knowledge. This is therefore a thought which does not fit easily into a Kantian framework of the forms of judgement; and, for Deleuze, it is the mark of Hume's empiricism. Second, to the extent that Hume subscribes to the thesis of the externality of all relations, to the same extent he subscribes to an atomism of the mind in its original state, for these two theses must go together. He castigates critics who complain that Hume 'pulverises' experience for failing to see that this is an essential component of empiricism, and required by the doctrine of associationism. As he says elsewhere, the whole point of empiricism is that it thinks of experience not in terms of forms imposed by the subject, but as an indefinite multiplicity of differences—for empiricism, it is all a matter of '*and* and *and*'.[12]

---

[11] Deleuze, *Empiricism and Subjectivity*, 99. I take the phrase 'modes of appearance' to be a reference to Hume's doctrine that the ideas of space and time originate not in impressions of space and time (there are no such impressions—space and time are not objects) but in the 'manner of appearance' of impressions of objects. For a detailed discussion cf. Frasca-Spada, *Space and Self in Hume's* Treatise. Frasca-Spada investigates the connections in Hume's thought between various 'manners' (manner of appearance, manner of conception) and the conception of the self. I think that Deleuze, too, would connect such 'manners' to the self, seeing in them the 'affection' of the mind which transforms a mere flux of perceptions into the mind of a subject.

[12] Gilles Deleuze with Claire Parnet, *Dialogues*, trans. H. Tomlinson and B. Habberjam (New York: Columbia University Press, 1977).

HUMAN NATURE AS AFFECTIVITY

The human mind considered only as a multiplicity of different, distinguish-able, and separable ideas is not human nature. Human nature, subjectivity, arises only as and when the multiplicity is affected, producing system: tendencies, dispositions, transitions, and associations. These are, in part, the 'extraordinary effects' of 'a kind of *attraction* . . . in the mental world' whose 'causes . . . are mostly unknown, and must be resolv'd into *original* qualities of human nature' (*Treatise*, 13). So the original qualities of human nature are the causes of 'attraction', not the causes of ideas—except in so far as ideas are, in turn, caused by human nature. Elsewhere Hume says that without the operations of the principles of association and of passions human nature would go to ruin. Thus human nature as the possible object of a science must be thought of as transcending the mind considered as a multiplicity.

In the case of the understanding, this transcendence of the given manifests itself above all in belief in the real existence of objects beyond the scope of sense and memory. We are familiar with Hume's account here. Although all three principles of association play a part in the enlivening of ideas, it is only causation which produces belief in the real existence of objects. For Deleuze the central point in this account is Hume's insistence that the idea of necessary connection arises from an impression of reflection. He argues that impressions of reflection are always impressions of how the mind is affected—by association, by passion, by habit—and so are reflections in the mind of principles of human nature. The mind becomes human nature as it finds the principles of human nature reflected in itself. As a result, Hume carefully distinguishes between ideas that arise from impressions of sensa-tion, which we can think of as effects of matter and its principles, and ideas that arise from impressions of reflection, the effects of human nature and its principles. From this follows the lack of interest which Hume, the empiricist, shows in sensation—he is not interested in the origin of the mind, but in its affects:

'Tis certain, that the mind, in its perceptions, must begin somewhere; and that since the impressions precede their correspondent ideas, there must be some impressions, which without any introduction make their appearance in the soul. As these depend upon natural and physical causes, the examination of them wou'd lead me too far from my present subject. (Ibid. 275–6)

From this also follows another important consequence. Those ideas which arise from impressions of reflection, or 'secondary' impressions, are not strictly representations of objects or their qualities. For example, none of the ideas of necessary connection, vice and virtue, property or justice, can represent objects or their properties simply given to the mind. These are realities for the human subject, but their explanation is impossible without reference to the principles of human nature.

This orientation of empiricism is, says Deleuze, Hume's 'fundamental project. It entails

> the *substitution of a psychology of the mind by a psychology of the mind's affections*. The constitution of a psychology of the mind is not at all possible, since this psychology cannot find in its object the required constancy or universality; only a psychology of affections will be capable of constituting the true science of humanity.[13]

There is therefore always a duality in empiricism between terms and relations, such that the second does not follow from the nature of the first. Here this duality appears between the origin of ideas in the mind and the mind's affections, which give it a nature. Subjectivity is revealed in the association of ideas and the association of impressions, especially of the passions. The self is the object of passions—'the concern we take in ourselves'. Hume explains and illustrates this thought in detail in *Treatise*, II. ii. 2, 'Experiments to confirm this system'. Here the idea, or rather the impression, of the self as an object of passion serves as a kind of focus or privileged term. The passions are unlike the ideas in that the transition of the mind in the case of ideas is a kind of oscillation—for example, from cause to effect and equally from effect to cause—whereas the transition of the passions from another to the self is easy, but harder from the self to another.

In Hume's 'experiments' in which the self appears as the object of passion, the relations and associations are movements of the mind, not ideas and impressions, but their synthesis. The principles of human nature determine the mind by producing these relations and associations between what are, in truth, different and distinct and distinguishable terms. This empiricist duality therefore has a consequence, which is that if we seek to make the self the object of an idea when we ask about 'personal identity as it regards our thought or imagination' (*Treatise*, 235), we are bound to fail. Because subjectivity is the way in which the atoms are related, what Hume sometimes calls a 'manner of appearance', because 'all our distinct perceptions are distinct existences', and, finally, because 'the mind never perceives any real connexion among distinct existences' (ibid. 636), the self as subject of experience does not appear as the object of an idea. In Deleuze's reading, therefore, there is no inconsistency between the so-called absence of the self in Book I and its 'presence' in Book II. After all, Hume himself pauses to remind us in Book II that 'Ourself, independent of the perception of every other object, is in reality nothing' (ibid. 340). Both positions are consequences of the empiricist thesis that relations are external to their terms.

[13] Deleuze, *Empiricism and Subjectivity*, 21.

TRANSCENDENTAL EMPIRICISM

We have so far explored a little of Deleuze's reading of Hume, concentrating on empiricism and subjectivity. Deleuze himself speaks of the project of a transcendental empiricism, and his references to Hume in his own philosophy suggest that his reading of Hume is in some way connected to his idea of transcendental empiricism.

In strictly Kantian terms the label sounds contradictory: the transcendental conditions the empirical so that if the transcendental were itself empirical, it would not be transcendental. However, the earlier discussion in this paper has already drawn attention to the criterion of empiricism that Deleuze extracts from Hume, and its difference from the way Kant himself characterizes empiricism. It is worth repeating here:

> the criterion of empiricism becomes evident. We will call 'nonempiricist' every theory according to which, *in one way or another*, relations are derived from the nature of things.[14]

If transcendental empiricism is a philosophy that thinks the transcendental according to *this* criterion of empiricism, then the concern is with relations *within* the transcendental. So Deleuze has in focus not relations between elements in the content of experience but relations between that which gives form to experience, which is to say, between the faculties. In Kant the faculties of sensibility, imagination, and understanding are linked together in their transcendental activity of giving form to experience through being, so to speak, so many specifications of a fundamental unity, the unity of apperception. These relations, it can be plausibly argued, derive from 'the nature of things'—in this case from the nature of the transcendental subject as an a priori unity outside space and time. In a transcendental empiricism, therefore, the faculties will be thought of, in their transcendental roles, as different, distinct, and separable, as each capable of constructing their objects for themselves, without there being, necessarily, a unity in experience which reflects the harmony of the faculties that Kant invokes and justifies through the postulation of a prior, necessary unity of the mind.

Kant, at least in the Analytic of the First *Critique*, is quite opposed to such a thought. Objective experience is, precisely, unified experience. We cannot have, as it were, areas of objective experience which are not necessarily coherent with each other. As ever, the objection is: what would make these all my experience? It is evident, however, that as Kant develops his thought through, first, the Dialectic of the First *Critique*, and, second, the

---

[14] Deleuze, *Empiricism and Subjectivity*, 109.

Introductions and the two parts of the Third *Critique*, on aesthetic judgement and teleological judgement, possibilities keep emerging in which objective experience is not as necessarily unified as all that. It is increasingly accepted that the constitutive structures given by the a priori forms of sensibility and understanding may not guarantee very much necessary unity. For example, Kant at various points confronts the possibilities that the manifold of intuition does not allow for the formation of empirical concepts at all, or for particular empirical laws, or for systems of laws.

In the Dialectic of the First *Critique* he responds with the thought of transcendental but regulative ideas, not constitutive principles. In the *Critique of Judgement* we find a distinction between determinant judgement and reflective judgement. Determinant judgement is judgement as it appears in the First *Critique*, the subsumption of particulars under concepts already given. In the end, such judgements apply the categories. Reflective judgement, in contrast, is the finding or creating of concepts to fit the particulars. When we are dealing with the particularity of empirical experiences, reflective judgement is a necessary condition of determinant judgement, for we must find, and are not given, empirical concepts which can then figure in judgements of the various possible logical forms, and thus *in certain circumstances*, be brought eventually under the categories, allowing for systematic knowledge. 'In certain circumstances', because the Third *Critique* is concerned fundamentally with areas of experience where only reflective, and not also determinant, judgement is possible. This *Critique* is Kant's exploration of two domains, namely works of art and biology, where, he claims, the objects of our experience cannot be regarded as only ordinary objects of the sort whose presence in experience is guaranteed by the transcendental activities of the faculties as given in the First *Critique*. These objects, Kant says, display in differing ways the character of law-likeness without a law. Consequently, reflective judgement is seen as in a certain way equally free of law. In aesthetic judgement, for example, the faculties are in 'free play', each of them doing their own thing, so to speak. In teleological judgement, reflective judgement has a transcendental principle, that of the purposiveness of nature for our judgement, which is simply *its own* rule.

So even in Kant the possibility of thinking the transcendental without the presupposition of an a priori unity between the faculties seems already to be recognized. I think, therefore, that Deleuze's transcendental empiricism can be seen as a rethinking of Kantian philosophy, which draws in the ways I have briefly described, on his reading of Hume. Hume is sometimes thought of as leaving a legacy preserved exclusively in the analytic tradition. Deleuze's work shows that he is also important in the continental tradition. This helps to form yet another bridge between the two traditions in which we can think today.

REFERENCES

Deleuze, Gilles, *Empiricism and Subjectivity: An Essay on Hume's Theory of Human Nature* (1953), trans. C. V. Boundas (New York: Columbia University Press, 1991).

—— *Nietzsche and Philosophy* (1962), trans. H. Tomlinson (London: Athlone, 1983).

—— *Kant's Critical Philosophy: The Doctrine of the Faculties* (1963), trans. H. Tomlinson and B. Habberjam (London: Athlone, 1984).

—— *Bergsonism* (1966), trans. H. Tomlinson and B. Habberjam (New York: Zone Books, 1988).

—— *Difference and Repetition* (1968), trans. P. Patton (London: Athlone, 1994).

—— *The Logic of Sense* (1969), trans. M. Lester with C. Stivale, ed. C. V. Boundas (London: Athlone, 1990).

—— *Spinoza* (Paris: Presses Universitaires de France, 1970).

—— and Guattari, Félix, *What is Philosophy?*, trans. G. Burchell and H. Tomlinson (London and New York: Verso, 1994).

—— with Parnet, Claire, *Dialogues*, trans. H. Tomlinson and B. Habberjam (New York: Columbia University Press, 1977).

Frasca-Spada, Marina, *Space and Self in Hume's* Treatise (Cambridge: Cambridge University Press, 1998).

Hume, David, *An Enquiry Concerning Human Understanding*, ed. L. A. Selby-Bigge, 3rd edn., rev. P. H. Nidditch (Oxford: Clarendon Press, 1975).

—— *A Treatise of Human Nature*, ed. L. A. Selby-Bigge, 2nd edn., rev. P. H. Nidditch (Oxford: Clarendon Press, 1978).

Kant, Immanuel, *Critique of Pure Reason*, trans. N. Kemp Smith (London: Macmillan, 1929).

—— *Critique of Judgement*, trans. J. Meredith (Oxford: Oxford University Press, 1952).

—— *Prolegomena to Any Future Metaphysics*, trans. P. Carus, rev. J. W. Ellington (Indianapolis: Hackett Publishing Co., 1977).

Livingston, Donald W., *Hume's Philosophy of Common Life* (Chicago: University of Chicago Press, 1984).

Sympathy and Comparison: Two Principles of Human Nature

SUSAN JAMES

———•———

Writing to his friend Michael Ramsay soon after he had completed the manuscript of *A Treatise of Human Nature*, Hume listed some of the authors whose ideas had influenced his philosophy. Before embarking on the new work, Hume urged Ramsey to

> read once over the Recherche de la Verite of Pere Malebranche, the Principles of Human Knowledge by Dr. Berkeley, some of the more metaphysical articles of Bayle's Dictionary; such as those [on] Zeno, and Spinoza, Descartes' Meditations would also be useful but don't know if you will find it easily among your Acquaintances. These books will make you easily comprehend the metaphysical parts of my reasoning and as to the rest, they have so little dependence on all former systems of philosophy, that your natural good sense will afford you Light enough to judge of their Force and Solidity.[1]

Following Hume's advice, recent commentators have explored the ways in which Book I of the *Treatise* is indebted to Malebranche's *De la Recherche de la vérité*.[2] However, also following his advice, they have said relatively little about the relationship between Malebranche's discussion of the passions and Hume's treatment of this topic in Book II. I shall suggest that Malebranche's influence on the *Treatise* is in fact more pervasive than the letter to Ramsay acknowledges, and that, far from being independent of all former systems of philosophy, Hume's account of the passions echoes and engages with *De la Recherche*. Despite their divergent aims and convictions, he and Malebranche both aspire to situate the passions within a scientific account of the mind and to explain a wide range of emotional dispositions by appealing to natural principles. I shall briefly discuss these structural similarities, before going on to show how Malebranche and Hume appeal to the same set of

---

[1] Complete letter reprinted in Richard H. Popkin, 'So, Hume did read Berkeley', *Journal of Philosophy*, 61 (1964): 773–8.

[2] Charles J. McCracken, *Malebranche and British Philosophy* (Oxford: Clarendon Press, 1983); John P. Wright, *The Sceptical Realism of David Hume* (Manchester: Manchester University Press, 1983); John Passmore, *Hume's Intentions*, rev. edn. (London: Duckworth, 1968); Peter Jones, *Hume's Sentiments: Their Ciceronian and French Context* (Edinburgh: University of Edinburgh Press, 1982).

mechanisms to explain a family of passions which, they believe, play an important part in shaping our individual and social lives—our feelings of esteem, contempt, pride, and humility. The continuities I shall identify suggest that Hume not only adopted some of Malebranche's views about the workings of the passions, but also attempted to overcome inconsistencies that remained unresolved in Malebranche's analysis. By examining these moves in the discussion of esteem and contempt, we can get a clearer view of the overlaps and divergences between the two philosophers and arrive at a broader understanding of the relationship between French and Scottish philosophy during the early eighteenth century.

My main concern, however, is to see how Malebranche's and Hume's interpretations of esteem and contempt bear on a pair of interconnected themes: the development of an increasingly naturalistic analysis of the passions and an effort to limit the political significance of these particular emotions. A persuasive claim that certain passions are natural and relatively stable human dispositions will have direct political implications, since politicians and political theorists will take account of it. The passions in question will help to determine what is regarded as politically possible, and will impose boundaries on both theoretical conceptions and practical policies. At the same time, purportedly scientific claims about the passions can legitimate political norms and institutions by representing them as consonant with human nature. I shall argue that Malebranche's and Hume's analyses of esteem and contempt function in this way, though each philosopher implicitly legitimates a different type of polity. By tracing their changing views about the character and role of this family of emotions, we can come to see how their theories of the passions are put to political use.

IMPULSES OF THE SOUL

For both Malebranche and Hume, the study of the passions belongs to the most important of all the sciences, the science of man. In the Preface to *De la Recherche*, Malebranche declares that 'Of all the sciences of which humans are capable, the science of man is the most worthy', a sentiment echoed in the Introduction to the *Treatise*, where Hume announces that 'There is no question of importance whose decision is not compriz'd in the science of man'.[3] Unfortunately, the two writers agree, this vital inquiry has been eclipsed by the popularity of natural philosophy and is in desperate

---

[3] 'De toutes les sciences humaines, la science de l'homme est la plus digne de l'homme.' Nicolas Malebranche, *De la Recherche de la vérité*, ed. Geneviève Rodis Lewis, 2 vols., in *Œuvres Complètes*, ed. Henri Gouhier (Paris: Librairie Vrin, 1972), i. 20 (hereafter *Recherche* and citations given in text). David Hume, *A Treatise of Human Nature*, ed. L. A. Selby-Bigge, 2nd edn., rev. P. H. Nidditch (Oxford: Clarendon Press, 1978), p. xxi (hereafter *Treatise* and citations given in text).

need of attention. Men spend their lives 'hanging on to a telescope or attached to a burner', Malebranche complains, because they gain more satisfaction from these glamorous studies than from the painful and distasteful task of entering into themselves. 'Being forever outside themselves, they never see the disorder within', and fail to appreciate that we should have 'greater esteem for the science that teaches us what we are than for all the others combined' (*Recherche*, i. 21, 22). As Hume elaborates, the imperfection of our attempts to gain a systematic understanding of the world has reached such a pitch that 'even the rabble without doors may judge from the noise and clamour, which they hear, that all goes not well within' (*Treatise*, pp. xvii–xviii). To remedy the situation, we must 'march up directly to the capital or center of these sciences, to human nature itself'. Once this citadel has been conquered, the surrounding terrain will capitulate, and it will be possible to construct a body of sciences capable of improving our knowledge of nature and natural religion, and bringing honour to the native country of its creator (ibid. pp. xx–xxi).

Hume's ambition is in a way more straightforward than the aims underlying *De la Recherche*, although the two projects overlap significantly. As Malebranche explains, his primary goal is to reveal the moral and scientific errors that arise from the mind's union with the body. If we are to avoid the mistakes endemic to our condition, we need to recognize that our faculties are fallible, and that our senses, imagination, and passions 'are altogether useless for discovering the truth and our good' (*Recherche*, i. 19). However, merely cataloguing these errors is not enough; we must also 'partially explain the mind's nature' by identifying their causes. 'Thus', Malebranche concludes, 'the subject of this work is the mind of man in its entirety' (ibid. 20). While Hume is not concerned to find methods for avoiding error, and is indifferent to the moral anxiety that drives Malebranche's undertaking, he shares its aspiration to reveal the 'ultimate principles' that cause our thoughts. For both philosophers, the key to the science of man lies in the natural impulses or original inclinations that shape our mental habits.

Among these, according to Malebranche, are natural inclinations in the body and the soul, given to us by God so that we may preserve ourselves. The soul's overarching impulse—a general inclination towards the good—manifests itself in several subsidiary inclinations, which include two kinds of self-love. On the one hand, our love of our own perfection or *grandeur* moves us to try to make ourselves independent (and to become as far as possible like God) by acquiring traits that give us power over other people, such as learning, wealth, or virtue.[4] On the other hand, we are moved by

---

[4] 'The reputation of being rich, learned and virtuous produces in the imagination of those around us, or who concern us most closely, dispositions that are very advantageous to us. It prostrates them at our feet; it excites them in our favour; it inspires in them all the impulses that tend to the preservation of our being and the increase of our *grandeur*' (ibid. 290).

a love of well-being to seek out pleasure and eschew pain. Alongside these impulses, God has equipped us with a further natural inclination that is always joined to the passions, an inclination to unify ourselves with the rest of his creation. This leads us to sympathize with things around us and especially with other men, so that 'their ills naturally afflict us, their joy delights us, and their *grandeur*, their abasement, their decline, seem to augment or diminish our own being' (*Recherche*, ii. 68).

In humans, these dispositions of the soul interconnect with motions of the body to form passions, which are also designed to help us survive. The soul's inclinations become sensible by virtue of being accompanied by movements of the animal spirits that we experience as feelings of love, hope, fear, and so on. A passion such as love or anger therefore consists of a complex concatenation of judgements, impulses, sensations, and bodily movements. It originates in a confused judgement of the soul as to how a given object is related to us. This is immediately followed by an impulse of the will to or from the object in question, which manifests itself in a feeling of delight (*douceur*) if the object is beneficial, or in a feeling of sadness, disgust, or bitterness if the object is displeasing. These sensations are accompanied by the feelings (*sentiments*) that we usually identify as passions, such as love, aversion, desire, joy, or sadness. And so on, through seven separate stages (ibid. 87–99). It is worth noting that, in describing the initial impulse of the will, Malebranche takes care to emphasize that 'reason alone is not enough to move [the soul]', and that feelings of pleasure and pain are needed to direct it to and from the objects of its judgements (ibid. 88).[5] Without these, the soul would be unable to respond to its own perceptions and would be trapped in a state of paralysis.

Our passions, then, are the register of our ability to assess objects, people, events, and states of affairs as broadly beneficial or harmful to us. While some passions are innate, they are modified from the time we are in the womb by our individual and social experiences—by the types of objects we encounter, by the relative force of particular feelings, and by patterns of association. Occupation, status, age, sex, and physiology all have an effect, so that each person comes to have their own passionate temperament, which nevertheless remains governed by the general principles operating in all human beings (*Recherche*, ii. 85–6). Passions are excited by anything we regard as beneficial or harmful to the body or the mind (ibid. 87); but Malebranche shares the standard view that our feelings for present, sensible things are stronger than those for things we have only imagined or heard about, or for those that are in principle imperceptible. 'Thus, the soul is more occupied by a simple pinprick than by lofty speculations, and the

---

[5] Compare Hume's celebrated claim that 'reason alone can never produce any action, or give rise to volition' (*Treatise*, 414).

pleasures and ills of this world make far more of an impression on it than the dreadful pains or infinite pleasures of eternity' (ibid. ii. 84, i. 177). This feature enables the passions to fulfil their function. Our chances of survival are enhanced by our disposition to respond most urgently to our immediate environment, the more so since passions prompt us to act. Other things being equal, fear prompts us to escape, and anger to avenge ourselves, although once again these dispositions are modified by our individual experience and cultural norms.

While Hume collapses some of the distinctions on which Malebranche's analysis is grounded, such as that between the soul's overarching impulse to good and its subsidiary striving for pleasure,[6] his account of the passions is constructed within a framework which has several features in common with the one we have just considered. To begin with the most schematic, Hume takes up and solidifies the view that passions are complex phenomena. Whereas Malebranche explicates a narrow sense of passion as a feeling by identifying its place and function in a sequence of judgements, sensations, and bodily movements, Hume treats passions as internally intricate con-catenations of impressions and ideas. They are composite states made up of two distinct elements that can be related in various ways. A further congru-ence arises from Hume's willingness to adopt Malebranche's impulses of the soul. This is perhaps most obvious in his treatment of pleasure or well-being, for just as Malebranche argues that the passions are underpinned by a natural striving for pleasure, so Hume grounds them on 'the chief spring or actuating principle of the human mind', our disposition to feel pleasure and pain (*Treatise*, 574). For both philosophers, the operations of pleasure or pain defy further natural explanation and form part of the bedrock on which the science of man is founded.

How, though, does Hume integrate Malebranche's other impulses into his philosophical system? To answer this question, we first need to examine Malebranche's account of the ways in which our natural love of *grandeur* and our sympathy for other human beings produce distinctive patterns of feeling and action. The striving for independence that constitutes our love of *grandeur* is manifested in the feelings surrounding esteem and contempt, which include veneration and respect for others, self-esteem or pride for ourselves, scorn for others, and abasement or humility (*Recherche*, ii. 120). Esteem and its relatives are our natural responses to the sensible property of *grandeur* or greatness, while contempt and its companions are what we feel for *petitesse*.

All these passions fix initially on comparative size, and each of us is consequently disposed to esteem things that are larger than we are, such as

---

[6] 'Beside good or evil, or in other words, pain or pleasure, the direct passions frequently arise from a natural impulse or instinct, which is perfectly unaccountable' (Hume, *Treatise*, 439).

the night sky, and to scorn things that are smaller, such as insects. However, because *grandeur* and *petitesse* are thickly descriptive qualities, they also extend to other scalar relations including distance, time, power, magnificence, learning, wisdom, virtue, and wealth. For example, we naturally esteem people for their relative magnificence or riches and are contemptuous of their shabbiness or poverty. As we have seen, however, the passions are more strongly excited by sensible than by merely imagined qualities, so that we are not equally responsive to all forms of *grandeur*. As Malebranche sighingly explains, 'a great house, a magnificent retinue, fine furniture, offices, honours, wealth, all appear greater and more real than virtue and justice' (ibid. 127). The way to arouse our esteem for these latter qualities is therefore to make them sensible, as when power is symbolized by monumental buildings, or justice by the daunting rituals of courts of law. These social manifestations of *grandeur* exploit our natural response to perceptible properties such as bulk or height, and associate the resulting passions with imperceptible qualities such as justice or virtue.

The urge to make ourselves independent that is contained in our impulse to *grandeur* works together with an equally basic inclination of the soul—the drive to unify ourselves with the rest of nature. This latter trait emerges as a disposition to sympathize with the passions of other people and is allied, so Malebranche argues, to a mechanical feature of our physiology. The structure of the nervous system ensures that human beings express their passions in their bodily gestures, expressions, and movements, thereby making them available for others to read (ibid. i. 208, ii. 121).[7] When we observe other people's emotions, we sympathize with them and experience answering passions of our own. In the case of esteem and contempt, this natural expressiveness gives rise to a sequence of exchanges, which can be most economically illustrated by an example, designed to draw out the main features of Malebranche's argument. When a tailor encounters a nobleman, he recognizes the nobleman's relative *grandeur*, while the nobleman in turn recognizes the tailor's relative *petitesse*. The tailor will feel esteem for the nobleman and humility at his own comparatively lowly condition, and will manifest these passions in his bearing and behaviour. Observing by these signs that the tailor esteems him, the nobleman's pride will be strengthened, and he too will express this change with his body (ibid. ii. 122). At the same time, though, some of his pride will be communicated to the tailor, so that, through his connection with someone greater than himself, the tailor's own self-esteem will be increased (ibid. i. 295–6). 'New honours for our relatives and friends, new acquisitions by those most closely related to us, the

---

[7] Malebranche concedes that we are capable of concealing a passion when it is surpassed by another very strong one. See *Recherche*, ii. 83.

conquests and victories of our prince, and even the recent discoveries of the New World, seem to add something to our substance' (ibid. ii. 68). In this type of passionate exchange, our desire for *grandeur* is at work, as are two separate patterns of sympathy. In some cases, as when the nobleman's self-esteem increases the self-esteem of the tailor, the passion expressed by one person arouses the same passion in someone else. In others, as when the tailor's humility increases the nobleman's pride, an initial passion is answered by a different one.

Malebranche presents a world in which people are naturally greedy for pride or self-esteem and therefore have a substantial psychological investment in the kind of process just illustrated. The mind gains pleasure from the contemplation of *grandeur* and from its sympathetic relationships with other things, and this shapes its efforts to sustain itself. To cast more light on this process, Malebranche composes a soliloquy in which the personified Mind muses on its own operations. 'It seems to me', it speculates, 'that I become greater . . . and expand when I embrace the idea of something great, [and that] I am something great by virtue of my connection with great things' (ibid. ii. 133). As it goes on to explain, it maintains its own existence and the perfection of its being by entertaining ideas which have an expansive effect on it, and this is why it pays attention to objects possessed of *grandeur*. When it does so, it feels the agreeable passion of esteem for these objects, and when they confirm it in its own greatness, its self-esteem is pleasurably reinforced. This psychic disposition to enjoy *grandeur* underlies the exchange of passions we have examined. In order to sustain a sense of self-worth, people need the esteem of others, and they gain it both through their encounters with those who are less great than they are and through their connections with those above them on the social scale. Our passionate interdependence extends throughout the ranks of society, moulding the relations between peasants and noblemen, kings and courtiers, masters and servants, parents and children, teachers and students. The general of an army depends for his self-respect on the esteem of his soldiers, who in turn depend on his *grandeur* for their sense of worth. He needs them as much as they need him.

HUMEAN MODIFICATIONS

The principles of the mind on which this account of esteem and contempt depends are taken over and rearticulated by Hume, who also appeals to them to explain the operations of the first passions he discusses in the *Treatise*, humility and pride. The pleasure we take in greatness, which for Malebranche constitutes our love of *grandeur*, is echoed in Hume's claim that 'the mere view and contemplation of any greatness . . . enlarges the soul and gives it sensible delight and pleasure' (*Treatise*, 432). In addition, Malebranche's view that our feelings of esteem and contempt depend on our disposition to compare ourselves to others is generalized by Hume, who argues that we habitually judge objects more by comparison than by their intrinsic qualities (ibid. 592–4).[8] Putting these two thoughts together, we arrive at a familiar sensitivity to scale, which so informs our passions that every object presented to our senses or imagination is accompanied by a proportional emotion or movement of the spirits. For example, a bulky object such as an ocean or a chain of mountains, or a large collection of objects such as a fleet or a crowd, will excite our admiration ('one of the most lively pleasures which human nature is capable of enjoying') and the greater the object, the greater the emotion (ibid. 373). Admiration or esteem is therefore sensitive to extension and number, and also to other dimensions of *grandeur* and *petitesse* such as virtue and vice, wit and folly, riches and poverty, happiness and misery (ibid. 374). Finally, our passions are modulated by our propensity to sympathize with others 'and to receive by communication their inclinations and sentiments, however different from, or opposed to, our own' (ibid. 316). This 'makes our minds mirrors to one another' and binds us together in a community of feeling (ibid. 365).

Bringing these principles to bear on pride and humility, Hume starts with the notion of pleasure. We feel proud of objects which give pleasure or the means to pleasure and which we associate with ourselves, such as our talents, wit, beauty, lineage, possessions, wealth, or power. Furthermore, our sensitivity to scale ensures that the greater the object, the greater the pride. In addition, pride and humility are heightened by comparison. For example, 'a rich man feels the felicity of his condition better by opposing it to that of a beggar', and we experience humility when we evaluate the good qualities of others in relation to our own (ibid. 315–16, 389–90). More generally, 'the same man may cause either respect, love or contempt by his condition and talents, according as the person, which considers him, from his inferior becomes his equal or superior. In changing the point of view, though the object remains the same, its proportion to ourselves entirely alters; which is the cause of the alteration in the passions' (ibid. 390). Lastly, as one would expect, sympathy is also at work. Because the admiration of other people reinforces our pride while their contempt undermines it, we cannot single-handedly sustain the feelings we have about our own condition and depend on the opinions of others to augment or diminish them.

---

[8] Both Malebranche and Hume acknowledge that the terms in which we compare objects may vary. We may estimate the *grandeur* or *petitesse* of an object by comparing it with ourselves (this nobleman is more magnificent than I am), by comparing it with humans in general (the night sky is vast by human standards), or by comparing it with what we regard as a normal case (a palace is large by the standards of ordinary buildings).

Thus, the sympathetic transfer of passions can strengthen or modify 'the vanity of power or the shame of slavery' (ibid. 315–16).[9]

These continuities indicate the existence of a shared set of principles, which are used by both Malebranche and Hume to explain the nature and role of pride and humility, esteem and contempt. For both writers, these passions are the fruit of natural dispositions of the mind, which give rise to widespread and predictable patterns of feeling. Hume, however, is the more vigorous of the two in trying to provide a scientific account of the passions, and in doing so he elaborates the principles on which Malebranche's theory is based. Some of his modifications, I shall suggest, can be read as efforts to tidy up loose ends and inconsistencies in the Malebranchian analysis, but others are attempts to extend the range of principles of which our passionate dispositions are effects.

As we have seen, Hume agrees with Malebranche that we are inclined to judge objects by comparison, and that passions such as pride and humility, admiration and scorn, are sensitive to degrees of greatness. We admire mountains more than hills, and writers of genius more than competent hacks. At the same time, though, we envisage geniuses as standing above us, and imagine the people for whom we feel contempt as placed far below. More generally, we associate anything good, whether genius, prosperity, heaven, or kings, with height; and anything bad, whether adversity, vulgar or trivial conceptions, hell, or peasants, we associate with lowness (ibid. 434). Why, Hume asks, should this be? It would be a mistake to reply that this is simply a matter of metaphor because, concealed in the image of height, there lies a natural principle of the mind. 'These methods of thinking, and of expressing ourselves, are not of so little consequence as they may appear at first sight' (ibid.). The metaphor arises from our experience of gravity, which in turn has an effect on the imagination. When we think of an object placed in a high position, we find it easier to move to ideas situated below it than to move in the other direction, so that 'we pass not without a kind of reluctance from the inferior to that which is situated above it, . . . as if our ideas acquired a kind of gravity from the objects' (ibid. 435). Having set this claim in place, Hume turns to a different point, that 'any opposition which does not entirely discourage us, rather has a contrary effect, and inspires us with more than ordinary *grandeur* and magnanimity. In overcoming an opposition we invigorate the soul and give it an elevation which is itself pleasurable. Furthermore, when the soul is invigorated it seeks opposition' (ibid. 433–4). Putting the two views together, he goes on to argue that when the soul moves from low to high ideas, it experiences a degree of difficulty or opposition. Overcoming opposition is pleasurable. So

---

[9] Hume here borrows a thought experiment from Arnauld, who points out in the *Port Royal Logic* that an *homme-machine*, however obedient and flattering, would be unable to satisfy our emotional needs.

the soul comes to associate anything that invigorates it with the movement from low to high, or, as Hume puts it, with an inclination for ascent. Among the objects that invigorate the soul are wealth, power, and virtue. So the soul comes to associate these with height or sublimity, and equally comes to associate poverty, slavery, and folly with lowness and descent.

In this argument, Hume grapples with an aspect of our understanding of *grandeur* and *petitesse* that Malebranche does not pause to explore, and introduces what seems on the face of things a thoroughly modern principle. Gravity not only rules nature, but also moulds the imagination and the patterns of impressions and ideas that depend on it. Interwoven with this Newtonian slant, however, is a more traditional concern with the motivating impulses of the mind. As we have seen, Malebranche conceives of the mind as striving to increase its own *grandeur* by contemplating ideas of greatness. In its quest for elevation it feeds off its own ideas by transferring their qualities to itself. A comparable process is evoked in Hume's argument. An underlying mechanism (the vigour that opposition induces in the soul) inclines the soul to seek out ideas that invigorate it, which, as it happens, are the passions associated with *grandeur*. 'Nothing invigorates and exalts the mind', Hume tells us, 'equally with pride and vanity' (ibid. 391). So although Hume throws the currency of Newtonianism into his discussion, his analysis of the relation between *grandeur* and height is more deeply indebted to an older conception of the soul's striving for perfection.

As well as introducing new principles to govern the mind, Hume takes up a puzzle left unresolved by Malebranche, concerning our responses to objects that are either ancient or of distant origin. Malebranche is profoundly distressed by the admiration which his contemporaries display for exotica (whether ancient amulets, the ordinances of the Great Mogul, Chinese clothes, or the worm-eaten slippers of some purported sage), and also by the esteem lavished on people who care about such things (*Recherche*, ii. 127–8). As he sees it, the interests of these *faux savants* are trivial, and their motives suspect (ibid. i. 281–2), but they are nevertheless more respected than true philosophers. Whether or not one shares his frustration, the claim that people are prone to venerate ancient and exotic objects poses two problems for his analysis of esteem and contempt. In *Recherche*, Malebranche upholds the widespread view that our passions for temporally and spatially remote objects are less strong than those for people and things close to us. Although any part of the creation excites some degree of sympathy, our affections are preoccupied by the here-and-now. Applying this principle, one would expect an ancient object such as an Egyptian amulet to excite contempt; and if our passions for spatially and temporally distant things are generally weaker than those for the near at hand, our feelings for the amulet should also be comparatively faint. Why, then, do people feel so strongly about them? Malebranche himself argues that veneration for old or exotic objects is aroused by their novelty, which, especially when combined with *grandeur*, causes a considerable agitation of the spirits (ibid. ii. 130). But since this passion, too, should presumably fade with spatial and temporal distance, the phenomenon remains in need of further explanation.

Hume's engagement with this problem is based on his usual premiss that the strength of our feeling for an object is usually inversely proportional to its distance from us, so that our strongest passions are reserved for ourselves and for objects contiguous to us in space or time (*Treatise*, 428–9). He agrees that intense admiration for the ancient and exotic is therefore anomalous. In explaining it, Hume begins with the normal case. Our feelings for remote objects are usually weak, because when we think about them, our thoughts are obliged to pass through the extent of space or time that divides them from us. In the process, our vivid awareness of ourselves continually recalls us, interrupting our mental journey; and the more interrupted the journey, the fainter are the ideas and affections we form at the end of it (ibid. 428). This is why 'the breaking of a mirror gives us more concern when at home, than the burning of a house when abroad, and some hundred leagues distant' (ibid. 429). Furthermore, our feelings for temporally remote objects are even weaker than for spatially distant ones, because it is easier for the mind to traverse spatial points which coexist than temporal ones which do not (ibid.). Why is it, then, that we feel a strong admiration for very distant and very old objects?

Taking up a hint offered by Malebranche, Hume first argues that admiration can be a response to the spatial or temporal distance between us and the object in question, which gets transferred to the object itself. In admiring an object, we admire the great extent of space or time between us and its point of origin. Thus, 'a great traveller, tho' in the same chamber, will pass for a very extraordinary person; as a Greek medal, even in our cabinet, is always esteemed a valuable curiosity' (ibid. 433). Hume also goes on to discuss what he takes to be two further asymmetries in our passionate responses to time and distance: that our esteem for ancient objects is even stronger than for exotic ones; and that we esteem things far in the past, such as our ancestors, more than things far in the future, such as our posterity. (Malebranche does not make either of these claims, so we can see Hume as embarking on a more detailed exploration of the area than his predecessor.) To explain these dispositions, Hume employs a combination of the principles we have already encountered. Addressing the first asymmetry, he reminds us that the effort required to pass through a series of temporal points is greater than that required to pass through a sequence of spatial ones. However, the fact that it is more difficult for the imagination to traverse time than space means that it is more invigorated and elevated when it succeeds in doing so, and the accompanying passions are stronger. It is not surprising, then, that 'all the relics of antiquity are so precious in our eyes and appear more valuable than what is brought from the remotest parts of the world', or that ancient busts are more esteemed than Japan tables (ibid. 433–6). Moving on to the second asymmetry, Hume asks why we tend to admire the distant past more than the distant future. Since we naturally experience time as flowing from past to future, he replies, the imagination moves more easily in this direction than in the opposite one. But resisting the flow (imagining objects in the past) is invigorating, and this invigoration habitually manifests itself in the passion of admiration (ibid. 430 f.).

In dealing with both these problems, Hume follows the programme set out by Malebranche, and tries to explain them by appealing to original dispositions of the mind. Still more ambitiously than Malebranche, however, he aims to integrate these principles into a naturalistic theory of great scope and power. Some of our most deeply ingrained mental habits are, in his view, caused by our persistent experience of physical principles. For instance, the operation of gravity shapes the imagination and passions, so that certain patterns of thought and feeling come easily to us, and others do not. The implications Hume draws from this and other principles may strike us as unduly baroque. Quite apart from their speculative audacity, they seem excessively *ad hoc*, and sometimes fail to achieve the explanatory tasks for which they are designed. The elaborate arguments I have just rehearsed, for example, leave intact the tension we find in Malebranche between the view that our passions for imperceptible objects are comparatively faint and the view that great distances create intense passions. Since spatial and temporal distances are not immediately sensible, why do they generate passions that are more intense than our feelings for present objects or those of recent origin?

To appreciate the character of Hume's innovations, we need to focus on the extent to which they rely on the traditional view that the mind takes pleasure in its own activity and looks for ways to invigorate itself. We find this assumption at work in philosophers such as Descartes and Spinoza, as well as Malebranche, who ground their theories of the passions on the assumption that we derive emotional satisfaction from objects and relationships that are broadly beneficial to us, and strive to experience this satisfaction as much as possible. One source of pleasure, Hume argues (appealing to an idea that goes back to Plato), is internal opposition; the mind takes pleasure in, and is invigorated by, its capacity to imagine against the grain of its own dispositions—against the grain, for example, of its natural tendency to move from high to low, or from past to future. Here again, Hume's analysis pulls in two directions. On the one hand, it has a Newtonian flavour which connects the science of man with the findings of natural philosophy. On the other hand, it relies on a mode of explanation that pre-dates the new science and emphasizes the emotions attached to the reflexive powers of the soul.

LEGITIMATING PASSIONS

While Hume shares Malebranche's view that we are naturally disposed to feel admiration and pride for *grandeur*, and takes trouble to explore the implications of this claim, we have yet to see what part these passions play in the economy of the passions, as Malebranche describes it. How powerful are they? How significant is their role in our relationships with one another? And what part do they play in political life?

If we return to Malebranche for a moment, we find that his answers are doubly equivocal. Our passionate responses to *grandeur* are in their own terms both beneficial and dangerous; and although they are part of our God-given nature, they are at the same time inimical to reason and true religion. At the first of these levels, the family of passions surrounding *grandeur* are among the natural ties that bind us to each other and strengthen civil society in a way that is ultimately advantageous. They sustain many unequal relationships such as those between parents and children or courtiers and kings, and provide rulers with a means to secure the admiration and loyalty of their subjects (*Recherche*, i. 331; ii. 70, 120–1). In addition, the desire for admiration inspires us to acts of emulation and courage. 'We would not win so many victories if soldiers and especially officers did not aspire to glory and command. Thus, all those composing armies, working only for their particular interests, nevertheless procure the advantage of the whole country' (ibid. ii. 72). Equally, however, these passions tend to the dissolution of societies. Contempt is the ultimate insult and the surest way of rupturing social bonds (ibid. 71–3); the whims of rulers can generate religious and political instability; and pride can easily swell to a point where it produces divisive levels of arrogance and self-entrancement (ibid. i. 333–4). The inextricability of the strengths and weaknesses of our passionate natures is especially vivid in Malebranche's discussion of social hypocrisy, which he views as vital to the maintenance of society. If people in positions of power are to win the admiration of those they command, they must conceal their feelings and avoid treating such people with open contempt. On the contrary, they must abase themselves before them and flatter them with false compliments, which will go some way towards relieving the pain suffered by those who feel themselves to be the meanest parts of the body politic (ibid. ii. 73).

Viewed in its own terms, the passionate life therefore has both strengths and weaknesses. Viewed from a philosophical standpoint, however, it is an unmitigated burden and a mark of our fallen condition. Because our passions are directed towards sensible objects, we are far too ready to esteem one another for our wealth, beauty, or power, and to neglect invisible yet superior forms of *grandeur* such as virtue or wisdom, or indeed the greatness of God (ibid. i. 489). We can overcome this practical error only by making use of reason, which, sometimes with the assistance of grace, redirects our attention from sensible to intelligible objects, and enables us to appreciate and admire true greatness.

Hume likewise allows that passions can disturb our judgements (*Treatise*, 321, 348), but he departs altogether from the last part of Malebranche's argument. Abstract reasoning about intelligible things will not, in his view, produce a science of man. In addition, however, he questions Malebranche's estimate of the dominant position occupied by the family of emotions surrounding esteem and contempt in the overall economy of human passion. According to Malebranche, we experience ever-changing degrees of esteem, pride, contempt, and humility as we measure ourselves against other people and things, and are driven by a continual desire to batten on to the great and lord it over the lowly. According to Hume, by contrast, our feelings of admiration and contempt are to some extent contained by other, equally fundamental passionate dispositions, and therefore have less far-reaching psychological and social consequences.

A first argument for this view results from an analysis of the relevant passions which is rather more detailed than anything Malebranche offers. At the beginning of Book II, Hume explains that pride and contempt are feelings that we have for ourselves when we compare other people's qualities with our own. A good deal later on, he identifies esteem and contempt as species of love and hatred directed towards others (ibid. 389). Often, though, we experience mixtures of these passions. Love and humility mixed together produce respect, while hatred and pride combine to cause contempt (ibid. 390). Moreover, as well as being a compound of two passions, respect and contempt arise from the combined operation of two familiar dispositions of the mind. When Hume admires a man's house and furniture, he sympathizes with the pleasure the owner takes in his possessions and feels a comparable pleasure. This is esteem. At the same time, he compares the man's possessions with his own, and if they are greater than his, he feels a degree of humility. The disposition to sympathize and the disposition to compare are therefore both at work whenever we feel respect, and the same goes for contempt.

The claim that both these dispositions are required in order to produce respect or contempt enables Hume to play down the potentially corrosive effects of comparison and to emphasize the more benign role of sympathy in our passionate responses. Our esteem for wealth, for example, is the fruit of the benevolent pleasure we take in the pleasures of others, and does not stem from any hope of our own advantage (ibid. 357–8). In support of this claim, Hume points out that people esteem the wealthy even when there is no expectation that this will serve their own interests; for example, prisoners of war are always treated with a respect suited to their condition, and ancestors receive a certain respect on account of their riches (ibid. 361). It is striking that Hume does not say anything at this point about the self-esteem that people acquire through their association with the great. While he agrees with Malebranche that we take pride in the reputation and fortune of people who are close to us, and cites this as the reason why we 'remove the poor as far from us as possible' and affect to be descended from a long succession of rich and honourable ancestors (ibid. 307), he marginalizes the disposition to compare ourselves to others on which these habits depend, and again emphasizes our ability to sympathize with other people's pleasure. Our investment in admiration and contempt as means of sustaining our own sense of self-worth, which is such a prominent feature of Malebranche's philosophy, is balanced by a more disinterested benevolence, and the struggle to clamber aboard the bandwagon of *grandeur* is eased by a more relaxed appreciation of property and wealth.

The suggestion that sympathy can balance and even outweigh comparison is also evident in Hume's discussion of the relative scope of these two principles. His starting-point here is the widely held assumption that we compare ourselves only with objects that resemble or are contiguous with us. Resemblance is the first relation at work here: since a mountain and a horse do not resemble one another, the mountain does not diminish the horse in our eyes (ibid. 378). Once a basis for comparison has been established, however, contiguity or proximity comes into play. Humans therefore compare themselves with other humans; but while a common soldier compares himself with his sergeant or corporal, he does not compare himself with his general. As Hume puts it, the distance between general and soldier 'cuts off the relation' (ibid. 377–8). When we encounter people whose circumstances are significantly different from our own, admiration and contempt cease to operate and give way to good will and compassion. Thus, a soldier will feel good will for a general and pity for a beggar. There is an illuminating transition here from Malebranche's image of a general whose need for approval spurs him on to acts of courage which will win the admiration of his troops, and of soldiers who gain their sense of worth from their general's *grandeur*, to Hume's interpretation of the interest that distant social ranks take in one another's fortunes. Although soldiers do not cease to sympathize with their general's pride in his own greatness, they do cease to compare themselves with him, and this limits the role of respect and contempt in social relations.[10]

Two further arguments also blunt the sharp edges of respect and contempt, and support the view that sympathy serves to confine them. Although Hume argues that many different qualities can arouse our pride, he adds that nothing excites it as much as virtue. Our love of the virtue of

---

[10] Malebranche allows that our admiration for ancient authors, unlike our admiration for living ones, does not jeopardize our own glory (*Recherche*, i. 283). However, he does not explain why this is so.

others, combined with an element of comparison, readily causes us to respect them. He here departs from Malebranche's sense that, because it is relatively difficult to make virtue perceptible, our admiration for it tends to be faint and to be easily eclipsed by our responsiveness to other forms of *grandeur*. We can detect virtue, Hume seems to be saying, by observing people's expressions, gestures, and actions, as well as by listening to what they say, and can imagine their virtue if their character or deeds are described to us. Since these experiences awaken our respect, we do not need to fear that this passion fastens only on worldly qualities, or that the force of our feelings for wealth, power, and so forth stands in the way of our appreciation of virtue. In fact, respect is just as sensitive to virtue, and for that matter to genius and learning, as to other forms of greatness, and therefore prompts us to respond to a whole range of important values.

Moving on to a further argument, Hume says some surprising things about pride and humility. Most of our passions, he argues, move us to act. For example, love gives rise to benevolence, a desire for the happiness of another, while hatred gives rise to anger, a desire for the misery of another, and both desires typically give rise to action. By contrast, pride and humility are pure emotions of the soul, unattended by desire, and do not immediately lead to action (*Treatise*, 367, 382). This makes them unique, and ensures that, unless they are mixed with other affections, they have no effect on what we do. Since both are dead ends as far as action is concerned, there is a sense in which the principle of comparison on which they are based has less effect overall than the principle of sympathy. This seems a peculiar claim for Hume to defend. Perhaps we cannot specify particular types of desire that are always associated with pride and humility, but, as Hume portrays these passions, they have plenty of consequences. In the first place, proper pride makes us sensible of our own merit and gives us confidence and assurance in all our projects and enterprises. It therefore seems to have at least an indirect effect on what we do. In the second place, we *express* our pride as much as we do our other passions, so that it enters into our passionate exchanges with other people. In fact, it is precisely because the manifestations of pride are naturally displeasing to others that Hume urges us (once again echoing Malebranche (*Recherche*, ii. 72–3)) to limit them. Although pride is not a bad thing in itself, good breeding and decency require us to conceal it (*Treatise*, 597). In these claims, we find Hume moving between the view that there is something about the passions of pride and humility themselves which limits their social consequences and the view that we should learn to limit these consequences for our own good.

The arguments I have discussed reflect a change of attitude toward admiration and contempt. For Malebranche, it is a natural fact about human beings that these are central and powerful passions. The impulses of the soul make us intensely sensitive to differences in greatness, and our sense of self-worth derives from affections based on comparison between ourselves and others. We can—and indeed should—try to modify the dimensions along which these comparisons are made, but comparison itself and the passions to which it gives rise are central to our existence and important to our survival. This view of our affections provides an indirect legitimation of hierarchical societies, in so far as it suggests that we are psychologically adapted to hierarchy, and even need it. The great need to manifest their greatness in order to attract the admiration on which their self-respect depends, while the lowly need to manifest their humility in order to collect the crumbs of self-esteem that fall from the great man's table. This being so, displays of pride, magnificence, wealth, and power—in fact all the trappings of seventeenth-century absolutism—are only to be expected.

As we have seen, Hume does not deny that humans are disposed to judge things more by comparison than by their intrinsic qualities; nor does he deny that this habit gives rise to pride and humility, admiration and contempt. In fact, he goes out of his way to identify the original principles of the mind on which these passions depend. At the same time, however, he constructs an economy of the passions in which the role played by these affections is comparatively limited. While we are naturally inclined to compare ourselves with others, we are also inclined to sympathize with their good or bad fortune, so that love and compassion do more to shape social relations than Malebranche allows (*Treatise*, 363). Thus, an aristocrat may feel contempt for a merchant whose wealth and position are fast approaching his own, but he is just as likely to sympathize with the pleasure which the merchant derives from his possessions and status. A woman may take a malicious delight in her neighbour's misfortune because it bolsters her own sense of superiority, but she is just as likely to feel pity and compassion. Alongside a limited psychological investment in hierarchical relations, we find an investment in collective good fortune.

This sunnier view is not original to Hume, but he goes further than other writers of his era in appealing to the economy of the passions to legitimate it. Although Shaftesbury and Hutcheson, for instance, emphasize the place of love and benevolence in social life, Hume sees that, in order to vindicate the centrality of these passions, he will have to explain what prevents them from being eclipsed by pride and contempt. In short, he modifies the strategy employed by Malebranche, and argues that although the comparative passions are part of our nature, they are also naturally limited by the operation of sympathy. This being so, pride and contempt are to be expected; but so are compassion and benevolence.

This shift has significant political implications. Hume is emphatic that social and political arrangements are incapable of suppressing the natural dispositions of the mind, so that 'the utmost politicians can perform is to extend the natural sentiments beyond their original bounds' (ibid. 500).

If Malebranche's claim that our passions are primarily competitive were right, politicians would have to work with this fact about us. But if, as Hume contends, we are as often moved by sympathy as by comparison, politicians have a more flexible foundation on which to build. They may be able to devise ways of extending the passions that are caused by these principles beyond their natural bounds, without going against the grain of human nature. As it turns out, the economy of the passions allows for sympathy and comparison, and is ideally suited to a society such as Britain, in which, according to Hume, the virtues of absolutism and republicanism are combined.

REFERENCES

Arnauld, Antoine, and Nicole, Pierre, *Logic, or the Art of Thinking*, ed. and trans. J. V. Buroker (Cambridge: Cambridge University Press, 1996).

Hume, David, *A Treatise of Human Nature*, ed. L. A. Selby Bigge, 2nd edn., rev. P. H. Nidditch (Oxford: Clarendon Press, 1978).

Jones, Peter, *Hume's Sentiments: Their Ciceronian and French Context* (Edinburgh: Edinburgh University Press, 1982).

Malebranche, Nicolas, *De la Recherche de la vérité*, ed. Geneviève Rodis Lewis, 2 vols., in *Œuvres Complètes*, ed. Henri Gouhier (Paris: Librairie Vrin, 1972).

McCracken, Charles J., *Malebranche and British Philosophy* (Oxford: Clarendon Press, 1983).

Passmore, John, *Hume's Intentions*, rev. edn. (London: Duckworth, 1968).

Popkin, Richard H., 'So, Hume did read Berkeley', *Journal of Philosophy*, 61 (1964): 773–8.

Wright, John P., *The Sceptical Realism of David Hume* (Manchester: Manchester University Press, 1983).

Hume's Ethical Conclusion

P. J. E. KAIL

—— •◆• ——

I

In the closing section of Book I of the *Treatise*,[1] Hume pauses to take stock. He imagines himself in a leaky, weather-beaten vessel, facing a boundless ocean, lamenting the irreparable 'wretchedness and weakness' of his faculties, reduced 'almost to despair'.

> I am first affrighted and confounded with that forelorn solitude, in which I am plac'd in my philosophy, and fancy myself some strange uncouth monster, who not being able to mingle and unite in society, has been expell'd all human commerce, and left utterly abandon'd and disconsolate. (p. 264)

Looking without, all he can expect is the enmity of metaphysicians, logicians, mathematicians, even theologians, and dispute, contradiction, anger, calumny, and detraction; looking within, he can find nothing but doubt and ignorance. 'All my opinions', he writes, 'loosen and fall of themselves, when unsupported by the approbation of others.'

One result of his labours in Book I is a 'manifest contradiction' between causal reasoning and the belief in the existence of the external world, which is ameliorated only by a 'trivial suggestion' of the fancy. Reason demands that this trivial suggestion should be rejected, and yet 'this resolution, [to follow reason], if steadily executed, wou'd be dangerous, and attended with the most fatal consequences'. Should we then 'reject refin'd and elaborate reasoning'? That would cut us off from all sciences and philosophy. We are left, so it seems, with no choice except between a false reason and none at all. Hume admits that he knows not what ought to be done, but points out that what ordinarily does happen is that such 'refin'd reflections' have little or no influence on us, even though we cannot establish it as a rule that they *ought* not to have any influence on us.

I would like to thank Marina Frasca-Spada, Martin Bell, Andrew Pyle, Sandy Stewart, and the reader for this volume for comments on earlier versions of this paper.

[1] David Hume, *A Treatise of Human Nature*, ed. L. A. Selby-Bigge, 2nd edn., rev. by P. H. Nidditch (Oxford: Clarendon Press, 1978).

Then he changes his mind.

This opinion I can scarce forbear retracting, and condemning from my present feeling and experience. The *intense* view of these manifold contradictions and imperfections in human reasoning has so wrought upon me, and heated my brain, that I am ready to reject all belief and reasoning, and can look upon no opinion even as more probable or likely than another. Where am I, or what? From what causes do I derive my existence, and to what condition shall I return . . . ? I am confounded with all these questions, and begin to fancy myself in the most deplorable condition imaginable, inviron'd with the deepest darkness, and utterly depriv'd of the use of every member and faculty. (Ibid. 268–9)

The palliative remedy for this philosophical melancholy and delirium is of course the Humean dinner and game of backgammon, 'some avocation and lively impression of my senses'. But what of philosophy? Why carry on? Does it follow that

I must seclude myself . . . from the commerce and society of men, which is so agreeable; and that I must torture my brain with subtilities and sophistries . . . Under what obligation do I lie of making such an abuse of time? And to what end can it serve either for the service of mankind, or for my own private interest? No: if I must be a fool, as all those who reason or believe any thing *certainly* are, my follies shall at least be natural and agreeable. Where I strive against my inclination, I shall have a good reason for my resistance; and will no more be led a wandering into such dreary solitudes, and rough passages, as I have hitherto met with. (Ibid. 269–70)

His reasons for continuing philosophy are then announced. He feels 'an ambition' to contribute to the instruction of mankind and of acquiring a name for himself. If he were to do anything else, he would be 'a loser in the point of pleasure'; and this, he says, is the 'origin of all my philosophy'. Philosophy is then distinguished from superstition in that the former generally does not disturb our natural conduct, whereas the latter can have harmful influences on behaviour—'the errors in religion are dangerous; those in philosophy only ridiculous'. Thus invigorated Hume is confident enough to offer a system 'which, if not true, (for that, perhaps, is too much to be hop'd for) might at least be satisfactory to the human mind', and which might 'bear the examination of the latest posterity'.

I felt it was worth revisiting the contents of Hume's conclusion in order to remind you of what a dramatic and peculiar text it is. In some ways, it is better to read this conclusion as the conclusion to Part 4 of Book 1, 'Of the sceptical and other systems of philosophy', rather than the whole of that book. Part 4 has a different tone from the others. In the first three parts Hume endorses the results of his investigation of human nature, and offers a naturalistic theory of belief and inference. In Part 4 the emphasis is on scepticism, and its relation to natural belief. Reason operating by itself would 'extinguish all belief and evidence'. Reason cannot justify our belief in the continued and distinct existence of the objects of our senses, and its deliverances contradict our belief in the external world. Nature constantly strives to reassert its grip on our psychology, even though reflection threatens to loosen it. Toward the conclusion, reflection seems to get the upper hand.[2] In effect, much of Part 4 demonstrates that nature and reason oppose each other, and this opposition leads to the crisis that Hume dramatizes in the conclusion. Reason is what is put to the test in Part 4, and there it is shown that when it operates alone, without the trivial suggestions of the fancy, it leads to disaster.[3]

What are we to make of all this drama? One line of thought to pursue is, roughly speaking, biographical. Hume famously wrote to a 'learn'd doctor', describing a mental crisis of some sort which he attributes to intense study, and the drama of the conclusion reflects Hume's own experiences. There is no doubt something to be said for this, but it won't be said here. My interest is to explore how the drama of the conclusion relates to Hume's wider philosophical concerns, and that I take to have a sufficient degree of independence from how the conclusion, and indeed Hume's philosophy as a whole, are conditioned by Hume's own personal experiences (this is not to deny that they have any bearing on our understanding of his enterprise). A related approach, which integrates the personal with the social and religious climate of the thinker, can be found in the work of Susan Manning. Manning sees the conclusion as expressing a secularized Calvinist attitude to the pursuit of knowledge: a vain hope is dashed by the imperfections of human reasoning.[4] Alternatively, but consistently with these other thoughts, one may see the conclusion as a Pyrrhonian moment of despair, a realization of the failure of reason. I do not think that these explanations are incorrect; there are certainly enough grains of truth in them to compose a noticeable heap, but there is still more to be said.

[2] For some different interpretations of this feature of the texts see e.g. Annette Baier, *A Progress of Sentiments: Reflections on Hume's Treatise* (Cambridge, Mass.: Harvard University Press, 1991), ch. 1; Don Garrett, *Cognition and Commitment in Hume's Philosophy* (New York: Oxford University Press, 1997), ch. 10; Donald W. Livingston, *Philosophical Melancholy and Delirium: Hume's Pathology of Philosophy* (Chicago: University of Chicago Press, 1998), part 1; David Owen, *Hume's Reason* (Oxford: Oxford University Press, 1999), ch. 9.

[3] This distinction between reason and the imagination masks the fact that demonstrative reason operates with ideas which fall under the scope of the imagination and that probable reason is itself the settled principles of the imagination. For a discussion, see Garrett, *Cognition and Commitment in Hume's Philosophy*, ch. 4. What Hume does here is to model probable reason on animal models of inference, models which Leibniz had thought of as 'pseudo reason' or 'the shadow of reason'. See P. J. E. Kail, *Projection and Realism in Hume* (Oxford: Oxford University Press, forthcoming), introduction and ch. 3.

[4] See Susan Manning, *The Puritan-Provincial Vision: Scottish and American Literature in the Nineteenth Century* (Cambridge: Cambridge University Press, 1990).

II

Here I will suggest that the conclusion to Book 1 is of a piece with Hume's ongoing concern with the impact of religious and philosophical views on ethical life. Hume questions the value of, and the motive for, the exercise of reason and the pursuit of truth at the expense of other natural inclinations, such as pleasure and company. This might not sound a particularly startling thesis to our ears, but its urgency for Hume is thrown into starker relief with the knowledge that a thoroughly Christian philosophical ethics in circulation at the time would have us believe that the exercise of reason at the expense of the pleasurable and the social is *the* central virtue. Underpinning this is the thought that reason is the respect in which we resemble God—the more we exercise reason, the more closely we resemble God. Hume's reaction is that solitary and unchecked activity leads to psychological disaster. Furthermore, though not explicitly stated in the *Treatise*, the resemblance thesis is open to attack. Without the resemblance thesis in place, the 'obligation' to exercise reason at the expense of natural inclination is questionable, to say the least. The activity of the philosopher in Part 4 of the *Treatise* embodies an 'artificial life' which Hume rejects.

Recent discussions of Hume's final choice of reason over superstition have emphasized the idea that for Hume doxastic norms are ultimately sanctioned by moral virtue.[5] The wise believer is one with doxastic virtues that are qualities which are useful or agreeable to himself and to others, entries in the catalogue of virtues. This feature surfaces in the questions Hume poses to himself in the conclusion, and the answers he offers. He asks of his philosophical seclusion from commerce and society 'what end can it serve either for the service of mankind, of my own private interest'? Whether, in other words, his philosophical pursuit is *useful* to others or himself. His answer is that the activity must be pursued only with 'good reason'—when, that is, it is within the scope of the natural and *agreeable* to himself. The use of philosophy for the instruction of humanity is another prospect which emboldens him, and the course of philosophy is the 'safest and most agreeable'. As is well known, Hume earlier in the *Treatise* offers us a choice between the principles of the imagination, which are permanent, irresistible and universal, and those which are weak, changeable, and not useful in the conduct of life (p. 225). The origin of all his philosophy is that he would be 'a loser in the point of pleasure', that he finds its pursuit, guided by the steady principles of the imagination, agreeable to himself. In the First

---

[5] See e.g. Owen, *Hume's Reason*, ch. 9, esp. pp. 212 ff.

Enquiry, Hume's ultimate objection to Pyrrhonian scepticism is its lack of utility:

[A] Pyrrhonian cannot expect, that his philosophy will have any constant influence on the mind: or if it had, that its influence would be beneficial to society. On the contrary, he must acknowledge, if he will acknowledge anything, that all human life will perish were his principles universally and steadily to prevail.[6]

Even this brief little sketch should be sufficient to persuade us that ethical and epistemic concerns are continuous for Hume. Here, though, I narrow the focus, and show how the conclusion to Book 1, and its attendant ethical undercurrents, can be greatly illuminated by a comparison with one of Hume's greatest, and most peculiar, influences, Nicolas Malebranche. Malebranche, in many ways, represents Hume's antithesis, and this can help us to understand the shape of Hume's conclusion and the ramifications it has for the rest of his philosophy. It must not be thought that I am implying that Hume's conclusion is directed solely at Malebranche; instead, Malebranche was uppermost in Hume's mind because Malebranche clearly expressed a general attitude and view of human beings present in many other authors whom Hume sought to attack.[7]

As David Fate Norton puts it, Hume's 'breadth of study and reading' suggests that 'no single writer or philosophical tradition can be relied upon to provide a comprehensive key to his thought'.[8] The point is well taken, but Malebranche's influence on Hume is both extensive and distinctive enough to merit special attention, attracting, as it has, the interest of a number of commentators.[9] In a letter to Michael Ramsey of 1737, Hume lists the authors Ramsey should read in preparation for the *Treatise*, and Malebranche heads the list. Examples, arguments, terminology, and even whole chunks of prose make their way into Hume's text, to such an extent that Charles McCracken conjectures that Hume had Malebranche open on his desk when he wrote the *Treatise*. Commentators have rarely paused,

---

[6] David Hume, *An Enquiry Concerning Human Understanding*, ed. L. A. Selby-Bigge, 3rd edn., rev. P. H. Nidditch (Oxford: Clarendon Press, 1975), 160.

[7] Pascal is another obvious target. See J. R. Maia Neto, 'Hume and Pascal: Pyrrhonism vs. Nature', *Hume Studies*, 18 (1991): 41–9.

[8] David Fate Norton, 'An introduction to Hume's thought', in David Fate Norton (ed.), *The Cambridge Companion to Hume* (Cambridge: Cambridge University Press, 1993), 1–32, at pp. 1–2.

[9] See e.g. Martin Bell, 'Sceptical doubts concerning Hume's causal realism', in K. Richman and R. Read (eds.), *The New Hume Debate* (London: Routledge, 2000), 122–37; Peter Jones, *Hume's Sentiments: Their Ciceronian and French Context* (Edinburgh: Edinburgh University Press, 1982); John Laird, *Hume's Philosophy of Human Nature* (London: Methuen, 1932); Charles McCracken, *Malebranche and British Philosophy* (Oxford: Clarendon Press, 1983); John Passmore, *Hume's Intentions* (Cambridge: Cambridge University Press, 1952); Nicholas Phillipson, *Hume* (London: Weidenfeld and Nicolson, 1989). See also Susan James's contribution to this volume.

however, to comment adequately on the oddity of this influence.[10] Malebranche's philosophy is one of the most baroque and explicitly Christian philosophies ever articulated, and Barnabite Gerdil, a rough contemporary of Hume, wrote that 'the philosophy of Malebranche leads straight to Christianity'.[11] Given Hume's attitude to Christianity, and his belief that Malebranche tried to conduct us on a trip to 'fairyland' (*Enquiry*, 72), it is worth asking why such a figure should play a substantial supporting role in the theatre of Hume's mind.

Certainly Malebranche was well known on both sides of the Channel—indeed, the *Spectator* advised that every lady should have a copy of his *De la Recherche de la vérité—Search after Truth*—in her cabinet.[12] But that by itself does not explain the extent of the influence. One reason why Malebranche may have had such an impact on Hume is his explicit claim that the science of man is a fundamental and 'experimental' science, which is of course how Hume conceived of his own project.[13] But Malebranche's science of man, or what he calls 'the true philosophy', is ultimately aimed at knowledge and love of the only thing worthy of love, the only real power: God. This view is articulated against the idea that man[14] is made in the image of God, a doctrine which a proper experimental investigation into human nature gives no support, as far as Hume is concerned. Edward Craig has argued that much of Hume's philosophy is targeted against a deeply entrenched and pervasive view of man as made in the image of God, a view which gets more concrete articulation in how our epistemic capacities were viewed potentially as the same kind of insight available to God, but obviously not as extensive (we can be infallible in key areas but not omniscient).[15] Malebranche is as explicit as one could be in his adherence to the Image of God doctrine, and if Craig is right, it is no surprise that he should have fascinated Hume.[16]

The Image of God doctrine deeply informs not only Malebranche's epistemology, but also his entire conception of human nature. He offers a

[10] Phillipson, *Hume*, is an exception here.

[11] Quoted in John Yolton, *Perceptual Acquaintance from Descartes to Reid* (Oxford: Basil Blackwell, 1984), 94.   [12] *The Spectator*, no. 37.

[13] See Nicolas Malebranche, *The Search after Truth*, trans. T. Lennon and P. Olscamp (Cambridge: Cambridge University Press, 1997), IV. vi. 2, p. 290, and *Treatise on Ethics*, trans. C. Walton (Dordrecht: Kluwer, 1993), I. v. 17, p. 80. 'Of all the sciences, knowledge of man is the most necessary to our subject. But it is only an experimental science, resulting from our reflection of what is happening within us. Reflection does not make us know the nature of the two substances of which we are composed.'

[14] The gendered term is of course something which has profound consequences.

[15] E. J. Craig, *The Mind of God and the Works of Man* (Oxford: Clarendon Press, 1987), chs. 1 and 2.

[16] Another point of resemblance, insufficiently emphasized by Craig, is the will, which makes itself felt in Descartes.

philosophical articulation of a view of fallen humanity in the opening pages of the *Search after Truth*:

The mind of man is by its nature situated, as it were, between its Creator and coporeal creatures . . . [the union between God and human mind] raise the mind above all things. Through it, the mind receives its life, its light, and its entire felicity . . . The mind's union with the body, on the contrary, infinitely debases man and is today the main cause of all his errors and miseries.[17]

This view is a not-too-distant cousin of the one in which Hume was immersed during his early religious education in the austere, page-a-day primer in morality, *The Whole Duty of Man*. From that Hume would have learned that he must be mindful of the great distance between himself and God, and consider himself as a poor worm of the earth, polluted and defiled, wallowing in all kinds of sins and uncleanliness. The body is a mere husk, but the soul requires care, for it is made in the image of God. Humility is a duty to ourselves, and breaches of our duty include placing our love and affections on the creatures rather than the Creator and taking pride in goods of nature—like wit and beauty—and goods of fortune, like possessions and privilege. Both these kinds of good are not due to the exercise of our free choice, and are therefore morally worthless. These themes occur in Malebranche and, *modulo* important differences between broadly Protestant and Catholic accounts of the consequences of Original Sin, are given distinct philosophical backing. If there was ever a concrete target for Hume's dislike of the consequences of religious thinking on our self-conception, it was Malebranche.

For Malebranche, the 'true philosophy', is the contemplation of the reason and power of God.[18] This is displayed to best effect in his ethics. In the first book of his *Treatise on Ethics*, we are told that virtue consists in the love of order, an order which is, like 'truth, justice and injustice', 'real and exist[s] for all intelligent beings; that which is true for man is also true for an angel, and for God himself.'[19] This order is an order of perfection, which consists in degrees of resemblance to the Reason of God—the more closely anything resembles God, the closer it gets to perfection. So a key

---

[17] Malebranche, *Search after Truth*, Introduction, p. xxxiii.

[18] Ibid., VI, i. 5, pp. 451–2. As Stephen Buckle has recently argued, Hume in the First *Enquiry* presents an attack that seems to have Catholicism as its target, but actually damages Christianity in general. See Buckle, *Hume's Enlightenment Tract: The Unity and Purpose of* An Enquiry Concerning Human Understanding (Oxford: Clarendon Press, 2001), 30 ff.

[19] Malebranche, *Treatise on Ethics*, I. i. 7, p. 46. Compare Hume, *Treatise*, 456: there are those 'who affirm that virtue is nothing but a conformity to reason; that there are eternal fitnesses and unfitnesses of things, which are the same to every rational being that considers them; that immutable measures of right and wrong impose an obligation, not only on human creatures, but also of the Deity himself'. Hume identifies Father Malebranche as he 'who first stated this abstract theory of morals' (*An Enquiry Concerning the Principles of Morals*, ed. L. A. Selby-Bigge, 3rd edn. rev. P. H. Nidditch (Oxford: Clarendon Press, 1975), 197 n.).

aspect of virtue is the attempt to increase our resemblance to God, by the exercise of reason. Like the good student of Augustine that he is, Malebranche thinks we have the capacity, hampered though it is by Original Sin, to undertake this, through the Grace of Jesus Christ. We require two cardinal virtues to attain this love of order and resemble the mind of God: 'strength of mind' and 'freedom of mind'. Strength of mind is acquired by habituation, and is the capacity to attend to a great degree only to clear and distinct ideas. We must assiduously avoid anything which 'flatters the senses and awakens the passions', (*Treatise on Ethics*, 77), and constantly work for the 'mortification' of the senses, imagination, and passions.

Malebranchian ethics simultaneously recognizes and condemns the mechanical pull of sympathy and the passions, and its relative importance to society. Sympathy and passion help us to 'gain the conservation of health and life, the union of man and woman, society, commerce, the acquisition of sensible goods', but, for all that, they are 'extremely contrary to true goods, goods of the spirit, goods due to virtue and merit' (ibid. 136–7). Such features of our embodiment give us an undue concern with the ordinary business of life, with the love of the created rather than the Creator, and draw us away from the love of virtue. Our natural inclinations drag us away from strength of mind, the focused attention on clear and distinct ideas. Strength of mind can, however, when coupled with 'freedom of mind', an acquired capacity to suspend consent except over matters which are clear and distinct, help us fight our natural inclinations. In summing up our duties to ourselves, Malebranche writes:

We must accustom ourselves to the effort of attention, and thereby acquire some strength of mind. We need consent only to evidence, and thereby conserve the freedom of mind . . . The world deceives us by way of our senses; it disturbs our minds by way of our imagination; it traps us and drops us into the worst unhappiness by way of our passions. We must break off the dangerous commerce we have with it by way of our bodies, if we want to augment the union we have with God by way of Reason. (Ibid. 222)

The most solidly virtuous man is he who 'goes back into himself most deeply, and who listens to the inner truth in the greatest silence of the senses, imagination and passions' (ibid. 57). Such solitary activity is coupled with the promise of happiness stemming from God's love.

We have here a model of virtue wherein we are to reason with the most accurate attention and assent only to the highest evidence, which requires us to shun the senses, imagination, passions, and the mechanical pull of sympathy. The justification for this practice is contingent on virtue consisting in increasing the resemblance we have between ourselves and God and the promise of happiness that God's grace may bring. Thus:

[Man] can sacrifice his peace of mind for the sake of Truth, and his pleasures for the sake of Order . . . He can, in a word, earn merit or demerit. For God is just;

He loves His creatures in proportion as they are loveable, in proportion as they resemble Him. (Ibid. 48)

Towards the end of his discussion of virtue, Malebranche considers two key vices, pleasure and pride. The vice of pleasure-seeking is more explicitly discussed in *The Search after Truth*, under the wonderful heading 'We must avoid pleasure, even though it makes us happy' (p. 307). Pleasure separates us from God, since we come to believe that the objects related to pleasure are genuinely the *cause* of that pleasure, and hence valuable. But God is the only true cause—and hence the only true cause of pleasure—and we attend to and love only him. Pride and pleasure are linked vices:

Finally, man is subject to two sorts of concupiscence: that of pleasures, and that of loftiness or greatness. People do not give this enough thought. When a man enjoys sensible pleasures, his imagination is polluted; and carnal concupiscence excites and fortifies it. So too, when he spreads himself out to the world, seeks status, makes friends, acquires a reputation, then his idea of himself expands and inflates his imagination, and the concupiscence of pride is renewed and augmented. (*Treatise on Ethics*, 133)

We then indiscreetly abandon ourselves to intercourse with the world and fearlessly embark on that stormy sea, as St. Augustine called it. . . . we 'make a name for ourselves', but a name which makes us more of a slave the more we do to 'make' it, since it is a name which ties us directly to creatures and separates us from the Creator—a name illustrious in the esteem of men, but a name of pride, which God will bring down. (Ibid.)

Again, pride separates us from God, since we come to value ourselves as autonomous and effective beings, and become concerned with the approval of other created beings. But all power is really God's, and only he is worthy of true esteem.

III

It is difficult to read this last passage without one's thoughts turning to Hume's conclusion. Hume questions his temerity to 'put out to sea' in his 'leaky weather-beaten vessel' (*Treatise*, 263). Ultimately, what persuades him to continue is that he will be a 'loser in the point of pleasure', and he feels an ambition of 'acquiring a name' (ibid. 271). Malebranche's ethics, which rejects pleasure and pride, is based on a highly abstract religious philosophy. It recommends a way of life which devalues aspects of human life which are pleasurable and useful to society in general. This marks out the man of Malebranchean virtue as living what Hume calls an *artificial life*.

A constant theme in Hume is the bad ethical effects of religious belief. Moral thinking has a natural basis in a set of virtues, those which are agreeable to their possessors and others, and those which are useful to their possessors and others. Our natural capacity to approve of useful qualities tends to be limited to local features, but it may be extended or augmented, by the help of custom and sympathy, to approve of conventions that are generally useful to society. These 'artificial' virtues lie on an intelligible continuum with the natural virtues, in that the basis of our approval of them, their utility, is the same as for some of the natural virtues. Their artificiality consists in the fact that they are human inventions—their virtue consists in their general utility. There are other 'artificial' practices which, however, are not virtues for Hume: those which are useless or, worse, damaging to their possessors or owners. Obviously there are natural vices, i.e. features which are displeasing or harmful and which are not human inventions. But Hume sometimes turns his attention to what we might call 'artificial vices'. Sometimes, adherence to artificially constructed bodies of commitment issues in what Hume calls 'artificial lives', that is, lives which are centred on the rejection of the natural virtues of the useful and the agreeable.

The notion of an artificial life surfaces in a number of places, including the Second *Enquiry*, 'A Dialogue', the *Natural History of Religion*, and the *History of England*. The defining characteristic of an artificial life is a rejection of the empirically justified set of virtues, a rejection motivated by theoretical commitments which, at the very best, lack justificatory status. The system of abstract thought issues in normative claims on the agent, enjoining courses of action which are rendered intelligible according to that set of abstract commitments. More often than not, the finger is pointed at abstract religious systems. Religion 'inspects our whole conduct, and prescribes an universal rule to our actions, to our words, to our very thought and inclinations'; and Pascal is offered as an example of a religiously inspired artificial life.[20] The example of the 'monkish virtues' in the Second *Enquiry* sums up the notion of an artificial life, and Hume's own critique of it, rather neatly:

And as every quality which is useful or agreeable to ourselves or others is, in common life, allowed to be a part of personal merit; so no other will be received, where men judge of things by their natural, unprejudiced reason, without the delusive glosses of superstition and false religion. Celibacy, fasting, penance, mortification, self-denial, humility, silence, solitude, and the whole train of monkish virtues; for what reason are they everywhere rejected by men of sense, but because they serve to no manner of purpose; they neither advance a man's fortune in the world, nor render him a more valuable member of the society; neither qualify him for the entertainment of company nor encrease his power of self-enjoyment . . . A gloomy, hair-brained enthusiast, after his death, may have a place in the calendar; but scarcely ever be admitted, when alive, into intimacy and society, except by those who are as delirious and dismal as himself.[21]

[20] 'A Dialogue', in *Enquiry Concerning the Principles of Morals*, 342–3.
[21] *Enquiry Concerning the Principles of Morals*, 270.

These monkish virtues are motivated by a comparison between humans and the infinite wisdom and virtue of God, which leads to a conception of oneself as a debased and pitiful creature. There is a 'secret comparison between man and beings of the most perfect wisdom'[22] which is, Hume argues in 'Of the dignity or meanness of human nature', inimical to human flourishing, promoting values which run contrary to the empirically justified values of pleasure and utility. Both Malebranche and *The Whole Duty of Man* recommend a view of oneself as almost entirely undesirable, corrupted by one's bodily, animal nature, when compared with infinite perfection.

If we see the conclusion of Hume's *Treatise* as based on an implicit rejection of this comparison (secret, or, in Malebranche's case, not so secret) between man and God, then an ethics which enjoins the pursuit of reason at the expense of other interests is an artificial one. And the textual details suggest that Hume had Malebranche squarely in mind. He begins by expressing the misery that his resolution to follow reason at the expense of natural inclination has brought him, and the metaphor of the immense sea, which occurs in Malebranche, opens this discussion. Malebranche's use of the metaphor is an allusion to Augustine's view of us as philosophical sailors who have 'chosen to proceed out on the deep . . . because a most treacherous calm weather of pleasure and honours entice them'.[23] Prior to Hume's citation of pleasure and the ambition to make a name for himself, he is left in forlorn solitude, unfit for human company, reduced almost to despair. Malebranche has warned that we may sacrifice our peace for the sake of Truth, but that sacrifice is justified by the resemblance to God that the exercise of reason increases. But Hume simply sees the loss of peace of mind due to the 'intense view' of these 'manifold contradictions', and the solitary exercise of reason is left with nothing to recommend it. He then records that mixing with company and allowing the senses to overcome his profound sceptical reasoning are a palliative to this philosophical melancholy and despair, and, *contra* Malebranche, as something that can be embraced without fear of justifiable ethical censure. Malebranche can no longer claim that the senses and company drag us away from the contemplation of God, and so should be avoided (*Treatise on Ethics*, II. xiv. 8).

Hume's next question involves a reflection on 'I must seclude myself . . . from the commerce and society of men, which is so agreeable; and that I must torture my brain with subtilities and sophistries . . . under what obligation do I lie of making such an abuse of time?' For Malebranche, such an obligation to seclude oneself from society and shut down the senses, imagination, passion, and sympathy derives from the thought that such things

---

[22] David Hume, *Essays, Moral, Political and Literary*, ed. Eugene F. Miller, rev. edn. (Indianapolis: Liberty Classics, 1987), 83.

[23] Augustine, *The Happy Life*, trans. L. Schopp (London: Herder, 1939), 43.

impede the solitary exercise of reason, which increases one's resemblance
to God. But again, without the theological background in place, this obligation to the unconditional exercise of reason is under pressure—and indeed
Hume rejects it.

No: if I must be a fool, as all those who reason or believe any thing *certainly*
are, my follies shall at least be natural and agreeable. Where I strive against my
inclination, I shall have a good reason for my resistance; and will no more be led
a wandering into such dreary solitudes, and rough passages, as I have hitherto met
with. (*Treatise*, 270)

Rejecting the obligation to philosophize in the manner of Malebranche,
Hume then offers reasons to pursue philosophy which are in line with the
natural virtues, qualities which are pleasing and useful to oneself and others,
features which Malebranche explicitly rejected as sinful. If Hume did not
continue with philosophy, he would be 'a loser in the point of pleasure', which
is the 'origin' of his philosophy. So there is one reason to continue which is
perfectly compatible with our natural patterns of evaluation. When it fails to
offer such a reward, there is no reason to continue to do philosophy.

Hume's further reason to continue with philosophy is that he feels an
'ambition [to contribute] to the instruction of mankind, and of acquiring a
name by my inventions and discoveries' (ibid. 271). This looks both
forward and back. Its looks back in being an allusion to Malebranche's
rejection of pride, the ambition of 'making a name for oneself', which he
saw as separating us from the Creator and joining us with other creatures;
again, this only makes sense on the supposition of the resemblance claim
and the abstract theology upon which it rests. It looks forward in the sense
that pride and the approbation of others play a vital role in Hume's ethics.
We said earlier that artificial lives denigrate features which contribute to
human flourishing. For Hume, pride and the approbation of others are
central to virtue, but can become devalued in an artificial life. Humility is
taken for a 'virtue' by the monkish, Hume thinks, because of the 'secret
comparison between man and beings of the most perfect wisdom', which
leads one to conceive of oneself as infinitely debased. But pride is central to
human flourishing in the following way.

Pride, for Hume, is both approval and awareness of one's virtues.
Without a due pride, the value of one's virtues fails to be recognized, and
this fact can impede their manifestation. We will not exercise virtues of
which we are unaware, or of which we disapprove (if you don't think you
are a good cook when you are one, or decry your skill, you will waste your
talent by staying out of the kitchen). A little over-confidence is actually
preferable, for Hume, than an underestimation of one's capacities:

Whatever capacity any one may be endow'd with, 'tis entirely useless to him, if he
be not acquainted with it, and form not designs suitable to it. 'Tis requisite on all

occasions to know our own force; and were it allowable to err on either side, 'twould be more advantageous to overrate our merit, than to form ideas of it, below its just standard. Fortune commonly favours the bold and enterprizing; and nothing inspires us with more boldness than a good opinion of ourselves. (Ibid. 597)

Pride's important role in virtue is not, however, self-supporting. It requires the recognition and support of others to be sustained:

But beside these original causes of pride and humility, there is a secondary one in the opinions of others, which has an equal influence on the affections. Our reputation, our character, our name are considerations of vast weight and importance; and even the other causes of pride; virtue, beauty and riches; have little influence, when not seconded by the opinions and sentiments of others. (Ibid. 316)

One's opinion of oneself, which is central to virtue, cannot be efficacious unless it is public, a view supported by the opinions of others. The solitary activity of Book I deprived Hume of any dependence on the opinions of others, and so, at the beginning of the conclusion of Book I, Hume's beliefs are almost lost: all his opinions 'loosen and fall of themselves, when unsupported by the approbation of others'. Freed from Malebranchian restrictions, especially the rejection of pride and the importance of reputation, Hume can call upon public approbation to support them. Philosophy can be public and human.

A final point about artificial lives is worth making here. The conclusion of Book I is Hume's self-conscious reflection on the business, method, and authority of philosophy.[24] Part 4 examines the relentless and solitary exercise of reason with no regard to other interests. We have already seen one model of human beings, Malebranche's, which attempts to render such an activity intelligible, and we have seen how Hume's conclusion may be regarded as a reflection upon, and a rejection of, that story, together with an endorsement of a 'careless' philosophy, one which is integrated with genuine, natural, and human evaluative concerns. For Malebranche, we have an obligation to search after truth.

In the conclusion to Book II of the *Treatise*, 'Of curiosity, or the love of truth', Hume turns his attention to the 'search after truth' and the reasons behind that passion. Malebranche's concern with the search after truth obviously owes much to the Augustinian tradition: truth and God are closely identified, partly because of a view that truth is independent of judgement, leading to an identification of the objective of God. For Hume, our interest in truth is explicable in more ordinary terms, in the thrill of the chase, the pleasure of discovery, and the utility of the quarry. Hume sees no *unconditional* value in truth or its pursuit. But then why are there people like Malebranche?

---

[24] See also Livingston, *Philosophical Melancholy and Delirium*, Part 1.

In typical fashion Hume brings to our attention a 'contradiction':

The difficulty on this head arises from hence, that many philosophers have con-sum'd their time, have destroy'd their health, and neglected their fortune, in search of such truths, as they esteem'd important and useful to the world, tho' it appear'd from their whole conduct and behaviour, that they were not endow'd with any share of public spirit, nor had any concern for the interests of mankind. Were they convinc'd, that their discoveries were of no consequence, they wou'd entirely lose all relish for their studies . . . which seems a contradiction. (Ibid. 450)

I take it that Hume is being ironic when he allows that these philosophers genuinely do think that their discoveries are important and useful. The contradiction is generated by those who pursue truth for no pleasure or utility, though the passion for truth is generated by those two features. A key way in which Hume thinks the contradiction is resolved is that though truth is originally sought after because of pleasure and utility, we can acquire an interest in truth *per se* simply through the exercise of the pur-suit. In the conditional search for *truths*, we can acquire an unconditioned interest in *truth*, one which can lead us into patterns of evaluation which make us neglect the useful and pleasing; the obsession with 'the Truth' can promote artificial lives.

What is being touched upon here is a problem that Nietzsche struggled with, the 'ascetic ideal' and the supposedly unconditional obligation to the truth. The relation between Christianity and truth, as explored by Nietzsche, is, I think, within the grasp of Hume's philosophy. Both seek a form of historical self-understanding, and offer 'genealogical' explanations about why patterns of evaluation have the shape they do. Hume's picture of the matter is less complex than Nietzsche's, but they share many affinities. Truth is but one value among others. What is surprising is that Hume seems not to connect the unconditional pursuit of truth and religious belief in the way Nietzsche did. But he had all the material in place and, it seems to me, came close to doing so.[25]

REFERENCES

Primary Sources

Augustine, *The Happy Life*, trans. L. Schopp (London: Herder, 1939).
Hume, David, *A Treatise of Human Nature*, ed. L. A. Selby-Bigge, 2nd edn., rev. P. H. Nidditch (Oxford: Clarendon Press, 1978).

[25] For a discussion see e.g. Ken Gemes, 'Nietzsche's critique of truth' in J. Richardson and B. Leiter (eds.), *Nietzsche*, Oxford Readings in Philosophy (Oxford: Oxford University Press, 2001), 40–58.

—— *An Enquiry Concerning Human Understanding*, ed. L. A. Selby-Bigge, 3rd edn., rev. P. H. Nidditch (Oxford: Clarendon Press, 1975).

—— *An Enquiry Concerning the Principles of Morals*, ed. L. A. Selby-Bigge, 3rd edn., rev. P. H. Nidditch (Oxford: Clarendon Press, 1975).

—— *Essays, Moral, Political and Literary*, ed. Eugene F. Miller, rev. edn. (Indianapolis: Liberty Classics, 1987).

Malebranche, Nicolas, *The Search after Truth*, trans. T. Lennon and P. Olscamp (Cambridge: Cambridge University Press, 1997).

—— *Treatise on Ethics*, trans. C. Walton (Dordrecht: Kluwer, 1993).

Secondary Sources

Baier, Annette, *A Progress of Sentiments: Reflections on Hume's Treatise* (Cambridge, Mass.: Harvard University Press, 1991).

Bell, Martin, 'Sceptical doubts concerning Hume's causal realism', in K. Richman and R. Read (eds.), *The New Hume Debate*, (London: Routledge, 2000), 122–37.

Buckle, Stephen, *Hume's Enlightenment Tract: The Unity and Purpose of An Enquiry Concerning Human Understanding* (Oxford: Clarendon Press, 2001).

Craig, Edward J., *The Mind of God and the Works of Man* (Oxford: Clarendon Press, 1987).

Garrett, Don, *Cognition and Commitment in Hume's Philosophy* (New York: Oxford University Press, 1997).

Gemes, Ken, 'Nietzsche's critique of truth', in J. Richardson and B. Leiter (eds.), *Nietzsche*, Oxford Readings in Philosophy (Oxford: Oxford University Press, 2001), 40–58.

Jones, Peter, *Hume's Sentiments: Their Ciceronian and French Context* (Edinburgh: Edinburgh University Press, 1982).

Kail, P. J. E., *Projection and Realism in Hume* (Oxford: Oxford University Press, forthcoming).

Laird, John, *Hume's Philosophy of Human Nature* (London: Methuen, 1932).

Livingston, Donald W., *Philosophical Melancholy and Delirium: Hume's Pathology of Philosophy* (Chicago: University of Chicago Press, 1998).

Maia Neto, J. R., 'Hume and Pascal: Pyrrhonism vs. nature', *Hume Studies*, 18 (1991): 41–9.

Manning, Susan, *The Puritan-Provincial Vision: Scottish and American Literature in the Nineteenth Century* (Cambridge: Cambridge University Press, 1990).

McCracken, Charles, *Malebranche and British Philosophy* (Oxford: Clarendon Press, 1983).

Norton, David Fate, 'An introduction to Hume's thought', in David Fate Norton (ed.), *The Cambridge Companion to Hume* (Cambridge: Cambridge University Press, 1993), 1–32.

Owen, David, *Hume's Reason* (Oxford: Oxford University Press, 1999).

Passmore, John, *Hume's Intentions* (Cambridge: Cambridge University Press, 1952).

Phillipson, Nicholas, *Hume* (London: Weidenfeld and Nicolson, 1989).

Yolton, John, *Perceptual Acquaintance from Descartes to Reid* (Oxford: Basil Blackwell, 1984).

Hume's Use of the Rhetoric of Calvinism

JAMES A. HARRIS

———•———

Close to the end of the *Enquiry Concerning Human Understanding* Hume claims that the 'best and most solid foundation' of 'Divinity or Theology' is '*faith* and divine revelation'.[1] The remark is made as Hume sums up the consequences of the limits of the understanding. Pure reason is unable to establish anything with regard to matters of fact. When it comes to proving the existence of things, we are dependent entirely upon experience; and thus belief in God 'has a foundation in *reason*, so far as it is supported by experience' (*Enquiry*, 165), but, Hume appears to be intimating, such belief is not well supported by experience, and so has no solid foundation in reason. Nevertheless, it has another basis, in what is revealed to men in Scripture. We must assume that Hume is drawing some kind of distinction between, on the one hand, 'Divinity or Theology', which 'proves the existence of a Deity, and the immortality of the soul', and, on the other, the volumes of writings on religion that he foresees will be committed to the flames when they are subjected to the test of whether they contain either '*abstract reasoning concerning quantity or number*' or '*any experimental reasoning concerning matter of fact and existence*' (ibid.). Systematic doctrinal theology may be destined for combustion, but there is a set of core beliefs which some seek to ground in experience, and which Hume thinks are better regarded as having their foundation in the fact that the Bible affirms them to be true. It is not the case, needless to say, that every sceptic who recommends that religious people rid themselves of the illusion that their belief is rational is properly regarded as a sceptic about religion: we know that Montaigne, for example, is sincere in his fideism in the 'Apology for Raymond Sebond', as is Pascal in the *Pensées*

Earlier versions of this paper were delivered at the 29th Hume Society Conference, held at Helsinki in 2002, and at Hume Studies in Britain II, held at Edinburgh in the same year. I am grateful to audiences on both occasions for their questions and comments. I should particularly like to thank my commentator at Helsinki, Wade Robison. My greatest debt is to M. A. Stewart, who, with his usual generosity, provided me with several pages of comments on a later version, and thereby improved the end result a great deal. All work on this paper was done during my tenure of a British Academy Postdoctoral Fellowship.

[1] David Hume, *An Enquiry Concerning Human Understanding*, ed. L. A. Selby-Bigge, 3rd edn., rev. P. H. Nidditch (Oxford: Clarendon Press, 1975), 165.

and (in all likelihood) Bayle in his *Historical and Critical Dictionary*. Such writers clearly do not regard belief in God or the immortality of the soul as in any sense weakened or endangered by demonstrations of its rational untenability. On the contrary, they see their attacks on the pretensions of reason as a means of clearing an obstacle in the way of seeing that, in Montaigne's words, 'the Christian faith . . . is, purely and simply, a gift depending on the generosity of Another' (that is, on the generosity of God himself).[2] But what are Hume's intentions here at the end of First *Enquiry*? Why does he use the language of fideism?

Before we consider possible answers to this question, we should note that there are several other places where Hume writes as one who believes that religious belief cannot be arrived at by reasoning, and who seeks to ground religious belief in a more direct encounter with the divine. In Section 8 of the same work, Hume concludes his treatment of the question of liberty and necessity with a declaration that 'mere natural and unassisted reason' is unable 'to explain distinctly, how the Deity can be the mediate cause of all the actions of men, without being the author of sin and moral turpitude': for 'whatever system she embraces, she must find herself involved in inextricable difficulties, and even contradictions, at every step which she takes with regard to such subjects' (*Enquiry*, 103). Section 10, 'Of Miracles', begins by insinuating that it is only 'by the immediate operation of the Holy Spirit' that belief is possible in what is revealed in Scripture (ibid. 109). So long as one regards the New Testament as a document that merely provides evidence about the life of a historical figure, Hume goes on to argue, one is bound not to be persuaded by its claims, for there are never good reasons to take reports of miracles as reliable. But this, he reiterates in the conclusion of the section, should not be taken as an attack on Revelation itself. The point is only to remind us that 'mere reason' is insufficient to convince us of '[o]ur most holy religion': '[W]hoever is moved by *Faith* to assent to it', Hume writes, 'is conscious of a continued miracle in his own person, which subverts all the principles of his understanding, and gives him a determination to believe what is most contrary to custom and experience' (ibid. 131). The essay 'Of the Immortality of the Soul' begins and ends in a similar spirit: 'it is the gospel, and the gospel alone, that has brought life and immortality to light,' Hume says in the opening paragraph; '[n]othing could set in a fuller light the infinite obligations which mankind have to divine revelation,' he says in the aftermath of his attack on metaphysical, moral, and physical arguments for immortality, 'since we find, that no other medium could ascertain this great and important truth'.[3] At the end, too, of the

---

[2] Michel de Montaigne, *The Complete Essays*, trans. by M. A. Screech (Harmondsworth: Penguin, 1991), 557.

[3] David Hume, *Essays Moral, Political, and Literary*, ed. Eugene F. Miller, rev. edn. (Indianapolis: Liberty Fund, 1987), 590, 598.

Dialogues concerning Natural Religion, Philo contrasts the person 'seasoned with a just sense of the imperfections of natural reason', who 'will fly to revealed truth with the greatest avidity', with 'the haughty dogmatist, persuaded that he can erect a complete system of theology by the mere help of philosophy', who 'disdains any further aid, and rejects this adventitious instructor': 'To be a philosophical sceptic is, in a man of letters,' he concludes, 'the first and most essential step towards being a sound, believing Christian.'[4]

It will be observed that Hume tends to restrict his fideistic pronouncements to opening and concluding paragraphs. David Berman has drawn attention to this as a characteristic feature of deistical texts. Berman shows that it is fairly common for a writer attacking the rationality of belief in a particular item of Christian doctrine to begin and end with an affirmation that the real basis of belief is to be found in revelation alone. Examining deist treatments of the immortality of the soul in particular, Berman distinguishes between irony and what he terms 'theological lying'.[5] One indulges in irony when one is sure that one's real meaning is easily understandable. One lies, by contrast, when one wishes to conceal one's real beliefs. Deists such as Collins, Tindal, Toland, and Blount, according to Berman, are not simply being ironic when they affirm the primacy of revelation. They are playing a rather more complicated game than that. There are three components to theological lying, on Berman's account. First, there is the literal meaning of the affirmation of revelation, employed to deceive the vulgar reader, so as to protect the writer from prosecution, and also protect those too tender-minded to be able to do without the doctrine in question. Secondly, there is the 'esoteric' message that a doctrine whose only support lies in revelation is not worth the respect of thoughtful and tough-minded people. This was signalled to other free thinkers (and also to clerical opponents versed in deist literature) by the cursory and formulaic nature of the appeal to revelation. Thirdly, and, Berman argues, most importantly, there is 'insinuation, or gently and covertly suggesting the second component (the radical message) to some of those ignorant of it'.[6] The deist hoped to do more than conceal his unbelief from some and to hint at it to others: he hoped that there would be those who would be so troubled by the contrast between the force of the attack on the rationality of belief in, say, the immortality of the soul and the brevity of the appeal to revelation that they would dismiss the doctrine altogether. Berman claims that Hume, in the essay on the immortality of the soul and elsewhere, uses this deist

---

[4] David Hume, *Dialogues Concerning Natural Religion and the Natural History of Religion,* ed. J. C. A. Gaskin (Oxford: Oxford University Press, 1993), 130.

[5] See David Berman, 'Deism, immortality, and the art of theological lying', in J. A. Leo Lemay (ed.), *Deism, Masonry, and the Enlightenment* (Newark: University of Delaware Press, 1987), 61–78. [6] Ibid., 72.

tactic. All that separates Hume from earlier writers is that his 'insinuation' is more obvious.[7]

Berman makes Hume's agenda (and that of the deists) a rather simple one: it is to rid readers of as many religious beliefs as possible. In this paper I wish to complicate this picture of Hume's intentions, by placing his use of fideistic language in its contemporary Scottish context. There are, of course, many contexts in which Hume's writings demand to be understood, but one of them is the Scottish one, and I shall concentrate upon it here to the exclusion of others. My point of departure is the fact that, while Berman portrays Hume's writings on religion (and those of the deists) as a series of broadside attacks on a monolithic, homogeneous system of belief, the truth is that in eighteenth-century Scotland no such monolith existed to be attacked. From the 1720s onwards, Scotland was the site of a running battle between would-be modernizers of religion and those who clung to the theology, and with it the anthropology, of the seventeenth century.[8] One focus of the dispute was the role which individual parishes should play in the selection of ministers: the modernizers upheld the right of the 'heritors', who paid the minister's wages, to determine appointments, while the reactionary party insisted that it was in the spirit of Presbyterianism that communities choose their own ministers. However, and as has been shown by Ian Clark, the central questions in this dispute were much more abstract, and had to do instead with relations between Church and State, and with whether the Church was to continue to consider itself an independent and inviolable community set up against the world and its temporal concerns, or to begin to see itself as a community which would work with the State in the pursuit of various kinds of 'improvement'.[9] The new programme had it that the preacher, instead of dwelling on Original Sin, predestination, the bondage of the will, and dependence on Christ's atonement, should seek to present the reasonableness of Christianity, and show how the life of politeness, benevolence, and industry had its surest foundation in the doctrines of natural religion. Hume regarded this modernizing attempt to involve religion in the renovation of Scottish society with great mistrust, and, so I shall suggest, invokes an old language of sceptical

---

[7] See David Berman, 'Deism, immortality, and the art of theological lying', in J. A. Leo Lemay (ed.), *Deism, Masonry, and the Enlightenment* (Newark: University of Delaware Press, 1987), 75–6. Berman does not regard Hume as a deist. Rather, he appears to regard the deists as having been, despite appearances, Humeans *avant la lettre*. In reality, according to Berman, the deists believed no more in natural religion than they did in revealed religion: their aim was to 'insinuate' that the former has just as little basis as the latter.

[8] For a general account of Scottish theology in the eighteenth century, see M. A. Stewart, 'Religion and rational theology', in A. Broadie (ed.), *The Cambridge Companion to the Scottish Enlightenment* (Cambridge: Cambridge University Press, 2003), 31–59.

[9] See Ian D. L. Clark, 'From protest to reaction: the moderate regime in the Church of Scotland', in N. T. Phillipson and R. Mitchison (eds.), *Scotland in the Age of Improvement* (Edinburgh: Edinburgh University Press, 1970), 200–24.

fideism in order to insinuate, to use Berman's word, its superficiality. For want of time and space necessary for a full treatment of the subject, attention will be restricted to Hume's appeals to faith and revelation in the First *Enquiry*.

The standard interpretation of the passages from the First *Enquiry* quoted above is that they are no more than exercises in mischief-making and heavy-handed irony.[10] My alternative, or supplementary, interpretation owes much to work recently published by M. A. Stewart on the context in which Hume rewrote Book I of the *Treatise of Human Nature* for publication in the form of a series of essays.[11] Stewart has argued that some (though not all) characteristic features of what we now call the *Enquiry Concerning Human Understanding* are to be seen as the product of Hume's failed attempt to secure the Edinburgh moral philosophy chair in 1745.[12] According to Stewart, the First *Enquiry* is, at least in part, 'effectively [Hume's] public attempt to rebut the accusations of his opponents'.[13] Hume's attack on Stoicism in Section 5, his rejection in Section 8 of the idea that the falsity of an opinion is indicated by its having 'dangerous consequences', and his clarification of the nature of his scepticism in Section 12 are three signs of his engagement with contemporary controversy.[14] More significant still are the distinctions between different species of philosophy made in Section 1, and the plea for freedom of philosophical speech in Section 11.[15] Hume's goal in the First *Enquiry* considered as a whole is to make the case for a different species of philosophy from the practically orientated Christian Stoicism favoured by those, most notably Francis Hutcheson and William Leechman, who had banded together to ensure that the Edinburgh chair went to William Cleghorn instead of Hume. The thing to keep in mind in connection with this episode of Hume's career is that, as Stewart puts it, 'it was not the extremists who went to such lengths to block Hume's chances. It was the leading liberals, opposing one systematic philosophy to

[10] See e.g. Antony Flew, *Hume's Philosophy of Belief* (London: Routledge, 1961), 162 (Hume concludes 'Of Liberty and Necessity' with 'a smirking genuflection of piety'); George Botterill, 'Hume on liberty and necessity', in P. Millican (ed.), *Reading Hume on Human Understanding* (Oxford: Oxford University Press, 2002), 289 (the final paragraph of the same essay is 'a very masterpiece of ironic disingenuity'); J. L. Mackie, *The Miracle of Theism* (Oxford: Oxford University Press, 1982), 29 (the conclusion of 'Of Miracles' is 'of course . . . only a joke'). For a more careful consideration of the conclusion of 'Of Miracles', see Stephen Buckle, *Hume's Enlightenment Tract: The Unity and Purpose of* An Enquiry Concerning Human Understanding (Oxford: Clarendon Press, 2001), 269–74. Buckle notes the fideistic pedigree of Hume's remarks, but in the end decides that Hume intends no more than 'an ironical allusion to the errors of the religious "enthusiasts" '.

[11] See M. A. Stewart, 'Two species of philosophy: the historical significance of the First *Enquiry*', in Millican (ed.), *Reading Hume*, 67–95.

[12] For a full account of this episode, see M. A. Stewart, *The Kirk and the Infidel* (Lancaster: Lancaster University, 1995). See also Roger Emerson, 'The "affair" at Edinburgh and the "project" at Glasgow', in M. A. Stewart and J. P. Wright (eds.), *Hume and Hume's Connexions* (Edinburgh: Edinburgh University Press, 1994), 1–22.

[13] Stewart, 'Two species of philosophy', 83.   [14] See ibid., 83–6.   [15] See ibid., 86–94.

another.'[16] Hume responds, therefore, with an attack on the philosophical system of the liberals; and this, it will be suggested here, provides a means of finding more than simple irony in his appeals to revelation at the expense of reason when considering the foundations of religious belief.

As Stewart describes the First *Enquiry*, it is to be understood as being in several important respects a reply to the accusations against Hume summarized in *A Letter from a Gentleman to his Friend in Edinburgh*. Part of Hume's answer to the charges made against the character of his philosophy is his clarification, in the *Enquiry* but also in the *Letter*, of the nature of his scepticism, and his rebuttal of the notion that he 'denies' the existence of causal connections anywhere in the universe. 'The attacks on his religious conformity were clearly harder to counter', Stewart says, 'and Hume seems to have decided that the best tactic here was to come clean.'[17] That is to say, Hume decided to be explicit where in the *Treatise* he had insinuated: so he came out into the open about the implications of his account of causal reasoning for natural religion (in 'Of a Particular Providence'), and for revealed religion too (in 'Of Miracles'). He also—and this is what I shall focus upon here—fought back with the claim that the species of philosophy most favourable to the interests of the Christian religion is in fact scepticism. There is irony, of course, in this claim: it would be absurd to imagine that Hume genuinely has the interests of the Christian religion in mind when he claims, as he does in the *Letter*, that one does an 'essential Service to Piety' when one shows the inability of human reason so much as to 'satisfy itself with regard to its own Operations', let alone with regard to the mysteries of the Incarnation and the Trinity.[18] But what Hume would have known was that the new species of philosophy advocated by Hutcheson, Leechman, William Wishart, and the others who blocked his candidacy for the Edinburgh chair had from its inception been under attack from a party in the Church of Scotland which was wholly serious in believing that reason, and philosophical reason in particular, was an inadequate basis for religious belief. This party clung to the traditional Calvinist view that human reason had been ruined by the Fall, and that faith, when it is granted to men, is not something that men can be said to have fashioned themselves, but is rather a gift from God himself, offered only to those who look to the Word, and the Word alone, for their salvation. When he sets up faith in opposition to reason, it is not some timeless form of piety that Hume adopts, but instead the rhetoric of these Calvinists, with whom he shared an opponent.

My suggestion, then, is that at least part of the reason why Hume is ostentatious in his claims about the value of Revelation is that he knew that

---

[16] Stewart, 'Two species of philosophy', 94.   [17] Ibid., 86.

[18] David Hume, *A Letter from a Gentleman to his Friend in Edinburgh*, ed. E. C. Mossner and J. V. Price (Edinburgh: Edinburgh University Press, 1967), 21.

therein lay a way to make out that it was the modernizers, and not he himself, who threatened the cause of traditional religion. The suggestion is not, to repeat, that Hume sincerely and earnestly sought to vindicate his philosophy by highlighting its affinities with Calvinism. Hume's use of the language of Calvinism is to be understood, rather, as a means of casting aspersions on the pretensions to religious wholesomeness frequently made by those who had frustrated his academic ambitions. Hutcheson's appointment at Glasgow had been contested by men unwilling to let go of the kind of Christianity that Scots had suffered for during the dark years of the seventeenth century.[19] Hutcheson had responded, in his inaugural lecture at Glasgow, with an apology for his new style of philosophy that culminates in the claim that to replace the 'selfish scheme' favoured by both Calvinists and natural lawyers such as Hobbes and Pufendorf with a theory of natural benevolence and sociability is better to serve the cause of religion: for that way, 'the benevolence towards mankind of the Deity, whom we should always gratefully worship and admire, is obvious from man's very constitution'.[20] It is characteristic of Hutcheson to seek to break down the distinction between moral philosophy, on the one hand, and natural religion, on the other. To describe human nature accurately is, according to Hutcheson, to illustrate divine benevolence, and to show that man has a place in the harmonious system that is the universe considered as a whole. It is precisely this aspect of Hutcheson's teaching that Leechman dwells upon in the 'account of the life, writings and character of the author' prefixed to Hutcheson's posthumous *System of Moral Philosophy*.[21] It is also this aspect of Hutcheson's teaching that Hume rejects when he distinguishes between the task of the anatomist and that of the painter. Hume's prominent use of fideistic language in his writings on religious topics was intended to remind the reader that the idea that philosophy might provide a foundation for religious belief was a relatively novel and controversial one. The intention, we may infer, was to discredit by whatever means possible the revolution in moral philosophy being engineered by Hutcheson, and so to imply a need for a return to the time when moral philosophy was one thing, and the teaching of natural religion another.

---

[19] See William Robert Scott, *Francis Hutcheson: His Life, Teaching, and Position in the History of Philosophy* (Cambridge: Cambridge University Press, 1900), 54–6. Hutcheson was elected to the chair of moral philosophy by a majority of just one vote.

[20] Francis Hutcheson, 'Inaugural lecture on the social nature of man', in *Francis Hutcheson: Two Texts on Human Nature*, ed. and trans. T. Mautner (Cambridge: Cambridge University Press, 1993), 147.

[21] See esp. Francis Hutcheson, *A System of Moral Philosophy* (London, 1755), 'The Preface, giving some Account of the Life, Writings, and Character of the Author', by William Leechman, i, pp. xxxii–iii. James Moore has argued that theodicy is more prominent in the *System of Moral Philosophy* than elsewhere in Hutcheson's writings: see 'Hutcheson's theodicy: the argument and the contexts of *A System of Moral Philosophy*', in P. Wood (ed.), *The Scottish Enlightenment: Essays in Reinterpretation* (Rochester, NY: University of Rochester Press, 2000), 239–66. I cannot argue the case here, but I think that theodicy is just as central to the texts of the 1720s.

It is time to move from stage-setting to particulars, and to a more detailed characterization of what I am claiming to be the Calvinist background of Hume's invocations of the language of fideism in the First *Enquiry*. Of special concern here, it will be remembered, are three moments in that book: the refusal to attempt a solution to the problem of evil at the end of Section 8, the characterization of faith itself as a miracle at the end of Section 10, and the claim made at the end of Section 12 that theology has its 'best and solid foundation' in '*faith* and divine revelation'. It should be noted that what follows is not, and should not be taken to be, the fruit of an exhaustive survey of the Scottish Calvinist tradition. There were surely distinctions made and differences developed within that tradition that go unremarked here. Nor is it being claimed that Hume himself read all, or indeed any, of the works quoted from below. It is improbable that Hume was a careful student of the Scottish theology of the post-Reformation period.[22] Hume never cites Scottish Calvinist texts, and the only time he quotes from a writer in order to support the claim that scepticism and religious belief are compatible, in the *Letter from a Gentleman*, the writer is the Catholic 'Monsieur *Huet* the learned Bishop of *Avaranches*' (p. 21). My purpose here is simply to identify affinities between the way in which Hume expresses himself at these three moments and the way Calvinists tended to express themselves when treating the same questions. It is unlikely that Hume chose to express himself in this way in ignorance of the resonances his language would have for his Scottish readership.

It is not necessary to spend a great deal of time demonstrating the echoes of Calvinism in Hume's remarks about the basis and nature of Christian faith in Sections 10 and 12. The idea that reason is no sure foundation for belief in God is ubiquitous in 'orthodox' Scottish Protestant theological texts. Robert Riccaltoun of Holkirk, for example, speaks for the mainstream Scottish Reformation tradition when he argues in the mid-eighteenth century that 'had mankind been left to themselves, they had never entertained a thought beyond the present state of things as they appear to our senses'.[23] Religion in lowland Scotland since the Reformation had been, in the main, a religion which followed Calvin in its estimation of faith, as opposed to works, as the supreme human achievement; and faith itself is in this tradition an act of Grace, something beyond what man is able to achieve for himself. The faculty of reason was not completely destroyed in the Fall, but what insight we have left, according to Calvin, 'is utterly blind and stupid in divine

---

[22] M. A. Stewart has pointed out to me, however, that the Hume family library did contain a collection of pamphlets concerning the controversy generated by John Simson, the Glasgow professor of divinity, in the late 1720s: see David Fate Norton and Mary Norton, *The David Hume Library* (Edinburgh: Edinburgh Bibliographical Society, 1996), 61.

[23] Robert Riccaltoun, *Works* (Edinburgh, 1771–2), iii. 185.

matters'.[24] 'The man who depends upon the light of nature', writes Calvin, 'comprehends nothing of God's spiritual mysteries.'[25] '[N]ature and reason are not onely unable to leade us to the true knowledge of God', according to John Knox, 'but also we affirme, that they have bene maistresses of all errors and idolatrie.'[26] In 1739 Archibald Campbell devoted *The Necessity of Revelation* to showing (in reply to Tindal) that 'mankind given up to themselves, and left wholly to their own industry to investigate the principles of religion from the nature and relations of things, are not able . . . to discern the immortality of the soul, or the being, the perfections, and providence of God'.[27] Again, when Hume says at the end of 'Of Miracles' that the honest man of faith 'is conscious of a continued miracle in his own person, which subverts all the principles of his understanding, and gives him a determination to believe what is most contrary to custom and experience', he is perfectly in accord with the spirit of Calvinism. What Hume has drawn attention to in the essay, in effect, is the fact that someone is deceiving himself who holds to the Bible as he holds to, say, what is told us about the Roman wars in Gaul by Julius Caesar. The faith that is the result of reading the Bible has another kind of ground altogether, and, as such, is available (in principle at least) to even the most untutored person, to the person who has made no study of, for example, the textual history of the Bible or the reliability of the purported witnesses of the events described in it. And this is something that the Calvinist not only allows, but insists upon. '[A]s God alone is a fit witness of himself in his Word', Calvin himself writes, 'so also the Word will not find acceptance in men's hearts before it is sealed by the inward testimony of Spirit.'[28] Scripture, according to Calvin, 'is its own authentication': 'it is not right to subject it to proof and reasoning'.[29]

There is, it cannot be denied, something plainly facetious in these passing invocations of the spirit of Calvinism. It is hard to imagine Hume being taken very seriously by anyone, least of all by the orthodox themselves, when he imitates the rhetoric of Calvinism in this way. Rather more significant, I shall now argue, is the use of Calvinist language at the close of 'Of Liberty and Necessity'. I believe that the closing paragraphs of Section 8 should be added to the evidence collected by Stewart to show that the First *Enquiry* was designed, at least in part, to be Hume's answer to Hutcheson, Leechman, Wishart, and company. For what Hume does in his treatment of the problem of evil is to juxtapose an argumentative strategy characteristic of the modernizing faction with the traditional Calvinist alternative, and to

---

[24] John Calvin, *Institutes of the Christian Religion*, trans. Ford Lewis Battles, ed. John T. McNeill (Philadelphia: Westminster Press, 1960), 278 (II. ii. 19).   [25] Ibid. 280 (II. ii. 20).

[26] John Knox, *Works*, ed. D. Laing (Edinburgh, 1846–64), v. 396–7.

[27] Archibald Campbell, *The Necessity of Revelation; or, An Inquiry into the Extent of Human Powers with respect to Matters of Religion* (London, 1739), 380.

[28] Calvin, *Institutes*, 78 (I. vii. 4).   [29] Ibid. 80 (I. vii. 5).

insinuate that intellectual honesty and a genuine commitment to truth are on the side of the Calvinists. To be more precise: Hume argues that the neo-Stoic solution to the problem, which amounts to an affirmation of the view that all evils, whether natural or moral, are in reality, and despite appearances, beneficial to the universe considered as a whole, is no more than a philosophical pipe-dream, a 'remote and uncertain' speculation which no human being can actually believe in. You can tell the man with gout or the victim of a crime that everything is for the best in this best of possible worlds—but he will not be able to believe you. Hume's point, here at least, is not that there is too much evil in the world for belief in providence to be rational.[30] It is, instead, that it is psychologically impossible for human beings to believe that any evil, no matter how limited in extent, is really a good. And this is because what an evil *is* is, simply, either physical pain or else something that bespeaks a moral character which is, in Hume's words, 'such as tend to public detriment and disturbance' (*Enquiry*, 103). There is, then, no possibility of solving the problem of evil as the modernizers sought to solve it, by arguing that, when seen from the right perspective, evil is not really evil at all. When one seeks, as Hutcheson says that he does, to analyse human sentiments and passions by means of attention to psychological reality, evil refuses to be explained away in this manner. Hume does not mention Hutcheson or any other contemporary by name here, but his contemptuous allusions to the doctrine that 'every thing is right with regard to the WHOLE' is fairly plainly directed at the proponents of the Stoic revival. Hutcheson (with the help of his colleague James Moor) had, after all, published his own translation of the *Meditations* of Marcus Aurelius in 1742.[31]

Hume's insistence on the reality of evil forces him on to the second horn of the dilemma he himself has raised for the defender of the doctrine of general providence. For if human actions really are criminal, and if human actions 'can be traced up, by a necessary chain, to the Deity', then, surely, 'we must retract the attribute of perfection, which we ascribe to the Deity, and must acknowledge him to be the ultimate author of guilt and moral turpitude in all his creatures' (*Enquiry*, 101). It is when faced with this conclusion that Hume adopts the language of fideism already quoted above. The usual interpretation of this move on Hume's part is to take him as hinting, broadly enough, that if religion has a problem with evil, then so much the worse for religion. And, as I have already admitted, this probably was Hume's own attitude to the problem. But what is interesting for present

---

[30] This is, however, Philo's point in Parts X and XI of the *Dialogues*; and also the Epicurean's in Section 11 of the First *Enquiry*, 138–9.

[31] For Hutcheson and Stoicism, and Hume and scepticism, see M. A. Stewart, 'The Stoic legacy in the early Scottish Enlightenment', in Margaret J. Osler (ed.), *Atoms, 'Pneuma', and Tranquillity: Epicurean and Stoic Themes in European Thought* (Cambridge: Cambridge University Press, 1991), 273–96.

purposes is that Hume has the weight of the Calvinist tradition behind him when he claims that the difficulties raised by the problem of evil are such as to evade solution by mere philosophy. It is in fact a central claim of the Christianity of the Calvinist tradition that human reason is unable to fathom how men can be at once predestined to sin and themselves wholly responsible for their sin. Not for Calvin the position that God permits, but does not ordain, moral evils; nor does Calvin accept a distinction between two divine wills, one of law, one of providence. God himself hardens the heart of the sinner. And yet, Calvin continues, 'We have . . . no reason to complain except against ourselves': 'man's ruin is to be ascribed to man alone'.[32] That we are responsible for our sins, conscience cannot deny, even though reason cannot make sense of its being true. The pains and terrors of a guilty conscience silence the objections of reason. Calvinist Scots repeatedly affirm the incomprehensibility of divine justice. Predestination to damnation may seem hard to square with the perfection of God; but, says Knox, if men 'enteryng within themself, do but in parte consider what is their natural condition, what is their ignorance', their objections will cease: the origin of evil 'doth everie wicked man so fynd within himself, that his owne conscience shall convict him, that no where elles is the cause of his iniquitie . . . to be soght, but onely within himself, and as proceeding of himself by instigation of the Devill, into whose power he is delivered . . . by the inscrutable and incomprehensible (but yet most just) judgementes of God'.[33] 'Our consciences condemn us, and so acquit the Deity,' writes Halyburton in his *Natural Religion Insufficient* of 1714. 'But without revelation, we can never understand upon what grounds we are condemned by ourselves, nor how the Deity is to be justified; and so this sentence of our conscience involves the matter more and increases the difficulty.'[34] As Hume would surely have known, there is nothing intrinsically irreligious in admitting that evil presents a problem 'which mere natural and unassisted reason is very unfit to handle'.

It is perhaps worth emphasizing the prominence of the 'all for the best' scheme in the writings of those in favour of the renovation of religion in Scotland. In the fashion of Shaftesbury, Leibniz, and Pope, these writers postulated an all-embracing scheme of providence in which what we call evil has a necessary place. This was not exactly to deny that evil exists, but it was to redefine evil as something which God himself brings into being, as part of a scheme the perfection of which we human beings, from our limited perspective, cannot hope properly to understand. Evil is no longer conceived as a negation or rejection of God, but is rendered comparable to, say, the

---

[32] Calvin, *Institutes*, 254 (II. i. 10). [33] Knox, *Works*, v. 350–1.
[34] Thomas Halyburton, *Natural Religion Insufficient; and Reveal'd Necessary to Man's Happiness in his Present State: or, a Rational Inquiry into the Principles of the Modern Deists* (Edinburgh, 1714), 114.

shadows necessary to the bringing out of the beauty of a landscape. Asks
Hutcheson: 'May not many natural Evils be necessary to prevent future
moral Evils, and to correct the Tempers of Agents, nay to introduce moral
Good?'[35] And again: 'Can there be *Forgiveness, Returns of good for evil*,
unless there be some *moral Evil*?'; 'May not all the present Disorders which
attend this state of *prevalent Order*, be rectified by the *directing Providence*
in a future Part of our existence?'[36] Similarly, George Turnbull argues 'that
many of the evils complained of in human life, moral as well as natural, are,
in the nature of things, necessary, absolutely necessary to many goods, without which human life could have no distinguishing excellence, nor indeed
any considerable happiness'.[37] William Dudgeon, too, affirms that 'there
can be nothing evil with respect to the whole creation': '[r]ight and wrong,
good and evil, are relative terms'.[38] And the same claim is made at the end
of Kames's *Essays on the Principles of Morality and Natural Religion*: there
Kames attempts 'to show, that pain and distress are productive of manifold
good ends, and the present system could not be without them'; and that 'All
our actions contribute equally to carry on the great and good designs of
Providence; and, therefore, there is nothing which in [God's] sight is evil; at
least, nothing which is evil upon the whole'.[39] Here we have a variety of
writers with a variety of agendas, but all seek to replace the Calvinist picture
of a mysterious God exercising his providence through predestination and
unpredictable, and undeserved, donations of grace with an intelligible,
law-governed, and, above all, benevolent scheme in which everything, evil
included, has a comprehensible place. The overriding objective was to
construct a metaphysical environment, so to speak, in which virtue in all its
forms might be regarded as *natural*, as simply part of the divinely ordained
fabric of the universe. Teaching and preaching could then be dedicated to
cultivating this natural virtue. It would no longer be necessary to look
directly to God for means of overcoming evil, since evil had been redefined
as merely a necessary means of maximizing goodness.

Hume, by contrast, regards it as a disaster for serious investigation of moral
subjects that the starting-point of philosophy be such sublime reflections as
these. The danger—amply demonstrated, Hume hints in his correspondence
with Hutcheson, in Hutcheson's own moral philosophy—is that teleology will
be reintroduced into the science of the mind: that ends will first be postulated,
and then the data distorted so as to 'prove' that the faculties of the mind serve

[35] Francis Hutcheson, *An Essay on the Nature and Conduct of the Passions and Affections, with Illustrations on the Moral Sense*, ed. A. Garrett (Indianapolis: Liberty Fund, 2002), 123.
[36] Ibid.
[37] George Turnbull, *The Principles of Moral Philosophy: An Enquiry into the Wise and Good Government of the Moral World* (London, 1740), ii. 329.
[38] William Dudgeon, *The Philosophical Works* (n. p., 1765), 220.
[39] [Henry Home, later Lord Kames], *Essays on the Principles of Morality and Natural Religion* (London, 1751), 370, 377.

those ends. Hume's primary purpose in the First *Enquiry* is to vindicate a style of philosophy different from the 'easy philosophy' that restricts its ambitions to the cultivation of virtue, and that fails to examine properly what the nature and basis of virtue are. The traditionalist wing of the Church of Scotland might have had no interest in Humean 'anatomy', but they shared Hume's antipathy to speculative and ill-grounded meditations of the neo-Stoic variety. In particular, they disliked the new view of divine providence, and the easy-going confidence in human abilities that went with it. This is especially clear in John Witherspoon's parody of the newly formed 'Moderate Party' in his *Ecclesiastical Characteristics* of 1754. Witherspoon includes in his pamphlet an 'Athenian Creed' (as distinct from the Athanasian Creed), which contains a declaration of belief 'that there is no ill in the universe, nor any such thing as virtue absolutely considered; that those things vulgarly called *sins*, are only errors in the judgment, and foils to set off the beauty of Nature, or patches to adorn her face; that the whole race of intelligent beings, even the devils themselves (if there are any), shall finally be happy; so that Judas Iscariot is by this time a glorified saint, and it is good for him that he hath been born'.[40] The *Ecclesiastical Characteristics* gives the 'all for the best' scheme a central place in the new order of things. Its sixth maxim is that 'It is not only unnecessary for a moderate man to have much learning, but he ought to be filled with a contempt of all kinds of learning but one, which is to understand Leibnitz's scheme well; the chief parts of which are so beautifully painted, and so harmoniously sung by Lord Shaftsbury, and which has been so well licked into form and method, by the late immortal Mr. H[utcheso]n'.[41] Witherspoon is no Bayle or Voltaire, but his satire has the virtue of making apparent the ways in which Hutcheson, Leechman, and their like offended the sensibilities of Calvinist traditionalists. In the process it shows that it was not necessarily a sign of scepticism about religion to reject the 'all for the best' scheme. The way in which Hume dismisses that scheme in 'Of Liberty and Necessity' is designed, I am suggesting, to contrast neo-Stoic *naïveté* with realism about the intractability of the problem of evil that he wants us to recognize as common ground between him and the Calvinist tradition. The point is not to masquerade as a Calvinist, but rather to emphasize the superficiality of the new philosophy.[42]

---

[40] [John Witherspoon], *Ecclesiastical Characteristics: or, the Arcana of Church Policy: Being an Attempt to open up the Mystery of Moderation*, 2nd edn. (Glasgow, 1754), 27.

[41] Ibid., 23.

[42] It is important to distinguish the Hutcheson–Leechman–Wishart axis of the 1740s, on the one hand, from the 'Moderate Party', on the other. Allegiances and agendas are changing rapidly by the mid-century. The Moderate Party is in many important respects a creation of the 1750s, and several of its members were friends of Hume's. One of the Party's first concerted actions was to defend Hume from the attempt on the part of the opposing 'Orthodox' or 'Highflying' or 'Popular' party to excommunicate him (and Kames) in 1755–6. Nevertheless, and as Witherspoon's pamphlet suggests, the philosophical-theological agenda of the early Scottish Enlightenment is taken up by the Moderates. See also Richard Sher, *Church and University in the Scottish Enlightenment: The Moderate Literati of Edinburgh* (Edinburgh: Edinburgh University Press, 1985), 175–86.

It was, in fact, not long before Hume's scepticism about the capacities of the understanding to solve deep metaphysical and theological problems was taken up by people whom no one could possibly accuse of being ironical. Thus the Common Sense philosopher James Oswald, as moderator of the General Assembly of the Church of Scotland in 1766 a scourge of the Moderate Party,[43] endorses Hume's criticism of the argument from design: 'for it will not be denied that the universe is a singularity that cannot be reduced to any genus with which we are acquainted; and, therefore, that we have not access to reason from works of art to the foundation of the universe, as we draw inferences from one species with which we are acquainted, to another which belongs to the same genus'.[44] And Oswald's recognition of the affinity of Humean scepticism with the anti-rationalism of the Calvinist tradition became more general with the 1805 controversy over the election of John Leslie to the Chair of Natural Philosophy at Edinburgh.[45] In a trial of strength between the leaders of the Moderate Party and the town council, an attempt was staged by some of the Moderates to block Leslie's candidacy with a trumped-up charge of atheism. The ground of the charge was a footnote in Leslie's *Experimental Inquiry into the Nature and Propagation of Heat*, in which he endorses Hume's treatment of the relation of cause and effect, and claims that 'The unsophisticated sentiments of mankind are in perfect union with the deductions of logic, and imply nothing more at bottom, in the relation of cause and effect, than a *constant and invariable sequence.*'[46] Both Dugald Stewart and Thomas Brown laboured, albeit in different ways, to show that there was nothing dangerous in the Humean theory. More significant for the purposes of this paper is the fact that a host of 'orthodox' opponents of Moderatism joined them, at least one arguing that Hume's attack on human reason is a proper reminder of the primacy of Revelation in religion. An anonymous pamphlet claims that Leslie has every right 'to discard all the ordinary framework of natural religion, and assert at the same time, his claim to the character of a sound theist': 'Many divines, to whom no one ever dreamed of attributing atheism, have maintained, that all the arguments which we derive from the light of nature to prove either the being or the providence of God, are either of a very inferior kind, or altogether inconclusive; and that

---

[43] See Richard Sher, *Church and University in the Scottish Enlightenment: The Moderate Literati of Edinburgh* (Edinburgh: Edinburgh University Press, 1985), 132.

[44] James Oswald, *An Appeal to Common Sense in Behalf of Religion* (Edinburgh, 1766–72), ii. 64–5.

[45] For an account of the affair, see Ian D. L. Clark, 'The Leslie controversy, 1805', *Records of the Scottish Church History Society*, 14 (1963): 179–97.

[46] John Leslie, *An Experimental Inquiry into the Nature and Propagation of Heat* (Edinburgh, 1804), 521–8 n. 16.

revelation, and revelation alone, is the grand source of all religious know-ledge.'[47] Admittedly, two of the examples the writer gives are unexpected: the Dutch Arminian 'Philip Limborch' and 'Faustus Socinus', who was usually represented by Calvinists as an arch-rationalist of the most dangerous kind. The third example given is Robert Riccaltoun, already cited above. The Leslie affair saw the first serious defeat sustained by the Moderates for decades, and attacks in the spirit of Hume on the over-estimation of natural religion grow increasingly common as the evangelical revival of the nineteenth century gathers steam.

The old view of Hume—presented most dramatically in Mossner's biography[48]—as leading an assault on the part of the Scottish forces of 'Enlightenment' against Calvinist bigotry now appears unduly simplistic. Its major flaw is that it neglects the fact that there were significant differ-ences of opinion separating Hume, on the one hand, and possibly also Smith, from other figures of the Scottish Enlightenment.[49] Hume's principal opponents, in the 1740s at least, did not come from the ranks of the 'orthodox', but were rather the forebears of the 'moderate literati' who dominated Scottish intellectual life during the second half of the eighteenth century. From the point of view of Francis Hutcheson and others with the same ambitions, Hume stood in the way of a new synthesis of moral philosophy and religion, a synthesis that would help to bring Scotland into the modern world by emphasizing active personal and political virtue (as opposed to an introspective and fragile experience of grace) as the mark of the genuine Christian. Or, at least, Hume would have stood in the way of that synthesis had he been charged with the teaching of moral philosophy in Scotland's capital city. The mainstream Scottish Enlightenment was from the first a practical movement dedicated to improvement and progress. By contrast, Hume's was the elevated and detached perspective of the observer of human affairs and of human weaknesses. Improvement and progress, from his point of view, were always unintended and accidental—and fragile and reversible as well. Hume's influence needed to be minimized, therefore, and this was why he ended up, eventually, as a librarian rather than a professor of philosophy. Hume's reaction to the concerted efforts of Hutcheson and company to keep him out of a position of importance was to do his best, first, to explain better the nature of his philosophical project,

---

[47] [Anon.], *A Letter to the Reverend Principal Hill on the case of Mr. John Leslie, Professor of Mathematics in the University of Edinburgh* (Edinburgh, 1805), 97–8.

[48] See Ernest Campbell Mossner, *The Life of David Hume*, 2nd edn. (Oxford: Clarendon Press, 1980), *passim*.

[49] See the papers by Stewart cited above; and also work by James Moore on the relationship between Hume and Hutcheson: e.g. and esp. 'Hume and Hutcheson', in Stewart and Wright (eds.), *Hume and Hume's Connexions*, 23–57.

and, secondly, to discredit the rather different project of his opponents. The suggestion made here has been that one of the ways in which Hume sought to insinuate the failings of the rival project was to hint at the affinities between his own scepticism and the hesitancy about the capacities of human reason characteristic of the Scottish post-Reformation theological tradition, thereby to highlight the superficiality of brash new fashions of thought.

The reader of Hume who wants an answer to the question of what Hume's own views really were about religious matters will have only been frustrated by what has been argued here. As I hope to have made quite clear, the title of this paper is not meant to imply that Hume himself was, deep down, and despite appearances, a Christian of the Calvinist variety. In fact, it seems to me that to use Hume's texts in order to attempt to characterize Hume's personal attitude towards religion is quite pointless. The interest of the *Dialogues Concerning Natural Religion*, for instance, is plainly not limited to working out which of the interlocutors 'speaks for Hume'. The same goes for the dialogue presented in Section 11 of the First *Enquiry*. When writing on religious issues, even if not using the dialogue form, Hume's arrangements are always polyphonic, and the best thing to say is probably that in every case all the voices are Hume's own. At any rate, a brief survey of the various hypotheses that have been proposed as to what Hume's 'real' views were should suffice to make anyone extremely wary of committing himself in this connection. Thus in his own lifetime Hume, as has already been mentioned, was popularly supposed to be an atheist; yet Hume's first biographer, Thomas Ritchie, says that the *Natural History of Religion* and the *Dialogues* are 'favourable to deism'.[50] A later biographer, John Hill Burton, claims that it is with Cleanthes, and not Philo, that the author of the *Dialogues* 'shows most sympathy'.[51] Thomas Henry Huxley wrote of Hume's 'shadowy inconsistent theism',[52] and Terence Penelhum has recently endorsed Huxley's judgment.[53] H. O. Mounce declares that 'The evidence is overwhelming that Hume never rid himself of his belief in God.'[54] The truth, however, is that Hume's texts, taken by themselves and independently of received opinions and familiar anecdotes, cannot settle the matter. The right question to ask is not what Hume privately thought, but why he chose to express himself as he did. This paper is intended to provide part of an answer to that question.

---

[50] Thomas Ritchie, *An Account of the Life and Writings of David Hume, Esq.* (London, 1807), 330.

[51] John H. Burton, *Life and Correspondence of David Hume* (Edinburgh, 1846), ii. 329–31.

[52] Thomas Henry Huxley, *Hume* (London: Macmillan, 1879), 156–7.

[53] In a paper on Huxley's book on Hume, given at the 29th Hume Society Conference in Helsinki in August 2002.

[54] H. O. Mounce, *Hume's Naturalism* (London: Routledge, 1999), 14.

REFERENCES

Primary Sources

[Anon.], *A Letter to the Reverend Principal Hill on the case of Mr. John Leslie, Professor of Mathematics in the University of Edinburgh* (Edinburgh, 1805).

Calvin, John, *Institutes of the Christian Religion*, trans. Ford Lewis Battles, ed. John T. McNeill (Philadelphia: Westminster Press, 1960).

Campbell, Archibald, *The Necessity of Revelation; or, An Inquiry into the Extent of Human Powers with respect to Matters of Religion* (London, 1739).

Dudgeon, William, *The Philosophical Works* (n. p., 1765).

Halyburton, Thomas, *Natural Religion Insufficient; and Reveal'd Necessary to Man's Happiness in his Present State: or, a Rational Inquiry into the Principles of the Modern Deists* (Edinburgh, 1714).

[Home, Henry, later Lord Kames], *Essays on the Principles of Morality and Natural Religion* (London, 1751).

Hume, David, *A Letter from a Gentleman to his Friend in Edinburgh*, ed. E. C. Mossner and J. V. Price (Edinburgh: Edinburgh University Press, 1967).

—— *Essays Moral, Political, and Literary*, ed. Eugene F. Miller, rev. edn. (Indianapolis: Liberty Classics, 1987).

—— *Dialogues Concerning Natural Religion and the Natural History of Religion*, ed. J. C. A. Gaskin (Oxford: Oxford University Press, 1993).

—— *An Enquiry Concerning Human Understanding*, ed. L. A. Selby-Bigge, 3rd edn., rev. P. H. Nidditch (Oxford: Clarendon Press, 1975).

Hutcheson, Francis, *A System of Moral Philosophy* (London, 1755).

—— 'Inaugural lecture on the social nature of man', in *Francis Hutcheson: Two Texts on Human Nature*, ed. T. Mautner (Cambridge: Cambridge University Press, 1993).

—— *An Essay on the Nature and Conduct of the Passions and Affections, with Illustrations on the Moral Sense*, ed. A. Garrett (Indianapolis: Liberty Fund, 2002).

Knox, John, *Works*, ed. D. Laing, 6 vols. (Edinburgh, 1846–64).

Leslie, John, *An Experimental Inquiry into the Nature and Propagation of Heat* (Edinburgh, 1804).

Montaigne, Michel de, *The Complete Essays*, ed. M. A. Screech (Harmondsworth: Penguin, 1991).

Oswald, James, *An Appeal to Common Sense in Behalf of Religion*, 2 vols. (Edinburgh, 1766–72).

Riccaltoun, Robert, *Works*, 2 vols. (Edinburgh, 1771–2).

Ritchie, Thomas, *An Account of the Life and Writings of David Hume, Esq.* (London, 1807).

Turnbull, George, *The Principles of Moral Philosophy: An Enquiry into the Wise and Good Government of the Moral World* (London, 1740).

[Witherspoon, John], *Ecclesiastical Characteristics: or, the Arcana of Church Policy: Being an Attempt to open up the Mystery of Moderation*, 2nd edn. (Glasgow, 1754).

Secondary Sources

Berman, David, 'Deism, immortality, and the art of theological lying', in J. A. Leo Lemay (ed.), *Deism, Masonry, and the Enlightenment* (Newark: University of Delaware Press, 1987), 61–78.

Botterill, George, 'Hume on liberty and necessity', in P. Millican (ed.), *Reading Hume on Human Understanding* (Oxford: Oxford University Press, 2002), 277–300.

Buckle, Stephen, *Hume's Enlightenment Tract: The Unity and Purpose of* An Enquiry Concerning Human Understanding (Oxford: Clarendon Press, 2001).

Burton, John H., *Life and Correspondence of David Hume*, 2 vols. (Edinburgh: William Tait, 1846).

Clark, Ian D. L., 'The Leslie controversy, 1805', *Records of the Scottish Church History Society*, 14 (1963): 179–97.

—— 'From protest to reaction: the moderate regime in the Church of Scotland', in N. T. Phillipson and R. Mitchison (eds.), *Scotland in the Age of Improvement* (Edinburgh: Edinburgh University Press, 1970), 200–24.

Emerson, Roger, 'The "affair" at Edinburgh and the "project" at Glasgow', in M. A. Stewart and J. P. Wright (eds.), *Hume and Hume's Connexions*, (Edinburgh: Edinburgh University Press, 1994), 1–22.

Flew, Antony, *Hume's Philosophy of Belief* (London: Routledge, 1961).

Huxley, Thomas Henry, *Hume* (London: Macmillan, 1879).

Mackie, J. L., *The Miracle of Theism* (Oxford: Oxford University Press, 1982).

Moore, James, 'Hume and Hutcheson' in M. A. Stewart and J. P. Wright (eds.), *Hume and Hume's Connexions* (Edinburgh: Edinburgh University Press, 1994), 23–57.

—— 'Hutcheson's theodicy: the argument and the contexts of *A System of Moral Philosophy*', in P. Wood (ed.), *The Scottish Enlightenment: Essays in Reinterpretation*, (Rochester, NY: University of Rochester Press, 2000), 239–66.

Mossner, Ernest C., *The Life of David Hume*, 2nd edn. (Oxford: Clarendon Press, 1980).

Mounce, H. O., *Hume's Naturalism* (London: Routledge, 1999).

Norton, David Fate, and Norton, Mary, *The David Hume Library* (Edinburgh: Edinburgh Bibliographical Society, 1996).

Scott, William Robert, *Francis Hutcheson: His Life, Teaching, and Position in the History of Philosophy* (Cambridge: Cambridge University Press, 1900).

Sher, Richard, B., *Church and University in the Scottish Enlightenment: The Moderate Literati of Edinburgh* (Edinburgh: Edinburgh University Press, 1985).

Stewart, M. A., 'The Stoic legacy in the early Scottish Enlightenment', in Margaret J. Osler (ed.), *Atoms, 'Pneuma', and Tranquillity* (Cambridge: Cambridge University Press, 1991), 273–96.

—— *The Kirk and the Infidel* (Lancaster: Lancaster University, 1995).

—— 'Two species of philosophy: the historical significance of the First *Enquiry*', in Peter Millican (ed.), *Reading Hume on Human Understanding* (Oxford: Clarendon Press, 2001), 67–95.

—— 'Religion and rational theology', in A. Broadie (ed.), *The Cambridge Companion to the Scottish Enlightenment* (Cambridge: Cambridge University Press, 2003), 31–59.

Quixotic Confusions and Hume's Imagination

MARINA FRASCA-SPADA

———•———

> It is a poor idea of fantasy which takes it to be a world apart from reality, a world clearly showing its unreality. Fantasy is precisely what reality can be confused with.
>
> Stanley Cavell, *The World Viewed*

In his *Dictionary*, under the entry 'Author', Samuel Johnson lists four definitions: (1) 'The first beginner or mover of any thing; he to whom any thing owes its original'; (2) 'The efficient; he that affects or produces any thing'; (3) 'The first writer of any thing; distinguished from the *translator* or *compiler*'; (4) 'a writer in general'. This wondrous progression from Heaven to Grub Street, backed with a variety of examples from Shakespeare, Milton, Dryden, Newton, the Bible, etc., reminds us once again how self-conscious eighteenth century 'authors' were.[1] Their egotism found its most typical expressions in the relationship they establish with their readers, and in their attitude towards the demarcation between reality and fantasy. Richardson, for example, was explicit on the special kind of attitude to reality at the basis of his relationship with his books and their readers.[2] As he put it in a letter to Warburton, who, in the preface he had prepared for *Clarissa*, acknowledged openly the fictional character of the work,

Will you, good Sir, allow me to mention, that I could wish that the *Air* of Genuiness [*sic*] had been kept up, tho' I want not the Letters to be *thought* genuine; only so far kept up, I mean, as that they should not prefatically be

I am grateful to Claire Davis, Silvia De Renzi, Anne Goldgar, Nick Jardine, Adrian Johns, Martin Kusch, Peter Lipton, Anne Secord, Jim Secord, Emma Spary, Wayne Waxman and Paul White for their encouragement, comments, and advice.

[1] Samuel Johnson, *A Dictionary of the English Language* (London, 1755).

[2] For a classic discussion of this see A. Hauser, *The Social History of Art*, 4 vols. (London: Routledge and Kegan Paul, 1962; 1st edn. 1951), iii. 65–6; on the boundary between reality and fantasy in Sterne see also J. Habermas, *The Structural Transformation of the Public Sphere: An Inquiry into a Category of Bourgeois Society*, trans. T. Burger with the assistance of F. Lawrence, 2nd edn. (Cambridge: Polity, 1989), 50.

owned *not* to be genuine: and this for fear of weakening their Influence where any of them are aimed to be exemplary; as well as to avoid hurting that kind of Historical Faith which Fiction itself is generally read with, tho' we know it to be Fiction.[3]

The differences and relations between history and fiction, and, more generally, the distinction between matter of fact and falsehood, and the balance of the plausible and the marvellous in historical (including natural-historical, medical, etc.) and fictional writings constitute a central concern for eighteenth-century authors and readers.[4] The subject of this article, very aptly summarized by the Cavell epigraph, is the difference between reading history and reading fiction, between the parts played by reality and fantasy in the enjoyment of reading, as eighteenth-century authors conceived of it on behalf of their readers. In particular, I focus on the ways readers' perceptions and sympathetic responses to historical and fictional writings were reflected on—described, explained, mocked, satirized—in an eighteenth-century novel, Charlotte Lennox's *The Female Quixote* of 1752, and in a contemporary abstract study of human perceptions and passions, David Hume's *Treatise of Human Nature*, of 1739–40.[5]

These nearly contemporary books make an odd pair, and reading them against each other requires justification. *The Female Quixote* was the work of a good, mid-ranking London author who was on friendly terms with Dr Johnson and Richardson. The novel, published in two 12mo volumes for Andrew Millar, was reasonably successful, being republished five times during Lennox's lifetime (2nd edn. July 1752; Dublin 1752 and 1763, London 1783 and 1799); and it is well known that it was a favourite of Jane Austen's. Today it is regarded as readable enough to be currently available in a popular format, among the Oxford Classics. When it was published in 1739–40, Hume's *Treatise* was the abstruse and pretentious metaphysics book of a young Scottish projector, and appeared in a second edition only in 1817.[6]

---

[3] Letter of 19 April 1748, cited in A. D. McKillop, *The Early Masters of English Fiction* (Lawrence, Kan.: University of Kansas Press, 1956), 42 and n. 44 (from the *Catalogue of American Art Association*, sale of 18/19 March 1925).

[4] See R. Mayer, *History and the Early English Novel: Matters of Fact from Bacon to Defoe* (Cambridge: Cambridge University Press, 1997), e.g. 3–4, 227–39.

[5] C. R. Lennox, *The Female Quixote*, ed. M. Dalziel, with an Introduction by M. A. Doody (Oxford and New York: Oxford University Press, 1989); Hume, *A Treatise of Human Nature*, ed. L. A. Selby-Bigge, 2nd edn., rev. P. H. Nidditch (Oxford: Clarendon Press, 1978).

[6] On the early reception of Hume's *Treatise* see E. C. Mossner, 'The continental reception of Hume's *Treatise*, 1739–1741', *Mind*, 45 (1947): 31–43; *idem*, 'The first answer to Hume's *Treatise*: an unnoticed item of 1740', *Journal of the History of Ideas*, 12 (1951): 291–4; *idem*, *The Life of David Hume* (Edinburgh: Nelson, 1954), 116 ff. Well-known early responses to the *Treatise* in books stretch from the not unfriendly, but uncomprehending, remarks of Henry Home (*Essays on the Principles of Morality and Natural Religion* (Edinburgh, 1751)), to the open hostility of James Beattie (*Essay on Truth* (Edinburgh, 1770)).

After a most unpromising start, it ended up a classic with a vengeance, in the canon of a surprising variety of philosophical traditions.[7]

As a consequence of its canonical status, when we read Hume's *Treatise* now, we are not likely to react to it with that mixture of puzzlement, curiosity, and open-minded expectation commonly aroused by past or alien products. We relate to it in a more direct way, because this book is now an essential part of our own, let us call it, philosophical instinct; and it is still possible to talk about Hume, and to respond to his work as if he were a living philosopher. Here I intend to consider this philosophy classic as part of a past culture, the eighteenth-century culture of feeling, and to show how, when Hume was writing his *Treatise*, the investigation of such matters as our perceptions and beliefs constituted—as Hume himself, among others, called it—a 'science of human nature', or 'science of man': a study associated with natural history, with medicine, with history, and with the 'polite' and 'conversable' sympathetic interest in other people, as well as with metaphysics and moral philosophy.[8]

In this respect, another eighteenth-century projector—Arabella, the female Quixote—will help us to read Hume's book: for, as I intend to show, she and Hume speak the same language and talk about the same things. This in turn may be of interest to philosophers too, if philosophy can be regarded, as Cavell again puts it, as a 'natural extension of conversation' and, more specifically, as 'a willingness to think not about something other than what ordinary human beings think about, but rather to learn to think undistractedly about things that ordinary human beings cannot help thinking about, or anyway cannot help having occur to them'.[9]

In the pages that follow, I organize my discussion in the form of a textual commentary, each section being focused on one or two passages either from Lennox or from Hume.

---

[7] For positivistic appropriations, see e.g. F. Zabeeh, *Hume, Precursor of Modern Empiricism*, 2nd edn. (The Hague: Martinus Nijoff, 1973), and D. F. Pears (ed.), *David Hume: A Symposium* (London: Macmillan 1963). For a history of the reception of Hume among the phenomenologists see G. Davie, *A Passion for Ideas: Essays on the Scottish Enlightenment* (Edinburgh: Polygon, 1994), ii. 7–8, and R. T. Murphy, *Hume and Husserl: Towards Radical Subjectivism* (The Hague: Martinus Nijoff, 1980), esp. the Introduction. And for the interest aroused more recently in deconstructionists and post-moderns, see Z. Parusnikova, 'Hume and post-modernism', *Hume Studies*, 19/2 (1993): 1–17. A striking and very influential 'continental' interpretation of Hume's philosophy is that of Gilles Deleuze in his *Empiricism and Subjectivity: An Essay on Hume's Theory of Human Nature* (1953), trans. C. V. Boundas (New York: Columbia University Press, 1991), on which see Martin Bell's article in this volume.

[8] See M. Frasca-Spada, 'The science and conversation of human nature', in W. Clark, J. Golinski, and S. Schaffer (eds.), *The Sciences in Enlightened Europe* (Chicago: University of Chicago Press, 2000), 218–45.

[9] S. Cavell, *Pursuits of Happiness: The Hollywood Comedy of Remarriage* (Cambridge, Mass.: Harvard University Press, 1981), 7, and *idem*, 'The thought of movies', in *Themes out of School: Effects and Causes* (Chicago and London: University of Chicago Press, 1988), 3–26, at p. 9.

BOOKS, HISTORY, AND BELIEF

It may be useful to begin by introducing the way in which the 'science of human nature' accounts for a reader's perceptions and beliefs. For this purpose, let us consider a page of Hume's *Treatise* on the nature of a reader's belief in a historical event narrated in a book. The context is the most famous part of Hume's philosophy: namely, his discussion of the idea of cause and effect.

In a nutshell, according to Hume we do not perceive—see, touch, etc.— any power or connection linking causes and effects: what we experience is, in fact, no more than sequences of conjoined events; so, for all we can tell, the sequences we call causal need not be sequences of connected events. Thus far, Hume is talking what a philosopher nowadays would call epistemology. The next steps of his discussion go further and further in a direction which philosophers tend to regard as psychological.[10] He remarks that, in spite of our inability to perceive it, we do believe that there is a connection linking cause and effect. Why? This belief, he says, is based on our habit to see a certain kind of event, which we call the cause, always followed by a certain other kind of event, which we call the effect of that cause. Experiencing a constant conjunction gives rise to a habit, and this produces the expectation that a certain cause will, as usual, be followed by a certain effect. In turn, the expectation consists simply in the particular way in which, as soon as we see the cause, we form the idea of the effect to follow: belief is the particularly strong, vivacious, firm, etc. 'manner' in which we conceive the idea. When we have the sense impression of the cause, we conceive a strong and vivacious idea of the effect with which it is habitually associated, because, Hume says, part of the force and vivacity of the sense impression of the cause is transferred to the idea of the effect.[11]

In thus anticipating the future with our expectation of a certain effect, our mind does not, in fact, take off in a flight of fancy. Quite the opposite: even though it is going beyond anything which is either present to our senses or

[10] This is indeed a standard way regarding Hume's discussion of belief and expectation. For a classic specimen of this interpretation see, e.g., A. J. Ayer, *Hume* (Oxford: Oxford University Press, 1980).

[11] See Hume, *Treatise*, 95–7 and 628–9. I discuss in more detail Hume's use of the force and vivacity terminology in connection both with impressions (as opposed to ideas) and with belief in 'Hume on sense impressions and objects', in M. Heidelberger and D. Stadler (eds.), *History of Philosophy of Science: New Trends and Perspectives*, Vienna Circle Institute Yearbook, 9/2001 (Dordrecht and London: Kluwer Academic Publishers, 2002), 13–24; and also in 'Belief and animal spirits in Hume's *Treatise*', *Eighteenth-Century Thought*, 1 (2003): 151–69. For an excellent treatment of belief in connection with the idea of cause and effect see A. Baier, *A Progress of Sentiments: Reflections on Hume's* Treatise (Cambridge, Mass., and London: Harvard University Press, 1991), 69–77; on the difficulties of Hume's theory of belief and its various interpretations see M. M. Gorman, 'Hume's theory of belief', *Hume Studies*, 10/1 (1993): 89–101.

remembered, the mind still must refer to a direct perception, that is, to an impression present or past. As Hume puts it, 'Tho' the mind in its reasonings from causes or effects carries its view beyond those objects, which it sees or remembers, it must never lose sight of them entirely, nor reason merely upon its own ideas, without some mixture of impressions' (*Treatise*, 82); the 'mixture of impressions' from the present and the past is indispensable for us to conceive and form our beliefs about the future.

Even though it is of paramount importance, this reference to an actual or remembered impression need not be immediate. In fact, it may be at the end of quite a long chain of argument: the cause itself may be either immediately perceived, or inferred from its own cause, and so on, until we reach a cause which is present to our senses or memory. It is to illustrate this point that Hume briefly considers our belief in historical matters. In particular, he mentions the assassination of Julius Caesar:

> To give an instance of this, we may chuse any point of history, and consider for what reason we either believe or reject it. Thus we believe that CÆSAR was kill'd in the senate-house on the *ides* of *March*; and that because this fact is establish'd on the unanimous testimony of historians, who agree to assign this precise time and place to that event. Here are certain characters and letters present either to our memory or senses; which characters we likewise remember to have been us'd as the signs of certain ideas; and these ideas were either in the minds of such as were immediately present at that action, and receiv'd the ideas directly from its existence; or they were deriv'd from the testimony of others, and that again from another testimony, by a visible gradation, 'till we arrive at those who were eye-witnesses and spectators of the event. 'Tis obvious all this chain of argument or connexion of causes and effects, is at first founded on those characters and letters, which are seen or remember'd, and that without the authority either of the memory or senses our whole reasoning wou'd be chimerical and without foundation. Every link of the chain wou'd in that case hang upon another; but there wou'd not be any thing fix'd to one end of it, capable of sustaining the whole; and consequently there would be no belief nor evidence. (Ibid. 83)

So, Hume first establishes that we believe in the historical fact of Caesar's death because this is 'establish'd on the unanimous testimony of historians': we know that historians agree on this—that is, we know something about history as an established body of knowledge. Then he shows that this knowledge involves reference to the 'chain of argument or connexion of causes and effects' underpinning our trust in the truthfulness of reports. It also involves our knowing how to read, our reading about this fact in this book, and our seeing this particular printed page. The sight of the printed page here has the crucial role of providing the emotional raw material, so to speak, of belief: the force or vivacity of conception. Our belief in the event of Caesar's assassination—that is, the specially strong and vivacious manner in which we conceive it—depends on the force and vivacity of the sense impressions that we, as readers, have of the characters on the page of our history book. It is based on a transference of emotional force and vivacity from the present impression of black signs on white paper to the idea of knives in the hero's flesh—the connection between them being guaranteed by the long tradition of reports and records whose existence is conceived as an integral part of the historical fact itself.[12]

There is, however, a problem with this theory: namely, that generally the longer the chain between the original sense impression and the believed idea, the feebler the resulting belief: ''Tis certain', Hume observes, 'that when an inference is drawn immediately from an object, without any intermediate cause or effect, the conviction is much stronger, and the persuasion more lively, than when the imagination is carry'd thro' a long chain of connected arguments, however infallible the connexion of each link may be esteem'd' (ibid. 144). It is in this connection that the topic of historical belief is taken up again, with an even more definite emphasis on the vivacity of the direct impression.

The reason why the length of an argument has a weakening effect on belief is straightforward: the vivacity constituting belief is directly dependent on the vivacity of the original impression, so it is weakened a bit at every step of the process of inference:

'Tis from the original impression, that the vivacity of all the ideas is deriv'd . . . and 'tis evident this vivacity must gradually decay in proportion to the distance, and must lose somewhat in each transition. . . . one must have a very strong and firm

---

[12] G. E. M. Anscombe, 'Hume and Julius Caesar', in *From Parmenides to Wittgenstein: Collected Philosophical Papers* (Oxford: Blackwell, 1981), i. 86–92, focuses on the 'chain of argument or connexion of causes and effects' in Hume's passage. She notices that the inference Hume actually describes there, from the historical record to the historical event, is not from cause to effect, but from effect to cause. This is not all that serious, she observes, since for Hume cause and effect are inferentially symmetrical; on the other hand, the presence of this minor slip is a sign that what Hume really had in mind as the foundation of our historical beliefs was a kind of cantilever procedure, with a hypothetical inferential chain from the assassination of Caesar to the characters on paper, and then an inferential chain from the latter back again to the former. But in her opinion this amended Humean theory is absurd. Our belief in the historical event is not the result of any such double chain of inference: belief in Caesar's assassination comes before any inference—in fact, our belief in such historical events as Caesar's assassination is foundational, in the sense that it makes us believe in the chain of records constituting history. In response to this, Donald Livingston ('Anscombe, Hume and Julius Caesar', *Analysis*, 35 (1974): 13–19) points out that, in fact, what Hume says is in full agreement with Anscombe's claim about our belief in historical facts not being generally based on an inferential chain: for Hume's statements about the chain of records constitute 'not a justification of belief, but an analysis of the structure of historical belief' (p. 14). Like Anscombe, Hume thinks that 'the record in hand of Caesar's death is an image through which we see "directly" not a long string of documents but Caesar's death' (p. 17); in fact, he seems to be saying that the chain of records is to be interpreted as a component of a 'temporally complex idea' of Caesar 'entailing the idea of our present situation and the idea of the correct temporal order between Caesar and ourselves' (p. 18). On Anscombe's article see also L. Pompa, *Human Nature and Historical Knowledge* (Cambridge: Cambridge University Press, 1990), 23 ff. (esp. 26–7 n. 30).

imagination to preserve the evidence to the end, where [it] is passed thro' so many stages. (Ibid.)

This observation applies to the assent commanded by the 'multitude of connected arguments' composing, for example, a mathematical demonstration or even something as elementary as a long series of additions: and if the chain is long enough, the effects of this decay of vivacity may be drastic (ibid. 181).[13] How are things with history? Here things may be particularly problematic, since

'tis evident there is no point of ancient history, of which we can have any assurance, but by passing thro' many millions of causes and effects, and thro' a chain of arguments of almost immeasurable length. Before the knowledge of the fact cou'd come to the first historian, it must be convey'd thro' many mouths; and after it is committed to writing, each new copy is a new object, of which the connexion with the foregoing is known only by experience and observation. Perhaps, therefore, it may be concluded from the precedent reasoning, that the evidence of all ancient history must now be lost; or at least, will be lost in time, as the chain of causes encreases, and runs on to a greater length. (Ibid. 144–5)

In fact, this is not so. History is the one exception to Hume's progression of diminishing belief, for 'it seems contrary to common sense to think, that if the republic of letters, and the art of printing continue on the same footing as at present, our posterity, even after a thousand ages, can ever doubt if there has been such a man as JULIUS CÆSAR' (ibid. 145). In the case of Julius Caesar, the length of the 'chain of argument' does not produce any decay in force and vivacity; it does not hinder the transference of vivacity from the visual impressions of the page to the ideas of the events narrated. We still think that our history book reports actual events in a reliable manner. This is for a very specific reason:

tho' the links are innumerable, that connect any original fact with the present impression, which is the foundation of belief; yet they are all of the same kind, and depend on the fidelity of Printers and Copists. One edition passes into another, and that into a third, and so on, till we come to that volume we peruse at present. There is no variation in the steps. After we know one, we know all of them; and after we have made one, we can have no scruple as to the rest. This circumstance alone preserves the evidence of history, and will perpetuate the memory of the present age to the latest posterity. If all the long chain of causes and effects, which connect any past event with any volume of history, were compos'd of parts different from each other, and which 'twere necessary for the mind distinctly to conceive, 'tis impossible we shou'd preserve to the end any belief or evidence. But as most of these proofs are perfectly resembling, the mind runs easily along them,

---

[13] For full discussions of this case see R. J. Fogelin, *Hume's Scepticism in the* Treatise of Human Nature (London: Routledge and Kegan Paul, 1985), ch. 2, 'Hume's Skepticism concerning Reason', 13–24.

jumps from one part to another with facility, and forms but a confus'd and general notion of each link. By this means a long chain of argument, has as little effect in diminishing the original vivacity, as a much shorter wou'd have, if compos'd of parts, which were different from each other, and of which each requir'd a distinct consideration. (Ibid. 146)

In other words, the crucial transference of vivacity and belief depends on the close resemblance of the however numerous links in the chain extending back in the past to the actual event. The chain may be very long, but every single link is, on its own, enough to represent the whole multitude in our imagination. So the passage of the mind through the whole chain, made ultra-fast and easy by reliance on the similarity of all the links, makes for an intact belief in Caesar's assassination, innumerable links and years later.

This similarity of the links is worth further unpacking. In his *The Ideology of Aesthetics* Terry Eagleton introduces Hume as the philosopher who 'not content with reducing morality to mere sentiment, threatens also to reduce knowledge to fictional hypothesis, belief to an intense feeling, the continuity of the self to a fiction, causality to an imaginative construct and history to a kind of text'.[14] The last remark is a very apt commentary on the page above, except on one point: when Hume talks about books, he does not mean texts, but concrete objects, the editions and the volumes produced in a number of copies. The faithfulness he has in mind concerns not only historians, but also printers and copyists: the guarantee of the truthfulness of our history book is given by the combined standards of 'the republic of letters, and the art of printing' (ibid. 145). So in the age of authors, this philosopher, future historian, and highly self-conscious author, by focusing his study of human nature on perception and the senses, identifies the very foundation of the reliability of history in the contribution of, among others, printers and copyists.

Now let us move away from the *Treatise* and the 'science of human nature' to consider the readers' reactions to different kinds of books, historical or fictional.

MATTERS OF FACT AND FALSEHOOD—OR, TWO SPIRITED YOUNG LADIES

. . . he that writes without Intention to be credited, must write to little Purpose; for what Pleasure or Advantage can arise from Facts that never happened? What Examples can be afforded by the Patience of those who never suffered, or the Chastity of those who were never solicited? The great End of History, is to shew how much human Nature can endure or perform. . . . Prove, therefore, that the

---

[14] Terry Eagleton, *The Ideology of Aesthetics* (Oxford: Blackwell, 1990), 45 and n. 22.

Books which I have hitherto read as Copies of Life, and Models of Conduct, are empty Fictions, and from this Hour I deliver them to Moths and Mould. (*Female Quixote*, 376–7)

In these words Arabella, the young protagonist of Lennox's novel, expresses her abhorrence for the books which have guided her life up to that point, should it turn out that they are not history, but romances, that is, 'falsehoods' and 'empty fictions'.[15] Her inflamed rhetoric tells both of her familiarity with the lofty style of romance and of her aptness to 'quick' and 'wild'—that is, romantic—imaginations. Less romantic young ladies were likely to react more moderately to such things and in fact, on occasion, even to take the opposite line and prefer 'empty fictions' to history. Consider the following vignette:

I remember I was once desired by a young beauty, for whom I had some passion, to send her some novels and romances for her amusement in the country; but was not so ungenerous as to take the advantage, which such a course of reading might have given me, being resolved not to make use of poisoned arms against her. I therefore sent her PLUTARCH's lives, assuring her, at the same time, that there was not a word of truth in them from beginning to end. She perused them very attentively, 'till she came to the lives of ALEXANDER and CAESAR, whose names she had heard by accident; and then returned me the book, with many reproaches for deceiving her.

This is from Hume's essay 'Of the Study of History'.[16] Novels and romances are, the author laments in the same gentle and patronizing vein, favourites of 'the fair sex': it is a pity that they should 'have such an aversion to matter of fact, and such an appetite for falsehood'. Perhaps it depends, he suggests, on the predominance these writings attribute to love in the world of men, and on the flattering image they offer of men's characters and behaviour.[17]

These two passages offer an interesting representation of a certain category of readers, polite young women, and of their reading and intellectual life. Consider how much power is attributed to the influence of fictional writings—romances and novels alike—on women's behaviour, by turning their delicate brains or affecting their soft hearts. This is a residue, I think, of

---

[15] In the *Female Quixote* 'fiction' is used as a synonym for 'falsehood': see e.g. p. 378, cited below (similarly in Johnson's *Dictionary*, s.v. 'Fiction', (3), with an explicit link to 'lie' as well). In the language of the *Treatise* 'fiction' is both 'falsehood', the 'fables' constituting the matter of poems and romances (e.g. the golden age, pp. 493–4), and the operation of the imagination through which, e.g., the mind constructs the idea of a perfect standard of equality by extrapolating it from the process of successive corrections in actual measurements (see p. 48); and we are told that the connections of this operation of the imagination with reason and the understanding pose very difficult questions (pp. 265–7).

[16] First published in 1741. On women's reading see also 'Of Essay Writing', of 1742. I cite from David Hume, *Essays Moral, Political, and Literary*, ed. E. F. Miller, rev. edn. (Indianapolis: Liberty Classics, 1987), 564.

[17] For the role of love in romance and novels, with the consequent power attributed to women, see e.g. J. Spencer, *The Rise of the Woman Novelist from Aphra Benn to Jane Austen* (Oxford: Blackwell, 1986), esp. ch. 6, pp. 181 ff.

the approach of the seventeenth-century physiological treatments of mental activity in terms of movement of the animal spirits: reading books may, especially in such nervous and sensitive people as women (and intellectuals), induce a dangerous increase in the speed and liveliness of the movement of the animal spirits in the brain, corresponding to over-excitement and over-heating of the imagination and leading, in extreme cases, to more serious disorders such as vapours or melancholia.[18] Later I shall add something more specific in this connection. Also note the emphasis on the instructive value of history: in Hume's words, its study is 'the best suited' to women, being at once 'more instructive than their ordinary books of amusement, and more entertaining than those serious compositions which are usually found in their closets'.[19] Finally, it is interesting that both young ladies were, to start with, mistaken about what their books were, and that the discovery of this mistake caused them to give up the reading. So, on the one hand, history and fiction are totally different: for historical writing is about 'matters of fact', while romances are about 'falsehood'. On the other hand, they may be similar enough to be easily mistaken for each other, at least by naïve readers.

[18] See A. Johns, 'The physiology of reading in Restoration England', in J. Raven, H. Small, and N. Tadmor (eds.), *The Practice and Representation of Reading in England* (Cambridge: Cambridge University Press, 1996), 138–61, and *idem*,'The physiology of reading', in M. Frasca-Spada and N. Jardine (eds.), *Books and Sciences in History* (Cambridge: Cambridge University Press, 2000), 291–314; specifically for the eighteenth century see G. J. Barker-Benfield, *The Culture of Sensibility: Sex and Society in Eighteenth-Century Britain* (Chicago and London: University of Chicago Press, 1992), ch. 1, 'Sensibility and the nervous system', pp. 1–37 (esp. 15–23); G. S. Rousseau, 'Nerves, spirits, and fibres: towards defining the origins of sensibility', *Blue Guitar*, 2 (1976): 125–53; also R. F. Brissenden, *Virtue in Distress: Studies in the Novel of Sentiment from Richardson to de Sade* (New York: Harper and Row, 1974), esp. 37–48; C. Lawrence, 'The nervous system and society in the Scottish Enlightenment', in B. Barnes and S. Shapin (eds.), *Natural Order: Historical Studies of Scientific Culture* (London: Sage, 1979), 19–39. J. P. Wright, *The Sceptical Realism of David Hume* (Manchester: Manchester University Press, 1983), contains fascinating material on Malebranche's talk about spirits as a possible source for Hume, and on its dissemination in English polite literature. For references to 'spirits' in Hume's work see e.g. *Treatise*, 60, 123, etc.; and see below. See also Frasca-Spada, 'Belief and animal spirits'.

[19] That history books contain a particularly happy combination of entertainment and instruction is not an isolated opinion. See e.g. Isaac Watts, *Improvement of the Mind; or a Supplement to the Art of Logic* (London, 1800), e.g. pp. 44 ff.; and Mrs Chapone's *Letters on the Improvement of the Mind, Addressed to a Young Lady* (London, 1773), letter 10, 'On the manner and course of reading history', make very clear the special suitability of history to young women— in fact, a whole letter is devoted to advising her young lady correspondent on how to improve her knowledge of history, how to combine solitary work and conversation, how to practise and improve her memory, from which works to start and which other books to read on what, etc. History books are also very prominent in the reading list addressed to young ladies in the anonymous (actually by Lady Sarah Pennington) *An Unfortunate Mother's Advice to her Absent Daughters* (London, 1761); (on the *Advice* see M. Ellis, *The Politics of Sensibility: Race, Gender and Commerce in the Sentimental Novel* (Cambridge: Cambridge University Press, 1996), 29–33). Hume himself was famously a voracious reader, in particular of historical works: see 'My Own Life', in Mossner, *Life of David Hume*, 611–15; and David F. Norton and Mary Norton, *The David Hume Library* (Edinburgh: Edinburgh Bibliographical Society, 1996).

Let us turn again to the 'science of human nature' and its ways of reflecting this pattern of differences and similarities. This time I intend to look at the diverse ways in which the operations of the imagination were said to combine with the operations of perception and of memory.

THREE CITIES AND THE IMAGINATION

Ideas are, according to Hume, exact, if paler, copies of former impressions of the senses or of passions: thinking comes after and reproduces feeling. This is, as he puts it, a general maxim of his science of human nature. But, strictly speaking, it applies in a direct, straightforward way only to simple perceptions:

I observe, that many of our complex ideas never had impressions, that corresponded to them, and that many of our complex impressions never are exactly copied in ideas. I can imagine to myself such a city as the *New Jerusalem*, whose pavement is gold and walls are rubies, tho' I never saw any such. I have seen *Paris*; but shall I affirm that I can form such an idea of that city, as will perfectly represent all its streets and houses in their real and just proportions? (*Treatise*, 3)

Many of the readers Hume was addressing were likely to have had perceptions of Paris at some stage or other, and to have corresponding memories; and they may well have been able to imagine the New Jerusalem, perhaps with the help of edifying pictures and descriptions. In this sense the complex ideas of both the perceived and remembered Paris and the fantasized New Jerusalem may be taken to copy impressions; but they are also both imagined, in so far as they are both constructed by the imagination as a sort of patchwork of former impressions taken to some extent out of context.

This point is illustrated again by the case of the distinction between ideas of memory and ideas of the imagination. An idea of memory, Hume writes, still 'retains a considerable degree of its first vivacity, and is somewhat intermediate betwixt an impression and an idea', while an idea of the imagination 'entirely loses that vivacity, and is a perfect idea' (ibid. 8). Memory preserves not only the simple ideas, but also 'their order and position', so that 'an historian may, perhaps, for the more convenient carrying on of his narration, relate an event before another, to which it was in fact posterior', but then, 'if he be exact', he also carefully 'takes notice of this disorder' (ibid. 9). The imagination, on the contrary, is completely free to rearrange simple ideas at pleasure: 'the fables we meet with in poems and romances put this entirely out of the question. Nature there is totally confounded, and nothing mentioned but winged horses, fiery dragons, and monstrous giants.' (ibid. 10). This all seems clear enough; and yet, in practice, things are not as straightforward as that:

> tho' it be a peculiar property of memory to preserve the original order and position of its ideas, while the imagination transposes and changes them, as it pleases; yet this difference is not sufficient to distinguish them in their operation, or make us know the one from the other; it being impossible to recall the past impressions, in order to compare them with our present ideas, and see whether their arrangement be exactly similar. (Ibid. 85)

So yet again, as in the case of the remembered Paris, memory itself can work only thanks to a decisive contribution from the imagination; and, yet again, a neatly laid-out distinction seems to slip away. In fact, the difference between the remembered and the imagined is in the different force and vivacity of our conception of them: 'Since therefore the memory is known, neither by the order of its *complex* ideas, not by the nature of its *simple* ones; it follows, that the difference betwixt it and the imagination lies in its superior force and vivacity' (ibid.).

Perhaps we may regard both the fictional New Jerusalem and the remembered Paris thus reconstructed by the imagination as emblems of fictional writing: the New Jerusalem as an emblem of romance and its fantasy, Paris as an emblem of the novel's verisimilitude and indirect connection with matters of fact. (As an emblem of history, we may be tempted to take the Rome through the streets of which, on a fatal early spring day, Julius Caesar walked to the Senate House; and this would highlight what crucial part the imagination must play in the case of history writing and reading as well.) Eighteenth-century critics and men of letters often appealed to the imagination as Hume does to account for readers' reactions to both historical and fictional writings. For example, in his *Elements of Criticism* of 1762, Lord Kames wrote that 'even genuine history has no command over our passions but by ideal presence only; and consequently . . . in this respect it stands upon the same footing with fable . . . what effect either may have to raise our sympathy, depends on the vivacity of the ideas they raise; and with respect to that circumstance, fable is generally more successful than history'.[20]

So whether the writings are historical or fictional, it is the imagination which moves us, which turns us from readers into spectators of the event being narrated; and frequently it is in fictional writings that we find the more inspiring pages.[21] Kames's account of the 'ideal presence' sounds very

---

[20] Henry Home of Kames, *Elements of Criticism* (Edinburgh, 1762), e.g. 95–6 (but the whole of Part 1, ch. 2, sect. vii, 'Emotions caused by fiction', is relevant in this connection).

[21] On Kames's 'ideal presence' see P. Meyer Spacks, *Desire and Truth: Functions of Plot in Eighteenth-Century English Novels* (Chicago: University of Chicago Press, 1990), 26 and 46–7: 'Emotional power measures fiction's worth.' In her *The Progress of Romance* of 1785, Clara Reeve puts it even more specifically: 'The effects of Romance, and true History are not very different. When the imagination is raised, men do not stand to enquire whether the motive be true

close to Hume's description of the role of the imagination in the page on Paris and the New Jerusalen: we conceive both without reference to any actual city as such, and the imagined 'existence' they possess in our thought is some quality of liveliness that we perceive during the evocation of ideas. So much so, that in Hume's passage the New Jerusalem has a more convincing tinge, and feels more, as it were, 'existent' than Paris, on account of those pavements of gold and walls of rubies, which inevitably capture our imagination more (and afford us more 'ideal presence') than the flat reference to the 'streets and houses' in Paris.[22]

Yet, we still think of the existent town and of the New Jerusalem in different ways. Both to Hume's young beauty and to Arabella, knowing whether their books tell them true stories does make a difference: indeed, they both stop reading when it turns out that things were not as they had supposed in this respect. Consider the case of a man who is reminded by another of some 'scene of action' in which they have been engaged together, and which he has forgotten:

Here the person that forgets receives at first all the ideas from the discourse of the other, with the same circumstances of time and place; tho' he considers them as mere fictions of the imagination. But as soon as the circumstance is mention'd, that touches the memory, the very same ideas now appear in a new light, and have, in a manner, a different feeling from what they had before. Without any other alteration, beside that of the feeling, they become immediately ideas of the memory, and are assented to. (*Treatise*, 628)

The very same ideas are first merely entertained, and then remembered; the passage of status from fictions to matters of fact does not alter their content in any way. But the 'alteration of the feeling' is what makes a difference, and it is a big difference indeed. In a similar way, Hume explains that the operation of the reader's imagination is affected by the knowledge that what one is reading is a true story:

If one person sits down to read a book as a romance, and another as a true history, they plainly receive the same ideas, and in the same order; nor does the incredulity of the one, and the belief of the other hinder them from putting the very same

or false.' Romance is just as good as history in inspiring men to perform great actions, and in this sense the character of Don Quixote, 'with all its virtues and absurdities', is, she suggests, 'more respectable, and more amiable' than many a respectable bourgeois 'wholly immersed in low, grovelling, effeminate, or mercenary pursuits'. Similarly in her opinion, one's reactions to Pamela's cases, however fictional, are a good test of the quality of one's heart and feelings. See *The Progress of Romance* (Colchester, 1785), i. 101–3, 106, 135. See also J. Priestley, *A Course of Lectures on Oratory and Criticism* (London, 1777), Lecture 12, esp. pp. 80–1.

[22] For very different discussions of these issues, both classic, see J. Bennett, *Locke, Berkeley, Hume: Central Themes* (Oxford: Clarendon Press, 1971), 294 ff., and C. V. Salmon, 'The central problem of David Hume's philosophy: an essay toward a phenomenological interpretation of the First Book of the *Treatise of Human Nature*', *Jahrbuch für Philosophie und phänomenologische Forschung*, 10 (1929): 299–449.

sense upon their author. His words produce the same ideas in both; tho' his testimony has not the same influence on them. The latter has a more lively conception of all the incidents. (Ibid. 97–8)

Hume is suggesting that the flavour of reality sharpens the imagination of one of these readers and increases the emotional intensity of her response to the story—she conceives the very same ideas and in the same order, but conceives them in a different manner. Similarly, the idea of the New Jerusalem may be conceived in a more or less lively manner according to whether we believe in its existence, regardless of the striking images whereby we may choose to describe it, so that the (undeniable) vivacity of the idea of an amazing, but non-existent New Jerusalem is distinct from the vivacity of the 'action of the mind' with which we conceive the idea of Paris, perhaps as relatively dull but as existing out there.[23]

One interesting implication of this view is that it may account for how we can believe in the existence of a Paris described in a dull manner, and entertain the thought of a New Jerusalem with plenty of 'ideal presence'—that is, how we may have a lively idea of a relatively dull object, and a faint idea of an exciting one. For 'an opinion or belief is nothing but an idea, that is different from a fiction, not in the nature, or the order of its parts, but in the *manner* of its being conceiv'd' (ibid. 628); in other words, 'ideas' have a nature and number of parts, on the one hand, and a manner of being conceived, on the other. So in the cases of Paris and the New Jerusalem the different liveliness of the manner of conception is not balanced by the opposite difference in the liveliness of the content—there is no transference of vivacity from one level to the other.[24] In a similar way, the science of human nature may also account for the ability to tell a dull fact from an exciting fiction, and to distinguish between believing in history and having fun with romances. But then, in principle, the best books we can read are those which present us with lively contents that we believe to be true facts: history books written in a lively manner. When we read good historical works, we get both the belief/vivacity of the act of the mind and the fun/vivacity of the evoked content. As Hume puts it:

The perusal of history seems a calm entertainment; but would be no entertainment at all, did not our hearts beat with correspondent movements to those which are described by the historian. The indifferent, uninteresting style of Suetonius, equally with the masterly pencil of Tacitus, may convince us of the cruel depravity of Nero or Tiberius: But what a difference of sentiment! While the former coldly relates the facts; and the latter sets before our eyes the venerable figures of

---

[23] For belief as an 'act' or 'action' of the mind see e.g. ibid. 97 n. and 107. I have discussed this in 'Belief and animal spirits'. J. McIntyre, 'Hume's passions: direct and indirect', *Hume Studies*, 26/1 (2000): 77–86, examines another distinction of a similar kind which is presented in Book II of the *Treatise*, that between calm and strong versus violent and weak passions.

[24] *Pace* Bennett, *Locke, Berkeley, Hume*, 294.

a Soranus and a Thrasea, intrepid in their fate, and only moved by the melting sorrows of their friends and kindred. What sympathy then touches every human heart! What indignation against the tyrant, whose causeless fear or unprovoked malice gave rise to such detestable barbarity! If we bring these subjects nearer: If we remove all suspicion of fiction and deceit: What powerful concern is excited, and how much superior, in many instances, to the narrow attachment of self-love and private interest! Popular sedition, party zeal, a devoted obedience to factious leaders; these are some of the most visible, though less laudable effects of this social sympathy in human nature.[25] (*Enquiry*, 181–2)

Note that even this lively and entertaining—in fact, genuinely exciting—history is very different from romance, for it seeks to arouse not wonder, as romances are meant to do with their winged horses, fiery dragons, and monstrous giants, but rather sympathy. In other words, in order to associate belief and fun, it seems that we must move from romantic enthusiasm to sympathetic feeling and sentiment.[26]

AVOIDING QUIXOTIC CONFUSIONS

I have suggested that Hume's account of belief implies a distinction within the notion of 'idea' between mental content and act of the mind: it is the force and vivacity of the second which, as I think Hume is intimating, makes the difference between reading history and reading fiction, and which explains the refusal, for opposite reasons, of the young beauty to go on reading his Plutarch, and of Arabella to go on reading her romances. But this is not the end of the story, for Hume's remarks on these matters are, in fact, rather vague; and the case of Arabella, the female Quixote, makes one uneasily aware that in practice the force and vivacity of the act of the mind may not always be distinguished as neatly as one might wish from the force and vivacity of exciting mental contents.

---

[25] In contemporary discussions about style in history writing a common theme is how to avoid the risk of being boring: see e.g. *The Guardian* no. 25, which discusses simple historical style, human nature and emotions; no. 60 is about style in history writing, and on the risk of boredom; the same emphasis on possible boredom is also in *The World*, no. 107 (Jan. 1755). On the other hand see K. Stewart, 'History, poetry, and the terms of fiction in the eighteenth century', *Modern Philology*, 26 (1968–9): 110–20, esp. p. 113, for contemporary criticism of Voltaire, Robertson, and Smollett, as historians whose history writing had degenerated into romance due to their lively imaginative style and their inventions.

[26] On Hume's balancing accuracy with a relatively moderate amount of feeling and sentiment in his *History of England*, see N. Phillipson, *Hume* (London: Weidenfeld and Nicolson, 1989). On sympathy and sentiment in the *History of England* see also D. T. Siebert, *The Moral Animus of David Hume* (London and Toronto: Associated University Presses, 1990), ch. 1, 'In search of the hero of feeling', pp. 25–61; J. C. Hilson, 'Hume: the historian as man of feeling', in J. C. Hilson, M. M. B. Jones, and J. R. Watson (eds.), *Augustan Worlds* (New York: Barnes and Noble, 1978), 205–22; and M. Frasca-Spada, 'The science and conversation of human nature'.

According to Michael McKeon, *Don Quixote* epitomizes the dialectical trajectory of the English novel: from the naïve belief that whatever one reads is true, through generalized scepticism, to the final stage of extreme scepticism and 'the saving faith of the extreme skeptic'—that is, the 'belief-without-really-believing', the 'instrumental and saving belief in romance'.[27] *Don Quixote* was very popular with English audiences virtually from its very publication; and it has been written that history of the different stages of its reception in England commands attention because it 'reflects the changing literary tastes of many generations of English readers'.[28] In particular, in the eighteenth century the book was translated, edited, and reprinted, in the original Spanish and in a number of its various English translations, innumerable times, as well as illustrated, travestied, and imitated. The knight of the mournful countenance was probably the most popular fictional hero with eighteenth-century authors.[29] The interest in *Don Quixote* was connected with, among other things, serious concerns about the relations between romance and history books, both on the authors' and on the readers' part. As far as authors were concerned, there was extensive discussion of fictional writers' techniques of mixing historical with imaginary characters and situations;[30] in the case of historical writing, a field in which drastic changes were taking place, there was plenty of scope for reflection on the amount of sentimentalization and dramatization allowed, and on the authenticating roles of footnotes and critical apparatus.[31] On the other hand, readers' responses to the intricate textures of matters of fact and falsehood presented to them both in history and in romance were an object of discussion from moral, religious, and medical points of view: reading the wrong books, or in the wrong way, could corrupt a reader's mind, ruin their

[27] M. McKeon, *The Origins of the English Novel, 1600–1740* (Baltimore: Johns Hopkins University Press, 1987), 282.

[28] See the classic article by E. B. Knowles, 'Cervantes and English literature', in A. Flores and M. J. Benardete (eds.), *Cervantes across the Centuries* (New York: Gordian Press, 1969), 277–303, esp. p. 277; also S. Staves, 'Don Quixote in eighteenth-century England', *Comparative Literature*, 24 (1972): 193–215.

[29] For detailed analyses of the reactions of eighteenth-century English authors to Cervantes see the recent excellent study by R. Paulson, *Don Quixote in England: The Aesthetics of Laughter* (Baltimore: Johns Hopkins University Press, 1998).

[30] For a rich collection of sources describing the different combinations of fantasy, verisimilitude, and history constituting the different kinds of 'falsehood' involved in romances and novels, see I. Williams (ed.), *Novel and Romance 1700–1800: A Documentary Record* (London: Routledge and Kegan Paul, 1970).

[31] On the tendency of eighteenth-century historiography towards a less sentimental rendering see Phillipson, *Hume*; on the generalization of the use of footnotes and direct references to sources in history works in this period see A. Grafton, *The Footnote: A Curious History* (London: Faber & Faber, 1997), esp. ch. 4, 'Footnotes and *philosophie*: an Enlightenment interlude', pp. 94–121, and ch. 7, 'Clarity and distinctness in the abysses of erudition: the Cartesian origins of the modern footnote', pp. 190–222 (which also discusses Hume's own views on the footnoting of history books).

soul, and damage their health.[32] Hume's tentative reflections in the *Treatise* and Lennox's humorously self-conscious representations in the *Female Quixote* are part of this picture.

Lennox's *The Female Quixote* derives its very structure from the definitions of histories, romances, and novels, on the basis of their contrasting attitudes to reality.[33] The protagonist Arabella is a fine young lady deriving all her knowledge of life from intensive reading of bad English translations of famous seventeenth-century French heroic romances (La Calprenède's 12-or-so-volume blockbusters *Cleopatra*, *Cassandra* and *Pharamond*, Madeleine de Scudéry's *Clelia* and *Artamenes*, etc.), which she takes for 'real Pictures of Life'.[34] Obvious difficulties arise when she leaves the sheltered and isolated environment in which she has been brought up. Believing love to be 'the ruling Principle of the World', she interprets everything in romantic terms: in her dream of female power, every trifling incident is the beginning of an adventure, every stranger a ravisher trying to abduct her, every servant a prince in disguise ready to die for her, and so on. She behaves accordingly, driving her aspiring fiancé nearly to distraction with her blunders and with her uncompromising insistence on a silent and heroic devotion.[35] A kind countess, taken with Arabella's beauty and intelligence in all but one matter, tries to sort her out. She explains to Arabella that 'adventures' are nothing a virtuous and sensible woman wishes for herself nowadays, and that romance is no good guide to behaviour because 'Custom . . . changes the very Nature of Things, and what was honourable a thousand Years ago, may probably be look'd upon as infamous now' (pp. 327–8).

The line of argument presented by the countess does not yet win Arabella's assent. For that she needs nothing less than a real adventure. In imitation of de Scudéry's divine Clelia, she escapes a supposed abduction by throwing herself in the Thames, and is nearly drowned. Following this, a wise and learned divine manages to sober her views by means of a full

---

[32] See the works cited above, n. 18. Also J. Brewer, *The Pleasures of the Imagination: English Culture in the Eighteenth Century* (London: Harper Collins, 1997), ch. 4, 'Readers and the reading public', pp. 167–97.

[33] See L. Langbauer, 'Romance revised: Charlotte Lennox's *The Female Quixote*', *Novel*, 18 (1984): 29–49 (on novel and romance in *The Female Quixote*); and Meyer Spacks, *Desire and Truth*, 12–33 (on reality and fiction in *The Female Quixote* and in eighteenth-century criticism).

[34] Arabella is, Langbauer acutely observes, 'a novelist's fantasy of wish-fulfilment. She is the ideal reader, completely given over to the sway of the text, attesting to the power of romance, a power the novelist desires for her form too' ('Romance revised', 30).

[35] On romance as fantasy of female power, and on Arabella's predicament, trapped between being a female Quixote and having to renounce both her dream of power and the possibility of being a heroine and having a history, see in particular L. E. Warren, 'Of the conversation of women: *The Female Quixote* and the dream of perfection', *Studies in Eighteenth-Century Culture*, 11 (1982): 367–80, esp. pp. 371 ff.; Spencer, *Rise of the Woman Novelist*, esp. ch. 6, pp. 181 ff.; and D. Ross, 'Mirror, mirror: the didactic dilemma of *The Female Quixote*', *Studies in English Literature 1500–1900*, 27 (1987): 455–73.

discussion of romance and history.[36] They dispute about historical truth in a very learned vein:

Your Ladyship knows, I suppose to what Authors these Writings are ascrib'd?—To the *French* Wits of the last Century, said *Arabella*.—And at what Distance, Madam, are the Facts related in them from the Age of the Writer?—I was never exact in my Computation, replied *Arabella*; but I think most of the Events happen'd about two thousand Years ago.—How then, Madam, resum'd the Doctor, could these Events be so minutely known to Writers so remote from the Time in which they happen'd? (p. 375)

The Doctor is suggesting that precisely the richness of detail which makes the events of romances so lively to the imagination, and therefore so easily taken for real facts, is what makes their truthfulness so unlikely.

Returning to the science of human nature: according to Hume, 'among the vulgar, quacks and projectors meet with a more easy faith upon account of their magnificent pretensions, than if they kept themselves within the bounds of moderation' (*Treatise*, 120). The reason is, he says, that the very amazement caused by their unbelievable reports 'so vivifies and enlivens the idea, that it resembles the inferences we draw from experience', thus producing something like a functional equivalent of belief. When they build their fictions around historical characters or situations, poets rely on another variety of transference of belief: 'The several incidents of a piece acquire a kind of relation by being united into one poem or representation; and if any of these incidents be an object of belief, it bestows a force and vivacity on the others, which are related to it' (ibid. 122). This is the basis of a whole series of possible errors and misunderstandings which, for the sake of brevity, we may identify as 'Quixotic'; and Arabella is a female Quixote because of her inability to tell the history from the fantasy in her books.[37] Such a lively imagination as Arabella's may indeed come close to a form of madness—and here is a description sketched by Hume in the language of animal economy, of this borderline between a lively imagination and 'madness or folly' which, even though it may well, in fact, refer to such serious matters as intoxication and vapours, seems to be tailor-made for her case:

When the imagination, from any extraordinary ferment of the blood and spirits, acquires such a vivacity as disorders all its powers and faculties, there is no means

[36] For Johnson's authorship of the chapter, first suggested by J. Mitford in *The Gentleman's Magazine*, NS 20 (Aug. 1843): 132, and 21 (Jan. 1844): 41, see M. Small, *Charlotte Ramsay Lennox* (New Haven: Yale University Press, 1935), 2 ff., 79–92; D. Isles, 'Johnson and Charlotte Lennox', *The New Rambler*, series C, no. 34 (1967): 34–48, esp. p. 43. See also M. Dalziel's note in her edition of *The Female Quixote*, 414–15, and Isles's appendix to it, 'Johnson, Richardson, and *The Female Quixote*', ibid. 422, expressing opposite views.

[37] See Meyer Spacks, *Desire and Truth*, 22–3, 26, etc. In fact, this is a typical definition of Quixotism: see Staves, 'Don Quixote in eighteenth-century England'. Ross, 'Mirror, mirror', 464, contains a good summary of Arabella's situation: 'she believes romance is history—told from a perspective that makes women central figures'.

to distinguish betwixt truth and falsehood . . . Every chimera of the brain is as vivid and intense as any of those inferences, which we formerly dignify'd with the name of conclusions concerning matters of fact, and sometimes as the present impressions of the senses. (Ibid. 123)

In Hume's terms, Arabella's problem is that she lets the liveliness of the 'chimeras' aroused in her brain by the contents of her romances bring about the liveliness of conception which Hume identifies with belief. The problem is: how do we routinely avoid Quixotic confusions, and how can these be cured when they occur? Does Hume offer any view?

Both in poetry and in madness, Hume writes, 'the vivacity they bestow on the ideas is not deriv'd from the particular situations or connexions of the objects of these ideas, but from the present temper and disposition of the person' (ibid. 630). The difference is that, contrary to madness, poetry produces an emotion which is 'still the mere phantom of belief or persuasion': 'There is no passion of the human mind but what may arise from poetry; tho' at the same time the *feelings* of the passions are very different when excited by poetical fictions, from what they are when they arise from belief and reality' (ibid. 630–1). Here the '*feeling*' is a third-order mental act: an impression of the senses gives rise to an impression of reflection (or passion), and this in turn *feels* differently according to whether the book arousing it is known to be a novel or a historical writing. Hume insists that the vivacity of a poetic fiction 'never has the same *feeling*' as that arising 'when we reason', and that the ideas presented in a poetical description 'are different to the *feeling*' from the ideas presented in a historical narration (ibid. 630, 631). The italicized '*feeling*' is repeated three times in this paragraph, together with references to 'the apparent agitation of the mind' and to 'that seeming vehemence of thought and sentiment' resulting from poetical enthusiasm; it is, I think, the sign of a struggle. After this, Hume comes up with a new suggestion: namely, that we distinguish between the two different kinds of mental states on the basis of a particular kind of reflexion.

We shall afterwards have occasion to remark both the resemblances and differences betwixt a poetical enthusiasm, and a serious conviction. In the mean time I cannot forbear observing, that the great difference in their feeling proceeds in some measure from reflexion and *general rules*. We observe, that the vigour of conception, which fictions receive from poetry and eloquence, is a circumstance merely accidental, of which every idea is equally susceptible; and that such fictions are connected with nothing that is real. This observation makes us only lend ourselves, so to speak, to the fiction: But causes the idea to feel very different from the eternal establish'd persuasion founded on memory and custom. They are somewhat of the same kind: But the one is much inferior to the other, both in its causes and effects. A like reflexion on *general rules* keeps us from augmenting our belief upon every increase of the force and vivacity of our ideas. (Ibid. 631–2)

So belief is a form of vivacity, but is not the same as 'the force and vivacity of our ideas', because belief is a force and vivacity somehow guided by 'reflexion and *general rules*'. Hume does not say much about either this 'reflexion' or the general rules, and my comments on this point are tentative. I think it is clear that in this passage he is discussing again the liveliness of poetic fictions as a temporary functional equivalent of belief, or of suspended disbelief. The most prominent feature of this feeling is its unconnectedness: its liveliness is 'a circumstance merely accidental', and every idea 'is equally susceptible' of it. In so far as it is dependent on the 'present temper and disposition' of the person, this lively feeling is an isolated emotional response and does not belong to, or fit, our view of the world: it does not involve consideration of the 'particular situations and connexions' which constitute the background for our yet-to-be-acquired beliefs and the way we routinely vet them, as it were. And 'reflexion' is, I think, a good name for the operation of balancing such distinctions as that between the liveliness of mental content and the liveliness of mental action. But this is not all.

In contrast with poetical fictions and follies, the ideas we believe in are presumably not entirely derived from 'the present temper and disposition of the person', and must depend on the 'particular situations or connexions of the objects of these ideas' (ibid. 630):

When the vivacity arises from a customary conjunction with a present impression; tho' the imagination may not, in appearance, be so much mov'd; yet there is always something more forcible and real in its actions, than in the fervours of poetry and eloquence. The force of our mental actions in this case, no more than in any other, is not to be measur'd by the apparent agitation of the mind. (Ibid. 631)

The 'general rules' may, I suggest, operate on the basis of the difference between the causal histories of the objects of the suspended disbelief generated by poetry and those of the objects of the belief commanded by history: that is, a difference in the 'chain of argument or connexion of causes and effects' behind them, to use the expression that Hume uses with regard to history in his discussion of the death of Julius Caesar (ibid. 83). By these means they help us establish the position of an idea with respect to, say, history, in so far as this is part of the established and public body of knowledge constituting our general frame of reference.[38]

---

[38] On the discussion in *Treatise*, 632, and the meaning and use of the 'general rules' see J. Laird, *Hume's Philosophy of Human Nature* (London: Methuen, 1932), 91–2; J. Passmore, *Hume's Intentions*, 3rd edn. (London: Duckworth, 1980), 10, 63–4, and *passim*; A.-L. Leroy, *David Hume* (Paris: Presses Universitaires de France, 1953), 69 ff.; L. W. Beck, 'A Prussian Hume and a Scottish Kant', in *Essays on Kant and Hume* (New Haven: Yale University Press, 1978), 111–29, esp. pp. 122 ff.; T. K. Hearn, Jr., '"General rules" in Hume's *Treatise*', *Journal of the History of Philosophy*, 8 (1970): 405–22; W. H. Walsh, 'Hume's concept of truth', in G. Vesey (ed.), *Reason and Reality*, Royal Institute of Philosophy Lectures, 5, 1970–1 (London: Macmillan, 1972), 99–116; Louis E. Loeb, 'Hume on stability, justification, and unphilosophical probability', *Journal*

CODA

So, the causal history of a romance written by a French author is different from that of the history written by Plutarch, behind which there is the whole tradition of historical writing, which involves the extended trust in witnesses, historians, and printers. General rules are, then, reflexive tools that we routinely apply to avoid confusions or to sort ourselves out when we do get confused: how was such-and-such a belief caused? How does it compare with other people's belief?

As a conclusion I would now like to examine how Arabella finally comes back to her senses. To the Doctor's last question—how do authors writing so long after the events have such detailed knowledge of them?—Arabella can provide a very good answer, which in turn triggers a series of unanswerable questions:

—By Records, Monuments, Memoirs, and Histories, answered the Lady.—But by what Accident, then, said the Doctor smiling, did it happen these Records and Monuments were kept universally secret to Mankind till the last Century? What brought all the Memoirs of the remotest Nations and earliest Ages only to *France*? Where were they hidden that none could consult them but a few and obscure Authors? And wither are they now vanished again that they can be found no more? (p. 375)

So Arabella's brain was 'turned' because she had failed to practice the 'general rules': 'How is any oral, or written Testimony, confuted or confirmed?—By comparing it, says the Lady, with the Testimony of others, or with the natural Effects and standing Evidence of the Facts related, and sometimes by comparing it with itself' (pp. 377–8). This criterion, pronounced by Arabella herself, is violated in all sorts of ways in La Calprenède's and de Scudéry's stories, where characters unmentioned in any history book appear, and geography and landscape are altered, nations and kingdoms created according to narrative convenience. This is enough to discredit her romances: she is finally convinced.

But romances are not only untruthful, insists the Doctor, they are also absurd and criminal. They are criminal, because they 'inflame our Passions' to the 'contemplation of Crimes' (p. 380): in their pursuit of personal glory, romance heroes and heroines behave like selfish monsters, unmoved even by needless bloodshed (pp. 380–2). And they are absurd, because they lack verisimilitude: 'the only Excellence of Falsehood . . . is its Resemblance to Truth', a criterion that romances fail by definition (p. 378). So fantastic narrative is not to be preferred to a narrative constrained by respect of

of the History of Philosophy, 33 (1995): 101–32, *idem, Stability and Justification in Hume's* Treatise (Oxford: Oxford University Press, 2002), ch. 4, 'Unphilosophical probability and judgements arising from sympathy'; and Richard Serjeantson's article in this volume.

verisimilitude, and heroic virtue is not to be preferred to a less flamboyant, but more humane, bourgeois morality. 'Truth—says the Doctor—is not always injured by Fiction': in fact, Richardson in his novels 'has found the Way to convey the most solid Instructions, the noblest Sentiments, and the most exalted Piety, in the pleasing Dress of a Novel, and, to use the Words of the greatest Genius of the present Age, "Has taught the Passions to move at the Command of Virtue"' (p. 377). The genius cited here is Dr Johnson, with whose benediction, if she has now lost *Cleopatra* and *Cassandra*, Arabella may still read the still fictional, but bourgeois and edifying *Clarissa*.

It is perhaps worth adding that *Clarissa* is (believe it or not) a far slimmer work than any of Arabella's favoured readings; but what it lacks in pages is more than balanced by Arabella's admission to the polite circle of its readers, so keen on Clarissa's cases, that they talk about her as if she really existed, while their very conversation protects them against the danger of overheating of the imagination, of brain-turning—in short, of Quixotic confusions.[39]

REFERENCES

Primary Sources

Beattie, James, *An Essay on the Nature and Immutability of Truth in Opposition to Sophistry and Scepticism* (Edinburgh: Printed for A. Kincaid and J. Bell, etc., 1770).
Chapone, Hester Mulso, *Letters on the Improvement of the Mind, Addressed to a Young Lady*, 2 vols. (London: Printed by H. Hughes, for J. Walter, 1773).
Home, Henry (later Lord Kames), *Essays on the Principles of Morality and Natural Religion* (Edinburgh: Printed by R. Fleming, for A. Kincaid and A. Donaldson, 1751).
—— *Elements of Criticism* (Edinburgh: Printed for A. Miller, London, and A. Kincaid & J. Bell, Edinburgh, 1762).
Hume, David, *A Treatise of Human Nature*, ed. L. A. Selby-Bigge, 2nd edn., rev. P. H. Nidditch (Oxford: Clarendon Press, 1978).
—— *Essays Moral, Political, and Literary*, ed. E. F. Miller, rev. edn. (Indianapolis: Liberty Classics, 1987).
Johnson, Samuel, *A Dictionary of the English Language* (London: Printed by W. Strahan, for J. and P. Knapton etc., 1755).
Lennox, Charlotte Ramsay, *The Female Quixote; or, the Adventures of Arabella*, 2 vols. (London: A. Millar, 1752).

---

[39] On conversation as the remedy against 'turning' of the brain see Warren, 'Of the conversation of women'; and on conversation, philosophy, and forms of entertainment see Cavell, *Pursuits of Happiness*, 12–13, 38–9.

—— *The Female Quixote*, ed. M. Dalziel, Introduction by M. A. Doody (Oxford and New York: Oxford University Press, 1989).

Pennington, Lady Sarah, *An Unfortunate Mother's Advice to her Absent Daughters: In a Letter to Miss Pennington* (London: Printed by S. Chandler, and sold by W. Bristow and C. Etherington, York, 1761).

Priestley, Joseph, *A Course of Lectures on Oratory and Criticism* (London, 1777).

Reeve, Clara, *The Progress of Romance, Through Times, Countries, and Manners: with Remarks on the Good and Bad Effects of it, on them respectively; in a Course of Evening Conversations*, 2 vols. (Colchester: Printed by W. Keymer, for the author, 1785).

Watts, Isaac, *Improvement of the Mind; or a Supplement to the Art of Logic* (London: Sold by T. Hurst, and W. Baynes, etc., 1800).

Williams, I. (ed.), *Novel and Romance 1700–1800: A Documentary Record* (London: Routledge and Kegan Paul, 1970).

Secondary Sources

Anscombe, G. E. M., 'Hume and Julius Caesar', in *From Parmenides to Wittgenstein: Collected Philosophical Papers* (Oxford: Blackwell, 1981), i. 86–92.

Ayer, Alfred J., *Hume* (Oxford: Oxford University Press, 1980).

Baier, Annette, *A Progress of Sentiments: Reflections on Hume's Treatise* (Cambridge, Mass., and London: Harvard University Press, 1991).

Barker-Benfield, G. J., *The Culture of Sensibility: Sex and Society in Eighteenth-Century Britain* (Chicago and London: University of Chicago Press, 1992).

Beck, Lewis White, 'A Prussian Hume and a Scottish Kant', in *Essays on Kant and Hume* (New Haven: Yale University Press, 1978), 111–29.

Bennett, Jonathan, *Locke, Berkeley, Hume: Central Themes* (Oxford: Clarendon Press, 1971).

Brewer, John, *The Pleasures of the Imagination: English Culture in the Eighteenth Century* (London: Harper Collins, 1997).

Brissenden, R. F., *Virtue in Distress: Studies in the Novel of Sentiment from Richardson to de Sade* (New York: Harper and Row, 1974).

Cavell, Stanley, *Pursuits of Happiness: The Hollywood Comedy of Remarriage* (Cambridge, Mass.: Harvard University Press, 1981).

—— 'The thought of movies', in *Themes out of School: Effects and Causes* (Chicago and London: University of Chicago Press, 1988), 3–26.

Davie, George, *A Passion for Ideas: Essays on the Scottish Enlightenment* (Edinburgh: Polygon, 1994).

Deleuze, Gilles, *Empiricism and Subjectivity: An Essay on Hume's Theory of Human Nature* (1953), trans. C. V. Boundas (New York: Columbia University Press, 1991).

Eagleton, Terry, *The Ideology of Aesthetics* (Oxford: Blackwell, 1990).

Ellis, M., *The Politics of Sensibility: Race, Gender and Commerce in the Sentimental Novel* (Cambridge: Cambridge University Press, 1996).

Fogelin, Robert J., *Hume's Scepticism in the* Treatise of Human Nature (London: Routledge and Kegan Paul, 1985).

Frasca-Spada, Marina, 'The science and conversation of human nature', in W. Clark, J. Golinski, and S. Schaffer (eds.), *The Sciences in Enlightened Europe* (Chicago: University of Chicago Press, 2000), 218–45.

—— 'Hume on sense impressions and objects', in M. Heidelberger and D. Stadler (eds.), *History of Philosophy of Science: New Trends and Perspectives*, Vienna Circle Institute Yearbook, 9/2001 (Dordrecht and London: Kluwer Academic Publishers, 2002), 13–24.

—— 'Belief and animal spirits in Hume's *Treatise*', *Eighteenth-Century Thought*, 1 (2003): 151–69.

Gorman, Michael M., 'Hume's theory of belief', *Hume Studies*, 10/1 (1993): 89–101.

Grafton, Anthony, *The Footnote: A Curious History* (London: Faber & Faber, 1997).

Habermas, Jürgen, *The Structural Transformation of the Public Sphere: An Inquiry into a Category of Bourgeois Society*, trans. T. Burger with the assistance of F. Lawrence, 2nd edn. (Cambridge: Polity, 1989).

Hauser, Arnold, *The Social History of Art*, 4 vols. (London: Routledge and Kegan Paul, 1962).

Hearn, T. K. Jr., ' "General rules" in Hume's *Treatise*', *Journal of the History of Philosophy*, 8 (1970): 405–22.

Hilson, J. C., 'Hume: the historian as man of feeling', in J. C. Hilson, M. M. B. Jones, and J. R. Watson (eds.), (*Augustan Worlds*, New York: Barnes and Noble, 1978), 205–22.

Isles, D., 'Johnson and Charlotte Lennox', *The New Rambler*, series C, no. 34 (1967): 34–48.

Johns, Adrian, 'The physiology of reading in Restoration England', in J. Raven, H. Small, and N. Tadmor (eds.), *The Practice and Representation of Reading in England* (Cambridge: Cambridge University Press, 1996), 138–61.

—— 'The physiology of reading', in M. Frasca-Spada and N. Jardine (eds.), *Books and Sciences in History* (Cambridge: Cambridge University Press, 2000), 291–314.

Knowles, E. B., 'Cervantes and English literature', in A. Flores and M. J. Benardete (eds.), *Cervantes across the Centuries* (New York: Gordian Press, 1969), 277–303.

Laird, John, *Hume's Philosophy of Human Nature* (London: Methuen, 1932).

Langbauer, L., 'Romance revised: Charlotte Lennox's *The Female Quixote*', *Novel*, 18 (1984): 29–49.

Lawrence, Chris, 'The nervous system and society in the Scottish Enlightenment', in B. Barnes and S. Shapin (eds.), *Natural Order: Historical Studies of Scientific Culture* (London: Sage, 1979), 19–39.

Leroy, André-Louis, *David Hume* (Paris: Presses Universitaires de France, 1953).

Livingston, Donald W., 'Anscombe, Hume and Julius Caesar', *Analysis*, 35 (1974): 13–19.

Loeb, Louis E., 'Hume on stability, justification, and unphilosophical probability', *Journal of the History of Philosophy*, 33 (1995): 101–32.

—— *Stability and Justification in Hume's* Treatise (Oxford: Oxford University Press, 2002).

Mayer, R., *History and the Early English Novel: Matters of Fact from Bacon to Defoe* (Cambridge: Cambridge University Press, 1997).

McIntyre, Jane, 'Hume's passions: direct and indirect', *Hume Studies*, 26/1 (2000): 77–86.

McKeon, Michael, *The Origins of the English Novel, 1600–1740* (Baltimore: Johns Hopkins University Press, 1987).

McKillop, A. D., *The Early Masters of English Fiction* (Lawrence, Kan.: University of Kansas Press, 1956).

Meyer Spacks, Patricia, *Desire and Truth: Functions of Plot in Eighteenth-Century English Novels* (Chicago: University of Chicago Press, 1990).

Mossner, Ernest C., 'The continental reception of Hume's *Treatise*, 1739–1741', *Mind*, 45 (1947): 31–43.

—— 'The first answer to Hume's *Treatise*: an unnoticed item of 1740', *Journal of the History of Ideas*, 12 (1951): 291–4.

—— *The Life of David Hume* (Edinburgh: Nelson, 1954); 2nd edn. (Oxford: Clarendon Press, 1980).

Murphy, R. T., *Hume and Husserl: Towards Radical Subjectivism* (The Hague: Martinus Nijoff, 1980).

Norton, David Fate, and Norton, Mary, *The David Hume Library* (Edinburgh: Edinburgh Bibliographical Society, 1996).

Parusnikova, Zuzana, 'Hume and post-modernism', *Hume Studies*, 19/2 (1993): 1–17.

Passmore, John, *Hume's Intentions*, 3rd edn. (London: Duckworth, 1980).

Paulson, R. *Don Quixote in England: The Aesthetics of Laughter* (Baltimore: Johns Hopkins University Press, 1998).

Pears, David F. (ed.), *David Hume: A Symposium* (London: Macmillan, 1963).

Phillipson, Nicholas, *Hume* (London: Weidenfeld and Nicolson, 1989).

Pompa, Leon, *Human Nature and Historical Knowledge* (Cambridge: Cambridge University Press, 1990).

Ross, D., 'Mirror, mirror: the didactic dilemma of *The Female Quixote*', *Studies in English Literature 1500–1900*, 27 (1987): 455–73.

Rousseau, G. S., 'Nerves, spirits, and fibres: towards defining the origins of sensibility', *Blue Guitar*, 2 (1976): 125–53.

Salmon, C. V., 'The central problem of David Hume's philosophy: an essay toward a phenomenological interpretation of the First Book of the *Treatise of Human Nature*', *Jahrbuch für Philosophie und phänomenologische Forschung*, 10 (1929): 299–449.

Siebert, Donald T., *The Moral Animus of David Hume* (London and Toronto: Associated University Presses, 1990).

Small, M., *Charlotte Ramsay Lennox* (New Haven: Yale University Press, 1935).

Spencer, J., *The Rise of the Woman Novelist from Aphra Benn to Jane Austen* (Oxford: Blackwell, 1986).

Staves, S., 'Don Quixote in eighteenth-century England', *Comparative Literature*, 24 (1972): 193–215.

Stewart, K., 'History, poetry, and the terms of fiction in the eighteenth century', *Modern Philology*, 26 (1968–9): 110–20.

Walsh, W. H., 'Hume's concept of truth', in G. Vesey (ed.), *Reason and Reality*, Royal Institute of Philosophy Lectures, 5, 1970–1 (London: Macmillan, 1972), 99–116.

Warren, L. E., 'Of the conversation of women: *The Female Quixote* and the dream of perfection', *Studies in Eighteenth-Century Culture*, 11 (1982): 367–80.

Wright, John P., *The Sceptical Realism of David Hume* (Manchester: Manchester University Press, 1983).

Zabeeh, Farhang, *Hume, Precursor of Modern Empiricism: An Analysis of his Opinions on Meaning, Metaphysics, Logic and Mathematics*, 2nd edn. (The Hague: Martinus Nijoff, 1973).

Hume's General Rules and the 'Chief Business of Philosophers'

R. W. SERJEANTSON

This essay addresses two recent questions in Hume scholarship, in order to raise a third. The first question concerns the experimental ambition of Hume's philosophy. Hume conceived the *Treatise of Human Nature* (1739) as 'an attempt to introduce the experimental method of reasoning into moral subjects'.[1] A number of recent studies have concurred in seeing this ambition as basically 'Newtonian' in inspiration.[2] I place it in a somewhat different context by explaining aspects of Book I of the *Treatise* in terms of Hume's self-conscious rejection of conventional accounts of the reasoning process that were formulated in the discipline of logic. I then turn to consider in detail Hume's account of 'general rules' as a species of probability, and relate them to earlier accounts of the role of 'rules' in philosophy. This aspect of my argument provides a point of entry into the second question that has been raised by recent commentators on Hume's writings: how far his account of reason is normative or obligatory.[3] I shall suggest that

I am grateful to Professor M. A. Stewart for correspondence about Hume's education, and to Dr Marina Frasca-Spada for her encouragement and advice.

[1] David Hume, *A Treatise of Human Nature*, ed. L. A. Selby-Bigge, 2nd edn., rev. P. H. Nidditch (Oxford: Clarendon Press, 1978), p. xi (title-page); see also p. xvi, on 'the application of experimental philosophy to moral subjects'.

[2] The modern version of the 'Newtonian' interpretation of Hume derives primarily from J. A. Passmore, *Hume's Intentions* (Cambridge: Cambridge University Press, 1952), esp. p. 43. See further James Noxon, *Hume's Philosophical Development: A Study of his Methods* (Oxford: Clarendon Press, 1973), 68–123 (esp. p. 76: 'The claim that Hume's philosophical development was profoundly affected by the Newtonian method is as probable as any assertion of an unacknowledged influence can be'). John P. Wright, *The Sceptical Realism of David Hume* (Manchester: Manchester University Press, 1983), 196–7, notes that the Newtonian interpretation of Hume's experimental ambition 'must be treated with some caution', but allows that 'Hume's goals resemble those of Newton'. M. A. Box, *The Suasive Art of David Hume* (Princeton: Princeton University Press, 1990), 88, states: 'it hardly needs substantiation here that Hume was following a program inspired by Newton's example'. For a *caveat* about Hume's knowledge and use of Newton's writings see Peter Jones, *Hume's Sentiments: Their Ciceronian and French Context* (Edinburgh: Edinburgh University Press, 1982), 11–12.

[3] See in particular Antonia LoLordo, 'Probability and skepticism about reason in Hume's *Treatise*', *British Journal for the History of Philosophy*, 8 (2000): 419–46, esp. pp. 443–6; also Marie Martin, 'The rational warrant for Hume's general rules', *Journal of the History of Philosophy*, 31 (1993): 245–57, esp. pp. 252–7.

the uncertainty of Hume's commentators on this question reflects an uncertainty in early modern philosophy about the function of rules in respect of reason. From these two vantage-points, I turn in the final part of this essay to address the larger question suggested by my title: what did Hume take to be the task or office of philosophy?[4]

THE 'EXPERIMENTAL METHOD' AND THE
DISCIPLINE OF LOGIC

What Hume calls the 'experimental method' came about as a consequence of developments in the discipline of natural philosophy between the later sixteenth and the early eighteenth centuries. In the course of the seventeenth century a new form of inquiry, dubbed by its practitioners 'experimental natural philosophy' and in good part pursued outside the universities, had arisen to challenge the claims of the natural philosophy taught in the schools. The latter neo-Aristotelian natural philosophy was characterized by explanations that were universal—which described what happened 'all, or most of the time' in the 'ordinary course of nature'. It was a natural philosophy that drew upon logical and metaphysical principles, often couched in the form of self-evident or precognitive axioms such as 'the whole is greater than the part' or 'nature does nothing in vain'. And it appealed to notions of generalized 'experience' rather than particular experiments.[5]

The new natural philosophy, by contrast—and particularly in its British instantiation—emphasized the particularity of natural phenomena. Experiments were conceived of precisely as ways of diverting nature from its ordinary course, with experimental natural philosophers deliberately seeking out marvellous and prodigious phenomena. Such natural philosophers, too, rejected both traditional logic as a means to direct their inquiries and traditional metaphysics as a means of explaining the phenomena they discovered. And in their essayistic and unsystematic reports they appealed not to a tacit consensus of 'experience', but instead described particular experiments in all their circumstantial detail. In the course of the seventeenth century, natural philosophy transformed itself (in Aristotelian terms) from a theoretical to a practical discipline.

The history of the philosophy of 'human understanding' in this period can in part be seen as an attempt to explain the implications of these

[4] This question has recently been raised, from a somewhat different perspective, by C. J. Finlay, 'Enlightenment and the university: philosophy, communication, and education in the early writings of David Hume', *History of Universities*, 16 (2000): 103–34, esp. pp. 115–28.

[5] See further Peter Dear, *Discipline and Experience: The Mathematical Way in the Scientific Revolution* (Chicago: University of Chicago Press, 1995), esp. pp. 15–25.

developments for reasoning and psychology.[6] Throughout the seventeenth century a number of works were written that attempted to give philosophical shape to these developments. Among these writings, which include some of the most justly celebrated philosophical works of the period, were Francis Bacon's *Novum organum* ('New instrument', 1620; Hume considered Bacon 'the father of experimental physicks'[7]); René Descartes's *Regulae ad directionem ingenii* ('Rules for the direction of the mind', written *c*.1628) and *Discours de la méthode* ('Discourse on the method', 1637);[8] Baruch de Spinoza's *Tractatus de emendatione intellectus* ('Treatise on the emendation of the intellect', *c*.1658); Nicolas Malebranche's *De la recherche de la vérité* (1674–75); Ehrenfried Walter von Tschirnhaus's *Medicina mentis* ('Medicine of the mind', 1695);[9] John Locke's *Essay Concerning Human Understanding* (1690) and Gottfried Wilhelm von Leibniz's dialogic commentary upon it, the *Nouveaux essais sur l'entendement humain* ('New essays on human understanding', written between 1703 and 1705, but first published only in 1765, and therefore unknown to Hume when he wrote the *Treatise*); George Berkeley's *Treatise Concerning the Principles of Human Knowledge* (1710, 1734), and indeed Hume's *Treatise of Human Nature*. By definition—since they are in good part written in reaction against it—such works do not fit neatly into the disciplinary categories by which the dominant Aristotelian philosophy of the sixteenth and earlier seventeenth centuries was so effectively structured. None the less, all of these works, as well as drawing upon natural philosophy, faculty psychology, and even medicine, take on a great part of their significance when seen in the context of the discipline of logic.[10]

---

[6] For background to this point, see Frederick S. Michael, 'Why logic became epistemology: Gassendi, Port Royal and the reformation in logic', in P. Easton (ed.), *Logic and the Workings of the Mind: The Logic of Ideas and Faculty Psychology in Early Modern Philosophy*, North American Kant Society Studies in Philosophy, 5 (Atascadero, Calif.: Ridgeview, 1997), 1–20; Gabriel Nuchelmans, 'Logic in the seventeenth century: preliminary remarks and the constituents of the proposition', in D. Garber and M. Ayers, (eds.), *The Cambridge History of Seventeenth-Century Philosophy*, 2 vols. (Cambridge: Cambridge University Press, 1998), i. 103–17, at pp. 104–5.

[7] David Hume, *An Abstract of a Book Lately Published*, in *Treatise*, 641–62, at p. 646.

[8] On Descartes's *Regulae* as a form of logic, see Eric Palmer, 'Descartes's *Rules* and the workings of the mind', in Easton (ed.), *Logic and the Workings of the Mind*, 269–82.

[9] Ehrenfried Walther von Tschirnhaus, *Medicina mentis*, 2nd edn. (Leipzig: Thomas Fritsch, 1695). On this work, see C. A. van Peursen, 'E. W. von Tschirnhaus and the *ars inveniendi*', *Journal of the History of Ideas*, 54 (1993): 395–410; Martin Schönfeld, 'Dogmatic metaphysics and Tschirnhaus's methodology', *Journal of the History of Philosophy*, 36 (1998): 57–76; Catherine Wilson, 'Between *medicina mentis* and medical materialism', in Easton (ed.), *Logic and the Workings of the Mind*, 251–68.

[10] This point is made effectively by Lorne Falkenstein and Patricia Easton, 'Preface', in Easton (ed.), *Logic and the Workings of the Mind*, pp. i–vii, at pp. ii–iii. See also Norman Fiering, *Moral Philosophy at Seventeenth-Century Harvard: A Discipline in Transition* (Chapel Hill, NC: University of North Carolina Press, 1981), 240 n. 3.

It was in the discipline of logic that questions about reason and the nature of knowledge were treated in conventional school philosophy. It is thus the discipline of logic that should underlie our attempts to understand the significance in the history of philosophy of the emphasis that emerged in the later seventeenth century on 'human understanding'. Indeed, this emphasis developed in part from works of logic themselves. A number were published which endeavoured to apply some of the different theories of the 'new philosophy' to logic.[11] Pierre Gassendi's (1592–1655) posthumously published *Institutio logica* ('Logical institution', 1658) incorporated Gassendi's neo-Epicurean account of knowledge into the discipline. *La Logique, ou l'art de penser* ('Logic, or the art of thinking', 1661; 5th ed. 1683) of the Port-Royalists Antoine Arnauld and Pierre Nicole—as well as taking a number of tacit side-swipes at Gassendi's logic[12]—incorporated aspects of the Cartesian philosophy of ideas into a logical structure.[13] The relation of a slightly later philosopher like John Locke to the discipline of logic—who was familiar both with Gassendi's writings and with the Port-Royal *Logique*—was less direct. Locke frequently engages in explicit and indeed intemperate criticism of school logic in his *Essay Concerning Human Understanding*. None the less, aspects both of the structure and of the content of the *Essay* make best sense when seen in the context of the discipline of logic.[14]

Logic was a central component of the 'ordinary Course of Education' that Hume passed through with success: he studied it at Edinburgh in 1724 under Professor Colin Drummond, notes on whose lectures survive.[15] Many fewer of the assumptions and terms of the discipline of logic survive in Hume's *Treatise* than in Locke's *Essay*. And in contrast to Locke's persistent sniping, Hume makes only two explicit attacks on logic in the *Treatise*—although

[11] See further Gabriel Nuchelmans, 'Deductive reasoning', in Garber and Ayers (eds.), *Cambridge History of Seventeenth-Century Philosophy*, i. 132–46, at p. 144.

[12] F. S. Michael, 'Why logic became epistemology', 12–16.

[13] Hume was familiar with the Port-Royal *Logique*, which he cites in the *Treatise*, 43 n. 1. For an illuminating comparison between the account of miracles in the *Logique* and Hume, see M. A. Stewart, 'Hume's historical view of miracles', in M. A. Stewart and John P. Wright (eds.), *Hume and Hume's Connexions* (Edinburgh: Edinburgh University Press, 1994), 171–200, esp. pp. 176–80.

[14] See Paul Schuurman, 'Locke's logic of ideas in context: content and structure', *British Journal for the History of Philosophy*, 9 (2001): 439–66; E. J. Ashworth, ' "Do words signify ideas or things?": the scholastic sources of Locke's theory of language', *Journal of the History of Philosophy*, 19 (1981): 299–326.

[15] Ernest Campbell Mossner, *The Life of David Hume*, 2nd edn. (Oxford: Clarendon Press, 1980), 611, 42. Charles Echelbarger, 'Hume and the logicians', in Easton (ed.), *Logic and the Workings of the Mind*, 137–52, has attempted without notable success to determine which texts Drummond might have been drawing on in his logic lectures, a set of notes on which survive in the National Library of Scotland, MS 3938. No works of logic are among those noted by Hume in his post-university memoranda (see Ernest Campbell Mossner, 'Hume's early memoranda, 1729–1740: the complete text', *Journal of the History of Ideas*, 9 (1948): 492–518).

both, as we shall see, are highly significant for understanding what he conceived the significance of that work to be.[16] None the less, many of Hume's most extravagant philosophical paradoxes take their force from the rejection of earlier philosophical pieties. Moreover, when Hume tried to stimulate interest in the *Treatise* with the *Abstract* of 1740, part of his attempt to promote it consisted in describing Book I of the work as a kind of logic.[17] Here Hume explains that the 'science of human nature' (the subject of the *Treatise*) comprehends 'logic', the *'sole end'* of which *'is to explain the principles and Operations of our reasoning faculty, and the nature of our ideas'*; Hume goes on to state that in the *Treatise*, he 'has finished what regards logic' (p. 646).

The logic of the *Treatise*, of course, is a very far cry indeed from the logic of the schools. Hume himself signals this when he writes in the conclusion of Book I that by publishing the work he had 'expos'd himself to the enmity of all . . . logicians' (p. 265). Among other striking departures from more conventional logical works, Hume distinguishes between impressions and ideas (II. i. 7); gives his own enumeration of the qualities of relation between objects rather than appealing to the Aristotelian categories (I. i. 6); repudiates (as we shall see) the logical division of the 'acts of the intellect'; and argues that all reasoning is an effect of custom, and hence (remarkably) that 'reason is nothing but a wonderful and unintelligible instinct in our souls'.[18] In the *Enquiry Concerning Human Understanding* he also went on to denounce 'all those pretended syllogistical reasonings, which may be found in every other branch of learning, except the sciences of quantity and number' (*Enquiry*, 122).[19] The motive for these radical developments also emerges from the *Abstract* of the *Treatise*. There Hume alludes to an observation in Leibniz's *Théodicée* (1710), about 'a defect in the common systems of logic, that they are very copious when they explain the operations of the understanding in the forming of demonstrations, but are too concise when they treat of probabilities'.[20] Hume follows Leibniz in censuring Locke's

---

[16] Hume, *Treatise*, 183 may constitute a third attack.

[17] This point is brought out clearly by Echelbarger, 'Hume and the logicians', 142–3. R. W. Connon and M. Pollard, 'On the authorship of "Hume's" *Abstract*', *Philosophical Quarterly*, 27 (1977): 60–6, furnish positive evidence for Hume's authorship of the *Abstract*.

[18] Hume, *Treatise*, 149, 115, 183; cf. Hume, *An Enquiry Concerning Human Understanding*, ed. Tom L. Beauchamp, The Clarendon Edition of the Works of David Hume (Oxford: Clarendon Press, 2000), 81 n. 20. Hume, *Treatise*, 179.

[19] I do not follow J. A. Passmore, 'Descartes, the British empiricists and formal logic', *Philosophical Review*, 62 (1953): 545–53, at p. 548, in seeing this statement as indicating that Hume 'admitted the usefulness of syllogistic reasoning in mathematics'.

[20] Hume, *Abstract*, in *Treatise*, 646–7. G. W. Leibniz, *Essais de Théodicée sur la bonté de Dieu, la liberté de l'homme et l'origine du mal*, in *Œuvres philosophiques de Leibniz*, ed. Paul Janet, 2 vols. (Paris: Félix Alcan, 1900), i. 1–442, at pp. 49–50 ('De la conformité de la foi avec la raison', §31). On this point see also Lorraine Daston, *Classical Probability in the Enlightenment* (Princeton: Princeton University Press, 1988), 266. Cf. Leibniz's then unpublished *Nouveaux essais*

Essay, Malebranche's *De la Recherche de la vérité*, and the *Logique* of Arnauld and Nicole for exemplifying this defect, and goes on to explain that it is above all as a contribution to an understanding of probability that the first part of the *Treatise* should be considered.[21]

Hume's explication of what he calls in the *Treatise* 'reasonings from cause and effect'—which historians of philosophy have tended to treat anachronistically as the 'problem of induction'—was therefore intended by him as a contribution to a logic of probability.[22] It is no coincidence, then, that it is in the course of explaining how to judge the relations of cause and effect that we find Hume alluding most explicitly to his logical heritage.

'GENERAL RULES' IN THE *TREATISE OF HUMAN NATURE*

We have seen that one of the principal intellectual problems faced by the new experimental natural philosophers of the later seventeenth century was the incorporation of the particularity of experience into a mode of philosophy—natural philosophy—which in its Aristotelian form had prized universality and shunned local detail. One of the means by which the new philosophers had achieved this was by writing self-consciously circumstantial experimental narratives.[23] John Locke's account in his *Essay* of the 'improvement of our knowledge', with its emphasis on the particular, rather than the general, origin of all knowledge, can be seen as a response to this development within natural philosophy.[24] Hume's *Treatise*, with its insistence that not only all knowledge, but even all reasoning, is a function of experience, can be seen as the *ne plus ultra* of this tendency.

sur l'entendement humain, ed. André Robinet and Heinrich Schepers, in *Sämtliche Schriften und Briefen, Sechste Reihe: Philosophische Schriften*, vol. vi (Berlin: Akademie-Verlag, 1962), 206, 373.

[21] For this and other reasons I dissent from the unduly simplistic argument of Paul Russell, 'Hume's *Treatise* and Hobbes's *The Elements of Law*', *Journal of the History of Ideas*, 46 (1985): 51–63, that Hobbes's *Elements of Law* provides the 'scope and structure' of Hume's *Treatise*. On Hume's critique of Locke's account of probability, see David Owen, 'Hume's doubts about probable reasoning: was Locke the target?' in Stewart and Wright (eds.), *Hume and Hume's Connexions*, 140–59.

[22] For two recent attempts to explain 'Hume's problem' non-anachronistically, see J. R. Milton, 'Induction before Hume', *British Journal for the Philosophy of Science*, 38 (1987): 49–74, and Dear, *Discipline and Experience*, ch. 1.

[23] Steven Shapin, 'Pump and circumstance: Robert Boyle's literary technology', *Social Studies of Science*, 14 (1984): 481–520. Ian Maclean, 'Evidence, logic, the rule and the exception in Renaissance law and medicine', *Early Science and Medicine*, 5 (2000): 227–57, contains learned and valuable suggestions about late Renaissance medical precursors of this development.

[24] John Locke, *An Essay Concerning Human Understanding*, ed. P. H. Nidditch (Oxford: Clarendon Press, 1975), 680: 'the immediate Object of all our Reasoning and Knowledge, is nothing but Particulars'. On this point, see further Margaret J. Osler, 'John Locke and the changing ideal of scientific knowledge', *Journal of the History of Ideas*, 31 (1970): 3–16.

If philosophy began from the particular circumstances of experience, however, Hume did not believe that it should remain there. Indeed, as we shall see, he regarded the ability to derive general principles from particular experiences as what distinguished philosophers from the 'vulgar'. Whereas Aristotle had thought that intellectual acumen consisted in the ability to grasp middle terms quickly, Hume explained the 'great difference in human understandings' in terms of an ability to formulate general rules from one's experience that would comprehend as wide a variety of circumstances as possible.[25] Hume's problem was to explain how this was accomplished.

The most systematic account that Hume provided of how the circumstances of experience become subject to general rules occurs in the third Part of Book I of the *Treatise of Human Nature*. Here Hume describes '*general rules*' (p. 146) as a species of probability: that is to say, a form of reasoning, 'still attended with uncertainty' (p. 124).[26] They are not a part of 'science', since Hume still understands 'science' in the Aristotelian sense of certain, or demonstrative, knowledge (ibid. 73).[27] But because Hume's conception of the scope of science was highly limited, his conception of the operation of such general rules is correspondingly extensive.

Why did Hume think we formed 'general rules'? He opens his account pessimistically, suggesting that general rules underlie prejudices—it is a general rule that 'An *Irishman* cannot have wit, and a *Frenchman* cannot have solidity'[28]—and that we do not for the most part modify such prejudices 'even contrary to' the exceptions provided by 'present observation and experience' (ibid. 146-7.[29] Hume goes on, however, to suggest that general rules are not simply, or indeed merely, a source of error. On the contrary, Hume argues that human understanding cannot operate without them. Our experience generates general rules about relations between causes and effects, and so when we encounter a cause like those we are already familiar with, 'the imagination naturally carries us to a lively conception of the usual effect' (ibid. 150).[30] General rules are part of the

---

[25] Aristotle, *Posterior Analytics*, trans. Jonathan Barnes, in *The Complete Works of Aristotle: The Revised Oxford Translation*, ed. Jonathan Barnes, 2 vols. (Princeton: Princeton University Press, 1984), i. 114–66, at p. 147 (1.34). Hume, *Enquiry Concerning Human Understanding*, 81 n. 20.

[26] The account by Thomas K. Hearn, Jr., 'General rules in Hume's *Treatise*', *Journal of the History of Philosophy*, 8 (1970): 405–22, is lucid and judicious. See also Martin, 'Rational warrant'. David Owen, *Hume's Reason* (Oxford: Oxford University Press, 1999), 148–9, notes that general rules constitute 'an important ingredient in Hume's account of probable reasoning'.

[27] On this point, see further Owen, 'Hume's doubts about probable reasoning', 142.

[28] This comment is both exemplary and ironic, and therefore cannot simply be taken as an expression of Hume's own prejudices. On this point see further Robert Palter, 'Hume and prejudice', *Hume Studies*, 21 (1995): 3–23, at p. 11.

[29] On this point see also Owen, *Hume's Reason*, 212–13.

[30] Charles J. McCracken, *Malebranche and British Philosophy* (Oxford: Clarendon Press, 1983), 279, notes the shared preoccupation of Hume and Malebranche with the capacity of the imagination to confuse constant conjunction with necessary connection.

accumulated experience that enables us to understand, and function in, the world.[31]

If we are philosophers, however, we also use general rules to correct these first impressions, in accordance with 'the more general and authentic operations of the understanding'.[32] Hume illustrates the way in which 'our general rules' are thus 'in a manner set in opposition to each other' with an example. He asks us to consider the case of a man hung from a high tower in an iron cage. This man, Hume asserts, 'cannot forbear trembling', even though 'he knows himself to be perfectly secure from falling, by the solidity of the iron which supports him' (ibid. 148–9). The general rule that great height presents a great danger is set against the general rule that iron provides a secure stay. The one kind of rule is supplied by the imagination, the other by the judgement. Hume does not draw the moral explicitly, but his account certainly implies that, tremble though he still might, a caged philosopher would tremble less than a less reflective prisoner.

Hume ascribed a good deal of importance to his 'general rules'; so much so, in fact, that in the *Treatise* he articulated a set of them to judge the relations between causes and effects. According to Hume's account of causation, it is in principle 'possible for all objects to become causes or effects to each other'. In order to determine 'when they really are so', Hume provides his set of eight general rules. These rules are intended to distinguish 'accidental circumstances' from 'efficacious causes'. They include such stipulations as 'The cause and effect must be contiguous in space and time'; 'The cause must be prior to the effect'; and 'There must be a constant union betwixt the cause and effect' (ibid. 173, 149).[33]

The inspiration for Hume's 'Rules by which to judge of causes and effects' has sometimes been ascribed to the four *Regulae philosophandi* printed at the beginning of Book III of Isaac Newton's *Principiae mathematica philosophia naturalis* ('Mathematical principles of natural philosophy') in the third edition of 1726.[34] Hume's own account of their nature, however,

[31] On this point, see also David Owen, 'Philosophy and the good life: Hume's defence of probable reasoning', *Dialogue*, 35 (1996): 485–503, at pp. 491–2.

[32] On this point, see also Noxon, *Hume's Philosophical Development*, 87; Martin, 'Rational warrant', 251; Owen, *Hume's Reason*, 212.

[33] On Hume's use of general rules in this context see further Owen, *Hume's Reason*, 206.

[34] Isaac Newton, *Philosophiae naturalis principia mathematica: The Third Edition (1726) with variant readings*, ed. A. Koyré and I. B. Cohen, with the assistance of A. Whitman, 2 vols. (Cambridge: Cambridge University Press, 1972), ii. 550–5. The *regulae* took their final form only in this third edition. Maurizio Mamiani, 'To twist the meaning: Newton's *Regulae philosophandi* revisited', in J. Z. Buchwald and I. B. Cohen (eds.), *Isaac Newton's Natural Philosophy* (Cambridge, Mass.: MIT Press, 2000), 3–14, provides a questionable recent interpretation. Hume alludes to Newton's third rule in *An Enquiry Concerning the Principles of Morals*, ed. Tom L. Beauchamp, The Clarendon Edition of the Works of David Hume (Oxford: Clarendon Press, 1998), 27; see further Wright, *Sceptical Realism of David Hume*, 198.

suggests a different context. Having articulated the eight general rules, Hume pauses to make the following polemical comment:

Here is all the LOGIC I think proper to employ in my reasoning; and perhaps even this was not very necessary, but might have been supply'd by the natural principles of our understanding. Our scholastic headpieces and logicians shew no such superiority above the mere vulgar in their reason and ability, as to give us any inclination to imitate them in delivering a long system of rules and precepts to direct our judgment, in philosophy. (ibid. 175)[35]

Two principal points emerge for our purposes from this passage.[36] The first is that Hume regarded the articulation of rules in philosophy (as distinct from the general rules that he had suggested we all frame in daily life) as being an aspect of the discipline of logic ('our scholastic headpieces and logicians'). This recognition casts doubt on the suggestion that Hume's principal inspiration here came from Newton's *regulae*. Whilst Hume goes on in the following sentences to discuss the example of natural philosophy, it is clear that he does not regard the formulation of such rules as being restricted to that discipline.[37] The second point to emerge from this passage is that, within the discipline of logic, Hume regarded rules as having the function of directing the 'judgment' ('a long system of rules and precepts to direct our judgment, in philosophy'), a comment that recalls the subtitle of the Port-Royal *Logique*: 'Containing, besides common rules (*règles communes*), several new observations for developing the judgment'.

Hume, then, in a rather conventional manner, regarded his rules as pertaining to the 'judgment'. His account of judgement, however, was quite different from the 'scholastic headpieces' whose works he knew through Professor Drummond's logic lectures. The typical account that school philosophers gave of the intellect or understanding (*intellectus*) divided its activities into three distinct roles: the so-called acts of the mind (*actus intellectus*).[38] (Hume employs this scholastic term in the *Treatise*.[39]) The three 'acts of the mind' consisted of 'apprehension' (*apprehensio*), judgement (*judicium*), and ratiocination (*discursus*).[40] The logics taught in

[35] 'Headpiece' (*OED*, 2nd edn., 4b): 'A man possessed of brains; a man of intellect'.

[36] Other aspects of the passage are brought out by Louis Loeb, 'Causal inference, association-ism, and scepticism in Part III of Book I of Hume's *Treatise*', in Easton (ed.), *Logic and the Workings of the Mind*, 283–306, at p. 290.

[37] Cf. Noxon, *Hume's Philosophical Development*, 82–3 (a valuable discussion), who charac-terizes this section as 'some remarks in the Newtonian spirit upon the difficulty and importance of devising experiments to exclude extraneous factors', and goes on to note the different concerns of Newton's and Hume's rules—the one with the physical world, the other with human experience— but concludes that they are none the less 'quite compatible'.

[38] Drummond taught this doctrine in his lectures: Echelbarger, 'Hume and the logicians', 140, 144.

[39] Hume, *Treatise*, 150: 'this act of the mind'.

[40] The details of terminology varied, but the structure remained constant. This account is taken from one of the most widely read school philosophers in the period, Franco Burgersdijk. The *actus*

the Scottish universities in the later seventeenth and earlier eighteenth centuries all endorsed this division.[41] Indeed, seventeenth- and earlier eighteenth-century works on logic were commonly organized according to this arrangement, with each act of the mind being accorded a separate section.[42] A number of works also added a fourth section on 'method' (*methodus*), although it should be noted that Drummond criticized this tendency in his logic lectures.[43]

Hume had decisively rejected this threefold division of the acts of the mind in a polemical footnote earlier in the *Treatise*:

We may here take occasion to observe a very remarkable error, which being frequently inculcated in the schools has become a kind of establish'd maxim, and is
universally received by all logicians. This error consists in the vulgar division of
the acts of the understanding, into *conception, judgment* and *reasoning*, and in the
definitions we give of them. Conception is defin'd to be the simple survey of one
or more ideas: Judgment to be the separating or uniting of different ideas:
Reasoning to be the separating or uniting of different ideas by the interposition of
others, which show the relation they bear to each other.

According to Hume, however, 'these distinctions and definitions are faulty in very considerable articles': there is only one act of the mind, and that is the first—conception (ibid. 96 n. 1).[44] This is an unusually explicit attack on the traditions of reasoning which the *Treatise* both emerges from and comprehensively rejects. It is aimed both at school logic and also at more self-consciously modern works in the discipline, such as those by Arnauld and Nicole and Isaac Watts, since their works too endorsed this division of the understanding.[45] In context, this attack is part of Hume's endeavour to explain the nature of belief. In respect of his larger philosophy, however, it relates to his account of reasoning as being an immediate and indeed an instinctive process. Hume's attacks on the logic of judgement invite us to consider a further question: how his account of 'general rules' relates to earlier accounts of the nature and function of rules in logic and philosophy more generally.

---

intellectus are found widely in early-modern Aristotelian philosophy, although they are nowhere distinguished in Aristotle's *Organon* or *De anima*; see further E. J. Ashworth, 'Editor's introduction', in Robert Sanderson, *Logicae Artis Compendium (1618)*, ed. E. J. Ashworth, Instrumenta Rationis, 2 (Bologna: Clueb, 1985), pp. ix–lv, at pp. xl–xli.

[41] Emily Michael, 'Frances Hutcheson's *Logicae compendium* and the Glasgow school of logic', in Easton (ed.), *Logic and the Workings of the Mind*, 83–96, at p. 88.

[42] On this point, see also F. S. Michael, 'Why logic became epistemology', 9.

[43] Personal communication from Prof. M. A. Stewart.

[44] Kant, by contrast, argued that all acts of the understanding could be reduced to judgements (see the discussion in Jill Vance Buroker, 'The priority of thought to language in Cartesian philosophy', in Easton (ed.), *Logic and the Workings of the Mind*, 97–107, at p. 104).

[45] This point is made by Echelbarger, 'Hume and the logicians', 144.

'RULES' IN EARLY-MODERN PHILOSOPHY

Historians of early-modern philosophy tend to concentrate on philosophers' explicit arguments, rather than the form in which they are couched or the presuppositions that underlie them. There is a case, however, for suggesting that this approach risks missing a good part of the significance of such works.[46] One such aspect of early-modern philosophy, which was rarely reflected upon but which permeated many parts of it, was its reliance upon 'rules'. In this regard, Hume's account of 'general rules' should be seen as a formalization of tendencies already implicit in early-modern philosophy.

Seventeenth-century philosophers draw so extensively upon rules that it is not a simple matter to determine where Hume stands in relation to their practices. As we have seen, Hume related his general rules concerning cause and effect explicitly to logic. Rules were certainly a significant component of works in this discipline. A celebrated vernacular logic of the sixteenth century was simply entitled *The Rule of Reason*.[47] Pierre Gassendi articulated the generally unspoken assumption that 'it is the task (*officium*) of logic to provide canons or rules (*Canones sive Regulas*) governing correct thinking'. He went on, however, to display a rather unusual degree of self-consciousness in his *Institutio logica* about his own use of such rules: 'the canons which we are proposing concerning each part are not to be taken as strict rules or injunctions (*Regulae seu praecepta*) stipulating some definite requirement as much as speculative propositions which offer something for consideration'.[48] Other self-consciously post-scholastic logicians expressed reservations about rules, whilst eventually succumbing to the temptation to provide them. This is the case, for instance, in Jean Le Clerc's *Logica, sive ars ratiocinandi* ('Logic, or the art of reasoning', 1692). Le Clerc, who had been a close associate of John Locke when the latter was living in exile in the Low Countries in the mid-1680s, drew a number of aspects of his logic from Locke's *Essay*. One of these was a suspicion of formal rules of reasoning. Le Clerc explained in a very Lockean manner that, whilst 'old Philosophers' (*veteres Philosophi*) had found it necessary to formulate explicit *regulae* for teaching and to moderate disputations, he regarded such rules as unnecessary for people of unimpaired intellect. None the less—Le Clerc eventually capitulates—he too will provide such rules of reasoning, although not in the same spirit as the old philosophers, but because they are true (*sed quia verae*

---

[46] This case is made by Quentin Skinner, *Reason and Rhetoric in the Philosophy of Hobbes* (Cambridge: Cambridge University Press, 1996), esp. pp. 14–15. For a valuable attempt to consider the various generic affiliations of the *Treatise*, see Box, *Suasive Art of David Hume*, 90–110.

[47] Thomas Wilson, *The Rule of Reason* (London: John Kingston, 1563; first pub. 1551).

[48] Pierre Gassendi, *Institutio logica* (1658), ed. and trans. Howard Jones (Assen: Van Gorcum, 1981), 2; translation (modified) from pp. 81–2. Gassendi's adoption of the Epicurean device of 'canons' is specific to his own philosophical project.

sunt), and because they can sometimes be of use.[49] Rules survived prominently in the best-known English contribution to the discipline written in the eighteenth century, Isaac Watts's *Logic* (1725). Watts regarded rules and general directions as an integral part of his work. He provides numerous 'general directions', 'particular rules', and indeed 'general rules' for directing the judgement and the reason. Watts particularly emphasized the utility of 'general rules' for guiding the judgement: they are necessary, he writes, 'in order to judge aright'.[50] Thus, while works of logic commonly took the form of sets of rules, the philosophical status of the rule itself was not so often considered.

In general, early-modern philosophers manifested a striking reluctance to reflect upon the nature of the rules that they crammed into their writings. They were normative, but unexamined. This tendency is particularly evident in the Cartesian tradition. Descartes's first sustained piece of philosophical writing was his *Regulae ad directionem ingenii* (first published in Latin in 1701 and hence potentially accessible to Hume). Like Hume, Descartes clearly regarded the function of his rules as being to 'direct the judgment', since his first *regula* is: 'The aim of our studies should be to direct the mind with a view to forming true and sound judgments about whatever comes before it.'[51] But he is reticent about the status that such rules themselves have within his philosophy. He did note with curiosity in his earliest surviving papers (the so-called *Cogitationes privatae*, unpublished until 1859) that he was 'making use of definite rules' in his thinking.[52] None the less, subsequent explicit reflection on their function in the *Regulae* is restricted to comments such as this one: 'a large number of rules is often the result of inexperience in the teacher'.[53] It is notable, however, that in his later writings Descartes placed much less emphasis on philosophical 'rules'. In the *Meditationes* (1641)—which was one of the works of metaphysics which Hume

[49] Jean Le Clerc, *Logica, sive ars ratiocinandi* (London: Awnsham and John Churchill, 1692), 150–1. For the (unsubstantiated) suggestion that Hume may have known Le Clerc's *Logica*, see Echelbarger, 'Hume and the logicians', 140. Cf. Locke, *Essay*, 670: 'If we will observe the Actings of our own Minds, we shall find that we reason best and clearest, when we only observe the connexion of the Proofs, without reducing our Thoughts to any Rule of syllogism.... The Understanding is not taught to reason by these Rules; it has a native Faculty to perceive the Coherence or Incoherence of its *Ideas*, and can range them right, without any such perplexing Repetitions.'

[50] Isaac Watts, *Logic; or, The Right Use of Reason, in the Enquiry after Truth. With a variety of rules to guard against error, in the affairs of religion and human life, as well as in the sciences* (Chiswick: Thomas Tegg, 1828), 183.

[51] René Descartes, *Regulae ad directionem ingenii*, in *Œuvres de Descartes*, ed. C. Adam and P. Tannery, 12 vols. (Paris: Vrin, 1964–76), x. 359–472, at p. 359. Translation from Descartes, *Rules for the direction of the mind*, in *The Philosophical Writings*, trans. R. Stoothoff, D. Murdoch, and J. Cottingham, 3 vols. (Cambridge: Cambridge University Press, 1985), i. 7–78, at p. 9.

[52] Descartes, *Cogitationes privatae*, in *Œuvres*, ed. Adam and Tannery, x. 214.

[53] Descartes, *Regulae*, x. 461 (*regula* 18). Translation from Descartes, 'Rules', in *Philosophical Writings*, i. 71.

recommended to his friend Michael Ramsay as preparatory reading for understanding the *Treatise*[54]—Descartes is not concerned with formulating rules at all.

Subsequent Cartesians were scarcely more explicit than their master about the status of the rules that they continued to elaborate so eagerly. The Port-Royal *Logique*, which incorporates material from Descartes's *Regulae*, contains a good number of rules relating to logical procedures, but little reflection upon their status. Arnauld and Nicole do comment that 'rules' about sophisms in logical argument, 'viewed merely as speculative truths', are 'useful for exercising the mind'.[55] Otherwise, however, the extensive deployment of *règles* in the *Logique* goes unexplained. The case of Malebranche, whose *De la Recherche de la vérité* Hume studied closely, is analogous.[56] The final book of the *Recherche* is framed according to 'rules that [the mind] must observe in the search after truth in order never to err'.[57] In the work, however, Malebranche does not explicitly reflect on the philosophical status of the rules he elaborates.

Hume's rules by which to judge of causes and effects, then, clearly take their generic form from earlier traditions of furnishing philosophical rules. But his suspicion of 'rules and precepts to direct our judgment, in philosophy' also reflects the unexamined status of such rules in earlier traditions. As early-modern logic had become increasingly concerned with questions of human understanding and knowledge, rather than neo-Aristotelian categorical and syllogistic logic, so the resort to 'rules' began to seem increasingly problematic. There is another aspect to 'rules' in early-modern philosophy which was considered more explicitly, however, and which also has an important bearing on Hume's account of their significance. This aspect was the use of axioms or maxims to regulate philosophical reasoning. In this regard, 'rules' formed a fundamental component of early-modern Aristotelian philosophy in general, and of the disciplines of logic, physics, and metaphysics in particular. It was of this tradition that Leibniz commented in the *Nouveaux essais* that 'There are certain philosophical rules— big books crammed with them—which people like to use'.[58] One such book, the Jena Aristotelian Daniel Stahl's (1585–1654) *Regulae philosophicae*

[54] Mossner, *Life of David Hume*, 627.

[55] Antoine Arnauld and Pierre Nicole, *La Logique ou l'art de penser*, ed. P. Clair and F. Girbal, 2nd edn. (Paris: Vrin, 1981), 178. Translation from Arnauld and Nicole, *Logic, or the Art of Thinking*, ed. and trans. J. V. Buroker (Cambridge: Cambridge University Press, 1996), 135.

[56] On Hume's relations to Malebranche, see McCracken, *Malebranche and British Philosophy*, esp. pp. 257–8.

[57] Nicolas Malebranche, *De la Recherche de la vérité*, in *Œuvres*, ed. G. Rodis-Lewis, 2 vols. (Paris: Gallimard, 1979), i. 1–1126, at p. 590. Translation from Malebranche, *The Search after Truth*, ed. and trans. T. M. Lennon and P. Olscamp (Cambridge: Cambridge University Press, 1997), 408.

[58] Leibniz, *Nouveaux essais*, 419. Translation from Leibniz, *New Essays*, 419.

('Philosophical rules', 1657) explains the value of rules precisely as inhering in their general nature. Stahl began his treatise by explaining that 'We have put together these Philosophical rules, which, on account of their generality (*propter generalitatem*), are conspicuously valuable in all disciplines'. Hume's account of rules retains the Aristotelian emphasis on generality. But he could not endorse a further aspect of these axiomatic *regulae*, which held them to be *praecognita*—that is, self-evident, and indeed prior to reasoning or experience.[59]

It was in their Aristotelian aspect as precognitive maxims that John Locke launched a devastating attack on general rules in Book IV, chapter 7, of the *Essay Concerning Human Understanding*. In his *Free and Impartial Censure of the Platonick Philosophie* (1666), Samuel Parker (who seems to be one of Locke's targets in this chapter) had attempted to rehabilitate such maxims by arguing that their basis was fundamentally empirical: '*general Axiomes* are only the results and abridgements of a multitude of single Experiments'.[60] Locke, by contrast, equated such rules of reasoning with Aristotelian metaphysical maxims that the mechanical philosophy had done so much to explode. Locke's objection to such maxims was that their self-evidence had both been taken for granted and also taken as a reason for supposing that they constituted a form of innate ideas. Locke did not regard such '*general Maxims*' as entirely useless: he acknowledged their function in teaching and in moderating excessively contentious disputation. He did, however, deny that they served any of the three chief constructive functions ascribed to them by 'Scholastick Men': viz., those of proving less general self-evident propositions, of being the foundation of sciences, and of helping in the 'new Discoveries of yet unknown Truths'. And he closed his chapter on maxims with a warning that they were potentially a potent source of error. As becomes even clearer when Locke returns to the question in the chapter 'Of the Improvement of our Knowledge', the basis of his critique of the scholastic understanding of general maxims is that they do not take account of the particularity of experience. For Locke, it is 'the particular instance' that gives 'Life and Birth' to the 'general Rule', and not the other way round.[61]

---

[59] Daniel Stahl, *Regulae philosophicae* (Oxford: J. Webb, 1663), 1. On this point see further Maclean, 'Evidence, logic, the rule and the exception', who discusses (pp. 235, 238) the senses of *generaliter*, and concludes persuasively (p. 256): 'The laws which [Renaissance doctors and jurists] invoke under the name of "axiomata," "praecognita," "regulae," "ordo" are different in kind from those which preoccupy such thinkers of the seventeenth century as Descartes and Newton. If there is a decisive shift in mental habit which occurred between these figures and the late Renaissance, it is perhaps to be located here rather than in the slavish and uncritical adherence to Aristotelian doctrines of which they were accused by their successors.'

[60] Samuel Parker, *A Free and Impartial Censure of the Platonick Philosophie* (Oxford: Richard Davis, 1666), 55. See also the discussion by Milton, 'Induction before Hume', 64.

[61] Locke, *Essay*, 591; see also 639–41. Ibid., 598, 630.

Locke is distinguished from Hume, then, by the destructive aspect of his account of the place of maxims or general rules in human understanding. This is largely explained by the fact that his understanding of them was restricted mainly to their scholastic use as axioms. In this respect Locke's interlocutor G. W. Leibniz had a more capacious view of the value of general rules. In his *Nouveaux essais* Leibniz argued in opposition to Locke that 'Discoverers have been delighted to catch sight of maxims and general truths when they have succeeded in arriving at them, since otherwise their discoveries would have remained quite incomplete'. Leibniz also drew attention to the restricted sense in which Locke had understood maxims by making the point that, far from it being 'only the Schools that are prone to form maxims', in fact it was 'a general and very reasonable human instinct'. As Hume would explain prejudices ('an *Irishman* cannot have wit') in terms of the kind of general rules that cannot be avoided, so Leibniz described 'the proverbs which are current in every nation' as being 'usually nothing but maxims accepted by the whole populace'.[62] Although he could hardly have known the *Nouveaux essais*, then, Hume's account of general rules is closer to Leibniz than to Locke. Whilst rejecting outright their Aristotelian content and metaphysical import, Hume retained the philosophical sense that general rules were a valuable, and indeed necessary, form of reason.

Having seen how the form and context of Hume's general rules ultimately derive from traditions of logic and school philosophy more generally, we are now in a position to return to the long-standing question of their natural philosophical—and, more specifically, experimental—inspiration. For philosophers as diverse as Locke and Arnauld, it was natural philosophy that had done most to damage the Aristotelian reliance on maxims and rules. As Arnauld and Nicole had pointed out in their *Logique*, the experiments of the new natural philosophy had provided exceptions to rules which had hitherto been thought indubitable—such as the rule that water always finds its own level.[63] As we have seen, this had led Locke to a suspicion of all general principles when faced with the necessary particularity of human knowledge. Not all natural philosophers shared this suspicion, however. As we have also seen, Newton retained his *regulae philosophandi* in the *Principia*, even citing the hoary maxim that 'Nature does nothing in vain' (*Natura agit nihil frustra*) in the gloss to his first rule.[64]

The author whose conception of 'general rules' perhaps came closest to that of Hume, however, was the Irish metaphysician George Berkeley (1685–1753). Hume was well acquainted with Berkeley's writings. He refers

[62] Leibniz, *Nouveaux essais*, 416, 421. Translations from Leibniz, *New Essays*, 416, 421.
[63] Arnauld and Nicole, *La Logique*, 317 (4.6). See further Milton, 'Induction before Hume', 59.
[64] Newton, *Philosophiae naturalis principia mathematica*, ii. 550.

to Berkeley at the beginning of the *Treatise of Human Nature* as 'a great philosopher', and his *Treatise Concerning the Principles of Human Knowledge* (1710; 2nd edn. 1734) he recommended to Ramsay as preparation for his own *Treatise* (p. 17 and n. 1).[65] In the *Principles*, Berkeley discusses 'general rules' in a manner that bears close comparison with Hume's account in the *Treatise*:

> If therefore we consider the difference there is betwixt natural philosophers and other men, with regard to their knowledge of the *phenomena*, we shall find it consists, not in an exacter knowledge of the efficient cause that produces them, . . . but only in a greater largeness of comprehension, whereby analogies, harmonies, and agreements are discovered in the works of Nature, and the particular effects explained, that is, reduced to general rules, . . . which rules grounded on the analogy, and uniformness observed in the production of natural effects, are most agreeable, and sought after by the mind; for that they extend our prospect beyond what is present, and near to us, and enable us to make very probable conjectures, touching things that may have happened at very great distances of time and place, as well as to predict things to come; which sort of endeavour towards omniscience, is much affected by the mind.

Berkeley went on to make it clear that he considered his 'general rules' to be analogous to 'Laws of Nature', that is, 'certain general laws that run through the whole chain of natural effects', which are 'learned by the observation and study of Nature'.[66]

Berkeley's account of 'general rules' is significant for our understanding of Hume for the emphasis he places on their desirability, their non-demonstrative status,[67] and their capacity to distinguish philosophers from 'other men'. His account is also none the less different from Hume's in several important respects. In the first place, Berkeley's consideration of general rules is restricted to the sphere of natural philosophy. Secondly, for Berkeley, the 'general rules' formulated by philosophers are a direct reflection of the regulation of nature effected by God ('or the intelligence which sustains and rules the ordinary course of things').[68] In something more than a simple play on words, human

---

[65] Mossner, *Life of David Hume*, 104, and 626–7. See also Hume, *Enquiry Concerning Human Understanding*, 116 n. 32. See further Richard H. Popkin, 'So, Hume did read Berkeley', *Journal of Philosophy*, 61 (1964): 773–8, and references therein.

[66] George Berkeley, *A Treatise Concerning the Principles of Human Knowledge*, ed. J. Dancy (Oxford: Oxford University Press, 1998), 141, 142. Analogously, Robert Boyle, *A Free Enquiry into the Vulgarly Received Notion of Nature* (1686), ed. E. B. Davis and M. Hunter (Cambridge: Cambridge University Press, 1996), 39, speaks of God settling 'such laws or rules of local motion'.

[67] Berkeley, *Principles*, 142 (§107): 'by a diligent observation of the *phenomena* within our view, we may discover the general laws of Nature, and from them deduce the other *phenomena*, I do not say *demonstrate* . . .'.

[68] Berkeley, *Principles*, 125 (§62). For discussion, see Michael Ayers, 'Natures and laws from Descartes to Hume', in G. A. J. Rogers and S. Tomaselli (eds.), *The Philosophical Canon in the 17th and 18th Centuries: Essays in honour of John W. Yolton*, (Rochester, NY: University of Rochester Press, 1996), 83–108, at pp. 101–4.

rules reflect divine rule. Hume may have accepted the basic structure of Berkeley's account of general rules, but he never accepted that they were under-written by the deity (*Treatise*, 159–60). Finally, and most characteristically, Berkeley does not regard the natural philosophers' 'general rules' as providing any knowledge about relations of cause and effect. Instead, they are simply a reflection of our perception of signs: 'Those men who frame general rules from the *phenomena*, and afterwards derive the *phenomena* from those rules, seem to consider signs rather than causes.'[69] Here again we may see Hume's account of general rules as a response to Berkeley. Hume acknowledges that it is 'only by signs' that we become sensible of effects (*Treatise*, 151). But he does not accept Berkeley's doubts about our ability to discern their causes, since that is precisely what his 'Rules by which to judge of causes and effects' are intended to accomplish.

With this account behind us we are now in a position to assess where Hume's *Treatise* stands in relation to previous accounts of 'general rules' in early-modern philosophy. The first, and perhaps most important, point to make is that in his hostility to long systems of 'rules and precepts to direct our judgment, in philosophy', Hume is an inheritor and in some senses the culmination of seventeenth-century tendencies towards a 'natural logic' rather than an 'artificial' account of ratiocination.[70] That is to say, Hume rejected any division between the acts of the understanding, and any account of the reasoning process that conceived it as being guided by a priori rules rather than by experience or custom. He rejected the putatively self-evident maxims and axioms of the neo-Aristotelian tradition, and also the Cartesian alternative offered by Arnauld and Nicole and by Malebranche, with their numerous but unexamined philosophical *règles*.

Locke's *Essay*, with its hostility to scholastic accounts of ratiocination, was an important precursor in its emphasis on the naturalness of the reason-ing process. But Hume did not follow Locke's wholly negative account of 'general rules' in reasoning. Locke had associated these rules with scholastic axioms and *praecognita*, and rejected them because he found them a positive impediment to knowledge gained from experience. Hume also implicitly rejects the scholastic account of the precognitive and self-evident character of general rules. But Hume, as Leibniz had also done, maintained the view that the mind is necessarily guided by general rules or maxims, which it forms to itself according to experience. The challenge—and it was a challenge that

---

[69] Berkeley, *Principles*, 142 (§108); see also p. 126 (§65): 'the connexion of ideas does not imply the relation of *cause* and *effect*, but only of a mark or *sign* with the thing *signified*'.

[70] See e.g. Pierre du Moulin, *The Elements of Logick* (London: Nicholas Bourne, 1624), sig. 7ᵛ; Descartes, *Regulae*, x. 440; Richard Burthogge, *Organum Vetus & Novum: Or, A Discourse of Reason and Truth. Wherein the Natural Logick common to Mankinde is briefly and plainly described* (London: Samuel Crouch, 1678); Locke, *Essay*, esp. pp. 672, 677. See also Passmore, 'Descartes, the British empiricists and formal logic', 548–9.

had been laid down above all by natural philosophers and theorized in particular by Berkeley—was to formulate these rules as subtly and effectively as possible, according to the diverse circumstances of experience. Perhaps the most important point to make, however, about Hume's uptake of the broadly natural-philosophical account of general rules is that he extended them beyond natural philosophy. Hume, remarkably, denied that there was any distinction between the kind of rules one formulates about nature, and the kind of rules one formulates about human affairs. This is one of his most striking paradoxes: his refusal to acknowledge in his account of human understanding the venerable distinction between natural and moral philosophy. This refusal is implicit in the *Treatise* in the example of the man in the iron cage; it is made explicit in the *Enquiry Concerning Human Understanding* when Hume states that natural and moral arguments are 'of the same nature, and derived from the same principles' (p. 69).

'THE CHIEF BUSINESS OF PHILOSOPHERS'

Hume never lost his conviction that philosophers were distinguished from the 'vulgar' by their ability to subsume the circumstantial multiplicity of experience within effective general rules.[71] He did restrain his desire to provide a formal account of this procedure, however, as can be seen when we turn to consider the role of rules and circumstance in the two *Enquiries*. In a notice written for posthumous publication, Hume advertised the *Enquiry Concerning Human Understanding* as containing 'most of the principles, and reasonings' of the *Treatise*. The part of this *Enquiry* that corresponds most closely to the account of 'general rules' in the *Treatise* (I. iii. 13) is a footnote in Section 5 attacking the conventional distinction made between 'reason' and 'experience'. Here Hume explains that all the sciences—whether natural, moral, or political— 'will be found to terminate, at last, in some general principle or conclusion, for which we can assign no reason but observation and experience', and he goes on to equate these principles with 'general and just maxims' (*Enquiry*, 1, 37–8 n. 8).

In the transition between the *Treatise* and the *Enquiries*, then, Hume's unphilosophical 'general rules' tend to become 'maxims'. This is confirmed by a comment in another long footnote in the section 'Of the Reason of Animals', in which Hume explains why, despite the fact that reasoning

---

[71] Here I am in agreement with Hearn, 'General rules in Hume's *Treatise*', 406, who notes that 'a natural tendency requiring correction by general rules . . . can be said to represent one of the basic ingredients in Hume's account of human nature and experience'. It follows that I dissent from the conclusion of Noxon, *Hume's Philosophical Development*, 192, that the later Hume decided that 'the student of nature has more to learn from history than from the experimental method'; Hume did not regard the two as contradictory.

concerning cause and effect is 'derived merely from custom', men none the less surpass animals, and some men other men, in reasoning. Part of his explanation concerns 'the forming of general maxims from particular observation' (ibid. 81 n. 20). There is a further telling reformulation of his account of general rules at the end of the first section of *An Enquiry Concerning the Principles of Morals* (1751), where Hume speaks of 'following the experimental method, and deducing general maxims from a comparison of particular instances' (p. 6).[72]

In his *Essays*, Hume likewise tends not to deploy his more technical vocabulary of 'general rules', but instead speaks fairly indifferently of 'maxims', 'rules', and 'general principles'. He retained, however, the basic framework of his understanding of the relationship between rule and circumstance, for he recapitulates it more than once. The most striking instance of this is in the introduction to the essay 'Of Commerce', first published in the *Political Discourses* of 1752. Here Hume distinguishes between '*shallow* thinkers' and '*abstruse* thinkers' according to their capacity for 'general reasonings'. Abstruse thinkers—philosophers—have the capacity to form accurate general rules from a multiplicity of circumstances: they are able to 'distinguish, in a great number of particulars, that common circumstance in which they all agree, or to extract it, pure and unmixed, from the other superfluous circumstances'. General principles, Hume continues, 'must always prevail in the general course of things', and 'it is the chief business of philosophers to regard the general course of things'.[73]

Hume's account of the office of the philosopher in this essay is therefore consistent both with the *Treatise* and with the *Enquiry Concerning Human Understanding*. In the 'Introduction' to the former, Hume had written that it was his task, as an experimental moral philosopher, to 'endeavour to render all our principles as universal as possible, by tracing up our experiments to the utmost, and explaining all effects from the simplest and fewest causes' (p. xvii). In the First *Enquiry*, Hume had reiterated this point, explaining that 'the endeavour of' moralists as well as of 'critics, logicians, and even politicians' has been to find 'general principles'. One of the best sources for such general principles was human history. In the *Enquiry Concerning Human Understanding*, Hume had explained that the 'chief use' of history 'is only to discover the constant and universal principles of human nature, by showing men in all varieties of circumstances and situations, and

[72] For discussion of the problematic sense of 'deducing' in this passage, see Owen, 'Hume's doubts about probable reasoning', 141. General rules do make a reappearance, however, in the Second *Enquiry*, 29, where we learn that 'General rules are often extended beyond the principle, whence they first arise; and this in all matters of taste and sentiment'. This can be seen as a hangover from Hume, *Treatise*, 572 (3.2.12). For further and more passing references to 'general rules' of morality in the second *Enquiry*, see pp. 76, 121.

[73] David Hume, *Essays Moral, Political, and Literary*, ed. Eugene F. Miller, rev. edn. (Indianapolis: Liberty Classics, 1985), 253–4.

furnishing us with materials from which we may form our observations and become acquainted with the regular springs of human action and behaviour' (pp. 11–12). Hume himself draws the moral here, explaining that history functions for the moral philosopher like 'so many collections of experiments', in just the way that the experiments of natural philosophers acquaint them with the nature of 'plants, minerals, and other external objects' (p. 64). Indeed, Hume retained his concern with the importance of general principles in the *Dialogues Concerning Natural Religion* (first drafted in the 1750s; published posthumously in 1779). In a celebrated passage in the first part of that work, Hume compares philosophy to 'common life', and explains that the progress of both consists in the acquisition of effective general principles:

He considers besides, that every one, even in common Life, is constrain'd to have more or less of this Philosophy; that from our earliest Infancy we make continual Advances in forming more general Principles of Conduct and Reasoning; that the larger Experience we acquire, and the stronger Reason we are endow'd with, we always render our Principles the more general and comprehensive; and that what we call *Philosophy* is nothing but a more regular and methodical Operation of the same kind.[74]

As we have seen throughout this essay, then, the task or office of the working philosopher—whether natural or moral—is to identify general rules that explain the widest possible range of phenomena in the world.[75]

The problem, on Hume's account, with formulating judicious general rules to account for experience is that it is difficult. 'All the rules of this nature are very easy in their invention, but extremely difficult in their application' (*Treatise*, 175). Indeed, it is precisely this difficulty that distinguishes philosophers, who are skilled at applying them, from the 'vulgar', who are not. The difficulty in formulating general rules arises from the particular details of experience of which they must take account, or, as Hume tends to call them, 'circumstances'. We recall that Hume's 'rules by which to judge of causes and effects' in the *Treatise* are intended to separate 'accidental circumstances' from 'efficacious causes' (p. 149). Likewise, in the *Enquiry Concerning Human Understanding*, Hume explains that 'The circumstance, on which the effect depends, is frequently involved in other circumstances, which are foreign and extrinsic. The separation of it requires great attention, accuracy, and subtlety'. For this reason, he goes on, 'The forming of

---

[74] David Hume, *Dialogues Concerning Natural Religion*, in *The Natural History of Religion*, ed. A. Wayne Colver, and *Dialogues Concerning Natural Religion*, ed. John Valdimir Price (Oxford: Clarendon Press, 1976), 151. Cf. Hume, *Enquiry Concerning Human Understanding*, 121: 'philosophical decisions are nothing but the reflections of common life, methodized and corrected'.

[75] For this point made from a rather different perspective, see Robert W. Connon, 'Hume's theory of mental activity', in D. F. Norton, N. Capaldi, and W. L. Robison (eds.), *McGill Hume Studies* (San Diego: Austin Hill Press, 1979), 101–20, esp. p. 117.

general maxims from particular observation is a very nice operation; and nothing is more usual, from haste or a narrowness of mind, which sees not on all sides, than to commit mistakes in this particular' (p. 81 n. 20).

It is skill in the involved business of separating adventitious from efficacious circumstances, then, that makes a philosopher. 'All general laws', wrote Hume in 'On the Rise and Progress of the Arts and Sciences' (first published in the *Essays, Moral and Political* of 1742), 'are attended with inconveniences, when applied to particular cases; and it requires great penetration and experience, . . . to discern what general laws are, upon the whole, attended with fewest inconveniences' (p. 116). This is why, as he explained at the beginning of 'Of Commerce', it is the ability of philosophers 'to abstract general rules or principles' that distinguishes them from '*shallow* thinkers' for whom 'Every judgment or conclusion . . . is particular' (pp. 253–5). 'Wise men', Hume had explained in the section of the *Treatise* on 'general rules', are more capable of forming and applying such maxims than are 'the vulgar' (p. 150). (A related concern underlies the distinction Hume makes at the beginning of the *Enquiry Concerning Human Understanding* between the 'easy and obvious' moral philosophy based on feeling, which is preferred by the 'generality of mankind', and the 'accurate and abstruse' philosophy based on speculation, which is the province of the 'profound philosopher' (pp. 5–6). Hume, then, regarded the task of the working philosopher to be the formulation of general rules, maxims, or principles by which to explain natural, and in his case particularly moral and political, phenomena. I should like to close by suggesting that it is this practical ambition that underlies many of his moral, political, and even literary essays.

A number of Hume's essays begin with the consideration of an established maxim or proverb. Thus 'Of Taxes' (first published in the 1752 *Political Discourses*) takes as its starting-point 'a prevailing maxim, among some reasoners' about taxation (p. 342).[76] Likewise, 'Of Interest' (also first published in that volume) takes its point of departure from the mercantilist maxim that ascribed lowness of interest to plenty of money, and then goes on to identify six connected 'circumstances' which go to prove that it in fact proceeds from 'the encrease of industry and commerce' (pp. 295, 297). And the essay 'Of Natural Characters' (which appeared in the first publication to which Hume put his name, the *Essays, Moral and Political* of 1748), provides an exemplification of the kind of general rules formulated by 'the vulgar', and the exceptions acknowledged by 'men of sense', that is very much in the manner of the account in the *Treatise*: 'We have reason to expect greater wit and gaiety in a FRENCHMAN than in a SPANIARD; though CERVANTES was born in SPAIN. An ENGLISHMAN will naturally be supposed to

[76] Hume, *Essays*, p. 342.

have more knowledge than a DANE; though TYCHO BRAHE was a native of DENMARK' (pp. 197–8).

Several of Hume's essays, too, are structured by the formulation of general maxims on the subjects in question. Perhaps the most striking example of this is the essay 'Of the Rise and Progress of the Arts and Sciences', which takes the form of a commentary on four observations explaining the factors promoting politeness and learning. Hume introduces these observations with this characteristic comment, which again recalls his account of general rules in the *Treatise*: 'this is so curious a subject, that it were a pity to abandon it entirely, before we have found whether it be susceptible of reasoning, and can be reduced to any general principles' (p. 115).

We may conclude our argument by asking whether Hume's account of the formation and function of general rules extended to questions of 'criticism'; that is to say, whether they also operate in the essays that he designated as literary in nature. That they indeed do emerges from his late essay 'Of the Standard of Taste' (first published in the *Four Dissertations* of 1757). 'All the general rules of art', wrote Hume there, 'are founded only on experience, and on the observation of the common sentiments of human nature'. None the less, he continued,

we must not imagine, that, on every occasion, the feelings of men will be conformable to these rules. Those finer emotions of the mind are of a very tender and delicate nature, and require the concurrence of many favourable circumstances to make them play with facility and exactness, according to their general and established principles. (*Essays*, 232)

With this observation, Hume confirmed (as we might by now expect) that the scope of his lifelong interest in formulating explanatory rules that conform generally yet precisely to the multiplicity of circumstances presented by experience extended from natural and moral philosophy to 'criticism'— a pursuit that was regarded in the eighteenth century as a form of applied logic.

REFERENCES

Primary Sources

Aristotle, *Posterior Analytics*, trans. Jonathan Barnes, in *The Complete Works of Aristotle: The Revised Oxford Translation*, ed. J. Barnes, 2 vols. (Princeton: Princeton University Press, 1984), i. 114–66.

Arnauld, Antoine, and Nicole, Pierre, *La Logique ou l'art de penser*, ed. P. Clair and F. Girbal, 2nd edn. (Paris: Vrin, 1981).

—— —— *Logic, or the Art of Thinking*, ed. and trans. J. V. Buroker (Cambridge: Cambridge University Press, 1996).

Berkeley, George, *A Treatise Concerning the Principles of Human Knowledge*, ed. J. Dancy (Oxford: Oxford University Press, 1998).

Boyle, Robert, *A Free Enquiry into the Vulgarly Received Notion of Nature*, ed. E. B. Davis and M. Hunter (Cambridge: Cambridge University Press, 1996).

Burthogge, Richard, *Organum Vetus & Novum: Or, A Discourse of Reason and Truth. Wherein the Natural Logick common to Mankinde is briefly and plainly described* (London: Samuel Crouch, 1678).

Descartes, René, *Cogitationes privatae*, in *Œuvres de Descartes*, ed. C. Adam and P. Tannery, 12 vols. (Paris: Vrin, 1964–76), x. 213–56.

—— *Regulae ad directionem ingenii*, in *Œuvres de Descartes*, ed. C. Adam and P. Tannery, 12 vols. (Paris: Vrin, 1964–76), x. 359–472.

—— *Rules for the Direction of the Mind*, in *The Philosophical Writings*, trans. R. Stoothoff, D. Murdoch, and J. Cottingham, 3 vols. (Cambridge: Cambridge University Press, 1985), i. 7–78.

Gassendi, Pierre, *Institutio logica* (1658), ed. and trans. H. Jones (Assen: Van Gorcum, 1981).

Hume, David, *The Natural History of Religion*, ed. A. Wayne Colver, and *Dialogues Concerning Natural Religion*, ed. John Valdimir Price (Oxford: Clarendon Press, 1976).

—— *A Treatise of Human Nature*, ed. L. A. Selby-Bigge, 2nd edn., rev. P. H. Nidditch (Oxford: Clarendon Press, 1978).

—— *Essays Moral, Political, and Literary*, ed. E. F. Miller, rev. edn. (Indianapolis: Liberty Classics, 1985).

—— *An Enquiry Concerning the Principles of Morals*, ed. T. L. Beauchamp, The Clarendon Edition of the Works of David Hume (Oxford: Clarendon Press, 1998).

—— *An Enquiry Concerning Human Understanding*, ed. T. L. Beauchamp, The Clarendon Edition of the Works of David Hume (Oxford: Clarendon Press, 2000).

Le Clerc, Jean, *Logica, sive ars ratiocinandi* (London: Awnsham and John Churchill, 1692).

Leibniz, G. W., *Essais de Théodicée sur la bonté de Dieu, la liberté de l'homme et l'origine du mal*, in *Œuvres philosophiques de Leibniz*, ed. Paul Janet, 2 vols. (Paris: Félix Alcan, 1900), i. 1–442.

—— *Nouveaux essais sur l'entendement humain*, ed. A. Robinet and H. Schepers, in *Sämtliche Schriften und Briefen, Sechste Reihe: Philosophische Schriften*, vol. vi (Berlin: Akademie-Verlag, 1962).

Locke, John, *An Essay Concerning Human Understanding*, ed. P. H. Nidditch (Oxford: Clarendon Press, 1975).

Malebranche, Nicolas, *De la Recherche de la vérité*, in *Œuvres*, ed. G. Rodis-Lewis, 2 vols. (Paris: Gallimard, 1979), i. 1–1126.

—— *The Search after Truth*, ed. and trans. T. M. Lennon and P. Olscamp (Cambridge: Cambridge University Press, 1997).

Moulin, Pierre du, *The Elements of Logick* (London: Nicholas Bourne, 1624).

Newton, Isaac, *Philosophiae naturalis principia mathematica: The Third Edition (1726) with Variant Readings*, ed. A. Koyré and I. B. Cohen, with the assistance of A. Whitman, 2 vols. (Cambridge: Cambridge University Press, 1972).

Parker, Samuel, *A Free and Impartial Censure of the Platonick Philosophie* (Oxford: Richard Davis, 1666).

Stahl, Daniel, *Regulae philosophicae* (Oxford: J. Webb, 1663).

Tschirnhaus, Ehrenfried Walther von, *Medicina mentis*, 2nd edn. (Leipzig: Thomas Fritsch, 1695).

Watts, Isaac, *Logic; or, The Right Use of Reason, in the Enquiry after Truth. With a variety of rules to guard against error, in the affairs of religion and human life, as well as in the sciences* (Chiswick: Thomas Tegg, 1828).

Wilson, Thomas, *The Rule of Reason* (London: John Kingston, 1563).

Secondary Sources

Ashworth, E. J. ' "Do words signify ideas or things?": the scholastic sources of Locke's theory of language', *Journal of the History of Philosophy*, 19 (1981): 299–326.

—— 'Editor's introduction', in Robert Sanderson, *Logicae Artis Compendium (1618)*, ed. E. J. Ashworth, Instrumenta Rationis 2 (Bologna: Clueb, 1985), pp. ix–lv.

Ayers, Michael, 'Natures and laws from Descartes to Hume', in G. A. J. Rogers and S. Tomaselli (eds.), *The Philosophical Canon in the 17th and 18th Centuries: Essays in Honour of John W. Yolton* (Rochester, NY: University of Rochester Press, 1996), 83–108.

Box, M. A., *The Suasive Art of David Hume* (Princeton: Princeton University Press, 1990).

Buroker, Jill Vance, 'The priority of thought to language in Cartesian philosophy', in P. Easton (ed.), *Logic and the Workings of the Mind: The Logic of Ideas and Faculty Psychology in Early Modern Philosophy*, North American Kant Society Studies in Philosophy, 5 (Atascadero, Calif.: Ridgeview, 1997), 97–107.

Connon, Robert W., 'Hume's theory of mental activity', in D. F. Norton, N. Capaldi, and W. L. Robison (eds.), *McGill Hume Studies* (San Diego: Austin Hill Press, 1979), 101–20.

—— and Pollard, M., 'On the authorship of "Hume's" *Abstract*', *Philosophical Quarterly*, 27 (1977): 60–6.

Daston, Lorraine, *Classical Probability in the Enlightenment* (Princeton: Princeton University Press, 1988).

Dear, Peter, *Discipline and Experience: The Mathematical Way in the Scientific Revolution* (Chicago: University of Chicago Press, 1995).

Echelbarger, Charles, 'Hume and the logicians', in P. Easton (ed.), *Logic and the Workings of the Mind: The Logic of Ideas and Faculty Psychology in Early Modern Philosophy*, North American Kant Society Studies in Philosophy, 5 (Atascadero, Calif.: Ridgeview, 1997), 137–52.

Falkenstein, Lorne, and Easton, Patricia, 'Preface', in P. Easton (ed.), *Logic and the Workings of the Mind: The Logic of Ideas and Faculty Psychology in Early Modern Philosophy*, North American Kant Society Studies in Philosophy, 5 (Atascadero, Calif.: Ridgeview, 1997), pp. i–vii.

Fiering, Norman, *Moral Philosophy at Seventeenth-Century Harvard: A Discipline in Transition* (Chapel Hill, NC: University of North Carolina Press, 1981).

Finlay, C. J., 'Enlightenment and the university: philosophy, communication, and education in the early writings of David Hume', *History of Universities*, 16 (2000): 103–34.

Hearn, Thomas K. Jr., 'General rules in Hume's *Treatise*', *Journal of the History of Philosophy*, 8 (1970): 405–22.

Jones, Peter, *Hume's Sentiments: Their Ciceronian and French Context* (Edinburgh: Edinburgh University Press, 1982).

Loeb, Louis, 'Causal inference, associationism, and scepticism in Part III of Book I of Hume's *Treatise*', in P. Easton (ed.), *Logic and the Workings of the Mind: The Logic of Ideas and Faculty Psychology in Early Modern Philosophy*, North American Kant Society Studies in Philosophy, 5 (Atascadero, Calif.: Ridgeview, 1997), 283–306.

LoLordo, Antonia, 'Probability and skepticism about reason in Hume's *Treatise*', *British Journal for the History of Philosophy*, 8 (2000): 419–46.

Maclean, Ian, 'Evidence, logic, the rule and the exception in Renaissance law and medicine', *Early Science and Medicine*, 5 (2000): 227–57.

Mamiani, Maurizio, 'To twist the meaning: Newton's *Regulae philosophandi* revisited', in Jed Z. Buchwald and I. B. Cohen (eds.), *Isaac Newton's Natural Philosophy*, (Cambridge, Mass.: MIT Press, 2000), 3–14.

Martin, Marie, 'The rational warrant for Hume's general rules', *Journal of the History of Philosophy*, 31 (1993): 245–57.

McCracken, Charles J., *Malebranche and British Philosophy* (Oxford: Clarendon Press, 1983).

Michael, Emily, 'Frances Hutcheson's *Logicae compendium* and the Glasgow school of logic', in P. Easton (ed.), *Logic and the Workings of the Mind: The Logic of Ideas and Faculty Psychology in Early Modern Philosophy*, North American Kant Society Studies in Philosophy, 5 (Atascadero, Calif.: Ridgeview, 1997), 83–96.

Michael, Frederick S., 'Why logic became epistemology: Gassendi, Port Royal and the reformation in logic', in P. Easton (ed.), *Logic and the Workings of the Mind: The Logic of Ideas and Faculty Psychology in Early Modern Philosophy*, North American Kant Society Studies in Philosophy, 5 (Atascadero, Calif.: Ridgeview, 1997), 1–20.

Milton, J. R., 'Induction before Hume', *British Journal for the Philosophy of Science*, 38 (1987): 49–74.

Mossner, Ernest Campbell, 'Hume's early memoranda, 1729–1740: the complete text', *Journal of the History of Ideas*, 9 (1948): 492–518.

—— *The Life of David Hume*, 2nd edn. (Oxford: Clarendon Press, 1980).

Noxon, James, *Hume's Philosophical Development: A Study of his Methods* (Oxford: Clarendon Press, 1973).

Nuchelmans, Gabriel, 'Logic in the seventeenth century: preliminary remarks and the constituents of the proposition', in D. Garber and M. Ayers (eds.), *The Cambridge History of Seventeenth-Century Philosophy*, 2 vols. (Cambridge: Cambridge University Press, 1998), i. 103–17.

—— 'Deductive reasoning', in D. Garber and M. Ayers (eds.), *The Cambridge History of Seventeenth-Century Philosophy*, 2 vols. (Cambridge: Cambridge University Press, 1998), i. 132–46.

Osler, Margaret J., 'John Locke and the changing ideal of scientific knowledge', *Journal of the History of Ideas*, 31 (1970): 3–16.

Owen, David, 'Hume's doubts about probable reasoning: was Locke the target?', in M. A. Stewart and J. P. Wright (eds.), *Hume and Hume's Connexions*, (Edinburgh: Edinburgh University Press, 1994), 140–59.

—— 'Philosophy and the good life: Hume's defence of probable reasoning', *Dialogue*, 35 (1996): 485–503.

—— *Hume's Reason* (New York: Oxford University Press, 1999).

Palmer, Eric, 'Descartes's *Rules* and the workings of the mind', in P. Easton (ed.), *Logic and the Workings of the Mind: The Logic of Ideas and Faculty Psychology in Early Modern Philosophy*, North American Kant Society Studies in Philosophy, 5 (Atascadero, Calif.: Ridgeview, 1997), 269–82.

Palter, Robert, 'Hume and prejudice', *Hume Studies*, 21 (1995): 3–23.

Passmore, J. A., *Hume's Intentions* (Cambridge: Cambridge University Press, 1952).

—— 'Descartes, the British empiricists and formal logic', *Philosophical Review*, 62 (1953): 545–53.

Peursen, C. A. van, 'E. W. von Tschirnhaus and the *ars inveniendi*', *Journal of the History of Ideas*, 54 (1993): 395–410.

Popkin, Richard H., 'So, Hume did read Berkeley', *Journal of Philosophy*, 61 (1964): 773–8.

Russell, Paul, 'Hume's *Treatise* and Hobbes's *The Elements of Law*', *Journal of the History of Ideas*, 46 (1985): 51–63.

Schönfeld, Martin, 'Dogmatic metaphysics and Tschirnhaus's methodology', *Journal of the History of Philosophy*, 36 (1998): 57–76.

Schuurman, Paul, 'Locke's logic of ideas in context: content and structure', *British Journal for the History of Philosophy*, 9 (2001): 439–66.

Shapin, Steven, 'Pump and circumstance: Robert Boyle's literary technology', *Social Studies of Science*, 14 (1984): 481–520.

Skinner, Quentin, *Reason and Rhetoric in the Philosophy of Hobbes* (Cambridge: Cambridge University Press, 1996).

Stewart, M. A., 'Hume's historical view of miracles', in M. A. Stewart and J. P. Wright (eds.), *Hume and Hume's Connexions* (Edinburgh: Edinburgh University Press, 1994), 171–200.

Wilson, Catherine, 'Between *medicina mentis* and medical materialism', in P. Easton (ed.), *Logic and the Workings of the Mind: The Logic of Ideas and Faculty Psychology in Early Modern Philosophy*, North American Kant Society Studies in Philosophy, 5 (Atascadero, Calif.: Ridgeview, 1997), 251–68.

Wright, John P., *The Sceptical Realism of David Hume* (Manchester: Manchester University Press, 1983).

Hume's 'Meek' Philosophy among the Milanese

EMILIO MAZZA

THE *COTERIE DE MILAN*

Pietro Verri (1728–97) was, as Friedrich-Melchior Grimm wrote in November 1766, 'a just spirit, not lacking in refinement' and 'one of the prime members of the *coterie de Milan*'. Two other members were Cesare Beccaria (1738–94), whose very countenance showed 'the marks of Lumbard goodness and simplicity', and Alessandro Verri (1741–1816), who, 'not yet twenty-four, and of a very agreeable countenance, ha[d] a graceful and fine understanding'. The *coterie*, which had been organized 'to cultivate letters and philosophy' was the centre of Enlightenment in Milan; and the Verri brothers and Beccaria were its key figures.[1] All three were members of the local 'Accademia dei Pugni' (1762–6), whose journal, *Il Caffè*, published from June 1764 to May 1766, contained, in Pietro's words, a number of things directed towards 'public utility', and pursued 'the end of disseminating useful knowledge among our citizens as Steele, Swift, Addison, Pope and others had already done elsewhere'.[2] Pietro Verri, who ended his career as a high-ranking official of the Austrian Government, was the author of the *Meditazioni sulla felicità* (1763), translated into French in May 1766, of the *Meditazioni sulla economia politica*

I am very grateful to Gianni Francioni and Marina Frasca-Spada for discussing this paper with me; I also wish to thank Aldo Coletto (Biblioteca Nazionale Braidense, Milan) and Barbara Costa and Sara Rosini (Archivio Verri, Fondazione Raffaele Mattioli per la Storia del Pensiero Economico, Milan) for their help.

[1] Friedrich-Melchior Grimm, *Correspondance littéraire, philosophique et critique, adressé à un Souverain d'Allemagne, depuis 1753 jusqu'en 1769, par le Baron de Grimm et par Diderot* (Paris: Longchamps et F. Buisson, 1813), v. 372–3. On the Verri brothers see Carlo Capra (ed.), *Pietro Verri e il suo tempo*, 2 vols. (Bologna: Cisalpino-Monduzzi, 1999); Carlo Capra, *I progressi della ragione: vita di Pietro Verri* (Bologna: il Mulino, 2002); Giorgio Panizza and Barbara Costa, *L'archivio Verri*, 2 vols. (Milan: Fondazione Raffaele Mattioli per la Storia del Pensiero Economico, 1997, 2000); Franco Venturi, 'La Milano del *Caffè*', in *Settecento riformatore* i: *Da Muratori a Beccaria 1730–1764* (Turin: Einaudi, 1972), i. 645–747; *idem*, 'Gli uomini delle riforme: la Lombardia', in *Settecento riformatore*, v, *L'Italia dei lumi 1764–1790* (Turin: Einaudi, 1987), v. (1). 425–834.

[2] Pietro Verri, 'Introduzione', in Verri *et al.*, *'Il Caffè' 1764–1766*, ed. G. Francioni and S. Romagnoli, 2nd rev. edn. (Turin: Bollati Boringhieri, 1993), 11–17, at p. 11; cf. also Alessandro Verri, 'Dei difetti della letteratura e di alcune loro cagioni', in *'Il Caffè'*, 539–60, at p. 542; Cesare Beccaria, 'De' fogli periodici', in *'Il Caffè'*, 411–19, at p. 418.

(1771) and other pieces on trade, of an essay on pleasure, and of the posthumous *Osservazioni sulla tortura*. His brother Alessandro wrote many articles for *Il Caffè*. He also wrote (but left unpublished) a *Saggio di Morale Cristiana* of 1763, and the *Saggio sulla storia d'Italia dalla fondazione di Roma fino alla metà del nostro secolo* of 1763–6, a historical work probably composed on the model of Hume's *History*. In addition, Alessandro translated Shakespeare and Bolingbroke into Italian, and was one of the most important Italian authors of the time for his tragedies and novels—in particular, for the internationally famous *Le notti romane* of 1792. The most distinguished product of the *coterie*, however, was undoubtedly Beccaria's *Dei delitti e delle pene* of 1764. In this work Beccaria articulated the view that the 'only and true' measure of crimes was the 'damage' done to society, and, in a chapter devoted to discussion of the death penalty, maintained that capital punishment was neither 'just', nor 'useful', nor 'necessary'.[3] The book was translated into French by Morellet at the end of 1765 (Hume, who had read the original 'with great care', seems to have approved of the translation), and inspired Voltaire to publish a *Commentaire* in September 1766.[4]

At the beginning of October 1766, invited by Morellet and the *philosophes*, Beccaria and Alessandro Verri left Milan for a six-month trip to Paris and London.[5] At the end of November, however, Beccaria unexpectedly decided to return to Milan, and so he and Alessandro parted company. Rather than going back home, Alessandro left Paris for London, where he remained until the beginning of February. He returned to Paris in mid-March and then travelled on through Piedmont, Liguria, and Tuscany. Finally, in the middle of May he arrived in Rome where he settled for life, devoting himself to literature; that is, to what was truly good for him ('il mio vero bene', as he calls it).[6]

In this essay I look at Hume through the lens of the correspondence held between Alessandro Verri and his brother Pietro from October 1766 to September 1782. In particular, I concentrate on the letters written during Alessandro's trip to Paris and London. After briefly reporting on Alessandro's reactions to cultural and intellectual life in the two European capitals, I focus on Hume's public image in Paris as discussed in the Verri brothers' correspondence, and introduce Alessandro's view of Humean

[3] Cesare Beccaria, *Dei delitti e delle pene: con una raccolta di lettere e documenti relativi alla nascita dell'opera e alla sua fortuna nell'Europa del Settecento*, ed. F. Venturi (Turin: Einaudi, 1994), 22, 23, 62; cf. Gianni Francioni, 'Prefazione', in François-Marie Arouet Voltaire, *Commentario sul libro 'Dei delitti e delle pene'*, ed. G. Francioni (Como-Pavia: Ibis, 1994), 7–28.

[4] André Morellet, *Lettres d'André Morellet*, ed. D. Medlin, J. C. David, and P. Leclerc, 2 vols. (Oxford: Voltaire Foundation, 1991), i. 42.

[5] Pietro and Alessandro Verri, *Viaggio a Parigi e Londra (1766–1767): Carteggio di Pietro e Alessandro Verri*, ed. G. Gaspari (Milan: Adelphi, 1980), 24, 37, 136, 445.

[6] Pietro and Alessandro Verri, *Carteggio di Pietro e di Alessandro Verri*, ed. A. Giulini, E. Greppi, F. Novati, and G. Seregni, 12 vols. (Milan: L. F. Cogliati, A. Giuffrè, 1910–42), i (1). 407.

philosophy as 'meek' ('mansueta').[7] Then, to elaborate on the contrast he draws between (Hume's) 'meek' philosophy and (the *philosophes'*) philosophical enthusiasm and fanaticism, I focus on the Verri brothers' and Beccaria's views of Hume's dispute with Rousseau: I argue that Alessandro, who championed Humean philosophy over that of the *philosophes* (and of his brother), effectively revived the Hume–Rousseau dispute in the course of the personal dispute that he was by now involved in with Beccaria. Finally, I take the opportunity to use Alessandro's reports on Hume to reassess Hume's position on religion. To do so I discuss the famous anecdote in which Hume is reported as having said that he had never seen an atheist. The anecdote, quoted as important evidence in some recent interpretations of Hume's views on religion, does indeed agree with other testimonies.[8] However, I propose that taking it at face value means attributing to Hume

---

[7] The expression 'filosofia mansueta' ('meek philosophy') applied to Hume sounds as odd in Verri's language as it does in English. Verri's 'mansueto' does literally mean 'meek'. The Italian 'mansueto [mansuetus]' was used at the time, and still is, especially with reference to such (meek) domestic animals as sheep and heifer (the wild animal can become 'tame and meek'). Alessandro and Pietro Verri use it also with reference to religion ('mansueta religione', 'Dio di mansuetudine'), Beccaria to eloquence ('mansueta eloquenza'). 'Meekness', Edward Bentham writes, 'is a virtue particularly exercised in regulating the passion of Anger. It implies a good degree of what we call easiness of temper, a freedom from mistrust, a disposition to believe well of our neighbour, a readiness to forgo our right for the sake of peace, as well as in the way of compassion' (Edward Bentham, *Introduction to Moral Philosophy*, 2nd edn. (Oxford: 1745)). According to Hume's *Treatise*, 'Meekness', together with 'beneficence, charity, generosity, clemency, moderation, equity', 'bear the greatest figure among the moral qualities, and are commonly denominated the *social* virtues, to mark their tendency to the good of society' (David Hume, *A Treatise of Human Nature*, ed. L. A. Selby-Bigge, 2nd edn. rev. P. H. Nidditch (Oxford: Clarendon Press, 1978), 578).

[8] Among those who have used the anecdote to discuss Hume's religious views see M. A. Box, *The Suasive Art of David Hume* (Princeton: Princeton University Press, 1990), 213–14 and n. 62; John H. Burton, *Life and Correspondence of David Hume*, 2 vols. (Edinburgh: William Tait, 1846), ii. 220 and n. 1; James Fieser, 'Hume's concealed attack on religion and his early critics', *Journal of Philosophical Research*, 20 (1995): 431–49, at pp. 433, 445; J. C. A. Gaskin, *Hume's Philosophy of Religion*, 2nd edn. (London: Macmillan Press, 1993), 220–1; Roberto Gilardi, *Il giovane Hume, Volume Primo: Il "background" religioso e culturale* (Milan: Vita e Pensiero, 1990), 66–7; Donald W. Livingston, *Philosophical Melancholy and Delirium: Hume's Pathology of Philosophy* (Chicago and London: University of Chicago Press, 1998), 73–4; H. O. Mounce, *Hume's Naturalism* (London and New York: Routledge, 1999), 106; Terence Penelhum, *Hume* (London: Macmillan, 1975), 166; *idem, David Hume: An Introduction to his Philosophical System* (West Lafayette, Ind.: Purdue University Press, 1992), 36, 187, 192 n. 22; *idem, Themes in Hume: The Self, the Will, Religion* (Oxford: Clarendon Press, 2000), 242; Richard H. Popkin, *The High Road to Pyrrhonism*, ed. R. A. Watson and J. E. Force (San Diego: Austin Hill Press, 1980), 59, 123 n. 62. Cf. also Laurence L. Bongie, *David Hume: Prophet of the Counter-Revolution*, 2nd edn. (Indianapolis: Liberty Press, 2000), 54; Jean-Claude Bourdin, *Préface* à P.-H. Thiry d'Holbach, *Œuvres Philosophiques*, 5 Tomes (Paris: ALIVE, 1998–9), i. pp. vii–xxi, at p. xiii; Nicholas Capaldi, *David Hume: The Newtonian Philosopher* (Boston: Twayne Publishers, 1975), 24; Ernest C. Mossner, 'Hume and the French men of letters', *Revue internationale de philosophie*, 6 (1952): 221–35, at p. 230; *idem, The Life of David Hume*, 2nd edn. (Oxford: Clarendon Press, 1980), 483–6; Norman Kemp Smith, 'Introduction', in David Hume, *Dialogues Concerning Natural Religion*, ed. N. Kemp Smith, 2nd edn. (Edinburgh: Thomas Nelson, 1947), 1–75, at pp. 37–8.

the position of 'the most religious philosophers': a position which, as I intend to show, clashes with much in his texts. My suggestion is, rather, that the anecdote is part of the complex confrontation between Hume and the *philosophes* over what kinds of strategy and philosophical style ought to be adopted when discussing religious matters.

MODEST VERSUS BOASTFUL PHILOSOPHERS

'I'd rather have a meek philosophy even when confronting the errors of vice and I would like its strengh to lie in truth, not in enthusiasm,' Alessandro Verri wrote to his brother Pietro in March 1768. And, in contrast with the 'arrogance of Gallic philosophy', he briefly sketched the virtues of Humean philosophy:[9]

This is the reason why I like Hume's style so much. Through his tranquil profundity Hume has conveyed and shown more things than all the French philosophers taken together, with the exception of Voltaire . . . By always doubting the forces of human Reason, Hume increases her rights, and by degrading her in appearance, he exalts her in reality. He pursues the truth step by step and plucks its feathers one by one without scratching the skin [Alessandro offers his peculiar version of Hume's parallel between philosophy, hunting and anatomy]. Hume's modesty charms people and by this advantage makes them ready to hearken to him . . . he has not made as much noise as other philosophers, and he has gained more followers. But the pompous, intolerant, bold and sneering airs of some philosophers have provoked an endless indignation.[10]

It is interesting that, in all probability, when referring to Hume's meekness and modesty Verri had in mind, besides the *Political Discourses* and the *History*, not the religiously castrated *Treatise*, but the more 'complete' and explicit *Enquiry Concerning Human Understanding*.[11] In fact, Alessandro was aware of Hume's radicalism in matters of religion. For in 'Del grand'essere', a short unpublished piece composed a few months after the letter cited above, he described Section XI of the *Enquiry*, 'Of a particular Providence and of a future State', as that in which Hume had attacked 'the most common proof of the existence of God . . . namely the argument from

[9] Verri and Verri, *Carteggio*, i(2). 204, 225.

[10] Ibid. 204–5. 'The modest philosopher', Alessandro writes in his 'Saggio di morale cristiana', 'does persuade and find more often people who agree with him than the haughty' (Alessandro Verri, 'Saggio di morale cristiana', unpublished, Archivio Verri, Fondazione Raffaele Mattioli per la Storia del Pensiero Economico, folder 484, fasc. 1, f. 24). With regard to 'the profound metaphysics of monsieur Hume, the truth and novelty of his views', cf. Cesare Beccaria, *Carteggio*, ed. C. Capra, R. Pasta, and F. Pino Pongolini, in *Edizione Nazionale delle Opere di Cesare Beccaria*, ed. L. Firpo and G. Francioni (Milan: Mediobanca, 1984), iv(1). 219.

[11] David Hume, *The Letters of David Hume*, ed. J. Y. T. Greig, 2 vols. (Oxford: Clarendon Press, 1932), i. 158.

effect to cause' and maintained that 'the assertion of the infinite and supreme attributes of the cause of that effect [i.e. the universe] is a gratuitous one'.[12] Nor could Alessandro have failed to appreciate that radicalism, since Hume's *Philosophical Essays*, in French translation, had already been called 'detestable' and 'full of very pernicious maxims' in the *Estratto della letteratura Europea* of 1759; and, in 1764, the *Estratto* had gone on to claim: 'the more Hume shows himself to be a little man when assaulting religion the more he is a great one when talking about politics, morals and history'. (The *Estratto*, first printed in Berne, then in Yverdon, and from the beginning of 1766 in Milan, was considered by Pietro 'in [his] hands'.[13]) In fact, on 19 January 1761 the French translation of these *Essays*, which Hume judged 'too bold and too metaphysical' for the French climate, had also earned a place on the Index of the books prohibited by the Roman Catholic Church.[14]

---

[12] Alessandro Verri, 'Del grand'essere' (unpublished), Archivio Verri, folder 492, quad. 'B', ff. 51–3, at f. 53; cf. David Hume, *Enquiry Concerning Human Understanding*, in *Enquiries Concerning Human Understanding and Concerning the Principles of Morals*, ed. L. A. Selby-Bigge, 3rd edn., rev. P. H. Nidditch (Oxford: Clarendon Press, 1975), 136. Since he writes 'Sul che David Hume essaÿ *of a providence, and future state*', Alessandro is doubtless not quoting from the 1748 edition of the *Philosophical Essays*, but more probably from the 1758 or a later edition of the *Essays and Treatises on Several Subjects*. The name 'Hume' appears on a list written by Alessandro after the first half of 1764 of important authors under the title of 'Metaphysics, and morals' (at first 'Metaphysics, and politics') and 'History' (Archivio Verri, folder 485). In 1769, when he was trying to achieve 'the miserable glory of the translator' (Verri and Verri, *Carteggio*, iv. 64), Alessandro refered to Hume's texts in three letters (ibid. ii. 124, 154; iii. 90–1): he quoted a passage from *The Sceptic* probably translated by himself (ibid. ii. 154) and declared his agreement with Hume's view and 'sceptical style' (ibid. iii. 90). Hume was a literary model for 'imitation'. In 1778, thinking of his own experience, Alessandro wrote: 'Hume has been very obscure for a long time and his History', as Wilkes once told him in Paris in November 1766 (Verri and Verri, *Viaggio*, 119; *idem*, *Carteggio*, iii. 90), 'has been much vilified' (ibid. iv. 149–50). His 'Storia d'Italia', probably inspired also by Hume's *History*, which was read both by Beccaria and Pietro, remained unpublished—he wrote in 1808—as a 'juvenile work, with bold judgments, bastard style, anxiety for paradoxes and lacking narrative for excessive hurry' (Archivio Verri, folder 489, fasc. 1). With regard to 'the Italian Historians' Hume had the 'Opinion that that Language has not producd one Author who knew how to write elegant, correct Prose, though it contains several Excellent Poets' (Hume, *Letters*, ii. 256); cf. Beccaria, 'Carteggio', iv(1). 223; Verri and Verri, *Carteggio*, xi. 280–1); Verri, 'Dei difetti della letteratura', 542.

[13] 'Review of D. Hume, *Essais Philosophiques*, 2 vols, Amsterdam, 1759', in *Estratto della letteratura Europea per l'anno MDCCLIX*, ii (1759), 269–70; 'Review of D. Hume, *Œuvres de M. Hume*, t. VI, 1764', in *Estratto della letteratura Europea per l'anno MDCCLXIV*, i (1764), 280–1; Verri and Verri, *Viaggio*, 131 (cf. p. 13).

[14] Hume, *Letters*, i. 192, 198, 227. *Index Librorum Prohibitorum . . . Benedicti XIV* (Parma: Apud Philippum Carmignani, 1783), 297; *Index Librorum Prohibitorum . . . Pii Septimi* (Rome: Ex Typographia Rev. Camerae Apostolicae, 1819), 410. Only the French translation of the *Philosophical Essays*, not 'all' of Hume's works (as Mossner suggested), earned a place on the Index on 19 January 1761. According to the *Acta Congregationis*, Hume is the 'audax' philosopher who 'Materialismum cum Pyrrhonismo ubique invehit . . . ut summa Religionis . . . capita sus deque misceat, atque subvertat', and 'Deismum, vel Atheismum, Pyrrhonismum undique, putidosque Materialistarum atque Fatalistarum errores omnium animis instillat'. Only on 10 September 1827, after the fourth Italian translation of the *History*, was the prohibition extended to this work, because

Alessandro's letter and his brother Pietro's reply belong, as we shall see, to a sort of philosophical journey, and we can look at Hume in the mirror of the Verri brothers' correspondence. Admittedly, in many cases this mirror reflects an entirely distorted image: for example, when Alessandro observes that 'a man of such genius in writing' is 'so defective in action', thus adopting what Hume had called 'the ancient prejudice industriously propagated by the dunces in all countries, *That a man of genius is unfit for business*'.[15] In Alessandro's published writings there are other kinds of complications. For example, in the 'Conversazione tenutasi nel caffè', Filone, that is Philo, that is Alessandro, praises Hume's *History* as an excellent philosophical history in the same breath as he defends Voltaire's *Histoire universelle* from the charge of being 'full of false facts' in spite of its 'poetry and grace'; but he ignores the fact that Hume himself thought that the *Histoire universelle* could not be 'depended on with regard to facts' in spite of its 'sometimes sound, and always entertaining general views'.[16]

Pietro's reply to his brother's letter is a standard one. In November 1766 he had judged the 'partisan spirit' of French philosophers to be a defensive need (Alessandro too was later to adopt this view, and explained the warmth and enthusiasm of Parisian philosophers as a reaction to the persecution of philosophical truths).[17] In March 1768 Pietro again underlines the

---

of its 'iniquitous' matter and 'seducing' manner, and to the *opera omnia* of the 'jam valde male famosus . . . David Hume' (Archivio storico della Congregazione per la Dottrina della Fede, Città del Vaticano, *Protocolli*, 1761, IIa 87, ff. 199^r, 203^v; *Protocolli*, 1827, IIa 109, ff. 230^r, 237^r, 240^v).

[15] Verri and Verri, *Carteggio*, ii. 366 (see also pp. 369–70, 381); David Hume, *Essays Moral, Political, and Literary*, ed. E. F. Miller (Indianapolis: Liberty Classics, 1987), 621 n. g.

[16] Alessandro Verri, 'Conversazione tenutasi nel caffè', in '*Il Caffè*', 163–5, at pp. 163–4; Hume, *Letters*, i. 326; cf. Alessandro Verri, 'Saggio di legislazione sul pedantismo', in '*Il Caffè*', 134–40, at p. 138; Alessandro Verri, ['Dell'universalità delle scienze'] (unpublished), Archivio Verri, folder n.n., ins. [5].

[17] Verri and Verri, *Viaggio*, 66; cf. pp. 48, 66, 88, 168; *idem, Carteggio*, iv. 111. In general Pietro defends Hume's right, as a 'wise and learned' man ('the profound thinker David Hume'), to treat and examine religious matters (*idem, Viaggio*, 389–90). Hume is the one who discovered 'the reflection concerning the impossibility of proving an infinite power' (*idem, Carteggio*, ii. 155). Yet, in the dispute with Rousseau, Pietro is 'convinced in favour of Rousseau' and considers Hume 'too cool and reasonable' to be innocent (*idem, Viaggio*, 88–9). Pietro, who has read Hume's *History* (*idem, Carteggio*, xi. 280–1, and see above, n. 12) and studied Hume's *Political Discourses* (cf. Pietro Verri, 'Estratti da Hume', MS, Archivio Verri, folder 374, fasc. 8, ff. 12^r–15^v), in the *Considerazioni sul Commercio dello Stato di Milano* (1763) defines Hume as an 'Author of Commerce', or an 'author of works of public economy', and in the *Dialogo sulle monete fra Fronimo e Simplicio* (1762) as a 'credited writer' on money. Moreover, in the *Considerazioni sul Commercio* Pietro discusses his views concerning 'the extraordinary increase of taxes' ('Of Taxes') and the 'annual increase of the noble metal in Europe' ('Of Money') (Archivio Verri, folder 377, fasc. 3–4; fasc. I, II, ff. 19–20 n. b, 271 n. a; folder 374, fasc. 7, ff. 2, 5). He also discusses Hume's essays 'Of Luxury' in the 'Considerazioni sul lusso' and 'Of Money' in the *Meditazioni sulla economia politica*, where he refers to him as 'a certain writer, otherwise an exact thinker' (Pietro Verri, 'Considerazioni sul lusso', in '*Il Caffè*', 155–62, at p. 155; 'Del lusso delle manifatture d'oro e d'argento', in '*Il Caffè*', 494–7; Pietro Verri, *Meditazioni sulla economia politica*, ed. R. De Felice (Milan: Bruno Mondadori, 1998), 54; Verri and Verri, *Carteggio*, iv. 46.

expediency of their attitude, and vindicates the role played by boastful as opposed to modest philosophers:

You are very English and you cannot stand the enthusiasm of the French. I agree with you. Yet it must be confessed that those who boast about philosophy have, perhaps, been more beneficial to human society than the modest philosophers. It was necessary to have someone rouse the multitude by means of a sort of very bold air of inspiration . . . a great deal of imposture and passion were required to awaken us. The peaceful and modest Bayle gained only a few followers, while the Encyclopedists, by means of a great deal of quackery, put philosophy in much more venerable and glaring colours, not in my eyes or yours but in the public's eyes.[18]

Here Pietro takes Bayle, rather than Hume, as a paragon of modesty, and acknowledges that 'the pomp of the Encyclopedists, and especially of Rousseau, is something evil'; and yet, he says, 'this evil in Europe has come in time to be very beneficial'.[19] Alessandro too is prepared to recognize the need for this 'philosophical imposture'; yet, he observes, 'between you and me, we regard this *sacred fire*, which fills their breast, as an enthusiasm that posterity will esteem as we esteem that of the Pythagoreans, the Stoics and other such sects'. He agrees that 'these *enfants perdus* of reason are necessary' and that, 'since they bring this benefit to humanity, we should venerate them, with all their sacred fury, as enthusiastic votaries of a benevolent Goddess'. But in conclusion he declares that he will 'always regard this orgasm [i.e. intense excitement] as a contagion, especially in writing'.[20] In 1778, with regard to Rousseau and Helvétius, Alessandro and Pietro were still to go through the same issues once again: such books, Alessandro protested, 'put me in agitation, they are drugs that disgust me . . . since I find in them the too-tiring raptures of enthusiasm'. This time Pietro was closer to his brother's view, denouncing the 'fanaticism' and 'the enthusiastic manner of writing brought into fashion by the Encyclopedists': 'true philosophy', he acknowledged, 'is more cautious . . . I am out of humour with the Encyclopedists.'[21]

ALESSANDRO'S 'PHILOSOPHICAL PILGRIMAGE'

Alessandro Verri and Cesare Beccaria's journey to Paris is briefly reported in Morellet's *Mémoires* and Grimm's *Correspondance*.[22] With regard to the

---

[18] Verri and Verri, *Carteggio*, i(2). 206–7.

[19] At the beginning of January Pietro wrote: 'all the books which have met with success in this age have been written with warmth; and all the improvements of philosophy arise from enthusiastical writers. Bayle has convinced the few; Rousseau, Voltaire and Diderot spread fire around' (ibid. iv. 111).

[20] Ibid. i(2). 207, 225 (cf. Alessandro Verri, *Saggio sulla storia d'Italia*, ed. B. Scalvini (Rome: Edizioni di storia e letteratura, 2001), 15).   [21] Verri and Verri, *Carteggio*, iv. 53–4, 65–6.

[22] André Morellet, *Mémoires Inédits*, 2nd edn., 2 vols. (Paris: Librairie Française de Ladvocat, 1822), i. 167–73; Grimm, *Correspondance littéraire*, v. 372–3; iv. 514–23; Verri and Verri, *Viaggio*, 353, 361.

'coterie de Milan', Grimm in 1765 reports that 'reason in Italy has made a prodigious progress'. This was by then a matter of common knowledge. In 1767 Alessandro was to relate that, according to Voltaire, '*l'Ecole de Milan* is making a considerable progress'.[23] Grimm goes on: 'we had the satisfaction here of meeting two members of this society: . . . Beccaria . . . and the cadet brother of the Earl of Verri. The latter . . . is the author of many pages in the *Caffè*.' This is close to Alessandro's self-portrait of 1766: 'In two years I have written a fifth of the first book of the *Caffè* and half of the second . . . and a *Storia d'Italia*.'[24] Grimm does not mistake Alessandro for Beccaria's 'companion', nor does he mistake him for his more famous brother Pietro, the author of the *Meditazioni*, two errors from which Alessandro seems to suffer often. This is probably the reason why Grimm appears to him 'a man of great merit and very amiable'—apart from the fact that, in any case, in Paris 'all is either *amiable* and *charming*, or *detestable* and *horrible*'.[25]

Alessandro was a provincial, 24-year-old, male traveller in the metropolis, where he found that 'the mind is distracted, and its dissipated passions are not directed towards any one object'.[26] It would be hard to list the many women (of every rank and condition, but especially prostitutes), who are a constant presence throughout his (and his brother's) letters. In Alessandro's view Paris was a sex paradise, and Paris was yet 'very chaste' in comparison with London, where every woman in the street was on the look-out for nothing more than sex and punch.[27] Some of his serious displays of London-mania are very funny: his praise of London and its adorable smoke in comparison with that of Paris, and of the London climate, milder than the Italian; his descriptions of the marvellous pavements and street lighting, of the pleasures of shopping in London, and of the true nature of the *grand tour* (i.e. to get clean and become refined in France, and to grow mild in Italy, only to return to gloomy London, there to be rude, sad, boorish, and brutish once more). Or take his reconstruction of the Englishman's food-chain of reasoning: he does not eat well, only 'beef and beer', therefore he is ruddy and fat, therefore he cannot perspire and is a great walker, therefore he's got big legs. Conclusion: 'one of the most dangerous diseases here is a neglected cold'.[28]

Among his reflections on Paris and London's 'police', on the 'cold and blind' laws and the 'worthy' thieves of England, where robbery is nothing but 'forced charity', there is in Alessandro's letters a 'macabre' episode that could be entitled 'To the scaffold'.[29] An 'interesting' narration, in Pietro's

[23] Grimm, *Correspondance littéraire*, iv. 514; Verri and Verri, *Viaggio*, 353, 361.
[24] Grimm, *Correspondance littéraire*, v. 372; Verri and Verri, *Viaggio*, 75 (cf. p. 115). The same thing happened with Morellet; cf. Morellet, *Mémoires Inédits*, i. 167; Verri and Verri, *Viaggio*, p. 39.
[25] Verri and Verri, *Viaggio*, 38, 24 (cf. pp. 40, 236, 334–5, 393, 398, 418, 433), 59, 75, 121.
[26] Ibid. 360 (cf. pp. 425, 431–2).
[27] Ibid. 355 (cf. pp. 28, 58, 115–16, 142–3, 174, 187–8, 275–6, 294, 352–3, 361–2, 366–7).
[28] Ibid. 143–4 (cf. pp. 148–9, 275–6).
[29] Ibid. 145 (cf. pp. 80–1, 92, 179), 146 (cf. pp. 169, 252, 271, 338–9), 256.

terms, for 'what a difference between the English and the Lombardo!'[30] Despite his (jurisprudential) background among philosophers denying the legitimacy and usefulness of capital punishment and torture, Alessandro, brother of the author of the *Osservazioni sulla tortura* and friend of the author of *Dei delitti e delle pene*, spent an enjoyable day outside London observing the brand new 'English way of being hanged'. All this without the least 'remorse': there was, he observed, no horror in this kind of spectacle because the abuse of capital punishment, as well as the nature of the climate, government and religion, made the English 'very cool in front of death'. The episode, together with another execution, suggested to Alessandro some general considerations.[31] Beccaria thought that there ought to be 'a correlation between crime and punishment', and that the best 'check' to crime was the 'infallibility' and 'extensiveness' of punishment, not its 'cruelty' and 'intensity': hence perpetual slavery rather than death.[32] Yet, the English put to death, as a matter of course, forgers and thieves as well as, say, uxoricides. Alessandro remarked: 'Here is the proportion between crimes and pain in England! ... In this respect I do not admire this Legislation ... Here cold and indifferent laws condemn, rather than men or their passions.'[33]

The Verri correspondence was not originally intended as a public one. Yet from the beginning Pietro planned that all the letters would be recorded in a book; and he communicated this plan to Alessandro. Alessandro knowingly used his letters as a diary, and he was evidently aware that he was to read them again, perhaps with his brother. After four months Pietro told Alessandro that the letters, all regularly numbered by him, should be circulated among some friends; he also told his brother that they should be published, and Alessandro responded by saying that he would pay more attention to what he wrote, making sure to take every opportunity to mortify Beccaria.[34] Somehow, what Pietro imagined as 'a small, delightful, instructive and interesting book' on his brother's journey to Paris and London (1766–7) became the twelve published volumes of Verri's correspondence (1766–82).[35]

Alessandro's journey is not only a sort of 'Sentimental Journey'; his letters from London are also a kind of 'Letters Concerning the English Nation', or 'Lettres philosophiques'. In fact, sometimes he seems to be running again through Voltaire's topics (the Quakers, the Stock Exchange, the different religious sects, Newton and his grave, etc.), and Hume's 'meek' philosophy seems to take the place of Locke's 'wise and modest' one.[36] According to Voltaire, 'philosophers ... are without enthusiasm'; according to Hume,

---

[30] Ibid. 263.   [31] Ibid. 251–6, 271.   [32] Beccaria, *Dei delitti*, 19, 59, 63, 64–5.

[33] Verri and Verri, *Viaggio*, 271.   [34] Ibid. 3, 45–6, 83–4, 138, 161, 311–12.

[35] Ibid. 280. The letters from 1783 to 1797 (Pietro's death) are still unpublished.

[36] François-Marie Arouet Voltaire, *Lettres philosophiques*, ed. F. Deloffre (Paris: Gallimard, 1986), 94; Verri and Verri, *Viaggio*, 144–5, 168, 170, 205, 336, 361 (cf. Voltaire, *Lettres philosophiques*, letters I–IV, VI, XIII–XIV).

'there is no enthusiasm among philosophers'; and according to Verri, 'even Hume, who seems capable of the greatest philosophical enthusiasm, in his essays often rails at this orgasm or sacred fire . . . by calling it . . . *philosophical devotion*'.[37]

This journey to Paris and London was, according to Pietro, a 'philosophical pilgrimage' and a 'walk through Europe', that is 'throughout the globe', during which Alessandro could pick '*scattered flowers* of literary history'.[38] Pietro advised Alessandro to try 'to make a name for himself, to become a renowned author and lay the foundations by which . . . we can exist in our own right even in the literary world'. While entertaining and instructing himself, he ought also to organize a sort of Italian branch of the Society of European Thinkers.[39] In Alessandro's view, the most important point in travelling 'with profit' (as opposed to travelling 'like trunks') was 'to make some good acquaintances and to cultivate honourable and useful correspondents'.[40]

The real journey produced at least three real effects. First, it destroyed the friendship between the Verri brothers and Beccaria. Second, it made Alessandro 'European not Milanese'; that is, it 'completely purged [him] of his native block-headedness' (in Pietro's words).[41] Third, it produced a correspondence through which Alessandro found himself, 'in spirit', back in Pietro's warm room holding a 'conversation', a '*tête à tête*' with him; while Pietro was able 'to travel again through Europe', sharing in his brothers 'feelings'.[42] The correspondence was also 'the ledger of so much bollocks [di tante coglionerie]' (in Alessandro's words).[43]

HUME'S PORTRAIT IN THE 'PHILOSOPHICAL MUSEUM'

In November 1766, just before going to London, Alessandro was thinking of Hume: 'I had hoped to meet him in London, but it will not be possible, because he has returned to Edinburgh, his home town.'[44] Unlike Paolo Frisi (1728–84), who was introduced to Hume through d'Alembert's letters and saw him for dinner a couple of times in the summer of 1766 (this seems to be all he has to say about it in his diary), Alessandro failed to meet Hume.[45]

---

[37] Voltaire, *Lettres philosophiques*, 94; Hume, *Enquiry*, 147; Verri and Verri, *Carteggio*, ii. 124. Unlike Voltaire and Hume, in his *Anti-Seneque, ou Discours sur le bonheur*, La Mettrie maintains that philosophy too has its own kind of 'fanaticism' (Julien Offray de La Mettrie, *Œuvres philosophiques* (Hildesheim: Georg Olms Verlag, 1988), 128).

[38] Verri and Verri, *Viaggio*, 121, 126, 230, 263 (cf. pp. 94, 168, 212, 237, 354, 446).

[39] Ibid. 226, 399–400 (cf. p. 130).   [40] Ibid. 380.   [41] Ibid. 129, 258.

[42] Ibid. 168, 193, 194, 204, 207, 240.   [43] Ibid. 150.   [44] Ibid. 119.

[45] National Library of Scotland, MS no. 23153, 6, ff. 434–6; 7, ff. 369–70; 9, f. 399; Paolo Frisi, 'Copia del "Diario" scritto dal matematico Paolo Frisi nel suo viaggio di Francia ed Inghilterra', Biblioteca Ambrosiana, Milan, BA 163a sup., 47^r–48^r.

This, however, did not prevent him from giving a brief second-hand portrait of Hume as a good man:

Monsieur Hume, as far as I am told, is possessed of that simplicity of manners that pleases infinitely more than the most studied politeness. From his portrait I see a rustic [lodigiana] countenance that promises no more than good sense. He is a very good man. Don't be surprised by this sparing praise. Goodness here is praised better than learning.[46]

It may be interesting to pause briefly on these lines. Let us consider the remark on Hume's countenance, allegedly so unexpected in a philosopher. Three weeks earlier Verri had pointed to Hume as living evidence of the great difference between authors and books (the same kind of Humean puzzle is described in Kant's *Anthropology*): '*Hume* is the best and simplest man in the world. Do you find him such in his audacious essays?'[47] Verri's physiognomical observation is evidently the Italian version of the Parisian *gros David*, Diderot's fat well-fed Bernardine monk, d'Alembert's Word made flesh, and Lord Charlemont's turtle-eating Alderman.[48]

That Parisians keenly and emphatically expressed a preference for goodness and simplicity of character over learning and sophisticated manners was something Verri had observed from day one: 'They maintain an entirely familiar philanthropic attitude towards one another. There is no pomp nor pedantry. They argue with one another heatedly and vigorously, but with all the good faith in the world,' Alessandro wrote in his first letter from Paris.[49] The French praised what they had, and were infectious: '[the Encyclopedists] are good people, they have no great profundity,' he writes after a month, 'but they are amiable. . . . Even I, by dint of being here, feel myself becoming better and milder, if I am not deceiving myself.'[50] Their mutual friendship, so free of diffidence, and their 'candour', were evidence of their goodness. They were the greatest philanthropists and the best-natured, most beneficent men: 'what makes them so worthy of our respect is their compassion, their humanity, their simplicity. For this they deserve our veneration.'[51]

---

[46] Verri and Verri, *Viaggio*, 119.

[47] Ibid. 61; Immanuel Kant, *Anthropology from a Pragmatic Point of View*, ed. and trans. M. J. Gregor (The Hague: Martinus Nijhoff, 1974), I, § 30, p. 49.

[48] Grimm, *Correspondance littéraire*, iv. 125, 338; Hume, *Letters*, i. 496 (cf. p. 437; David Hume, *New Letters of David Hume*, ed. R. Klibansky and E. C. Mossner (Oxford: Clarendon Press, 1954), 76; NLS MS no. 23155, 35, f. 367; 36, f. 431; 37, f. 21; 38, f. 25; 105, f. 97); James Caulfield, Earl of Charlemont, *Memoirs of the Political and Private Life of James Caulfield, Earl of Charlemont*, ed. F. Hardy, 2nd edn., 2 vols (London: T. Cadell and W. Davies, 1812), i. 15. Cf. also Lytton Strachey, 'Hume' (1928), in *Portraits in Miniature and Other Essays* (London: Chatto and Windus, 1931), 141–53, at p. 150.

[49] Verri and Verri, *Viaggio*, 24–5 (cf. pp. 101–2). For this remark on the *philosophes'* 'good faith', cf. Morellet, *Mémoires Inédits*, i. 135.

[50] Verri and Verri, *Viaggio*, 86 (cf. pp. 119, 336).   [51] Ibid. 48–9, 246–7.

All this was so much the case, Alessandro concluded, that 'in order to praise each other or someone else they don't begin by saying that he knows physics or algebra, but that *he is definitely a good chap* . . . as they say of us; and they would use the same expressions for d'Alambert, Diderau [*sic*] or any other great man'—David Hume not excepted, we may add, since they called him *le bon David*. Alessandro fancied that were his brother to go to Paris they 'would not say that [he was] possessed of genius and [was] a great man, since they do not use these sorts of expressions . . . To say *he is definitely a good chap* is a praise that they would bestow on Neuton [*sic*].'[52]

All this is consistent with what a satisfied Hume wrote to Hugh Blair in April 1764 about Paris: 'what gave me chief Pleasure was to find, that most of the Elogiums bestowd on me, turnd on my personal Character; my Naivety and Simplicity of Manners, the Candour and Mildness of my Disposition &c.' But it is not entirely consistent with the second *Enquiry*: 'I have often observed', Hume writes, 'that, among the French, the first questions, with regard to a stranger, are, "Is he polite? Has he wit?". In our own country, the chief praise bestowed, is always that of a "good-natured, sensible fellow".'[53]

I am not so sure that the French were entirely serious, as Alessandro seems to believe, when they said of a great man *he is definitely a good chap*. Certainly in 1762, in Keith's letters, Hume was already *le bon and doux David*. But Keith was the same person who called him, 'par plaisanterie' as he put it, the '*Defensor of the Faith*' and kept making fun of him throughout his stay in Paris.[54] At the same time Verri's insistence on the goodness of the Encyclopedists was also a way of highlighting both their anti-religious enthusiasm and their philosophical weakness. And Hume, as opposed to the *philosophes*, showed not only good nature and simplicity, but also modesty and profundity.

With regard to the French anti-religious enthusiasm, Verri says clearly that only d'Alembert 'is possessed of genius and does not know any enthusiasm. The two things here are often confused.'[55] With the sole exception of Rousseau (and Alessandro agreed with Pietro and Hume that the

---

[52] Verri and Verri, *Viaggio*, 48, 240.

[53] Hume, *Letters*, i. 437; Hume, *Enquiries*, 262; cf. Emilio Mazza, 'La mamma di Hume: interpretazioni di un detto apocrifo', in *Il mestiere di studiare e insegnare filosofia: saggi in onore di Franco Alessio* (Milan: Wise, 2000), 143–52.

[54] Jean Jacques Rousseau, *Correspondance complète de Jean Jacques Rousseau*, critical edn. R. A. Leigh, 52 vols. (Geneva: Institut et Musée Voltaire, Les Délices; Oxford: Voltaire Foundation, 1965–98), xiii. 149; xvii. 252; NLS MS no. 23158, 19, f. 414 (cf. NLS MS no. 23155, 99, f. 84; 100, f. 135; 105, ff. 97, 100; 108, f. 101; 109, f. 129; 112, f. 85; 113, f. 89; 115, f. 137; 116, f. 223; 117, f. 219). The same Keith 'pleasantly' called Rousseau 'the *honest savage*' (Hume, *Letters*, i. 372).   [55] Verri and Verri, *Viaggio*, 118.

'philosophical persecution' of him was probably due also to his 'unforgivable crime' of having a religion),[56] the *philosophes* spoke of religion *ad nauseam*, and were radical:[57]

Only one thing can I not forgive these great men: they are almost fanatical against the orthodox: if they could, they would establish the Inquisition against those who are not of their own opinion. There are many satellite people in this society who, without examining the matter, have abandoned the system in order to give themselves an air of superiority.[58]

Furthermore, they claimed that the Inquisition is very powerful in Italy, but they had the Bastille and were forbidden even to sell the *Encyclopédie*;[59] and they believed in miracles and the efficacy of prayers in spite of all their claims that 'there is no religion here!' In a word: philosophical fanaticism and vulgar bigotry went hand in hand in Paris.[60] In 1767 Pietro reported Frisi's melancholic view of the Encyclopedists as people 'who, with the exception of D'Alembert, do not study all that much . . . and among whom nobody, except Diderot, ever read the *Encyclopédie*'; and Alessandro comments only that this is 'partly true and partly exaggerated'.[61]

With regard to the weakness of the French as philosophers, Alessandro's argument was very straightforward. The *philosophes*—d'Alembert not excepted (again he agreed with Hume in this)—may well have been good men, but they were not particularly good philosophers: they were possessed of simplicity and humanity, but were not precise in their reasoning and logic. Beccaria was actually superior to every single one of them; thus Alessandro and his brother could reveal themselves also to be superior, since they were certainly superior to Beccaria. It was the Verri brothers who were the true Parisian *philosophes*.[62]

In general, modesty, shyness, and taciturnity were Alessandro's acknowledged features (Hume too, according to Grimm, was no great talker).[63] Among the *philosophes*, by contrast, there was a lot of chattering; nobody minded 'how' he talked, and everyone thought 'as best as he could':[64] 'the French are great chatterboxes indeed. They want to chat about everything and philosophize on everything, and they bring into their conversation their theatrical declamation. They despise reason while they seem to be in pursuit of it.'[65] Observing from London the Parisian 'philosophical museum',

[56] Ibid. 88, 166; Hume, *Letters*, ii. 13.
[57] Verri and Verri, *Viaggio*, 168 (cf. pp. 28, 38, 40–1, 44, 47, 49, 118, 200).
[58] Ibid. 48.   [59] Ibid. 38, 83.   [60] Ibid. 122, 44, 47.   [61] Ibid. 388, 403.
[62] Ibid. 24, 48, 86–7, 118–19, 247–8; Hume, *Letters*, ii. 13.
[63] Verri and Verri, *Viaggio*, 39 (cf. pp. 104, 113, 176, 179); Grimm, *Correspondance littéraire*, iv. 458; v. 125.   [64] Verri and Verri, *Viaggio*, 39, 47–8 (cf. pp. 101–2).
[65] Ibid. 39.

Alessandro was embarrassed by their lack of 'precision of reasoning' and by their 'poetry and heated imagination':[66]

they were all so far surpassed in logic by Beccaria, who often reduced to the minimal terms an ocean of words and bad reasonings; and, as far as I've heard, neither d'Alambert [*sic*] himself nor any of the others have Beccaria's precision nor yours, and perhaps, I'll modestly say, not even mine . . . If you carefully observe, the warmth of their writing announces the truth, but break up and ponder their ideas. [67]

In short, they were very similar to Italian men of letters, the Verri brothers excepted.[68] The most illustrious victim of Alessandro's pen was Morellet. This paradoxical 'madman', 'good but absurd', well known and generally despised as such, was simply incapable of arguing:[69]

A hundred times I heard him argue . . . and be reduced to nonsense and end up with saying that his opinion was founded on long meditation on the subject and that, in order to account for it, it was necessary to follow a long chain of reasoning, which was not possible in conversation.[70]

Hume's views on the French were not very different: his judgement on Helvétius's philosophical abilities, for example, was no more flattering. And, curiously, Helvétius himself seems on occasion to have entertained similar sentiments about Hume.[71]

'ALL THE CAFFETTISTI IN LONDON': ALESSANDRO'S ANGLOMANIA

Pietro thought Paris an 'amiable' place and London a 'ferocious' one.[72] When Alessandro played off London against Paris (if Paris was great, London was immense; London merchants were more reliable than Parisian ones, etc.), there was at least one clear-cut reason for this preference. His enthusiasm for London was, at least in part, due to 'the absence of Beccaria', a fact of which Pietro reminded him many times; and to some extent it should also be considered as a reaction against 'passionate and capricious', tumultuous and fanatical Parisian society. Alessandro acknowledged that he was happy to be 'alone' because he was 'independent'; that he started 'to travel, live and breathe' only when he was far from Beccaria ('without

---

[66] Verri and Verri, *Viaggio*, 246–7, 335.   [67] Ibid. 247.   [68] Ibid. 276.
[69] Ibid. 244, 366 (cf. pp. 60, 108, 245–6).   [70] Ibid. 244–5.
[71] Claude-Adrien Helvétius, *Correspondance générale d'Helvétius*, 4 vols. (Oxford: Voltaire Foundation, 1984–98), ed. A. Dainard, M.-T. Inguenaud, J. Orsoni, and D. Smith, iii(1991). 108.
[72] Verri and Verri, *Viaggio*, 4 (cf. pp. 133, 155).

that beast', as he puts it); and that Beccaria excited in his breast a sort of 'loathing' towards Paris.[73] He did not, however, totally agree with Pietro's ascription of this 'enthusiasm for London' to his 'personal passions': 'You suppose that London's people are ferocious, but I tell you they are more humane than any other people.'[74]

To him London was freedom and tranquillity and that coolness which derives from the acquisition of truth: 'many truths here are common . . . tolerance of opinions . . . is a trivial truth . . . there's not a great enthusiasm for truth where its possession is cool and its acquisition free and not prohibited.'[75] Alessandro had such a passion for English laws and customs that he started to study the language; he considered it so sweet and graceful that he even found the English 'th' easy and harmonious.[76] His was a perfect case of Anglomania, the same *anglomanie* which, according to Walpole, 'was worn out' in Paris and remained only as '*manie* against the English'.[77] Alessandro liked to mimic the English, and wore an English 'frack'—the 'modest frack' of the 'great and modest' English—from the very first day.[78] He loved English simplicity—for example, he adored English furniture and carriages. He praised the purity and cleanliness of English women and English houses, but was willing to accept England's contradictions to it (for example, when at the 'Klob', he was not given a napkin, and was obliged to drink from a 'shared' glass).[79]

He was so in love with London that in Paris, where he behaved like an Englishman and was pleased to be mistaken for one, he would say: 'I'm too English to love Paris.'[80] Moreover, he claimed, Beccaria's *Delitti* did not sell well in England; nor was Beccaria himself so highly esteemed, his maxims being regarded as common truths.[81] Only once did Alessandro admit to being upset by England and its licentiousness (this was probably only because someone called him a 'French dog'), and even then he finished his letter by reasserting his love for London: 'Oh London, London! If I could bring you here you'll see that I have reason to love London.'[82] Only a few days after his arrival he had already decided it was the most suitable town in which to live: 'How nice it would be,' he wrote, 'if we could bring here all the Caffettisti.'[83]

---

[73] Ibid. 150, 155, 164, 179, 196, 325.   [74] Ibid. 293 (cf. pp. 176–7, 293–4).

[75] Ibid. 169–70 (cf. pp. 148, 168, 195–6, 235, 256).

[76] Ibid. 188, 217 (cf. pp. 60, 104, 140).

[77] Horace Walpole, *The Letters of Horace Walpole*, ed. P. Toynbee, 16 vols. (Oxford: Clarendon Press, 1903–5), vi. 435; cf. Arturo Graf, *L'anglomania e l'influsso inglese in Italia nel secolo XVIII* (Turin: Ermanno Loescher, 1911).

[78] Verri and Verri, *Carteggio*, i(1) 421–2; *idem*, *Viaggio*, 140 (cf. pp. 143, 218–19, 251, 297).

[79] Verri and Verri, *Viaggio*, 140, 149, 178, 206, 289–90 (cf. p. 306).

[80] Ibid. 351, 362. According to his father, Alessandro does not 'prefer the English rather than the French', but he is '*finally disabused of the French*' (ibid. 342).

[81] Ibid. 148 (cf. pp. 249, 259, 320).   [82] Ibid. 218–19, 221.   [83] Ibid. 142.

'ANOTHER SCENE LIKE THAT BETWEEN HUME
AND ROUSSEAU'

The dispute between Hume and Rousseau—'such a scandalous literary case . . . this great plague of philosophy'—added complexity to the Verri brothers' positions.[84] Alessandro, who usually criticizes the *philosophes* as enthusiasts, sympathizes with Hume (and the *philosophes*) against Rousseau—that is, with modesty against enthusiasm. But he also sympathizes with Rousseau against the *philosophes* who were attacking him; that is, he is again against enthusiasm.[85] Pietro, who usually defends the *philosophes* from Alessandro's criticism, sympathizes with Rousseau against Hume (and the *philosophes*); that is, he attacks the *philosophes* (and Hume) for their being enthusiastically against Rousseau (Hume is suspiciously 'too cool and reasonable in every point of the dispute').[86] Pietro does not see any madness in Rousseau's conduct. And Beccaria, who is supposed to be another Rousseau (according to the monk Fernando Facchinei, the author of one of the first criticisms of Beccaria's book, Beccaria 'aspires to be considered the Italian Rousseau'), calls Rousseau a 'madman', just as the Verris call Beccaria the same, even if sometimes they treat him simply as an enemy.[87]

   A man of 'great imagination' and 'passion', Beccaria could only live in the present.[88] He was excessive.[89] He set out for Paris as if he were going to the scaffold.[90] Good-natured only in appearance, timorous and anxious at night, after the first day of his journey, in Novara, Beccaria already wanted to go back to Milan.[91] As Alessandro reports: 'I heard a voice waking me up saying: "look there! look there!" It was our friend, thinking that someone was getting in through the window.'[92] Similarly, Rousseau, at Senlis, in the middle of the night thought he heard Hume's voice saying 'Je tiens Jean-Jacques Rousseau'.[93] Prey to puerile foolishness and deep melancholy—that is, to 'home-sickness' or 'wife-sickness' (she 'punished his crime of leaving for Paris with a disproportionate punishment', according to Galiani's cruel

---

[84] Verri and Verri, *Viaggio*, p. 167 (cf. p. 201); 'Review of D. Hume, *Exposé succinct de la contestation*, London, 1766', in *Estratto della Letteratura Europea per l'anno MDCCLXVI*, iii (1766), 262–5, at pp. 262–3.   [85] Verri and Verri, *Viaggio*, 40, 118–19, 166–7, 346.

[86] Ibid. 87–9, 133, 201, 224, 476.

[87] Ibid. 22–3, 94, 209, 210, 239, 249, 270, 292, 304, 312, 326, 334, 341, 344–5, 366, 372, 374, 379, 383–4, 393; Ferdinando Facchinei, *Dalle 'Note ed osservazioni sul libro intitolato "Dei delitti e delle pene"* ', in Beccaria, *Dei delitti*, 164–77, at p. 175.

[88] Verri and Verri, *Viaggio*, 141, 240 (cf. pp. 23, 27, 54, 63, 76, 78, 86, 90, 159, 293, 305, 345), 135–6 (cf. pp. 110, 239).   [89] Ibid. 240, 292.

[90] Ibid. 31, 77, 458.   [91] Ibid. 53, 76 (cf. pp. 22, 26, 77), 99 (cf. pp. 239, 304).

[92] Ibid. 53, 76 (cf. pp. 22, 27, 77).

[93] Hume, *New Letters*, 151 (cf. pp. 142, 145, 162; Hume, *Letters*, ii. 29–30, 63, 399; David Hume, *Exposé succint de la contestation qui s'est élevée entre M. Hume and M. Rousseau*, ed. J.-P. Jackson (Paris: ALIVE, 1998), 140).

bon mot reported by Alessandro), Beccaria, 'idiotically' in Pietro's opinion, remained in Paris for only five weeks.[94] As d'Holbach contemptuously said: 'his mind was never in Paris at all.'[95]

In the dispute the Verris both sided passionately against Beccaria. Alessandro represented Beccaria as an enthusiast and himself as a reasonable moderate: they were, it is clear, even though he does not say it in as many words, another Rousseau and another Hume. Beccaria's accusation against the Verris, as reported by Pietro, was in turn very similar to Rousseau's against Hume: they tried to discredit him in front of the Republic of Letters. Like Rousseau, Beccaria was at first only a sad extravagant madman, but in the end a wicked one, jealous of everything and ungrateful. As in the case of Rousseau, according to the *philosophes* and the disaffected Hume, at least after 1766, Beccaria's only merits were eloquence and style.[96] The Verris claimed, with some justification, to have been Beccaria's ghost writers: they had suggested the subject-matter, given him materials (Alessandro was a criminal lawyer), and Pietro had corrected the final version.[97] After Paris they got excited when they heard of objections to and criticisms of the book, and were disappointed at their weakness.[98] They planned first to expose him as a 'plagiarist', then to criticize him publicly though anonymously, and finally to give him personally their manuscript criticisms.[99]

Eventually, when he wanted to prevent Pietro from starting 'a harsh and open war' against Beccaria (but only because he thought that the 'master-stroke' against him would be a public cold refutation of his work), Alessandro openly voiced the view that they were playing a provincial version of the Hume–Rousseau piece at 'the theatre of slanderous Milan': 'I wouldn't fancy reproducing another scene like that between Rousseau and Hume. The public are eagerly awaiting the occasion to speak ill of us.'[100]

ATHEISTS AT D'HOLBACH'S TABLE

In a letter from Paris, October 1766, having reported the *philosophes'* unjust judgements regarding Rousseau, Alessandro laments that they

[94] Verri and Verri, *Viaggio*, 40, 90, 94, 183, 238, 329 (cf. pp. 56, 78); *idem, Carteggio*, i(1). 429–30; 457 (cf. *idem, Viaggio*, 29).   [95] Verri and Verri, *Viaggio*, 356.

[96] Ibid. 340, 374 (cf. Hume, *Letters*, ii. 91; cf. ii. 103; i. 366, 373–4).

[97] Verri and Verri, *Viaggio*, 330, 332, 469 (cf. pp. 194, 304, 329, 350, 374); Gianni Francioni, 'Nota al testo', in C. Beccaria, 'Dei delitti e delle pene', ed. G. Francioni, in *Edizione Nazionale delle Opere di Cesare Beccaria*, ed. L. Firpo and G. Francioni (Milan: Mediobanca, 1984), i. 215–368.

[98] Verri and Verri, *Viaggio*, 319, 332, 364, 393–4.

[99] Ibid. 157, 346–7, 349–50; Verri and Verri, *Carteggio*, ii. 150–1.

[100] Verri and Verri, *Viaggio*, 344–6 (cf. pp. 118–19).

consider Hume 'weak-minded' only because he does not positively deny the existence of a God:

Atheism is so much in fashion here that they regard any one who has not such a positive opinion as they as weak-minded. For this reason David Hume is, in his principles, considered weak-minded. There's no remedy, the existence of a Being ought not to be believed. There is, properly speaking, a spirit of conspiracy. I don't like this. This universal attitude of the Learned makes many into infidels: they do not know why and how they are such. I shall never be lenient to anyone who is light-hearted on this most important matter.[101]

This account echoes other reports. Gibbon's *Autobiography*, for example, expresses disapproval for 'the intolerant zeal' of the *philosophes*: 'they laughed at the scepticism of Hume, preached the tenets of atheism with the bigotry of dogmatists, and damned all believers with ridicule and contempt.' And Carlyle remembers that they 'laugh'd at Andrew Stuart for making a Battle in Favour of a Future State'. According to George Horne, who relates the testimony of James Macdonald, they 'disapproved of certain religious prejudices not yet shaken off, which hindered Hume from aspiring to perfection'. Most of them 'were deep in Materialism, and have discarded the belief of a God, which our worthy Scottish philosopher refused to do: "So that poor Hume," says Sir James, "who on your side of the water was thought to have too little religion, is here thought to have too much".'[102] These accounts are connected with the famous anecdote reported by Diderot in 1765. As d'Holbach was to write in his *Système*, Diderot maintains that in England 'the Christian religion is almost extinguished . . . The deists . . . are numberless. There is scarcely an atheist; and those who are such, disguise it.' He says also that the first time 'the English philosopher' found himself at d'Holbach's table, he declared 'that he didn't believe in atheists, that he had never seen any of them'. And d'Holbach replied: 'Monsieur, count how many we are here.' They were eighteen, as Diderot observes, and the Baron added: 'It is not a misfortune that I can show you fifteen of them at once. The three others still don't know what to think about it.' Diderot concludes that 'a people who think that belief in a God, rather than good laws, makes men honest, do not seem . . . much advanced'. In 1781 Sir Samuel Romilly repeats the anecdote and ascribes to Diderot the Baconian and Spinozian observation, agreeable with Hume's First *Enquiry*

---

[101] Verri and Verri, *Viaggio*, 40.

[102] Edward Gibbon, *Memoirs of My Life and Writings*, ed. A. O. J. Cockshut and S. Constantine (Keele: Keele University Press, Ryburn Publishing, 1994), 381; Alan Charles Kors, *D'Holbach's Coterie: An Enlightenment in Paris* (Princeton: Princeton University Press, 1976), 104–5; John H. Burton (ed.), *Autobiography of the Rev. Dr Alexander Carlyle of Inveresk* (Edinburgh and London: William Blackwood and Sons, 1860), 278; W. J., 'Original Letter of Bishop Horne, 6 June 1764', *Gentleman's Magazine*, 63 (1793): 687b–688a, at p. 688a.

and with the *Natural History of Religion*, that the English are guilty of jumbling up theology and philosophy.[103]

This anecdote is reported in many twentieth-century studies of Hume, sometimes as evidence that he was not an atheist, that he thought it impossible to be such, and even that he was a deist, if not a Christian.[104] As Kors suggests with regard to d'Holbach's answer, perhaps Hume's assertion should not be assumed to be literally true: it could be a hyperbolic sceptical attempt to startle d'Holbach's positive atheism, or an irony directed at him ('don't wonder if I should return a Jesuit,' Walpole wrote from Paris), or one of those poses that unmask themselves due to their very excess.[105] Hume's texts make it easier to imagine him a sceptic with regard to the existence of 'the cause or causes of order in the universe' rather than to the existence of atheists.[106]

In December 1763, after a few months with his French men of letters, Hume seemed to be happy: 'they now begin to banter me, and tell droll stories of me . . . so that you see I am beginning to be at home.'[107] And he wrote to Blair that they were 'really very agreeable . . . living in entire or almost entire Harmony among themselves', as the philosophers in those 'happy times' that Hume desired to revive. They are also 'quite irreproachable in their Morals', like Bayle's *virtuous atheists*. In the same letter Hume remarked: 'It woud give you . . . great Satisfaction to find that there is not a single Deist among them.'[108]

---

[103] Denis Diderot, *Correspondance*, ed. G. Roth, 5 vols. (Paris: Les Editions de Minuit, 1955–9), v. 132–4 (cf. David Hume, *The Natural History of Religion*, in *idem, Four Dissertations*, ed. J. Immerwahr (Bristol: Thoemmes, 1995), 73–4); Paul-Henri Thiry d'Holbach, *Système de la Nature*, in *Œuvres Philosophiques*, ii. 609 and n. 48; Samuel Romilly, *Memoirs of the Life of Sir Samuel Romilly*, 2nd edn., 3 vols. (London: John Murray, 1840), i. 179; Hume, *Enquiry*, 12–13; *idem, Natural History*, 68–71; cf. also Thomas Carlyle, 'Diderot' (1833), in *Critical and Miscellaneous Essays*, 5 vols. (London: Chapman and Hall, 1899), iii. 177–248, at p. 230. In his description of Hume's supposed scepticism concerning the existence of atheists, Diderot seems to describe his own attitude as the author of *Pensées philosophiques* and the translator of Shaftesbury's *Inquiry*.

[104] Among those who have used the anecdote to maintain (1) that Hume is not an atheist *à la* d'Holbach, cf. Gaskin, *Hume's Philosophy of Religion*, 220–1; J. C. A. Gaskin, 'Hume on religion', in D. F. Norton (ed.), *The Cambridge Companion to Hume* (Cambridge: Cambridge University Press, 1993), 313–44, at p. 322; Gilardi, *Il giovane Hume*, 66–7; Popkin, *High Road to Pyrrhonism*, 59; Penelhum, *David Hume*, 36, 187, 192 n. 22; (2) that Hume doubts that there are any real or serious atheists, cf. Livingston, *Philosophical Melancholy and Delirium*, 73–4; Mounce, *Hume's Naturalism*, 106; Popkin, *High Road to Pyrrhonism*, 123 n. 62. The anecdote can also (more justly) be read in connection with Hume's distinction between 'personal convictions' and public behaviour (Penelhum, *Themes in Hume*, 242) or with Hume's 'ironic coyness' and 'agnostic' view (Box, *Suasive Art*, 213–14 and n. 62). The only reader, as far as I know, that quotes Diderot's letter under the bare and slightly ambiguous head of 'Hume humoriste' is the editor of the French translation of the first *Enquiry*; cf. David Hume, *Enquête sur l'entendement humain*, ed. D. Deleule (Paris: Le Livre de Poche, 1999), 25; David Berman, *A History of Atheism in Britain: From Hobbes to Russell* (London: Croom Helm, 1988), 101–9.

[105] Kors, *D'Holbach's Coterie*, 41–4; Walpole, *Letters*, vi. 352.

[106] Cf. Hume, *Dialogues Concerning Natural Religion*, 227.   [107] Hume, *Letters*, i. 417.

[108] Ibid. 173, 419 (cf. pp. 496–7); Hume, *Natural History*, pp. ii–iii.

So, Hume said to d'Holbach and to the 'sheiks in the Rue Royale' that he had never seen an atheist, and to Blair and 'the Clergy' (or his 'Protestant Pastors') that he had never seen a deist—in both cases not even among the *philosophes*. In his turn Blair admonished Hume that in Paris he was considered 'as being somewhat bigotted in one article', that of religion.[109] In February 1773 Hume remembered that the Baron's house was 'a common receptacle for all men of letters and ingenuity'; he remembered also that Keith and Helvétius used to consider the affected 'contempt of all religion' commendable, and that 'both of them used to laugh at me for my narrow way of thinking in these particulars'.[110] By the by, it is interesting that, doubtless from a different point of view, even Hume's brother thought him 'rather narrow-minded' in his religious principles; an observation associated, by Horne in his *Letters on Infidelity*, with Hume's Parisian sojourn and his 'religious prejudices'.[111] Let us also remember that the radical ('downright atheist') Keith started teasing the '*Defensor of the Faith*' at least one year before his arrival in Paris; and that long after his departure Helvétius and others repeatedly suggested to him that he should write that Ecclesiastical History which d'Alembert had declared would be so 'useful':[112] a project (apparently cherished by Alessandro too) that Hume never got round to pursuing, adducing as his justification in 1762 sometimes prudence and love of peace and sometimes literary satiety and laziness.[113] In

---

[109] NLS MS no. 23153, 51, ff. 156–7.

[110] Hume, *Letters*, ii. 274–5 (Verri and Verri, *Viaggio*, 449).

[111] For Hume's brother's testimony, cf. Samuel J. Pratt, *Supplement to the Life of David Hume* (London: J. Bew, 1777), 33–4; George Horne, *Letters on Infidelity* (1784), 2nd edn. (Oxford: Clarendon Press, 1786), 50–1.

[112] John H. Burton (ed.), *Letters of Eminent Persons Addressed to David Hume* (Edinburgh and London: William Blackwood and Sons, 1849), 13–14, 183–4, 69–70, 185–6, 218; Jean-Baptiste le Rond d'Alembert, *De l'abus de la critique en matière de religion*, in *Œuvres complètes de d'Alembert* (Geneva: Slatkine Reprints, 1967), i (2). 549–72, at pp. 567, 570; Grimm, *Correspondance littèraire*, v. 196–7; NLS MS no. 23155, 113, f. 89. On Hume's use of ecclesiastical history as confirmation of his reflections, cf. Hume, *Natural History*, 70; *idem*, *Essays*, 62 n. 9. On Keith as a 'downright atheist', cf. James Boswell, 'An Account of my last Interview with David Hume', in C. McC. Weis and F. A. Pottle (eds.), *Boswell in Extremes 1776–1778* (London: Heinemann, 1970), 11–15, at p. 11.

[113] Hume, *Letters*, i. 352, 369; Alessandro Verri, 'Alcune Memorie spettanti alla storia Ecclesiastica da me compilate nel 1763', MS, Fondazione Raffaele Mattioli per la Storia del Pensiero Economico, Archivio Verri, folder 488, fasc. 3. With regard to ecclesiastical history, cf. Girolamo Imbruglia, ' "My ecclesiastical History": Gibbon tra Hume e Raynal', in G. Imbruglia (ed.), *Ragione e immaginazione: Edward Gibbon e la storiografia europea del Settecento* (Naples: Liguori Editore, 1996), 55–101; Mossner, 'Hume and the French men of letters', 232–4; Rudolf Metz, 'Les Amitiés françaises de Hume et le mouvement des idées', *Revue de littérature comparée*, 9/4 (1929): 644–713, at p. 698; Ronald Grimsley, 'D'Alembert and Hume', *Revue de Littérature Comparée*, 35/4 (1961): 583–95, at pp. 591, 593, 595; Flavio Baroncelli, *Un inquietante filosofo perbene: saggio su David Hume* (Florence: La Nuova Italia, 1975), 8, 53. On Hume's consciousness of his bad reputation and the 'regeneration' of it by Lord Hertford's 'so high a character for piety', cf. Hume, *Letters*, i. 393, 423, 428.

short, they seemed to be trying to provoke Hume into a less cautious, more militant attitude towards religious matters.

In general, we could suppose that the difference between Hume and his 'friend' d'Holbach was the difference between the sceptical conclusion of Hume's *Natural History* and the atheistical view expressed in d'Holbach's *Le bon sens*.[114] Hume, however, sometimes does not seem satisfied with the view that 'Truth in these Subjects is beyond human Capacity' and seems to think that 'more Curiosity and Research gives a direct opposite Turn from the same Principles', as he writes to Elliot in 1751. In *Dialogues* Part 4, for example, this turn seems to be that of Stratonician atheism *à la Bayle*.[115] This is probably what Blair meant when he suggested to Hume to go 'but one Step farther' so as to make sure to have his statue erected in Paris and to be even more completely worshiped there: 'If you will show them the MSS of certain Dialogues perhaps that honour may still be done you.'[116]

Admittedly, the Hume reported to have said, 'I never saw an atheist', may remind the reader of a few of his passages on atheism and 'total' scepticism; and one might well be tempted tentatively to take that Hume at face value.[117] Yet, according to Hume—who in his works recognizes many kinds of scepticism and atheism, praises 'true' and 'mitigated' scepticism, and calls his philosophy 'very sceptical'[118]—this assertion is typical of those 'divines and graver philosophers' (such as Cheyne and Derham) who contradict themselves.[119]

---

[114] Hume, *Letters*, ii. 275; *idem, Natural History*, 116–17; Paul-Henri Thiry d'Holbach, *Le Bon Sens*, ed. J. Deprun (Paris: Editions rationalistes, 1971), 123–5.

[115] Hume, *Letters*, i. 151–2 (cf. *idem, Treatise*, pp. xiv–xv); *idem, Dialogues*, 161–4.

[116] NLS MS no. 23153, 51, f. 157; NLS MS no. 23154, 67, f. 353.

[117] On the possibility of 'total' scepticism (a 'fantastic' sect): Hume, *Treatise*, 183; *idem, Enquiry*, 149 (cf. David Hume, *A Letter from a Gentleman to his Friend in Edinburgh*, ed. E. C. Mossner and J. V. Price (Edinburgh: Edinburgh University Press, 1967), 19); *idem, Dialogues*, 139: on the 'extravagant' sceptics as only 'a few': *idem, Treatise*, 214; on the 'sceptical' principles in religious matters of 'a few' philosophers: *idem, Natural History*, 3; *idem, Dialogues*, 215, 227 (cf. pp. 226, 223); on the possibility of 'speculative atheist': *idem, Enquiry*, 146; *idem, Dialogues*, 139, 218.

[118] For Hume's different kinds of scepticism: Hume, *Treatise*, 224, 273, 639; *idem, Enquiry*, 41, 150, 161–2; for Hume on atheism, cf. Ernest C. Mossner, 'Hume's early memoranda, 1729–1740: the complete text', *Journal of the History of Ideas*, 9 (1948): 492–518, at pp. 501, 503; Hume, *New Letters*, 11; *idem, Letters*, i. 154–5; *idem, Dialogues*, 139–40, 158–60; *idem, Natural History*, 25–7, 32 and n. a.

[119] William Derham, *Physico-Theology*, 11th edn. (Glasgow: R. Urie and Company, for J. Barry, 1745), 428–30; George Cheyne, *Philosophical Principles of Religion Natural and Revealed*, 5th edn. (London: George Strahan, 1736), 178. On the rarity of atheists, Francis Bacon, *Of Atheism*, in *The Works of Francis Bacon*, ed. J. Spedding *et al.*, 14 vols. (London: Longman, 1861), vi. 413–15, at p. 414; on Derham's view, cf. d'Holbach, *Système*, 592; on the existence of speculative atheists, cf. Pierre Bayle, *Pensées diverses sur la comète*, ed. A. Prat, rev. P. Rétat (Paris: Société des Textes Français Modernes, 1994), ii. 18, 71; George Berkeley, *Alciphron: or, the Minute Philosopher in Seven Dialogues*, in *The Works of George Berkeley*, ed. A. A. Luce and T. E. Jessop, 9 vols. (Edinburgh: T. Nelson, 1948–57), iii. 23; cf. D. Berman, 'The repressive denials of atheism in Britain in the seventeenth and eighteenth centuries', *Proceedings of the Royal Irish Academy*, 82/9 (1982): 211–45.

As he remarks, *à la* Collins, at the beginning of Section XII of the First *Enquiry*:

There is not a greater number of philosophical reasonings, displayed upon any subject, than those, which prove the existence of a Deity, and refute the fallacies of *Atheists*; and yet the most religious philosophers still dispute whether any man can be so blinded as to be a speculative atheist.[120]

And a similar 'palpable contradiction' is observed by Philo in the *Dialogues*.[121] D'Holbach, who had read Hume's work and admired his genius, makes almost the same remark as the *Enquiry* in the chapter of the *Système* which asks 'Do the atheists exist?'; and he explains the divines' attitude by 'the absurd ideas that they ascribed to their adversaries'.[122] The difference between d'Holbach and Hume appears sometimes to be only a question of style and prudence, if not of simulation and hypocrisy.[123] Hume refuses to 'take off the mask'. Like Diderot's Englishman, he feels, he writes in the section 'Of unphilosophical probability' in Book I of the *Treatise*, a predilection for that kind of 'conceal'd', 'indirect', and 'oblique' attack where 'appearances are saved' and violations more easily overlooked or excused.[124]

Yet, unlike Diderot and d'Holbach, Hume is not so positive about the possibility of radically curing the 'frailty of human reason' and the 'irresistible contagion of opinion', and of being entirely free from these religious 'sick men's dreams'. For, he asks in the *Natural History*, 'when will the people be reasonable?' On these occasions, when religion appears to him a 'natural malady', Hume seems to indulge in a sort of superstitious atheism and sympathizes with that affected, not altogether sincere and sometimes simply pretended Ciceronian devotion, with that kind of happy and poetical paganism that 'sits so easy and light on men's mind', and approaches 'much nearer' disbelief than conviction.[125]

The *philosophes* did not laugh at Alessandro and did not call him weak-minded; yet, the young Italian in Paris had his own direct experience of their professed atheism. One morning of November 1766, *chez* d'Holbach, he witnessed an extraordinary and secret event: the Baron's reading of his catechism, the summary of his entire work intended 'to prove with, at once, great passion and precision, that Religion is the main source of all human evils'.[126]

---

[120] Hume, *Enquiry*, 149. For a similar remark by Collins, see Anthony Collins, *A Discourse of Free-Thinking* (New York: Garland, 1984), 104.   [121] Hume, *Dialogues*, 220–1.
[122] Burton (ed.), *Letters of Eminent Persons*, 252–3; d'Holbach, *Système*, 592–3.
[123] Hume, *Letters*, i. 439 (cf. i. 189–90, 326–7, 336, 351, 374; ii. 130, 248; NLS MS no. 23153, 51, f. 157).
[124] Hume, *Treatise*, 150–3; (cf. Hume, *Essays*, 461 n. 273, 463 n. 278); Diderot, *Correspondance*, v. 133.   [125] Hume, *Natural History*, 81–6, 91, 93, 115, 117.
[126] Verri and Verri, *Viaggio*, 120–1. This 'manuscript work', 'written in 18 months' and 'jealously kept', which could become 'three good volumes in-4°' containing 'his system', was d'Holbach's *Système*.

THE VICIOUS RELIGIONIST

The moderate Alessandro endeavoured to attack the (atheistic) enthusiasm of the *philosophes* by appealing to the French commonplace of Hume's supposed simplicity, good nature, and mitigated religious attitude. To do so, however, Alessandro was obliged to reduce Hume's philosophy to the position of those moderates who commonly attacked Hume and were attacked by him. And it is unfortunate that this reduction could scarcely be founded on Hume's own writings on religion.

Unlike Hume, Verri seriously believed in 'true religion' (which he identified with 'pure morals'), as distinguished from its false and adulterate species; and he thought that there was more to true religion than its abuses or corruptions, that is more than, as Hume would have it, the religion which had 'in fact, prevailed' and had 'commonly been found' in the world.[127] In his 'Saggio di morale cristiana' Alessandro also maintained that the principles of religion, its eternal revealed truths, 'kept men within the bounds of their duty' and rendered them 'both better and happy'.[128] For someone who intended to champion Hume's (however meek) philosophy, this view was not only very remote from Hume's unfeigned sentiments, but also embarrassingly close to Cleanthes' position and to the apologetic footnote Hume temporarily added to Book II of his *History* in order to defend himself from the accusations of atheism and to promote a work that he thought composed '*ad populum*, as well as *ad clerum*'. In this footnote, having declared sophistical the inference from the several historical examples of 'the abuse of religion' to the 'disadvantage of religion in general', Hume affects to conclude: 'the proper office of religion is to reform men's lives, to purify their hearts, to inforce all moral duties, and to secure obedience to the laws and civil magistrate.'[129]

But this was not Philo's opinion in Part 12 of the *Dialogues*; nor was it that of the author of the *Natural History of Religion*.[130] In Section XIV of

---

[127] A. Verri, 'Saggio di morale cristiana', ff. 1, 3, 15, 37; Hume, *Dialogues*, 223; *idem, Natural History*, 115. Alessandro's *true* religion is a 'pure morals, whose foundations are the instructions of a God who infinitely loves his work' (A. Verri, 'Saggio di morale cristiana', f. 3). On 'true religion' according to Hume, cf. Hume, *Dialogues*, 140, 189, 219, 223; *idem, Essays*, 73. On 'true religion' as a 'very equivocal expression', cf. Antoine Arnauld and Pierre Nicole, *La Logique ou L'art de penser*, ed. P. Clair et P. Girbal, 2nd edn. (Paris: Vrin, 1993), 67, 69. According to Toland, it commonly happens that an author 'aims at more' than he declares and 'cunningly disguise[s] some bad principles under the fair Pretence of defending the true Religion' (John Toland, *Christianity not Mysterious*, ed. P. McGuinness, A. Harrison, and R. Kearney (Dublin: The Lilliput Press, 1997), 7).   [128] A. Verri, 'Saggio di morale cristiana', ff. 45, 101.

[129] Hume, *Letters*, i. 189 (cf. i. 204, 214, 218, 221, 231, 237); David Hume, *The History of Great Britain, ii: Containing the Commonwealth, and the Reigns of Charles II and James II* (London: Printed for A. Millar, 1756), 449–50 n. (cf. Mossner, *Life of David Hume*, 306–7); Hume, *Dialogues*, 219–20.

[130] Hume, *Dialogues*, 221–3; *idem, Natural History*, 100–1, 104–8, 116. On the *Dialogues*, their strategy and historical context, see Giancarlo Carabelli, *Hume e la retorica*

the *Natural History* Hume maintains that, even if we could find a (popular) religion that expressly declares that 'nothing but morality could gain the divine favour', and institute an order of priests to inculcate this opinion 'in daily sermons' and 'with all the arts of persuasion', yet 'so inveterate are the people's prejudices, that for want of some other superstition, they would make the very attendance on these sermons the essentials of religion, rather than place them in virtue and good morals'. Morality is and can only be the 'least part' of religion, and 'always the least observed and regarded'.[131] Not only does religion not enforce morality; it commonly corrupts it. The section title, 'Bad influence of popular religions on morality', just because it was added later in order 'to see the scope of the discourse' (and does not exactly match the content), can be considered as a kind of slogan.[132]

With regard to d'Holbach's view that religion is connected with vice, and theological notions were and will be perpetually contrary to sound morals, Alessandro remarked in 1766:[133] 'he is such a very furious atheist that you must be careful not to be of a different opinion, if you do not want him to become suspicious of your morals.' And Pietro, certainly less of a modern zealot, with regard to the *Système de la Nature*, in 1770 admonished: 'the book . . . is so impious that, I am told, it endeavours to prove the horrible paradox, that none of those who believe in the existence of a Deity can be virtuous.'[134] At least concerning the relationship between religion and morality, Hume had not disguised his sentiments, which are very near to d'Holbach's and opposite to Alessandro's. In March 1751 Hume had written to Elliot: 'The worst speculative Sceptic ever I knew, was a much better Man than the best superstitious Devotee and Bigot.'[135] And in Section XIV

dell'ideologia: uno studio dei "Dialoghi sulla religione naturale" (Florence: La Nuova Italia, 1975). On Hume's paganism in the *Natural History*, see Emilio Mazza, ' "So easy and light": paganesimo e scetticismo nella *Natural History of Religion*', in L. Turco (ed.), *Filosofia, scienza e politica nel Settecento britannico* (Padua: Il Poligrafo, 2003), 189–209.

[131] Hume, *Natural History*, 103–5.

[132] Hume, *Letters*, i. 250–1; *idem, The Natural History of Religion*, ed. A. W. Colver (Oxford: Clarendon Press, 1976), 81, 86.

[133] D'Holbach, *Système*, 543. Claude-Adrien Helvétius, *De l'esprit*, in *Œuvres complètes d'Helvétius*, 7 vols. (Hildesheim: Georg Olms, 1967), ii(3). 131–3.

[134] Verri and Verri, *Viaggio*, 121; *idem, Carteggio*, iv. 30 (cf. pp. 10, 26). In the same period Galiani found d'Holbach's *Système* 'too long' and not so original; cf. Ferdinando Galiani and Louise d' Epinay, *Correspondance, 1769–1772*, ed. D. Maggetti and G. Dulac, 2 vols. (Paris: Editions Desjonquères, 1992–3), i. 196–7. According to Boswell, Hume remembers that he 'once hinted something as if I believed in the being of a God', and the 'downright atheist' Keith ('one of the men' or 'the man' of 'the greatest honour' Hume 'ever' knew) 'would not speak to me for a week' (Boswell, 'Account of my last interview', 14).

[135] Hume, *Letters*, i. 154 (cf. p. 106; David Hume, *The History of England, from the Invasion of Julius Caesar to the Revolution in 1688*, ed. W. B. Todd, 6 vols. (Indianapolis: Liberty Classics, 1983), vi. 153). On the virtuous atheist, cf. Anthony Ashley Cooper, 3rd Earl of Shaftesbury, *An Inquiry Concerning Virtue, or Merit*, in *Complete Works*, 7 vols. (Stuttgart and Bad Cannstatt: F. Frommann and G. Holzboog, 1981–98), ii(2). 28–9; Pierre Bayle, 'Arcesilas', in *Dictionnaire historique et critique*, 6th edn., 4 vols. (Amsterdam and Leiden, etc.: P. Brunel *et al.*, 1740),

of the *Natural History* he declared 'unsafe' the inference from religious fervor to a man's good morals.[136]

In fact, according to Boswell's 'Last interview', he thought it unnecessary to hide 'his singular notion that men of religion were generally bad men':

he then said flatly that the Morality of every Religion was bad, and . . . was not jocular when he said 'that when he heard a man was religious, he concluded he was a rascal, though he had known some instances of very good men being religious'.[137]

Hume thought it necessary to deliver this opinion openly; at least, Philo did in the posthumous *Dialogues*:

when we have to do with a man, who makes a great profession of religion and devotion; has this any other effect upon several, who pass for prudent, than to put them on their guard, lest they be cheated and deceived by him?[138]

As Hume put it in 'Of National Characters': 'all the prudent men are on their guard, when they meet with any extraordinary appearance of religion'.[139]

On the whole, we may conclude that, in order to believe that Hume was a follower of Cleanthes' view (religion enforces the motives of morality) only because he was not a fanatical and dogmatic atheist, you need not be an eighteenth-century young Italian, brother of a more famous thinker, Pietro, who had openly supported French philosophy and maintained that 'all the improvements of philosophy arise from enthusiastical writers'.[140] Like some of our present-day readers, Alessandro was also pursuing a precise project. He was defending 'a modest and tranquil philosophy' against the abuses of a 'malicious folly', as he writes in the 'Saggio di morale cristiana'. Or, according to the conclusion of his *Saggio sulla storia d'Italia*,

i, rem. K, p. 288; *idem, Pensées diverses*, 107, 122–7, 135–8; *idem, Écrits sur Spinoza*, ed. F. Charles-Daubert and P.-F. Moreau (Paris: Berg, 1983), 23.

[136] Hume, *Natural History*, 108.   [137] Boswell, 'Account of my last Interview', 11.

[138] Hume, *Dialogues*, 221.

[139] Hume, *Essays*, 200 n. 3. Even though the same 'prudent' men, as far as they are such, 'confess, that there are many exceptions to this general rule, and that probity and superstition, or even probity and fanaticism, are not altogether and in every instance incompatible'. According to Shaftesbury, we 'sometimes' meet with instances which seem to make against the 'general supposition' that religion and virtue are 'inseparabile companions': 'we have known people who, having the appearance of great zeal in religion, have yet wanted even the common affections of humanity and shown themselves extremely degenerate and corrupt. . . . in general, we find mere moral principles of such weight that, in our dealings with men, we are seldom satisfied by the fullest assurance given us of their zeal in religion till we hear something further of their character. If we are told that a man is religious, we still ask, "What are his Morals?" But, if we hear at first that he has honest moral principles and is a man of natural justice and good temper, we seldom think of the other question, "Whether he be religious and devout?"' (Shaftesbury, *An Inquiry Concerning Virtue or Merit*, in *Characteristics of Men, Manners, Opinions, Times*, ed. L. E. Klein (Cambridge: Cambridge University Press, 1999), 163; cf. La Mettrie, *Discours Préliminaire*, in *œuvres philosophiques*, i. 24).

[140] Verri and Verri, *Viaggio*, 66, 88; *idem, Carteggio*, iv. 111.

he was supporting that 'numerous but not vociferous party, who in silence and solitude are preparing for posterity a more tranquil philosophy'. For 'true philosophy fears and does not look for enthusiasm'.[141]

The paradox is that on this occasion the task of defending 'the profound thinker David Hume' was left to Pietro, who respected him chiefly as an 'Author of Commerce' and did not love him so much for his behaviour with regard to Rousseau. In April 1767 Pietro vindicated Hume's right, as a 'wise and learned' man, to examine religious matters in order to 'correct and encrease' our ideas and to 'direct their organization towards the public good'. 'God forbid', he writes, 'to approve he who attacks our Religion; but . . . those who enter into it in order to destroy abuses and superstitions deserve our praise for their patriotism and courage.'[142] Alessandro, at least since September 1768, knew Hume's views concerning miracles, providence, and a future state. He even ascribes to Hume the sentiments of the character who, in the dialogue of Section XI, 'loves sceptical paradoxes' and speaks in Epicurus's name, rather than the view, however pronounced in the first person, that religious doctrines have an 'influence' on life and morals. It is not unlikely that Alessandro knew all this already in March 1768, when he was celebrating Hume's 'modesty' and 'tranquil profundity', but he did not seem particularly struck by it. He would rather speak, as in 1769, of Hume's raillery on 'philosophical devotion' and of his 'sceptical style' in politics.[143] It was Alessandro's turn at the castrating knife. He cut off the noble irreligious parts of Hume's work, so that it could appear as meek as possible.

REFERENCES

Primary Sources

Arnauld, Antoine, and Nicole, Pierre, *La Logique ou l'art de penser*, ed. P. Clair and P. Girbal, 2nd edn. (Paris: Vrin, 1993).

Bacon, Francis, *Of Atheism, in The Works of Francis Bacon*, ed. J. Spedding *et al.*, vi (London: Longman, 1861), 413–15.

Bayle, Pierre, *Dictionnaire historique et critique*, 6th edn., 4 vols. (Amsterdam and Leiden, etc.: P. Brunel *et al.*, 1740).

—— *Écrits sur Spinoza*, ed. F. Charles-Daubert and P.-F. Moreau (Paris: Berg, 1983).

---

[141] A. Verri, 'Saggio di morale cristiana', f. 72; cf. ff. 35, 59–60; *idem, Saggio sulla storia d'Italia*, 15, 320. In his 'Saggio di morale cristiana' Alessandro quotes from Helvétius' *De l'esprit*: 'only the great man can be modest' (Verri, 'Saggio di morale cristiana', f. 60; Helvétius, *De l'esprit*, iii (6). 15). The same 'sweet' Helvétius (Verri and Verri, *Viaggio*, 49, 61, 117, 335–6), still someone who 'has reasoned profoundly' in 1769 (*idem, Carteggio*, ii. 382), will be attacked in 1778 (ibid. x. 53–4, 65–6).   [142] Verri and Verri, *Viaggio*, 389–90.
[143] Hume, *Enquiry*, 132, 134, 140, 147; Verri and Verri, *Carteggio*, i(2). 204–5; ii. 124; iii. 90–1.

—— *Pensées diverses sur la comète*, ed. A. Prat, rev. P. Rétat (Paris: Société des Textes Français Modernes, 1994).

Beccaria, Cesare, *Dei delitti e delle pene: con una raccolta di lettere e documenti relativi alla nascita dell'opera e alla sua fortuna nell'Europa del Settecento*, ed. F. Venturi (Turin: Einaudi, 1994).

—— 'Dei delitti e delle pene', ed. G. Francioni, in *Edizione Nazionale delle Opere di Cesare Beccaria*, ed. L. Firpo and G. Francioni (Milan: Mediobanca, 1984), i. 215–368.

—— 'Carteggio', ed. C. Capra, R. Pasta, and F. Pino Pongolini, in *Edizione Nazionale delle Opere di Cesare Beccaria*, ed. L. Firpo and G. Francioni (Milan: Mediobanca, 1984), iv.

Bentham, Edward, *Introduction to Moral Philosophy*, 2nd edn. (Oxford, 1745).

Berkeley, George, *Alciphron: or, the Minute Philosopher in Seven Dialogues*, in *The Works of George Berkeley*, ed. A. A. Luce and T. E. Jessop, 9 vols. (Edinburgh: T. Nelson, 1948–57), iii.

Boswell, James, 'An account of my last interview with David Hume', in C. McC. Weis and F. A. Pottle (eds.), *Boswell in Extremes 1776–1778*, (London: Heinemann, 1970), 11–15.

Burton John H. (ed.), *Autobiography of the Rev. Dr Alexander Carlyle of Inveresk* (Edinburgh and London: William Blackwood and Sons, 1860).

—— (ed.), *Letters of Eminent Persons Addressed to David Hume* (Edinburgh and London: William Blackwood and Sons, 1849).

Caulfield, James, *Memoirs of the Political and Private Life of James Caulfield, Earl of Charlemont*, ed. F. Hardy, 2nd edn., 2 vols. (London: T. Cadell and W. Davies, 1812).

Cheyne, George, *Philosophical Principles of Religion Natural and Revealed*, 5th edn. (London: George Strahan, 1736).

Collins, Anthony, *A Discourse of Free-Thinking* (New York: Garland, 1984).

D'Alembert, Jean-Baptiste le Rond, *De l'abus de la critique en matière de religion*, in *Œuvres complètes de d'Alembert* (Geneva: Slatkine Reprints, 1967), i (2). 549–72.

Derham, William, *Physico-Theology*, 11th edn. (Glasgow: R. Urie and Company, for J. Barry, 1745).

Diderot, Denis, *Correspondance*, ed. G. Roth, 5 vols. (Paris: Les Editions de Minuit, 1955–9).

Facchinei, Ferdinando, *Note ed osservazioni sul libro intitolato "Dei delitti e delle pene"*, in C. Beccaria, *Dei delitti e delle pene: con una raccolta di lettere e documenti relativi alla nascita dell'opera e alla sua fortuna nell'Europa del Settecento*, ed. F. Venturi (Turin: Einaudi, 1994), 164–77.

Frisi, Paolo, 'Copia del "Diario" scritto dal matematico Paolo Frisi nel suo viaggio di Francia ed Inghilterra', MS, Biblioteca Ambrosiana, Milan, BA 163a sup., 47^r–48^r.

Galliani, Ferdinando, and d'Epinay, Louise, *Correspondance, 1769–1772*, ed. D. Maggetti and G. Dulac, 2 vols. (Paris: Editions Desjonquères, 1992–3).

Gibbon, Edward, *Memoirs of My Life and Writings*, ed. A. O. J. Cockshut and S. Constantine (Keele: Keele University Press, Ryburn Publishing, 1994).

Grimm, Friedrich-Melchior, *Correspondance littéraire, philosophique et critique, adressé à un Souverain d'Allemagne, depuis 1753 jusqu'en 1769, par le Baron de Grimm et par Diderot*, ed. J. F. Michaud and F. Chéron, 6 vols. (Paris: Longchamps et F. Buisson, 1812).

Helvétius, Claude-Adrien, *De l'esprit*, in *Œuvres complètes d'Helvétius*, 7 vols. (Paris: P. Didot; facsimile reprint in 3 vols. of vols. i–vi, Hildesheim: Georg Olms, 1967–9).

—— *Correspondance générale d'Helvétius*, 4 vols., ed. A. Dainard, M.-T. Inguenaud, J. Orsoni, and D. Smith (Oxford: Voltaire Foundation, 1984–98).

d'Holbach, Paul-Henri Thiry, *Œuvres philosophiques*, 5 vols. (Paris: ALIVE, 1998–9).

Horne, George, *Letters on Infidelity*, 2nd edn. (Oxford: Clarendon Press, 1786).

Hume, David, *A Treatise of Human Nature*, ed. L. A. Selby-Bigge, 2nd edn. rev. P. H. Nidditch (Oxford: Clarendon Press, 1978).

—— *A Letter from a Gentleman to his Friend in Edinburgh*, ed. E. C. Mossner and J. V. Price (Edinburgh: Edinburgh University Press, 1967).

—— *Enquiries Concerning Human Understanding and Concerning the Principles of Morals*, ed. L. A. Selby-Bigge, 3rd edn., rev. P. H. Nidditch, (Oxford: Clarendon Press, 1975).

—— *Four Dissertations*, ed. J. Immerwahr (Bristol: Thoemmes, 1995).

—— *Exposé succinct de la contestation qui s'est élevée entre M. Hume and M. Rousseau*, ed. J.-P. Jackson (Paris: ALIVE, 1998).

—— *The History of Great Britain, ii: Containing the Reigns of James I and Charles I* (Edinburgh: Printed by Hamilton, Balfour and Neill, 1754).

—— *The History of Great Britain. ii: Containing the Commonwealth, and the Reigns of Charles II and James II* (London: Printed for A. Millar, 1756).

—— *The History of England, from the Invasion of Julius Caesar to the Revolution in 1688*, ed. W. B. Todd, 6 vols. (Indianapolis: Liberty Classics, 1983).

—— *Dialogues Concerning Natural Religion*, ed. N. Kemp Smith, 2nd edn. (Edinburgh: Thomas Nelson, 1947).

—— *The Natural History of Religion*, ed. A. W. Colver (Oxford: Clarendon Press, 1976).

—— *Essays Moral, Political, and Literary*, ed. E. F. Miller (Indianapolis: Liberty Classics, 1987).

—— *Enquête sur l'entendement humain*, ed. D. Deleule (Paris: Le Livre de Poche, 1999).

—— *The Letters of David Hume*, ed. J. Y. T. Greig, 2 vols. (Oxford: Clarendon Press, 1932).

—— *New Letters of David Hume*, ed. R. Klibansky and E. C. Mossner (Oxford: Clarendon Press, 1954).

Index Librorum Prohibitorum . . . Benedicti XIV (Parma: Apud Philippum Carmignani, 1783).

Index Librorum Prohibitorum . . . Pii Septimi (Rome: Ex Typographia Rev. Camerae Apostolicae, 1819).

Kant, Immanuel, *Anthropology from a Pragmatic Point of View*, ed. and trans. M. J. Gregor (The Hague: Martinus Nijhoff, 1974).

La Mettrie, Julien Offray de, *Anti-Seneque, ou Discours sur le bonheur, in œuvres philosophiques* (Hildesheim: Georg Olms Verlag, 1988).

Morellet, André *Mémoires Inédits*, 2nd edn., 2 vols. (Paris: Librairie Française de Ladvocat, 1822).

—— *Lettres d'André Morellet*, ed. D. Medlin, J. C. David, and P. Leclerc, 2 vols. (Oxford: Voltaire Foundation, 1991).

Pratt, Samuel J., *Supplement to the Life of David Hume* (London: J. Bew, 1777).

Review of D. Hume, *Essais Philosophiques*, in *Estratto della letteratura Europea per l'anno MDCCLIX*, ii (Amsterdam, 1759), 269–70.

Review of D. Hume, *Œuvres de M. Hume*, t. VI, 1764, in *Estratto della letteratura Europea per l'anno MDCCLXIV*, 1 (1764), 280–1.

Review of D. Hume, *Exposé succinct de la contestation*, in *Estratto della letteratura Europea per l'anno MDCCLXVI*, iii (London, 1766), 262–5.

Romilly, Samuel, *Memoirs of the Life of Sir Samuel Romilly*, 2nd edn., 3 vols. (London: John Murray, 1840).

Rousseau, Jean Jacques, *Correspondance complète de Jean Jacques Rousseau*, ed. R. A. Leigh, 52 vols. (Geneva: Institut et Musée Voltaire, Les Délices; Oxford: Voltaire Foundation, 1965–98).

Shaftesbury, Anthony Ashley Cooper, 3rd Earl of, *An Inquiry Concerning Virtue, or Merit*, in *Complete Works*, ii (Stuttgart and Bad Cannstatt: F. Frommann and G. Holzboog, 1981–98).

—— *An Inquiry Concerning Virtue or Merit*, in *Characteristics of Men, Manners, Opinions, Times*, ed. L. E. Klein (Cambridge: Cambridge University Press, 1999).

Toland, John, *Christianity not Mysterious*, ed. P. McGuinness, A. Harrison, and R. Kearney (Dublin: The Lilliput Press, 1997).

Verri, Alessandro, 'Saggio di morale cristiana', MS, Archivio Verri, Fondazione Raffaele Mattioli per la Storia del Pensiero Economico, folder 484, fasc. 1.

—— ['Dell'universalità delle scienze'], MS, Archivio Verri, folder n.n., ins. [5].

—— 'Alcune Memorie spettanti alla storia Ecclesiastica da me compilate nel 1763', MS, Fondazione Raffaele Mattioli per la Storia del Pensiero Economico, Archivio Verri, folder 488, fasc. 3.

—— *Saggio sulla storia d'Italia*, ed. B. Scalvini (Rome: Edizioni di storia e letteratura, 2001).

Verri, Pietro, Estratti da Hume, MS, Archivio Verri, folder 374, fasc. 8.

—— *Dialogo tra Fronimo e Simplicio sul disordine delle monete nello Stato di Milano* (Lucca, 1762).

—— *Considerazioni sul Commercio dello Stato di Milano* (1763), ed. C. A. Vianello (Milan: Università L. Bocconi, 1939).

—— *Meditazioni sulla economia politica*, ed. R. De Felice (Milan: Bruno Mondadori, 1998).

—— and Verri, Alessandro, *Carteggio di Pietro e di Alessandro Verri*, ed. A. Giulini, E. Greppi, F. Novati, and G. Seregni, 12 vols. (Milan: L. F. Cogliati, A. Giuffrè, 1910–42).

—— —— *Viaggio a Parigi e Londra (1766–1767): Carteggio di Pietro e Alessandro Verri*, ed. G. Gaspari (Milan: Adelphi, 1980).

Pietro Verri, Alessandro Verri *et al.*, *'Il Caffè'* *1764–1766*, ed. Gianni Francioni and S. Romagnoli, 2nd rev. edn. (Turin: Bollati Boringhieri, 1993).

Voltaire, François-Marie Arouet, *Commentario sul libro 'Dei delitti e delle pene'*, ed. G. Francioni (Como-Pavia: Ibis, 1994).

—— *Lettres philosophiques*, ed. F. Deloffre (Paris: Gallimard, 1986).

Walpole, Horace, *The Letters of Horace Walpole*, ed. P. Toynbee, 16 vols. (Oxford: Clarendon Press, 1903–5).

Secondary Sources

Baroncelli, Flavio, *Un inquietante filosofo perbene: saggio su David Hume* (Florence: La Nuova Italia, 1975).

Berman, David, 'The repressive denials of atheism in Britain in the seventeenth and eighteenth centuries', *Proceedings of the Royal Irish Academy*, 82/9 (1982): 211–45.

—— *A History of Atheism in Britain: From Hobbes to Russell* (London: Croom Helm, 1988).

Bongie, Laurence L., *David Hume: Prophet of the Counter-Revolution*, 2nd edn. (Indianapolis: Liberty Press, 2000).

Box, M. A., *The Suasive Art of David Hume* (Princeton: Princeton University Press, 1990).

Burton, John H., *Life and Correspondence of David Hume*, 2 vols. (Edinburgh: William Tait, 1846).

Capaldi, Nicholas, *David Hume: The Newtonian Philosopher* (Boston: Twayne Publishers, 1975).

Capra, Carlo, *I progressi della ragione: vita di Pietro Verri* (Bologna: il Mulino, 2002).

—— (ed.), *Pietro Verri e il suo tempo*, 2 vols. (Bologna: Cisalpino-Monduzzi, 1999).

Carabelli, Giancarlo, *Hume e la retorica dell'ideologia: Uno studio dei "Dialoghi sulla religione naturale"* (Florence: La Nuova Italia, 1975).

Carlyle, Thomas, 'Diderot' (1833), in *Critical and Miscellaneous Essays*, 5 vols. (London: Chapman and Hall, 1899), iii. 177–248.

Fieser, James, 'Hume's concealed attack on religion and his early critics', *Journal of Philosophical Research*, 20 (1995): 431–49.

Francioni, Gianni, *Prefazione* to François-Marie Arouet Voltaire, *Commentario sul libro 'Dei delitti e delle pene'*, ed. G. Francioni (Como-Pavia: Ibis, 1994), 7–28.

Gaskin, J. C. A., *Hume's Philosophy of Religion*, 2nd edn. (London: Macmillan Press, 1993).

—— 'Hume on religion', in David F. Norton (ed.), *The Cambridge Companion to Hume* (Cambridge: Cambridge University Press, 1993), 313–44.

Gilardi, Roberto, *Il giovane Hume, Volume Primo: Il "background" religioso e culturale* (Milan: Vita e Pensiero, 1990).

Graf, Arturo, *L'anglomania e l'influsso inglese in Italia nel secolo XVIII* (Turin: Ermanno Loescher, 1911).

Grimsley, Ronald, 'D'Alembert and Hume', *Revue de Littérature Comparée*, 35/4 (1961): 583–95.

Imbruglia, Girolamo, ' "My ecclesiastical History": Gibbon tra Hume e Raynal', in G. Imbruglia (ed.), *Ragione e immaginazione: Edward Gibbon e la storiografia europea del Settecento* (Naples: Liguori Editore, 1996), 55–101.

Kors, Alan Charles, *D'Holbach's Coterie: An Enlightenment in Paris* (Princeton: Princeton University Press, 1976).

Livingston, Donald W., *Philosophical Melancholy and Delirium: Hume's Pathology of Philosophy* (Chicago and London: University of Chicago Press, 1998).

Mazza, Emilio, 'La mamma di Hume: interpretazioni di un detto apocrifo', in *Il mestiere di studiare e insegnare filosofia: saggi in onore di Franco Alessio* (Milan: Wise, 2000), 143–52.

—— ' "So easy and light": paganesimo e scetticismo nella *Natural History of Religion*', in L. Turco (ed.), *Filosofia, scienza e politica nel Settecento britannico* (Padua: Il Poligrafo, 2003), 189–209.

Metz, Rudolf, 'Les Amitiés françaises de Hume et le mouvement des idées', *Revue de littérature comparée*, 9/4 (1929): 644–713.

Mossner, Ernest C., 'Hume's early memoranda, 1729–1740: the complete text', *Journal of the History of Ideas*, 9 (1948): 492–518.

—— 'Hume and the French men of letters', *Revue Internationale de Philosophie*, 6 (1952): 221–35.

—— *The Life of David Hume*, 2nd edn. (Oxford: Clarendon Press, 1980).

Mounce, H. O., *Hume's Naturalism* (London and New York: Routledge, 1999).

Panizza, Giorgio, and Costa, Barbara, *L'archivio Verri*, 2 vols. (Milan: Fondazione Raffaele Mattioli per la Storia del Pensiero Economico, 1997, 2000).

Penelhum, Terence, *Hume* (London: Macmillan, 1975).

—— *David Hume: An Introduction to his Philosophical System* (West Lafayette, Ind.: Purdue University Press, 1992).

—— *Themes in Hume: The Self, the Will, Religion* (Oxford: Clarendon Press, 2000).

Popkin, Richard H., *The High Road to Pyrrhonism*, ed. R. A. Watson and J. E. Force (San Diego: Austin Hill Press, 1980).

Strachey, Lytton, 'Hume', (1928), in *Portraits in Miniature and Other Essays* (London: Chatto and Windus, 1931), 141–53.

Venturi, Franco, 'La Milano del *Caffè*', in *Settecento riformatore, i: Da Muratori a Beccaria 1730–1764* (Turin: Einaudi, 1972), i. 645–747.

—— 'Gli uomini delle riforme: la Lombardia', in *Settecento riformatore, v: L'Italia dei lumi 1764–1790* (Turin: Einaudi, 1987), v (1). 425–834.

Hume's Fragments of Union and the Fiction of the Scottish Enlightenment

SUSAN MANNING

This essay offers a literary critic's perspective on some striking features of Hume's writing that resonate transatlantically through contexts well beyond the philosophical circles in which they are usually discussed. It is part of a larger argument about relationships between Scottish philosophy and American Romantic literature, a comparative study which looks at principles of connection: political, psychological, and grammatical, and the analogies that are developed between them in Scottish Enlightenment writing.[1] Here I shall first just outline the context and some of my assumptions. I take it as given in what follows that the parliamentary Union between England and Scotland in 1707 and the confederation of the United States in the American Revolution were, respectively, defining historical moments for the idea of nationhood in Scotland and America; in both cases the political event initiated a drive towards coherent narratives of self and nation which give particular character to the forms taken by literature in the Romantic period. Unifying 'stories' are held in tension with a kind of structural resistance, a fragmenting, dissolving impulse. Both extremes find epistemological, historical, and psychological expression in Scottish and American literature. My larger argument, then, looks at how the impulse to create narrative is cut into or frustrated by the fragmentation of the form, either as deliberate literary manner—such as elisions, missing episodes—or in the embedded structures of the exposition itself.

This tension between union and fragmentation took several forms, and led to a special interest in the principles of connection, the things that may join, or keep apart, the elements. This is the area where experience coheres—or fails to—where selves, and nations, may define themselves. The syntactic and grammatical dimensions of the tension between eloquence and silence, for example, not only concern Hume and William James, but

---

[1] Susan Manning, *Fragments of Union: Making Connections in Scottish and American Writing* (Basingstoke: Palgrave, 2002). The original version of this essay was given as a plenary lecture at the Hume Society's annual conference at Williamsburg, Virginia, in July 1999; a shorter version was delivered in Cambridge in September 1999.

preoccupy writing by James Boswell, Henry Mackenzie, and Thomas Jefferson. What all these examples have in common, in my reading of them, is an avowed purpose of linking or joining (in collaboration, celebration, or lament), and a fixation with the nature of the spaces or interludes that fragmented or frustrated the impulse to union, and thereby preserved the fragments from incorporation in the whole. More fundamentally, they are representations in language of elements of experience that resist articulation in words. Punctuation, or its absence, becomes some kind of analogy for the resistances that halt the coherent telling of experience.

In this essay I trace how the frequently made analogy between nation and self (or, to put it another way, between the structure of the political commonwealth and that of the human mind) developed into a literary-grammatical model for composition that would have enormous ideological potency for writers like Emerson, Whitman, Emily Dickinson, and William James. Hume's *A Treatise of Human Nature* was the starting-point for this conjunction. There is, I shall argue, a certain kind of silenced political vocabulary embedded in Hume's account of personal identity, which metamorphoses into psychological terms in the exposition of the *Treatise*. Hume established a 'grammar of selfhood' based in the terminology of arguments about national identity that influenced not only American political rhetoric (as Douglass Adair and, more recently, Donald Livingston have argued), but the forms of Scottish and American literature.[2]

I want to approach this discussion by way of an example of the kind of vocabulary that structured the political arguments prior to 1707: an anonymous pamphlet printed in Scotland in 1706 that embodies the mutual saturation of political and personal, discursive and fictional discourses in the debate surrounding the Union. 'The Comical History of the Marriage-Union betwixt *Fergusia* and *Heptarchus*' dramatizes the wooing of 'a Lady of venerable Antiquity, of a competent Estate and Fortune' by the 'young, lusty, very opulent and rich' Heptarchus who dwelt on her 'South Border'.[3] This plan has been proposed by Judith (Queen Anne) to 'keep her Dominions from being dismember'd on her Demise' (p. 7). Like the prudent old maid she is, Fergusia puts up a spirited resistance to Heptarchus's sudden and violently renewed suit, pointing to their ancient 'confederacy' and recalling an earlier proposal which 'preserves my Independency and Sovereignty' (p. 11). Heptarchus is passionate in his protestations: 'No, I can never be happy, till

---

[2] See Douglass Adair, ' "That politics may be reduced to a science": David Hume, James Madison, and the Tenth *Federalist*', in Donald W. Livingston and James T. King (eds.), *Hume: A Re-Evaluation* (New York: Fordham University Press, 1976), and Donald Livingston, *Philosophical Melancholy and Delirium: Hume's Pathology of Philosophy* (Chicago and London: University of Chicago Press, 1998).

[3] Anon., 'The Comical History of the Marriage-Union betwixt *Fergusia* and *Heptarchus*' (printed in *Scotland* upon that occasion; and reprinted in *England*, 1706), 3, 7; subsequent page references are given in parentheses in the text.

you and I become one Flesh, and be intirely Incorporated' (p. 12). Fergusia is
not fooled:

Incorporated! . . . It looks plaguely like your Love to your Bag-Pudding, that
you'd devour me, and bury me in the midst of your self; . . . at least it looks like
Jonah's Punishment, swallowed up in the Belly of the Whale. This is the Notion
I have of Incorporating; and if this be it, I had better live unmarried still: And
indeed, Heptarchus, I'm jealous there is a Snake in the Grass; for your People have
oft bragged, I would not be a Breakfast to them. (p. 12)

She reminds him slyly of their old 'Covenant', 'which was the nearest
Union we had together', and professes herself willing to renew that, but
makes no bones about her distaste for the disempowering consequences of
his present proposal:

It's plain by this Union, all I have becomes yours, and is perfectly at your Disposal,
and nothing you have becomes mine, so as to be at my Disposal; because there is
no Ballance of Power in my hand as will be in yours. (p. 18)

Pointing to other ill-assorted European unions of unequals, Fergusia
prophesies secession and divorce should this marriage be forced upon her:
'what *Norway* is in respect to *Denmark*, since its Union, I'll be with respect
to *Heptarchia*. *Sweden* and *Denmark* never flourished, when united; but
now separated, are become both formidable States' (p. 24). In a word,
she's not convinced, and resists his blandishments with self-preserving
urgency:

It's plain Self-Murther! This Surrender, this Incorporation, by coming under the
Power of a Government, wherein I can make no Balance, makes me as much
subjected and dependent on the absolute Will and Determination of your People,
in all my Concerns, Civil and Sacred, as if I were your conquered Slave. (p. 26)

The point of this little excursus into anti-Unionist political pamphleteer-
ing is twofold: first, to sketch in, very briefly, the prevailing contours of the
debate and some of the terms in which it was conducted: marital union,
division, and dismemberment; confederacy and incorporation; balance of
power and secession; self-sacrifice, subjection, and enslavement. Secondly,
highlighting this little fictional drama of reluctant wooing draws attention,
in advance, to a structural analogy which underlies Hume's arguments
about personal identity. I need to stress that I am concerned primarily with
the texture of Hume's prose: its construction, vocabulary, and tone—and
with the implications of his language use for subsequent writers. I'm not
making the claim that Hume's political *beliefs* were even covertly anti-
Unionist: unsurprisingly, in a man born four years after the Treaty's ratifica-
tion in 1707, whose lifetime saw the economic benefits brought to Scotland
in the mid-century by the Union, all his writing suggests that in terms of
consciously held opinion—and in biographical terms we can penetrate no

further—he was unequivocal about the advantages of the Union to both Scotland and England.[4]

But *A Treatise of Human Nature* was very much of its time and place, in more than the empirical thrust of its inquiries. I focus on this early work precisely because it gives in their rawest—and therefore for my purposes most revealing—state the form and structure of ideas that Hume later refined and subtilized. The two *Enquiries* and the essays are altogether smoother and suaver: more directly influential in some ways, but ultimately less potent. (I shall return to the question of influence at a later point.) Once we pay attention to Hume's vocabulary and the texture of his language in the *Treatise*, evidence presents itself at every turn that his thinking at this crucial formative stage expresses itself in terms of union and fragmentation. It is the form of this argument, as much as its propositions, that persists in the prose (and on occasion poetry) of the Scottish Enlightenment, which in turn helps to determine the shape of literary, political, and philosophical debate in the early years of the American Republic. Consciously or otherwise, Hume's antagonists and detractors typically adopted aspects of his rhetorical strategy that reinforced the pattern and ensured its transmission, particularly, into structures of expression in American Enlightenment and Romantic writing. There is, then—to put it no more strongly—an embedded political analogy within the vocabulary of union and fragmentation which structures the expression of Hume's ideas about personal identity. I shall go on to argue, further, that from a literary point of view, the laws of association which underpin his 'system' are predicated on grammatical and syntactic relationships as much as philosophical principles. Hume's ideas about the nature of human experience, that is, emerge from the *Treatise*'s dynamic play between political, epistemological, and grammatical frames of reference.

The political analogy is explicit in the text, though its implications are in no sense insisted upon: 'the true idea of the human mind', he writes,

is to consider it as a system of different perceptions or different existences, which are link'd together by the relation of cause and effect, and mutually produce, destroy, influence and modify each other. Our impressions give rise to their correspondent ideas; and these ideas in their turn produce other impressions. One thought chaces another, and draws after it a third, by which it is expell'd in its turn. In this respect, I cannot compare the soul more properly to any thing than to a republic or commonwealth, in which the several members are united by the reciprocal ties of government and subordination, and give rise to other persons, who propagate the same republic in the incessant changes of its parts. And as the same individual republic may not only change its members, but also its laws

---

[4] The essay 'On the Protestant Succession', probably written during or shortly after the 1745 Jacobite Rising, is a clear example of Hume's support for Hanover and the Union. On Hume's response to the events of 1745, and the timing of this essay's composition, see Ernest C. Mossner, *The Life of David Hume*, 2nd edn. (Oxford: Clarendon Press, 1980), 177 f.

and constitutions; in like manner the same person may vary his character and disposition, as well as his impressions and ideas, without losing his identity.[5]

The terms persist into the later essay, 'Of National Characters', which develops this idea of a nation as 'nothing but a collection of individuals'; national identity comes into being through the operation of a 'sympathy or contagion of manners'.[6] Interestingly, Hume describes the bonds holding together the 'English *Nation*' (that is, the united countries of England and Scotland) as the least cohesive and homogenizing of all: 'Hence the *English*, of any people in the universe, have the least of national character'; he finds the 'particular manners of the English not to hav[e] the same effect' in 'the neighbouring country of *Scotland*'.[7]

Analogous beliefs about the inevitability of internal disunion in the absence of sympathetic bonding appear to have determined Hume's early support for colonial independence in America, against the prevailing temper of opinion amongst Edinburgh literati. As early as 1768 he wrote of his 'long[ing] to see America ... revolted totally & finally'; it was his settled opinion that 'our Union with America ... in the Nature of things, cannot long subsist'.[8] A pamphlet by his friend and cousin John Home advocating war against the Americans provoked the sceptical reply:

I make no doubt, since you sound the trumpet for war against the Americans, that you have a plan ready for governing them, after they are subdued; but you will not subdue them, unless they break in pieces among themselves—an event very probable. It is a wonder it has not happened sooner.[9]

The vocabulary carries into Hume's 'Idea of the Perfect Commonwealth', which proposes an associative structure of 'hundreds' comprising the fragments of the ideal union—a system in line with Thomas Jefferson's views, despite the latter's contempt for what he regarded as Hume's Tory principles of political economy. Another essay, 'Of the First Principles of Government', describes 'collected' groups as 'quite unfit for government'; while 'dispersed' they are 'more susceptible of reason and order'.[10] This principle of aggregated fragments is actually what unites a big republic internally: according to Douglass Adair, James Madison drew on this aspect of Hume's thought

---

[5] Hume, *A Treatise of Human Nature*, ed. L. A. Selby-Bigge, 2nd edn., rev. P. H. Nidditch (Oxford: Clarendon Press, 1978), 261; subsequent page references are given in parentheses in the text.

[6] Hume, *Essays Moral, Political, and Literary*, ed. Eugene F. Miller, rev. edn. (Indianapolis: Liberty Classics, 1987), 198, 204. [7] Ibid. 207.

[8] *The Letters of David Hume*, ed. J. Y. T. Grieg, 2 vols. (Oxford: Clarendon Press, 1932), ii. 184, 210.

[9] *New Letters of David Hume*, ed. Raymond Klibansky and Ernest C. Mossner (Oxford: Clarendon Press, 1954), 210. On this point, see also Livingston, *Philosophical Melancholy and Delirium*, 307–8.

[10] Hume, *Essays*, 36. See Adair, ' "That politics may be reduced to a Science" ', 404–17, esp. p. 410.

in *The Federalist* no. 10, where 'he took these scattered and incomplete fragments [of political theory in Hume's essays] and built them into an intellectual and theoretical structure of his own'.[11]

Hume's later writings, then, support and develop the political implications which are largely submerged in the philosophical rhetoric of the *Treatise*. But for my purposes, the embedded, metaphorical nature of the vocabulary in the epistemological context permits a richer ambiguity and suggestiveness; his discussion of the possible forms of 'union', for example, recalls the federative and incorporative alternatives canvassed in 'Heptarchus and Fergusia'. Read in the context of Queen Anne's instructions to the marquis of Queensberry to block any move in the Scottish Parliament towards federal union, on the grounds that 'nothing can prove a solid and lasting settlement for the Peace and happiness of our Subjects of this Island but that of an entire Union', Hume's apparently abstract analysis of our ideas of space and time acquires new and more ambiguous resonance:

> Suppose two bodies containing no void within their circumference, to . . . unite in such a manner that the body, which results from their union, is no more extended than either of them; 'tis this we must mean when we talk of penetration. But 'tis evident this penetration is nothing but the annihilation of one of these bodies, and the preservation of the other, without our being able to distinguish particularly which is preserv'd and which annihilate. Before the approach we have the idea of two bodies. After it we have the idea only of one.
>
> Taking then penetration in this sense, for the annihilation of one body upon its approach to another, I ask any one, if he sees a necessity, that a colour'd or tangible point shou'd be annihilated upon the approach of another colour'd or tangible point? On the contrary, does he not evidently perceive, that from the union of these points there results an object, which is compounded and divisible, and may be distinguish'd into two parts, of which each preserves its existence distinct and separate, notwithstanding its contiguity to the other? (p. 41)

Philosophically speaking, Union is a convention of connection, not an inherent principle; its 'necessity' is experiential rather than inherent in the nature of things: 'in no single instance [is] the ultimate connexion of any object . . . discoverable either by our senses or reason . . . 'Tis their constant union alone, with which we are acquainted' (p. 660). But 'unions' (like republics, like whole stories) break down into fragments of meaning: 'Every

---

[11] Adair, ' "That politics may be reduced to a science" ', 411. The sceptical epistemology extends into the expression of the political philosophy. The inaccessibility of political unity in late eighteenth-century Germany, and the desire for single nationhood, led to the elevation of 'Unity' into a philosophical and aesthetic ideal, achievable only at the level of the individual mind. See e.g. A. W. Schlegel (1809): 'in the mental domain of thought and poetry, inaccessible to worldly power, the Germans, who are separate in so many ways from each other, still feel their unity', *Course of Lectures on Dramatic Art and Literature*, trans. J. Black, rev. A. J. W. Morrison (London, 1846), 6, quoted in David Simpson (ed.), *Origins of Modern Critical Thought: German Aesthetic and Literary Criticism from Lessing to Hegel* (Cambridge: Cambridge University Press, 1988), 5.

thing, that is different, is distinguishable; and every thing, that is distinguishable, may be separated' (p. 36). His most contentious proposition, regarding the integrity of personal identity, is a direct corollary of this thought:

what we call a *mind*, is nothing but a heap or collection of different perceptions, united together by certain relations, and suppos'd tho' falsely, to be endow'd with a perfect simplicity and identity. Now as every perception is distinguishable from another, and may be consider'd as separately existent; it evidently follows, that there is no absurdity in separating any particular perception from the mind; that is, in breaking off all its relations, with that connected mass of perceptions, which constitute a thinking being. (p. 207)

The possibility of perceptual secession must be accommodated, at least in the abstract: 'This uniting principle among ideas is not to be consider'd as an inseparable connexion' (p. 10). 'That term of unity', he asserts, 'is merely a fictitious denomination, which the mind may apply to any quantity of objects it collects together; nor can any such an unity any more exist alone than number can, as being in reality a true number' (p. 30). 'Union', that is, in this context is an imaginary principle, a fiction—but it is also (once the philosopher steps, as he must, outside the circle of empirical introspection) a 'fact' established by custom and habit, and what stabilizes our sense of identity. Union, identity, integrity are the imagined products of aggregated fragmentary observations; our world 'is the universe of the imagination, nor have we any idea but what is there produc'd' (pp. 67–8). This would be a crucial insight for Scottish and American Romantic fiction.

Inquiring what kind of bond might be able to hold elements together without totally subsuming and annihilating one within another (Fergusia's anticipated 'incorporation' into Heptarchus's 'Bag-Pudding'), Hume concludes that the problems associated with personal identity belong to language rather than to philosophy: that is, they have to do with the *verbal relationship* between the parts (the fragments) which are themselves the objects of philosophical scrutiny. The *connectives*, which cannot be observed by empirical introspection, are the products of expression and dissolve under scrutiny:

all the nice and subtle questions concerning personal identity can never possibly be decided, and are to be regarded rather as grammatical than as philosophical difficulties. Identity depends on the relations of ideas; and these relations produce identity, by means of that easy transition they occasion. But as the relations, and the easiness of the transition may diminish by insensible degrees, we have no just standard, by which we can decide any dispute concerning the time, when they acquire or lose a title to the name of identity. All the disputes concerning the identity of connected objects are merely verbal, except so far as the relation of parts gives rise to some fiction or imaginary principle of union. (p. 171)

At this point, the *nature* of the grammar of 'relations' which permit the mind's easy transition from fragmentary perception to unitary sense of identity becomes crucial, for it is by means of this connective tissue that we do or do not cohere as individuals (and the analogy with nationhood still lurks in the background of this account). The events a writer creates 'must be connected together by some bond or tie': the connection between the structure of language and the structure of thought becomes an increasingly important part of the epistemological argument, and one which Hume attempted to clarify in his subsequent redaction of the *Treatise* in Section III of *An Enquiry Concerning Human Understanding* (1748):

Among different languages, even where we cannot suspect the least connexion or communication, it is found, that the words, expressive of ideas, the most compounded, do yet nearly correspond to each other: A certain proof, that the simple ideas, comprehended in the compound ones, were bound together by some universal principle, which had an equal influence on all mankind.[12]

He elaborated on the nature of the connective tissue in 'An Abstract of a Book lately Published, Entituled, *A Treatise of Human Nature*, &c', published anonymously in 1740 to correct misapprehensive readings of the *Treatise*. The *Abstract* extends the structures of union and separation which characterize the expression of the original argument: 'The author [that is, Hume himself] asserts, that the soul, as far as we conceive it, is nothing but a system or train of different perceptions, those of heat *and* cold, love *and* anger, thoughts and sensations; all united together, but without any perfect simplicity or identity.'[13] It's a vision of Union without integrity, an infinite syntactic parataxis. 'Everything', as the American poet Elizabeth Bishop would later put it, 'only connected by "and" and "and"':[14]

every thing, that exists, is particular: And therefore it must be our several particular perceptions, that compose the mind. I say, *compose* the mind, not *belong* to it. The mind is not a substance, in which the perceptions inhere. (*Abstract*, 659)

Mind, that is, has a 'federative' not an 'incorporative'—or corporeal—structure; its syntax is paratactic, not hypotactic: there is no 'core' of identity other than the sum of the parts, which may, philosophically if not experientially speaking, be regarded separately. We do, however, *experience* wholeness or integrity; Hume's explanation for this aspect of personal identity draws on terms that resonate through later arguments both about political secession (in, for example, the rhetoric of Jefferson's *Declaration of Independence* or Crèvecoeur's *Letters of an American Farmer*) and

---

[12] David Hume, *An Enquiry Concerning Human Understanding*, ed. L. A. Selby-Bigge, 3rd edn., rev. P. H. Nidditch (Oxford: Clarendon Press, 1975), 23.

[13] Hume, *Abstract*, in Hume, *Treatise.*, ed. Selby-Bigge, p. 657; my emphasis.

[14] Elizabeth Bishop, 'Over 2000 illustrations and a complete concordance', in *The Complete Poems of Elizabeth Bishop* (New York: Farrar, Strauss and Giroux, 1969, 1978), 67.

associationist aesthetics. In effect, he articulates a narrative of mind, an account of how we *compose* the fiction of personal identity:

Our imagination has great authority over our ideas; and there are no ideas that are different from each other, which it cannot separate, and join, and compose into all the varieties of fiction. But notwithstanding the empire of the imagination, there is a secret tie or union among particular ideas, which causes the mind to conjoin them more frequently together, and makes the one, upon its appearance, introduce the other. Hence arises . . . the connection of writing: and hence that thread, or chain of thought, which a man naturally supports even in the loosest *reverie*. (*Abstract*, 662)

The imagination casts an imperial jurisdiction over its fragmented constituency of impressions; but their true unity is furnished by the principles of association:

so far as regards the mind, these are the only links that bind the parts of the universe together, or connect us with any person or object exterior to ourselves. For as it is by means of thought only that any thing operates upon our passions, and as these are the only ties of our thoughts, they are really *to us* the cement of the universe, and all the operations of the mind must, in a great measure, depend on them. (Ibid.)[15]

Our *experience* even of 'the union of cause and effect resolves itself, under analysis, into 'a customary association of ideas . . . identity is nothing really belonging to these different perceptions, and uniting them together; but is merely a quality, which we attribute to them, because of the union of their ideas in the imagination, when we reflect upon them' (*Treatise*, 260). This 'secret tie or union' which directs the imagination is, then, the aggregative process of association: contiguity rather than causation is the 'connective tissue' which holds together disparate perceptions and ideas, and forms 'to us, the cement of the universe'. The 'Abstract' identifies this use of the principle of association as the *Treatise*'s most fundamental originality.

The sequence of associations has a narrative character: 'We always follow the succession of time in placing our ideas, and . . . pass more easily to that, which follows immediately after [an object or event], than to that which went before it' (ibid. 430). Even after association has unified fragmentary perceptions into integrated experience, the 'total' experience (or narrative) retains the traces—though not, perhaps, the memory—of its constitutive elements. [16] Hume explains how the 'easy transition or passage of the imagination, along the ideas of these different and interrupted perceptions . . . makes us ascribe

[15] As Donald W. Livingston has recently put it, 'the defining characteristic of specifically historical thought for Hume is . . . narration' (*Hume's Philosophy of Common Life* (Chicago and London: University of Chicago Press, 1984), 6.

[16] On nineteenth-century developments of this theory of association and its relationship to memory, see Cairns Craig, 'T. S. Eliot, I. A. Richards and empiricism's art of memory', *Revue de metaphysique et de monde*, 1 (1998): 113–17.

to them a perfect identity', while 'The interrupted manner of their appearance makes us consider them as so many resembling but still distinct beings . . . The perplexity arising from this contradiction produces a propension to unite these broken appearances by the fiction of a continu'd existence' (ibid. 205). As long as we acquiesce unthinkingly in the fiction, then, we remain 'whole' to our own perception. But once we reflect on the process of this 'self-composition', it dissolves, like a conjurer's act interrupted.

Hume's compatriot James Boswell's diaries articulate the anxiety when separate 'units' won't cohere because the imagination cannot find a single 'smooth' passage between them. His *London Journal* embodies the young man's wish to attain 'a composed . . . character'; the exercise of diary writing is a conscious attempt to find an appropriate style for the expression of identity, to tell a single, consistent narrative of self.[17] Uneasiness and depression fragment his sense of self and reduce the diarist to silence; the return of composure puts him 'in fine humour for composition' (p. 188). Writing out self-contradictory elements of experience bestows at least the connective tissue of remembered sequence:

> Sunday 28 November. . . . I went to St. James's Church and heard service and a good sermon on 'By what means shall a young man learn to order his ways', in which the advantages of early piety were well displayed. What a curious, inconsistent thing is the mind of man! In the midst of divine service I was laying plans for having women, and yet I had the most sincere feelings of religion. I imagine that my want of belief is the occasion of this, so that I can have all the feelings. I would try to make out a little consistency this way. (p. 62)

In these journals, Boswell is, literally, writing himself into existence as the product of his moment-by-moment perceptions.

Book I of the *Treatise* systematically pursues the line of inward-facing empiricism, but its narrative issues in conclusions that enforce the disintegration of that system: turning the methods of empirical scrutiny inwards so that the mind considers its own workings is a hazardous activity analogous (as I've argued in another context) to a Calvinist understanding of the pursuit after unlawful knowledge; this is, philosophically and personally, a dead end.[18] Not only universal scepticism, but internal distress and the fragmentation of connected narrative, ensue:

> Where am I, or what? From what causes do I derive my existence and to what condition shall I return? Whose favour shall I court, and whose anger must I dread? What beings surround me? And on whom have I any influence, or who have any influence on me? (*Treatise*, 269)

---

[17] *Boswell's London Journal*, 1762–63, ed. Frederick A. Pottle (London: Heinemann Ltd., 1952), 56; subsequent page references are given in parentheses in the text.
[18] Susan Manning, *The Puritan-Provincial Vision: Scottish and American Literature in the Nineteenth Century* (Cambridge: Cambridge University Press, 1990), 38–40.

This is the consequence of a brief predominance of the reasoning faculty over the feelings, an outcome that is potentially disastrous for the sense of integrated self-hood. The solipsistic moment breaks, famously, on the return of relationships: unmitigated empirical introspection, it emerges, is a fragmenting narrative strategy of Hume's exposition—a prelude to the introduction of sympathy as the 'cement of the [social] universe'. Here we see just why it is that 'Reason is, and ought only to be, the slave of the passions' (ibid. 415). The union of the faculties can be accomplished only on such incorporative terms. Sympathy becomes the subject of the subsequent books of the *Treatise*, and indeed the main subject of Hume's continuing philosophical reflections. Where logic (analytic thought) fragments, writing (communicable feeling) establishes connections. These, Hume is clear, are the continuities of fiction, but they are nothing short of *necessary* fictions. 'Union', as we have seen, is a product of the imagination, which holds together the infinitely divisible sequence of perceptions. The analogies between the political compound of Union and the philosophical, psychological, and grammatical forms of the *Treatise* and its narrative sequels, the essays, exist primarily not at the level of political philosophy, but in terms of the rhetoric of sympathy and division.[19] Sympathy, in Hume's account, unites—but it also separates. A point of connection is not the same as a merger: 'sympathy is the chief source of moral distinctions' (p. 394). Hume's solution to his self-created epistemological conundrum enacts before the fact the paradox of *e pluribus unum*.

By the end of Book I Hume has demonstrated both the uselessness and the untenability of empirical thinking in its analytic or fragmentary phase, and the imperative need to put it back into a social context. We may see this mirrored in the different rhetorical structure—of communicability rather than solitary mastery—he adopted in subsequent works, where (not wanting to be blighted by the consequences of his own thinking) he fractured the system, and reinvented it as a series of social communications. The importance of maintaining the tension between unity and fragmentation in Hume's writing extends, in formal terms, beyond the *Treatise of Human Nature*. The *Treatise* was his 'system', and it remained—as a unified expression of the nature and operation of mind—substantially unaltered after 1740. This, however, was not the form in which most readers encountered his thought; nor was it divided only after publication: a private letter to Henry Home, Lord Kames, makes it clear that Hume had already detached a portion of the argument (which would become the essay 'Of Miracles') from the whole, a division which, in rendering the work 'safer', also camouflaged its overt challenge and thereby perhaps diminished its impact

[19] Livingston argues that there is no 'image of the American regime in Hume's "Idea of a Perfect Commonwealth" ' (*Philosophical Melancholy*, 324).

on publication.[20] Following his disappointment at the initial reception of the *Treatise* (which, as Hume famously put it himself, quoting Pope, 'fell *dead-born from the press*'), he devoted the remainder of his life to repackaging ideas by which he essentially continued to stand, in discrete essays designed explicitly for social consumption.[21] In 1775 he ordered his London printer William Strahan to publish an 'Advertisement' which was subsequently pre-fixed to all editions of the *Enquiries* up to the end of the nineteenth century, and which emphasized the jejeune status of the earlier work: with reflection, 'he was sensible of his error in going to the press too early, and he cast the whole anew in the following pieces, where some negligences in his former reasoning and more in the expression, are, he hopes, corrected'.[22] This dis-sociation of the parts of the system was not so much condescension to an audience unprepared to digest the difficulty of systematic philosophy, as a logical continuation of the *Treatise*'s inquiry into the nature of the connective tissue which binds the fragmentary perceptions of self. Where the 'whole' had failed of its aim, the 'pieces' perhaps would succeed in reaching an audience. It is worth noting that Hume directs his self-criticism almost exclusively at the *expression* of the *Treatise*: breaking up the connected argument, he spun off the dangerous, and misunderstood, unitary logic into separate redac-tions (the *Essays and Treatises on Several Subjects*) which put the elements of the system into different contexts of relation. In the essays, a carefully calculated, easy, sociable address replaced the *Treatise*'s tone of philosophic iconoclasm. Communication was of the essence: clarity, transparency, and availability became Hume's major stylistic preoccupations, and redirected the focus of attention on to the question of the relationship between identity and expression. Social exchange depends on our assuming not only the reality of the writer and of his audience, but the real possibility of ideas being passed between them in words. It is the great achievement of these essays to find a voice in which scepticism, individual isolation, subjectivity, personal relativity, Pyrrhonism itself, all become available for discussion in the intensely *social* context of the Scottish Enlightenment. The concerns are demonstrably continuous. In topics ostensibly distant from the analysis of mind, similar forms of argument recur: we have already seen how the confluence of terms describing personal and national identity persists into Hume's writing about national character; in an economic context, an essay 'Of Commerce' discusses the relationship between the greatness of the state,

[20] See Jerome Christensen, *Practicing Enlightenment: Hume and the Formation of a Literary Career* (Madison: University of Wisconsin Press, 1987), 94–5.

[21] *Epilogue to the Satires*, ii. 226, in *Pope: Poetical Works*, ed. Herbert Davis (Oxford: Oxford University Press, 1966, 1978).

[22] Hume, *Enquiry Concerning Human Understanding*, 83. Hume located the failure of the *Treatise* to please its initial audience not in philosophical error, but 'in the positive Air, which prevails in that Book, & which may be imputed to the Ardor of Youth'. See *Letters*, i. 187.

that of the sovereign, and the happiness of his subjects in the vocabulary of separation and union.[23]

Scottish Common-Sense writing is almost universally opposed to the fragmenting implications of Hume's empirical analysis; it is, by and large, emphatically a literature of union. Adam Smith and Lord Kames are perhaps the nearest, in print, to allies that his *Treatise* enlisted. Most of the other important figures—Reid, Campbell, Beattie, Blair—were clergymen either too politically cautious or too alarmed by the implications of infidelity to countenance the claims of association over those of subordination. Given that the *Treatise* was not republished in Hume's lifetime and achieved only very limited circulation (although greater notoriety), it may seem quixotic to assert its cardinal importance for the development of an idiom of union and fragmentation across psychological, political, philosophical, and aesthetic contexts. This is none the less demonstrably the case, through at least three mechanisms of propagation. First, consciously or otherwise, Hume's antagonists incorporated the vocabulary of his analysis in their refutations. Secondly, the terms and structures of his argument provided a sufficiently powerful model that writers such as Smith adopted the aesthetic and rhetorical consequences of its *form* of argument even as they challenged its theological, political, or ethical implications. Thirdly, the 'unacceptable' element of sceptical fragmentation in Book I of Hume's *Treatise* is in fact inseparable from the 'common-sense' moral philosophy based in sympathy propounded in the later phases of its argument; adopting and developing their own versions of sympathy, as Reid, Smith, and Beattie did, they confirmed the tendency for subsequent moral philosophy and fiction to turn their attention away from the civic responsibilities of the individual towards a focus on internal feelings.[24]

Thomas Reid's and James Beattie's 'refutations' of Hume, for example, effectively propagated the union–fragmentation tensions in his thought in the very form of their negations, at the same time as their stories of the self extended the implications of his analogy between identity and grammar.[25] The vocabulary of fragmentation and the structure of his argument percolate

---

[23] Hume, *Essays*, 258, 262.

[24] See David Fate Norton, *David Hume: Common-Sense Moralist, Sceptical Metaphysician* (Princeton: Princeton University Press, 1982), and Thomas Miller, *The Formation of College English: Rhetoric and Belles Lettres in the British Cultural Provinces* (Pittsburgh: University of Pittsburgh Press, 1997), 216.

[25] It was largely through the medium of his antagonists' writing that the *Treatise's* conceptual and verbal structures of union and fragmentation continued and expanded their currency in subsequent Scottish-American literary culture. See e.g. Reid's incorporation of Hume's currency of connection, fragmentation (divisibility), and union in *An Inquiry into the Human Mind on the Principles of Common Sense* (1764), ed. Derek R. Brookes (Edinburgh: Edinburgh University Press, 1997), 91–4, 121–2, 132, 176, and *idem, Essays on the Intellectual Powers of Man* (1785), ed. A. D. Woozley (London: Macmillan, 1941), 172–3.

(inadvertently on Beattie's part, we must assume) into the *Essay on Truth*: the universe, he says, 'is a vast collection of things';[26] 'What shall we say to this collection of strange phrases?'[27] If the *Essay on Truth* does not take Hume's epistemological or ethical argument any further, it unwittingly propagates it, through direct quotation and unconscious adoption of his rhetorical tissue and narrative patterns.

Body and spirit are utterly annihilated; and there remains nothing (for we must again descend into the gibberish of metaphysic) but a vast collection, bundle, mass, or heap, of unperceived perceptions. Such, if Mr Hume's words have any meaning, is the result of his system.[28]

All three writers were agreed on the inseparability of language analysis from the understanding of mind. Beattie's later 'Theory of Language' asserts that 'the principles of grammar form an important, and very curious, part of the philosophy of the human mind'.[29] According to Dugald Stewart, Adam Smith's unpublished Glasgow lectures in moral philosophy taught that 'the best method of explaining and illustrating the various powers of the human mind' was 'an examination of the several ways of communicating our thoughts by speech, and from an attention to the principles of . . . literary compositions'.[30] Even more influential was Reid's axiom that 'the very language of mankind, with regard to the operations of our minds, is ana-logical' (*Essays*, 30). Although he perceived that within its own terms Hume's logic was unassailable, and that successful refutation could lie only in changing the premises of the argument, Reid attempted to reclaim some a priori ground for personal identity from what he took to be Hume's reduct-ive phenomenalism (analysis from the point of view only of immediate objects of perception) by addressing his objections in the same linguistic framework. Discussing causal connection, for instance, he gives the exam-ple of magnetism, where with 'a little attention', we 'conceive a power of virtue in the magnet as the cause, and a motion in the iron as the effect; and although these are things quite unlike, they are so united in the imagination,

---

[26] James Beattie, *An Essay on the Nature and Immutability of Truth in Opposition to Sophistry and Scepticism*, 2nd edn. (Edinburgh: Kinkaid and Bell, 1771), with a new introduction by Roger J. Robinson (London and Bristol: Routledge/Thoemmes Press, 1996), 121.   [27] Ibid. 325.

[28] Ibid. 281. Beattie also propagates Humean structures of thought in his repeated citations of the *Treatise*. See e.g. his quotation on 'connections'(p. 160), on self as 'heap or collections of dif-ferent perceptions' (pp. 278, 482, 517), 'successive perceptions constituting the mind' (p. 279), on the connections between successive events (p. 323), 'the soul, which considers the union of two or more objects' (p. 330), 'a cause in an object precedent and contiguous to another, and so united with it' (p. 332).

[29] Beattie, 'The Theory of Language', in *Dissertations Moral and Critical* (London: W. Strahan and T. Cadell, 1783, and Edinburgh: W. Creech, 1783); facsimile reprint in *The Works of James Beattie*, 10 vols., vol. v, with a new introduction by R. J. Robinson (London: Routledge/ Thoemmes, 1996), 308. The nature and function of conjunctive terms in the work of Scottish Enlightenment discussions are considered more fully in my *Fragments of Union*, chs. 5 and 6.

[30] Quoted by Miller, *Formation of College English*, 169.

that we give the common name of *magnetism* to both' (ibid. 41–2). Our common use of language tends to join things which are in reality separate and separable, so that a single word which in fact signifies a connection, a conjunction, is taken by the imagination to be a unity. The mind's tendency to unite cause and effect is, Reid implies, a condition of inadvertence: separation of sensation from source may be achieved by a conscious 'act of the mind' (ibid. 42). Acts of the mind are acts of union, in that they make clear the elements that have been joined. Reid is convinced, however, that these connections have a status, a 'reality' that Hume does not accord them. As Manfred Kuhen puts it, 'Reid, while admitting that he could not explain how exactly the principles of common sense brought about the "real connexion" between our perceptions, nevertheless argued that there was such a connection, and that it could only be brought about by what he called "the principles of common sense".'[31]

Between the *Inquiry into the Human Mind on the Principles of Common Sense* (1764) and his *Essays on the Intellectual Powers of Man* (1785), Reid turned, under the influence of new theories of 'Universal Grammar', away from Lockean explanations towards the relation between mind and language to elucidate the 'connexion'. He conducts a running dialogue between the structure of language and the principles of perception, locating the self in the flow of experience from one sensation to another, so that identity is assured by a series of relationships between discrete memory fragments, rather as objects have a kind of permanence even as they alter through time. His analysis transforms Hume's fleeting objects of perception into mental *actions*:

Sensation, imagination, memory, and judgment, have, by the vulgar, in all ages, been considered as acts of the mind. The manner in which they are expressed in all languages, shews this. (*Common Sense*, 44)

The 'act of union' in Reid is, so to speak, a verb—the mind *acts* union, does not simply passively receive its impression, as in Hume's version.[32] Perception is an 'act of the mind' (ibid. 168) which is conscious, and may be reflected upon, although it cannot be analysed into simpler fragmentary components. To have a mind is to perform mental acts. This passage also gives an early indication of the analogy between language and the structure of consciousness that Reid would explore at greater length in his *Intellectual Powers of Man* some twenty years later. Here, the subject–verb–predicate

---

[31] Manfred Kuhen, 'Reid's Contribution to "Hume's Problem" ', in Peter Jones (ed.), *The 'Science of Man' in the Scottish Enlightenment: Hume, Reid and their Contemporaries* (Edinburgh: Edinburgh University Press, 1989), 132.

[32] See Leith Davis's fine analysis of 'Union' as enacted in the writing of eighteenth-century pro-Union writers like Defoe. Her *Acts of Union* (Stanford, Calif: Stanford University Press, 1998) appeared when my own argument was too well advanced to take full advantage of its perceptive readings.

structure is taken to reflect our experience of agency and act.[33] It is, once again, the *syntax* of experience that underpins identity. The transitional areas of philosophical and psychological inquiry correspond conceptually to the 'unfixed' connective parts of a sentence: grammar and syntax provide the cement to make sentences cohere internally; style determines the nature of the connections across sentences, one with the next; philosophical argument describes the relationship between mind and world.

Where Humean associationism, strictly pursued, implies a federative concept of (personal and national) identity, Reid's psychology inclines towards an incorporative model. The current unhappily divided state of philosophy exemplified by Hume's *Treatise*, Reid argues, is the consequence of a monstrous, unnatural 'union' that yokes two incompatible hypotheses concerning the 'intercourse that is carried on between the mind and the external world' (*Essays*, 91): first, 'that the mind, like a mirror, receives the images of things from without, by means of the sense', and secondly (the insight of modern empiricism), that sensations 'are not resemblances of any thing in bodies' (ibid. 93). 'This opinion', he continues,

surely looks with a very malign aspect upon the old hypothesis; yet that hypothesis hath still been retained, and conjoined with it. And what a brood of monsters hath this produced!

The first-born of this union . . . was, That the secondary qualities of body were mere sensations of the mind . . . The progeny that followed is still more frightful: . . . No causes nor effects; no substances, material or spiritual; no evidence even in mathematical demonstration; no liberty nor active power; nothing existing in nature, but impressions and ideas, following each other, without time, place, or subject. (Ibid. 94)

The product of an unnatural union, in other words (and as Fergusia had prophesied), is a universe reduced to a bundle of fragments. The 'true' union occurs at the level of first principles, prior to our capacity for separating analysis, and incorporates the relation of cause and effect into the very structure of the human mind.

In historiography, Hume's friend William Robertson articulated a similar incorporative principle in his view that 'There can be no union, and by consequence there can be no society, where there is no subordination'.[34] Robertson's *History of Scotland* (1759) not only took it for granted that the Union was incorporative rather than federative, but described its benefits enthusiastically in terms of the dissolving of local peculiarities into a single,

---

[33] Reid's analogy between the structures of mind and of language was probably, though he nowhere acknowledges it, suggested to him by George Turnbull, his tutor at Marischal College. See George Turnbull's *Principles of Moral Philosophy* (London, 1740).

[34] 'Reasons of Dissent from the Judgment and Resolution of the Commission, March 11, 1752', cited by Richard B. Sher, *Church and University in the Scottish Enlightenment: The Moderate Literati of Edinburgh* (Edinburgh: Edinburgh University Press, 1985), 45.

unified, national identity.[35] 'Robertson's achievement', as Richard Sher has put it, 'was to portray Anglo-Scottish relations not as they were but as polite society might wish them to be.'[36] The rhetorical sweep of the Unionist histories made their stories hugely compelling political parables of national development and—most importantly in relation to the fear of violent revolution—continuity. During discussion of Thomas Jefferson's draft 'Declaration of Independence' in America, disquiet was expressed about the danger that Union might lead to loss of sovereignty for individual states. According to Jefferson, Benjamin Franklin (referring perhaps to 'Fergusia and Heptarchus') dismissed this by crafty recourse to the parable of Jonah and the whale; noting that 'at the time of the Union between England and Scotland the latter had made the objection which the smaller states now do . . . [T]hat it would again happen as in times of old, that the whale would swallow Jonas, but he thought the prediction reversed in event and that Jonas had swallowed the whale, for the Scotch had in fact got possession of the government and gave laws to the English'.

John Witherspoon, Edinburgh graduate, Presbyterian divine and Principal of Princeton College in New Jersey, incensed by what he regarded as Franklin's sophistry, responded with the need to distinguish between 'an incorporating & a federal union. The union of England was an incorporating one; yet Scotland had suffered by that union: for that it's [*sic*] inhabitants were drawn from it by the hopes of places & employments'. The American proposals, on the other hand, were based on the view that 'All men admit that a confederacy is necessary.[37]

Hume's *History of England* (1754–62) makes clear the extent to which his thought increasingly became aligned with, rather than antagonistic to, the discourse of his milieu. Hume the historian, we might say, told a more unequivocally Unionist story than Hume the philosopher. Like William Robertson's, Tobias Smollett's, and James Macpherson's Anglo-Scots histories, Hume's made a complete separation between Scotland's independent past and the British present. As far as Scotland was concerned, in the First *Enquiry* he suggested that the 'great chain of events' which constituted connected history began at the Union, when as part of Great Britain, the old backward, feud-torn assemblage of warring factions was given the possibility of a connected future.[38] It can be no coincidence that these North British

---

[35] *Works of William Robertson*, 12 vols. (London: Printed for William Baynes and Son, 1824), iii. 155–6: 'At length the union having incorporated the two nations, and rendered them one people, the distinctions which had subsisted for many years gradually wear away . . . The Scots . . . were at once put into possession of privileges more valuable than those which their ancestors had formerly enjoyed.' [36] Sher, *Church and State*, 102.

[37] Thomas Jefferson, *Autobiography*, in *Writings*, ed. Merrill D. Peterson, Library of America (Cambridge: Cambridge University Press, 1984), 28–9. See also Livingston, *Philosophical Melancholy*, 331.

[38] Hume, *Enquiry Concerning Human Understanding*, ed. T. L. Beauchamp (Oxford: Oxford University Press, 1999), 103. (The passage discussed here did not appear in 1777 edition of the *Enquiry*, and is therefore not printed in the Selby-Bigge edition either.)

histories were (unlike the *Treatise*) produced in the aftermath of the Jacobite Rising of 1745, which subjected the Union to its severest test; for a short period, fragmentation appeared to be a real political possibility. Just as the parable of Jonah and the whale, like all stories, could be told more than one way, both Robertson and Hume as Unionist historians were perfectly aware of why they told the story of Scotland as they did: ''tis requisite', as Hume put it,

that the writer have some plan or object . . . in his first setting out, if not in the composition of the whole work . . . [Events or actions in narratives] must be related to each other in the imagination, and form a kind of Unity, which may bring them under one plan or view, and which may be the object or end of the writer in his first undertaking. (*Enquiry*, 102)

Union is a principle of historiographic composition. Hume's narrative of human understanding is less ideologically—as well as less expediently—and more sceptically mounted.

The final sections of Book I of Hume's *Treatise* pointed in what look like two radically different directions for fiction: first, radical subjectivity and the prison-house of language: 'this is the universe of the imagination, nor have we any idea but what is there produc'd' (p. 68). This is the fragmenting perception, which gave rise to tales of psychic disintegration. The alternative, imperative succession to this was the education of 'sentiments' as the cement of social relationship. However, as I have suggested, Hume's next move made it clear that to see one's own existence as an autonomous fragment is to neglect the union of society of which one is a fragment. The ties of sympathy preoccupied Enlightenment writers of fiction because they were only too aware of the fragmenting consequences of intense self-reflection.

A bizarre oriental tale by William Duff, an Aberdeenshire minister who is usually remembered as the author of *An Essay on Original Genius* . . . (1767), gives a measure of just how interwoven the Union debate, revalorized by Hume's vocabulary of union and fragmentation, became with that of sympathy in Scottish fiction. *The History of Rhedi* (1773) is precipitated by the son of wise Amur being 'tor[n] . . . to pieces' by a wild boar as the family flees from tyranny. This tragedy of dismemberment brings them into contact with the hermit Rhedi, whose sympathy with their feelings takes the form of reciprocating their sad story with his own woeful tale of his quest for 'union' with Selima (the word is used many times, notably in connection with a prior 'treaty' of marriage claimed by Rhedi's rival, a politically motivated 'alliance which was equally creditable and advantageous to both parties, and which would unite their families in the bonds of consanguinity and friendship').[39]

---

[39] William Duff, *The History of Rhedi, The Hermit of Mount Ararat: An Oriental Tale* (London: T. Cadell, 1773), 13, 35, 67–68. I am grateful to Martin Moonie for drawing this tale to my attention. Subsequent references to *Rhedi* are identified by page number in the text.

From this, he urges, they should learn the Stoic lesson of 'the instability of human happiness, which, though heedless mortals fancy to be solid and permanent as the strongly based promontory of the Hellespont, ... is tottering as the broken fragment of a tower which falls from the ruined domes of Palmyra on the head of the unhappy traveller, and instantly crushes him to pieces' (p. 66).

The prospect of eternal separation from his beloved, by this threatening 'treaty of union', distracts Rhedi completely, and the political allegory relocates to the site of personal disunion in an intriguingly Humean fashion, as his composure fragments in a disconnected succession of emotional states:

all the passions which can agitate and tear the human heart arose in my mind at once.—Love, rage, jealousy, hatred, terror, and despair alternately reigned and mingled with each other in my soul, in their utmost fury, and produced a conflict, whose violence rouzed me to phrenzy, and almost terminated in my dissolution. (p. 85).

Describing the form of Rhedi's 'dissolution', the prose itself fragments to paratactic listing of emotions abstracted from the self that feels them. Selima, Rhedi's beloved, escapes certain death at the Sophy's vengeful hand through his misunderstanding of the nature and source of her displayed emotions; from this point, 'sympathy' rather than fragmentation dominates the narrative, but it is unstable and liable to misinterpretation by onlookers. Rhedi, as the book's title emphasizes, is a hermit, able to sympathize precisely because he is 'inured to misfortune' (p. 21). The sympathy which enables understanding may operate most effectively in separation: like the Humean philosopher in 'Of Essay Writing', Rhedi lives 'secluded from the world', but the encounter at his place of retreat with the distressed family re-engages his social sympathies. Hume's writing is consistent on the mutual advantages of social association: 'The Separation of the Learned from the conversible World' is detrimental to both (*Essays*, 534). Scottish Enlightenment fiction devotes considerable attention to articulating the distinction between disengagement and social alienation.

Rhedi's distance from social absorption represents one option for shaping the fragments of immediate sensation into meaning. Henry Mackenzie, even as a young man, routinely invoked the trope of age and personal disconnectedness as a narrative perspective. The associative powers of memory create a space that does not demand resolution into either union or absolute separateness. Like oriental tales, fragments are anti-historical: they disrupt narratives of experience, whether of self or of nation. Mackenzie's first and most celebrated fiction *The Man of Feeling* (1770) is structurally ruinous: a series of fragmentary leaves rescued from the wadding of a fictional curate's gun evoke a staccato, disconnected succession of moments in the life of a man of sensibility. They are a series of sympathetic climaxes which record the protagonist Harley's emotional responses without the connective tissue, the cementing texture of continuous experience which might render these moments meaningful as part of a single life story. In the final episode, Harley's heart simply bursts on emotional overload.

Structurally fragmented fictions like *The Man of Feeling* imply a kind of pessimism about the 'social cement' of sympathy, a pessimism that Mackenzie carries further into the realms of individual identity and integrity in *Julia de Roubigné*, which locates the beginning of internal disintegration in the breakdown of the dialogic forms of epistolary fiction. The editor's 'introduction' to *Julia* makes a point of refusing to link the incomplete 'bundle of papers' (the fragments of the now irrecoverable complete story of the fatal union of Julia and Montauban) by connecting narrative, because 'they are made up of sentiment, which narrative would destroy'.[40] The implication is that the private intensities of feeling are not accessible to connected exposition, and are best apprehended 'in [their] smallest character'. 'The state of the mind', reflects the narrator, may be more readily apprehended 'from very trifling, than from very important circumstances' (p. 5). An epistolary novel where the confidants never reply, *Julia* explores highly developed emotional relationships whose primary characteristic is failure of sympathetic communication. The fragmentary remains of their story embodies the breakdown of sociability which prefigures a disastrous outcome for the union of the virtuous but self-isolating protagonists Julia and Montauban:

I am somehow afraid of writing to you, which is only another sort of thinking. Do not therefore expect to hear from me again until after Tuesday at soonest [the day of Julia's union with Montauban] . . . Set down Tuesday next for your Julia— but leave its property blank.—Fate will fill it up one day! (p. 73)

Fragmenting the form occludes the relations between parts, and embodies a kind of negative resistance to the uniting features of communicable narrative: 'It is not', as the narrator says, 'so much on story, as sentiment, that their interest with the Reader must depend' (p. 85). Once married, Julia and Montauban become increasingly remote from one another; their union is blighted by mutual suspicion and failures of communication, 'the delicate cords, which preserve the unity of the marriage-engagement' untwisted by both characters' preference for the solitary consolations of writing over speaking (p. 82). As the denouement approaches, emotional disconnectedness is mirrored in the fragmentation of their syntax:

If I have recollection enough—Oh! my Maria—I will be calm—it was but a dream—will you blush for my weakness? Yet hear me—(p. 154).

---

[40] H. Mackenzie, *Julia de Roubigné*, ed. Susan Manning (East Lothian: Tuckwell, 1999), 4, 5; subsequent page references are given in parentheses in the text.

I thought I heard her maid upon the stairs—it is not yet the time.—Hark! it was not my wife's bell—the clock struck eleven—(p. 156).

The break-up of narrative signifies more than the collapse of social exchange; it is an early image in Scottish fiction of imaginative integrity violated by the failure of sympathy to act as connective tissue between self and society.

It might well be argued that the closest fictional cognate to Hume's *Treatise* would be something like *Tristram Shandy*, or in another vein the introspective psychology of *Clarissa*.[41] Scottish Enlightenment fiction has nothing (barring a few pale imitations in magazine journalism) to compare with the range and suppleness of these empirical enquiries of the self.[42] So what, if anything, makes the preoccupation with union and fragmentation I've been describing a feature of *Scottish* literature, rather than simply a product of its empirical era? At this point (and this is in no sense a complete answer), I would offer two suggestions. First, the alliance of the political, the social, and the personal which characterizes aspects of the pre-1707 Union debate and which, I've suggested, subsequently structures Hume's philosophical exploration of the tensions between union and fragmentation, remains active in the Scottish and the American examples, as it does not in English literature. It is notable that Samuel Johnson's *Dictionary of the English Language* offers no political definition under 'Union': his examples come from the conjugal, spiritual, and ecclesiastical realms. Webster's *American Dictionary* of 1828, on the other hand, makes explicit reference to both the Scottish and the American political unions in its definitions. Political and personal stay mutually present in the texture of the stories these pieces tell: the integrity of selfhood (or its disintegration) is mirrored by that of nation conceived as an association of different parts. Disintegration of nation, or disunion, threatens integrity of personal identity. The alternative to full social integration and transparent communication is complete disaster.

A second possibility is that self-consciousness about language use gives a particular urgency to Scottish and American attention to the syntactic and grammatical dimensions of union and fragmentation. There is abundant evidence that Hume and his compatriots Thomas Reid, Boswell, Beattie, Macpherson, and others regarded these issues of personal identity and the experience of consciousness as intimately connected to—and indeed only expressible in terms of—the structures of language, *because of* their experience of being linguistically marked in an increasingly Anglophone post-Union Britain. These 'North Britons' were identifiable, and identified, by their distinctive non-English use of the language: in inflection, in Scotticisms or

---

[41] In this context, Hume's appreciation of Jean-Jacques Rousseau's *La Nouvelle Héloise* is interesting; see *Letters*, ii. 28.

[42] See, e.g., the Shandean manner of 'Peter Pennyless' in 'The Influence of Riches', *The Weekly Magazine, or Edinburgh Amusement*, Thursday, 15 March 1770.

Scots-specific words, and in embedded syntactical differences. They went to great lengths to remove the evidence of their pre-Union national origins from the surface of their writing, but there was always a danger that traces of personal and national difference lurked, resistant, like a virus in the deep structures of their language use, a form of self-definition that refused to be tamed to conscious projects of national or individual self-construction. Rüdiger Schreyer cites an early fragment of Adam Smith's writing which suggests that

language may be considered as a theory of nature, a popular system, which joins in 'the fancy' the multitude of unconnected phenomena of this world, which are, strictly speaking, only objects of perception. The linguistic system-builders thus resemble philosophical system-builders, who endeavour 'to find out something which may fill up the gap, which, like a bridge, may so far at least unite those seemingly disjointed objects, as to render the passage betwixt them smooth, and natural, and easy'.[43]

Naturalness and ease, the hallmarks of style (which Gilles Deleuze has called 'the foreign language within language') eludes these Anglo-Scots.[44]

Another way of describing this would be to say that in the main (the most notable exceptions being found in the prose of the philosophers themselves) the published stories of self and nation told by Scottish writing of the Enlightenment are so preoccupied with integration and unity—with holding themselves together, as it were—that they tend to impose a coherence which does not articulate negative and disintegrative states. These do, however, mark their texts in gaps, expressive lacunae, and fragmentary modes which qualify if they do not belie the more connected story. Even at its most 'integrated', Scottish Enlightenment writing preserves the register of resistance and discontinuity in vocabulary and syntactic forms which shape the distinctive character of Scottish Romanticism. And this, I suggest, is some kind of measure of the literary legacy of David Hume.

REFERENCES

Primary Sources

Anon., 'The Comical History of the Marriage-Union betwixt *Fergusia* and *Heptarchus*' (printed in *Scotland* upon that occasion; and reprinted in *England*, 1706).
Beattie, James, *An Essay on the Nature and Immutability of Truth in Opposition to Sophistry and Scepticism*, 2nd edn. (Edinburgh: A. Kinkaid, J. Bell,

---

[43] Citing *Early Writings of Adam Smith*, ed. J. R. Lindgren (New York: Kelly, 1967), 40, in his essay ' "Pray what Language did your wild Couple speak, when first they met?"—Language and the Science of Man in the Scottish Enlightenment', in Jones (ed.), *The 'Science of Man' in the Scottish Enlightenment*, 171.

[44] Gilles Deleuze, *Essays Critical and Clinical*, trans. Daniel W. Smith and Michael A. Greco (London and New York: Verso, 1998), 113.

and E. & C. Dilly, 1771; Facsimile reprint in *The works of James Beattie*, 10 vols., vol. iii, with a new introduction by R. J. Robinson (London: Routledge/ Thoemmes, 1996).

—— 'The theory of language' in *Dissertations Moral and Critical* (London: W. Strahan and T. Cadell, 1783, and Edinburgh: W. Creech, 1783; facsimile reprint in *The Works of James Beattie*, 10 vols., vol. v, with a new introduction by R. J. Robinson (London: Routledge/Thoemmes, 1996).

Bishop, Elizabeth, *The Complete Poems of Elizabeth Bishop* (New York: Farrar, Strauss and Giroux, 1969, 1978).

Boswell, James, *Boswell's London Journal, 1762–63*, ed. F. A. Pottle (London: Heinemann Ltd., 1952).

Duff, William, *The History of Rhedi, The Hermit of Mount Ararat: An Oriental Tale* (London: T. Cadell, 1773).

Hume, David, *A Treatise of Human Nature*, (1739–41), ed. L. A. Selby-Bigge, 2nd edn., rev. P. H. Nidditch (Oxford: Clarendon Press, 1978).

—— *An Enquiry Concerning Human Understanding* (1748), ed. L. A. Selby-Bigge, 3rd edn., rev. P. H. Nidditch (Oxford: Clarendon Press, 1975).

—— *An Enquiry Concerning Human Understanding* (1748), ed. T. L. Beauchamp (Oxford: Oxford University Press, 1999).

—— *Essays Moral, Political, and Literary*, ed. E. F. Miller, rev. edn. (Indianapolis: Liberty Classics, 1987).

—— *The Letters of David Hume*, ed. J. Y. T. Greig, 2 vols. (Oxford: Clarendon Press, 1932).

—— *New Letters of David Hume*, ed. R. Klibansky and E. C. Mossner (Oxford: Clarendon Press, 1954).

Jefferson, Thomas, *Writings*, ed. M. D. Peterson, Library of America (Cambridge: Cambridge University Press, 1984).

Mackenzie, Henry, *Julia de Roubigné*, ed. S. Manning (East Lothian: Tuckwell, 1999).

Reid, Thomas, *Essays on the Intellectual Powers of Man* (1785), ed. A. D. Woozley (London: Macmillan, 1941).

—— *An Inquiry into the Human Mind on the Principles of Common Sense* (1764), ed. Derek R. Brookes (Edinburgh: Edinburgh University Press, 1997).

Robertson, William, *Works of William Robertson*, 12 vols. (London: printed for William Baynes and Son, 1824).

Turnbull, George, *Principles of Moral Philosophy* (London, 1740).

Secondary Sources

Christensen, Jerome, *Practicing Enlightenment: Hume and the Formation of a Literary Career* (Madison: University of Wisconsin Press, 1987).

Craig, Cairns, 'T. S. Eliot, I. A. Richards and empiricism's art of memory', *Revue de metaphysique et de monde*, 1 (1998): 113–17.

Davis, Leith, *Acts of Union* (Stanford, Calif.: Stanford University Press, 1998).

Deleuze, Gilles, *Essays Critical and Clinical*, trans. D. W. Smith and M. A. Greco (London and New York: Verso, 1998).

Jones, Peter, (ed.), *The 'Science of Man' in the Scottish Enlightenment: Hume, Reid and their Contemporaries* (Edinburgh: Edinburgh University Press, 1989).

Livingston, Donald W., *Hume's Philosophy of Common Life* (Chicago and London: University of Chicago Press, 1984).

—— *Philosophical Melancholy and Delirium: Hume's Pathology of Philosophy* (Chicago and London: University of Chicago Press, 1998).

—— and King, James T. (eds.), *Hume: A Re-Evaluation* (New York: Fordham University Press, 1976).

Manning, Susan, *The Puritan-Provincial Vision: Scottish and American Literature in the Nineteenth Century* (Cambridge: Cambridge University Press, 1990).

—— *Fragments of Union: Making Connections in Scottish and American Writing* (Basingstoke: Palgrave, 2002).

Miller, Thomas, *The Formation of College English: Rhetoric and* Belles Lettres *in the British Cultural Provinces* (Pittsburgh: University of Pittsburgh Press, 1997).

Mossner, Ernest C., *The Life of David Hume*, 2nd edn. (Oxford: Clarendon Press, 1980).

Norton, David Fate, *David Hume: Common-Sense Moralist, Sceptical Metaphysician* (Princeton: Princeton University Press, 1982).

Sher, Richard B., *Church and University in the Scottish Enlightenment: The Moderate Literati of Edinburgh* (Edinburgh: Edinburgh University Press, 1985).

Simpson, David (ed.), *Origins of Modern Critical Thought: German Aesthetic and Literary Criticism from Lessing to Hegel* (Cambridge: Cambridge University Press, 1988).

Hume—and Others—on Marriage

SARAH M. S. PEARSALL

Our Youth, however well inclined, are too apt to be disgusted by the Formality of Precepts; and to slight the most important Truths, when inculcated by the dry Maxims of Philosophy, or enforced in a magisterial Manner: But the Case is quite otherwise, when the World is thus set before them; when the Consequences of Virtue and Vice are exhibited in Characters and Events drawn from Nature and real Life, and the Human Heart is laid open, and all the Springs that gave it Motion exposed to View.[1]

Man is a sociable, no less than a reasonable being . . . It seems, then, that nature has pointed out a mixed kind of life as most suitable to human race . . . Indulge your passion for science, says she, but let your science be human, and such as may have a direct reference to action and society . . . Be a philosopher; but, amidst all your philosophy, be still a man.[2]

What happens when the 'dry Maxims of Philosophy' are exhibited in 'Characters and Events drawn from Nature and real Life'? When philosophical theories are set next to the individual stories of Hume's contemporaries, both the philosophical theories and the individual stories are illuminated. The benefits are twofold. First, in knowing more about the philosophical shifts, and the kinds of vocabulary in circulation, it is possible to understand more about the way contemporaries, caught up in the exigencies of

I would like to thank David Armitage, Joyce E. Chaplin, Elaine Forman Crane, Jan Lewis, and Laurel Thatcher Ulrich, as well as the editors of this volume and an anonymous reader for Oxford University Press, for insightful comments on previous drafts, although I am of course responsible for any errors. Thanks, too, to Mark Spencer, who graciously shared his unpublished work on the circulation of Hume's texts. For helpful comments at early stages, I would also like to thank the audiences and commentators at the International Seminar on the History of the Atlantic World, Harvard University, in August 2000 and the Hume Studies in Britain Conference, Cambridge University, in September 2000.

[1] *The Complete Letter-Writer*, 4th edn. (London: Stanley Crowder and Co. and Henry Woodgate, 1757), no page number.

[2] David Hume, *Enquiries Concerning Human Understanding and Concerning the Principles of Morals* (1777), ed. L. A. Selby-Bigge, 3rd edn., rev. P. H. Nidditch (Oxford: Clarendon Press, 1975), 8–9.

daily life, deployed, subverted, and occasionally ignored these theories and
these vocabularies. In understanding the ways in which these theories and
vocabularies played out in the lived experience of individual couples, the
complexities and the limitations both in the philosophies and in the men who
created them are clarified. This essay considers the issue of marriage and
authority, and in particular the ways in which marital negotiations
were expected to proceed. It traces the shift that occurred from Locke
to Hutcheson to Hume, in which marriage became less of a contractual
commitment in which one party ruled, and became instead a partnership of
'mutual friendship'. It also explores the marital correspondence of one
couple, James and Margaret Parker, who found themselves at odds over
where their family should settle in the aftermath of the American Revolution.
This paper, in placing the theories against the lived experience, considers how
both well-known philosophers and more obscure writers created visions of
marriages, and of household relations, which were in some ways in tension
with the legal and financial disparities that continued to exist between
members of eighteenth-century households.

Scholars of the British–Atlantic world in the eighteenth century who have
focused on issues of gender and authority, particularly within the family,
are increasingly devoting attention to the Scottish Enlightenment and to its
effects on marriage and gender relations. Historians such as Rosemarie
Zagarri, Elaine Forman Crane, Jan Lewis, and Ruth H. Bloch have considered shifting views of gender relations in Scottish Enlightenment thought.[3]
Zagarri has traced the ways in which a Scottish emphasis on the virtues of
sensibility and the family translated into certain elements of what has been
termed 'Republican motherhood'. She has also argued that a Scottish view
of rights, in which duty and obligation were paramount, was central to early
republican American notions of women's rights. Bloch, too, has emphasized
that Scottish Enlightenment ideas, along with religious values and sentimental fiction, helped to transform views of romantic and sexual love in

---

[3] Rosemarie Zagarri, 'Morals, manners, and the republican mother', *American Quarterly*, 44
(1992): 192–215; *eadem*, 'The rights of man and woman in post-Revolutionary America', *William
and Mary Quarterly*, 55 (1998): 203–30; Elaine Forman Crane, 'Political dialogue and the spring
of Abigail's discontent', *William and Mary Quarterly*, 56 (1999): 745–74; *eadem*, *Ebb Tide in New
England: Women, Seaports, and Social Change, 1630–1800* (Boston: Northeastern University
Press, 1998); Jan Lewis, 'The republican wife: virtue and seduction in the early Republic', *William
and Mary Quarterly*, 44 (1987): 689–721; *eadem*, ' "Of every age sex & condition": the representation of women in the Constitution', *Journal of the Early Republic*, 15 (1995): 359–87; and Ruth
H. Bloch, 'Changing conceptions of sexuality and romance in eighteenth-century America', *William
and Mary Quarterly*, 60 (2003): 13–42. This article was originally written for the International
Seminar on the History of the Atlantic World in August 2000 and the Hume Studies in Britain
Conference in September 2000. Since that time, Ruth Bloch's article has appeared, and it seems
that we have independently reached certain shared conclusions about the ambivalent nature of a
number of Scottish Enlightenment writings on women and marriage. I have taken account of her
insightful article (which I first saw as a conference article in 2001) in this revised version.

eighteenth-century America. Still, the effect of Scottish Enlightenment ideas and terminology on marriage in particular remains understudied. While Susan Moller Okin has argued, in many ways persuasively, that the rise of the ideal of the sentimental family 'had catastrophic implications for the future of women's rights and freedoms', she does not consider any Scottish theorists.[4] None the less, her work, like Bloch's, has important implications for the ways in which languages of marriage as friendship had clear limitations for women.

On the other hand, those scholars who focus on the place of gender in Scottish Enlightenment theories, and more especially in the writings of David Hume, have often elided the historical contexts of that thought or its ramifications outside the area of philosophy.[5] Scholarship on the relationship of David Hume to issues of gender has tended to focus more on the question of whether David Hume was sexist, and on the ways in which feminists today might make use of his work.[6] I am more interested in determining why Hume and others wrote as they did, what kinds of shifts their visions represented, and what effects their writings had on others. This essay, while offering thoughts on the first two questions, focuses primarily on the last of these questions. After all, Hume stressed the virtues of sociability and sympathy, and the need to make 'direct reference to action and society'. If Hume was a philosopher *par excellence*, he was also still a man, and shifting notions of masculinity affected him. In turn, his notions of ideal masculine behaviour influenced others. He was one of the writers who most explicitly addressed ideal masculine behaviour and the necessity of 'gallantry' in a polite man's approach to the world. This essay, then, focuses on shifting notions of elite manliness, notions in which Hume was himself enmeshed.

In order to delve into the ways in which the theories and the realities played off against each other, it is helpful to understand what was happening in various husband–wife correspondences. I focus here on the transatlantic correspondence between James Parker, in Britain, and Margaret Parker, in Virginia. The Parkers represent one couple among many, but they provide a particularly useful case study of the nuances of these vocabularies. These marital letters, with their appeals to a 'dearest Friend' and assertions that happiness could only come in reunion, sound like they might have come from an eighteenth-century sentimental novel. Both husbands and wives deplored the circumstances that separated them, and both appealed to their

[4] Susan Moller Okin, 'Women and the making of the sentimental family', *Philosophy and Public Affairs*, 11 (1982): 65–88.

[5] See e.g. Annette C. Baier, 'Hume on women's complexion', in Peter Jones (ed.), *The 'Science of Man' in the Scottish Enlightenment; Hume, Reid, and their Contemporaries* (Edinburgh: Edinburgh University Press, 1989), 33–53, and Vicki J. Sapp, 'The philosopher's seduction: Hume and the fair sex', *Philosophy and Literature*, 19 (1995): 1–15.

[6] See Anne Jaap Jacobson (ed.), *Feminist Interpretations of David Hume* (University Park, Pa.: Pennsylvania State University Press, 2000).

unending sympathy for one another. Both sides also invoked their characters as good, loving spouses. Yet it is clear that these spouses sometimes had different visions of the right path for themselves and their family.

So, when husbands and wives ended up in disagreement within a 'happy marriage', how did they cope with difference? How was the new language of sensibility and sympathy, so prevalent in the late eighteenth-century transatlantic world, deployed in the rhythms of marriage? These cases reveal both the complicated manœuvres couples performed as well as the cultural contexts in which they did so. Even Okin, who characterizes the rise of the sentimental family ideal as a negative one for women, concedes that 'some women may have benefited in their personal lives from the increased emphasis on affection in marriage'.[7] Indeed, I argue that some women found in what I term 'the coercive language of affection' a kind of limited power, in part due to a shifting understanding of what constituted an ideal husband and man.[8] They were able to call upon their husbands by invoking their own affection and their husbands' sympathy, thus deploying loving language to particular ends. Such languages, however, should not obscure the inequalities that lay at the heart of these relationships, inequalities that mirror those in the philosophical theories highlighted by Bloch. At the same time, husbands too deployed this language, and in so doing aligned themselves to the 'gallantry' counselled by writers such as David Hume. These couples relied on crafted visions of longing and romance, and these fictions both alleviated their situation and also obscured the inequalities that lay at its heart.

Scholars have devoted much useful attention on the popular literature, including novels, which shaped this culture. Certainly, as I and others have argued elsewhere, the language of sensibility informed all kinds of familial

---

[7] Okin, 'Women and the making of the sentimental family', 74.

[8] Scholarship dealing with divorce and marital strife in early America includes: Merril D. Smith, *Breaking the Bonds: Marital Discord in Pennsylvania, 1730–1830* (New York: New York University Press, 1991); Norma Basch, *Framing American Divorce: From the Revolutionary Generation to the Victorians* (Berkeley: University of California Press, 1999); and Cornelia Hughes Dayton, *Women before the Bar: Gender, Law, & Society in Connecticut, 1639–1789* (Chapel Hill, NC: University of North Carolina Press, 1995). Lisa Wilson raises the possibility of conflict within loving marriages, but this discussion is very brief and focuses on negative assessments of women's anger. See Lisa Wilson, *Ye Heart of a Man: The Domestic Life of Men in Colonial New England* (New Haven: Yale University Press, 1999), 88–97. See also Nancy F. Cott, *Public Vows: A History of Marriage and the Nation* (Cambridge, Mass.: Harvard University Press, 2000). The scholarship on British marriage and divorce includes Lawrence Stone, *The Family, Sex and Marriage in England, 1500–1800* (New York: Harper & Row, 1977) as well as idem, *Road to Divorce: England, 1530–1987* (Oxford: Oxford University Press, 1990) and idem, *Broken Lives: Separation and Divorce in England, 1660–1857* (Oxford: Oxford University Press, 1993). Also see Alan Macfarlane, *Marriage and Love in England: Modes of Reproduction, 1300–1840* (Oxford: Oxford University Press, 1986); John R. Gillis, *For Better, For Worse: British Marriages, 1600 to the Present* (Oxford: Oxford University Press, 1985), and R. B. Outhwaite (ed.), *Marriage and Society: Studies in the Social History of Marriage* (New York: St. Martin's Press, 1982). There is also recent treatment in Joanne Bailey, *Unquiet Lives: Marriage and Marriage Breakdown in England, 1660–1800* (Cambridge: Cambridge University Press, 2003).

negotiations, and those between spouses were no exception.[9] Schoolbooks, novels, newspapers, and magazines combined to present newer kinds of vocabularies for these negotiations. But behind these popular writings were the works of philosophers. It is therefore helpful to attend to the marital models offered by social theorists such as John Locke, Francis Hutcheson, and David Hume, and to the shift that occurred from Locke to Hutcheson and Hume. These philosophers all offered understandings of how marriage should function in theory, and how disagreements should be reconciled. These thinkers thus crafted fictions of ideal marriages, and how decision making would proceed in them. After examining the words of the philosophers, the essay will turn to the words of the Parkers.

John Locke famously presented a contractual model of marriage that was in some ways egalitarian. Locke contended: '*Conjugal Society* is made by a voluntary Compact between Man and Woman; and tho' it consist chiefly in such a Communion and Right in one anothers Bodies, as is necessary to its chief End, Procreation; yet it draws with it mutual Support, and Assistance, and a Communion of Interest too, as necessary not only to unite their Care, and Affection, but also necessary to their common Off-spring.'[10] Locke emphasized that the 'Compact' was entered into freely by both the man and the woman; he also sketched a limited egalitarian vision in which both partners found 'mutual Support'. Locke also took care to convey that as this compact was voluntary, it could be ended by either party, maintaining that the husband had no more power over his wife's life than she had over his. Locke continued: 'The *Power of the Husband* being so far from that of an absolute Monarch, that the *Wife* has, in many cases, a Liberty to *separate* from him; where natural Right, or their Contract allows it' (p. 320).

Much as Locke posited that marriage was a voluntary 'communion of Interest', he also acknowledged that marriage did not obliterate difference. He allowed that 'the Husband and Wife, though they have but one common Concern, yet having different understandings, will unavoidably sometimes have different wills too'. Locke recognized the problem that might arise even in a contractual marriage: that the husband and wife would sometimes seek distinct ends. While mentioning this potential pitfall, Locke moved swiftly on to the standard understanding of how these differences should be resolved: 'it therefore being necessary, that the last Determination, *i.e.* the

---

[9] See Sarah Knott, 'A cultural history of sensibility in the era of the American Revolution' (D.Phil. thesis, Oxford, 1999), ch. 4, and Sarah M. S. Pearsall, ' "The late flagrant instance of depravity in my family": the story of an Anglo–Jamaican cuckold', *William and Mary Quarterly*, 60 (2003): 549–82. The classic coverage of sensibility is G. J. Barker-Benfield, *The Culture of Sensibility: Sex and Society in Eighteenth-Century England* (Chicago: University of Chicago Press, 1992).

[10] John Locke, *Two Treatises of Government*, ed. Peter Laslett (Cambridge: Cambridge University Press, 1988), II, ch. 7, 78, p. 319.

Rule, should be placed somewhere, it naturally falls to the Man's share, as the abler and the stronger' (p. 321).[11] Locke, in agreement with the legal situation of *femme covert*, gave the power to make decisions in the face of conflict to the man. According to Locke, man's authority lay both in his superior physical strength and in his greater ability. It was a fairly brutal conclusion, for 'Rule' within the family depended in part on physical prowess. Moreover, the 'Determination' of decisions was not a process of negotiation between equals; rather, it was equated simply with government. As Okin rightly points out, there was little about love and affection in Locke's model.[12]

Scottish Enlightenment philosophers developed a somewhat contrasting model of marital relations. While the acknowledgement of male superiority continued to lie at the heart of these formulations, there was a much greater emphasis on equality and affection between men and women. Bloch, too, has noted that marriage as friendship informed such writings, even as assumptions of gender difference underlay them.[13] Francis Hutcheson stressed the love that should lie at the heart of an egalitarian marriage. Marriage and the family were in fact central to Hutcheson's moral theory, for it was in the circle of the family that sympathy, which led ultimately to benevolence, virtue, and love of God, originated:

The sensible Pleasure alone must . . . be esteemed at a very low rate: But the Desires of this kind, as they were by Nature intended to found the most constant uninterrupted Friendship, and to introduce the most venerable and lovely Relations, by Marriages and Families, arise in our Hearts, attended with some of the sweetest Affections, with a disinterested Love and Tenderness, with a most gentle and obliging Deportment, with something great and heroick in our Temper.[14]

For Hutcheson, 'Marriages and Families' represented among 'the most venerable and lovely Relations' available to human beings. Affection was vital for the development of morality. Understanding this background helps to follow better Hutcheson's formulation of marriage.

Hutcheson stressed the importance of marital friendship: 'Nature has designed the conjugal state to be a constant reciprocal friendship of two.'[15]

---

[11] Daniela Gobetti argues: 'In this passage, Locke merely hints at the possibility of conflict, but this possibility is a reason strong enough to assign power to one party, not surprisingly, the man. A new description of woman's fate in life supersedes the egalitarian assumptions which are necessary for hypothesizing a contractual procedure between two adults'. See Daniela Gobetti, *Private and Public: Individuals, Households, and Body Politic in Locke and Hutcheson* (London: Routledge, 1992), 81.   [12] Okin, 'Women and the making of the sentimental family', 69.
[13] Bloch, 'Changing conceptions', 37–38, 41.
[14] Francis Hutcheson, *An Essay on the Nature and Conduct of the Passions and Affections with Illustrations on the Moral Sense* (1742), ed. Paul McReynolds, 3rd edn. (Gainesville, Fla.: Scholars' Facsimiles & Reprints, 1969), 309–10.
[15] Francis Hutcheson, *A System of Moral Philosophy (1755)*, ed. Bernhard Fabian, facsimile edn. (Hildesheim: Georg Olms Verlag, 1990), II, III, I, v, p. 15.

Throughout his discussion of marriage, Hutcheson constantly deployed words and phrases such as 'united', 'harmony', 'friendly partnership', and 'mutual affection'.[16] Hutcheson thus outlined a different formulation of marriage from that of Locke. Where Locke acknowledged conflict and placed the 'Rule' with the husband, Hutcheson instead explicitly focused on the fact that neither party ruled: 'The tender sentiments and affections which engage the parties into this relation of marriage, plainly declare it to be a state of equal partnership or friendship, and not such wherein the one party stipulates to himself a right of governing in all domestic affairs, and the other promises subjection' (p. 163). In what seems a much more egalitarian vision than Locke's, Hutcheson declared that 'government' had no place in marriage. Indeed, Hutcheson explicitly condemned polygamy because it relied on fear and coercion, rather than on affection: 'And hence we see that where this practice prevails, the women are every way treated as slaves: no friendly regards had to their satisfactions; chains and prisons, and guards must confine them, and not the bonds of love and friendship' (p. 161). Marriage should not be a relationship between masters and slaves, or even between ruler and ruled, but between people bound by 'love and friendship'.

However, Hutcheson, like Locke, claimed that there might be a looming superiority in men, although he did not feel that this situation should result in a right to authority: 'Grant that there were generally superior strength both of body and mind in the males, this does not give any perfect right of government in any society.' Hutcheson softened Locke's formulation, contending that the man's 'superior strength' would only extract greater respect from the weaker spouse: 'It could at best only oblige the other party to pay a greater respect or honour to the superior abilities.' Moreover, Hutcheson did not assume men's supremacy in all areas: 'And this superiority of the males in the endowments of mind does not at all hold universally. If the males more generally excel in fortitude, or strength of genius, there are other as amiable dispositions in which they are generally surpassed by the females' (p. 163). Hutcheson invoked a distinction that would continue to receive attention in later eighteenth- and nineteenth-century thought: that women have the power of superior social capacities, while men have greater intellectual and bodily fortitude.

Hutcheson's thoughts on these separate talents informed his discussion of how conflict in marriage should be resolved:

Where husband and wife disagree in points of management; in smaller matters, this deference may be due to the one who has the greatest abilities, and manages the most important affairs, that the other should courteously yield, tho' against his

---

[16] See e.g. ibid. II, III, I, v, pp. 151–3, 156, 159, 161–3. Subsequent page references are given in parentheses in the text.

or her private opinion. If ordinarily these superior abilities are in the husband, and his greater strength, and other circumstances of body, fit him to be employed in the more momentous affairs, it may more generally be the duty of the wife to submit. (Ibid.)

Clearly, there were limits to Hutcheson's egalitarianism. The submission of the wife ultimately lay at the core of his formulation, too. Still, his impartial treatment of the question (and his careful inclusion of 'his or her') emphasized the even-handedness of his general principles. While men's superiority was implied, it was not held to be 'natural' or utterly universal.

Also, Hutcheson felt that this resolution should apply only in 'smaller matters'. He presented a more radical vision in his discussion of larger ones: 'But in matters of great importance to the happiness of a family, if they cannot agree, nature suggests no other method of deciding such controversies, but a submission to common friends as arbitrator.' Hutcheson did not specify the gender of these friends, and he did not place the power of decision in men's hands. None the less, he then undermined this radical solution: 'Domestic matters indeed seem to be divided into two provinces, one fitted for the management of each sex, in which the other should seldom interfere, except by advising.' As in his treatment of the differing virtues of men and women, here is an early formulation of how 'separate spheres' might work. Such a model did give some control to women, who then enjoyed 'management' of their area. But it also conveys the limits of egalitarianism, particularly when Hutcheson has just acknowledged that the husband generally 'manages the most important affairs' (ibid.).

Like Francis Hutcheson, David Hume emphasized equality and affection in marriage. Hume, in his essay 'Of love and marriage', expressly dealt with questions of authority within marriage.[17] He elaborated on the 'Scythian women', who secretly planned and then executed a rebellion against their husbands. Hume moved from this tale to a consideration of modern women: 'I know not if our *Scottish* ladies derive any thing of this humour from their *Scythian* ancestors; but, I must confess that I have often been surprised to see a woman very well pleased to take a fool for her mate, that she might govern him with the less controul.' He contended that women's twisted desire for authority was men's fault, an oblique criticism of Locke's formulation of men's 'Rule' in marriage: 'I am afraid it is the fault of our sex, if the women be so fond of rule, and that if we did not abuse our authority, they would never think it worth while to dispute it. Tyrants, we know, produce rebels; and all history informs us, that rebels, when they

---

[17] David Hume, *Essays Moral, Political, and Literary*, ed. Eugene F. Miller, rev. edn. (Indianapolis: Liberty Classics, 1987). According to Eugene Miller, the editor, 'This essay appeared in the first edition *of Essays, Moral and Political, 1741*, and in subsequent editions up to and including *Essays and Treatises on Several Subjects, 1760*, after which it was withdrawn' (p. 557). Subsequent page references are given in parentheses in the text.

prevail, are apt to become tyrants in their turn.' So, Hume concluded, 'For this reason, I could wish there were no pretensions to authority on either side; but that every thing was carried on with perfect equality, as between two equal members of the same body.' Hume hoped that both men and women would 'embrace those amicable sentiments' of equality in marriage (pp. 559–60).

In contrast to Locke, Hume envisioned marriage as a state of 'perfect equality'. Unlike Locke, who explicitly acknowledged the potential for conflict within marriage, Hume felt marriage should not involve a struggle over will. After relating the tale of the rebellious Scythian women, Hume proceeded to tell a different story: a modification of Plato's theory that men and women were divided from an original androgyny, and so sought, in marriage, their perfect union. While Hume conceded that Plato's claims needed to be altered so as to allow for the problems of 'care', he none the less reiterated his belief in the unification of man and woman and the possibility of 'perfect equality', in which man and woman combined to 'form one perfect and happy creature'. Hume argued that when man and woman found their ideal partner, they then joined 'with the greatest fondness and sympathy' (pp. 560–2).

Emphasizing this union, in 'Of polygamy and divorces', Hume refuted Locke's views on divorce. Hume felt that men and women were not bound merely in a contract but also 'by all the ties of nature and humanity' (p. 181). So convinced was Hume of the power of these bonds that he condemned divorce.[18] Hume adduced three reasons for refusing divorce: it would be a problem for the children of the union; men and women would forget their 'frivolous quarrels' if they knew they had to remain married; and finally, if the union was not protected, quarrels would be pursued. This last point is the most relevant because Hume claimed: 'nothing is more dangerous than to unite two persons so closely in all their interests and concerns, as man and wife, without rendering the union entire and total. The least possibility of a separate interest must be the source of endless quarrels and suspicions.' Hume felt that even *allowing* for the possibility of 'separate interest' would have a very bad effect on both wife and husband: 'The wife, not secure of her establishment, will still be driving some separate end or project; and the husband's selfishness, being accompanied with more power, may be still more dangerous' (p. 189). Unlike Locke, Hume posited that recognizing that wives and husbands might have 'a separate interest'

---

[18] Thomas Paine, in the guise of 'an American savage', would later use this Platonic theory to argue the exact opposite; for each person should be able to dissolve a union that was not the true one: 'God made us all in pairs: each has his mate somewhere or other; and tis our duty to find each other out since no creature was ever intended to be miserable', *The Pennsylvania Magazine*, (April 1775): 152, as quoted in Jay Fliegelman, *Prodigals and Pilgrims: The American Revolution against Patriarchal Authority, 1750–1800* (Cambridge: Cambridge University Press, 1982), 124.

was dangerous to the family and to society. What Hume had in mind by the word 'interest' is ambiguous. He may have been referring to finances, and to the possibility that if husband and wife were not united financially, it would result in acrimony. But his use of 'interests and concerns' in the passage immediately before this one suggests that 'interests' may refer more broadly to their needs and desires. In certain respects, it was a more egalitarian vision than was Locke's, as it did not rely on the 'Rule' of the man. On the other hand, it raises a question that Hume largely ignored: how can a loving marriage survive the possibility of 'separate interest?'

In another essay, Hume, like Hutcheson, condemned polygamy, not because it made women slaves but because it made men tyrants. Hume posited that the male sovereignty found in polygamy 'is a real usurpation, and destroys that nearness of rank, not to say equality, which nature has established between the sexes. We are, by nature, their lovers, their friends, their patrons: Would we willingly exchange such endearing appellations, for the barbarous title of master and tyrant?' (p. 184). Men were *naturally* not 'masters' (or, as Locke might have phrased it, 'Rulers'), but lovers, friends, and patrons. The final title implied an imbalance of power between man and woman, but it also conveyed the benevolence of men's treatment of wives in monogamy.

Like Locke and Hutcheson, Hume did emphasize that men enjoyed greater intellectual and physical strength than women. Nevertheless, Hume entirely reversed Locke's conclusions, claiming that this supremacy should result not in men's government, but in their greater solicitude: 'As nature has given *man* the superiority above *woman*, by endowing him with greater strength both of mind and body; it is his part to alleviate that superiority, as much as possible, by the generosity of his behaviour, and by a studied deference and complaisance for all her inclinations and opinions.' While Locke utilized that formulation to place the 'Rule' with the husband, Hume used it to argue that men thus owed their wives a kind of learned deference, even if such deference did not come 'naturally'. Ultimately, though, such largesse served to increase the man's 'authority'. For, Hume continued, invoking the contrast between civilized and barbarous lands: 'Barbarous nations display superiority, by reducing their females to the most abject slavery; by confining them, by beating them, by selling them, by killing them. But the male sex, among a polite people, discover their authority in a more generous, though not a less evident manner; by civility, by respect, by complaisance, and, in a word, by gallantry' ('Of the rise and progress of the arts and sciences', p. 133).

Here, then, are two roughly distinct visions of marriage. In the Lockean one, conflict was acknowledged, and marriage was likened to a government in which the husband was 'naturally' the ruler. In the Humean/Hutchesonian paradigm, there was little place for government, but equally there was little allowance for separate wills. In this latter vision, marriage should be harmony, friendship, and perfect equality. These philosophers spun their visions of ideal marriages and imagined happy marriages that did not actually exist. Yet the question remains: when a wife pursued one 'end' and the husband another, how did they deal with the conflict of interest that arose within the marriage? In the transatlantic family letters of this period, there are echoes of both the Lockean and the Humean/Hutchesonian notions; the ability of men to make the final decisions always lies at the heart of these correspondences. None the less, like these theorists, spouses also crafted idealized visions of their own marriages, and often subsumed differences in languages of romance and perfect friendship.

The works of Locke, Hutcheson, and Hume were popular in later eighteenth-century North America and Britain.[19] Locke, of course, has been repeatedly linked with the founding of the American republic. Discussing mainland North America in the revolutionary and early republican period, Rosemarie Zagarri contends: 'the general influence of the Scottish Enlightenment is indisputable.'[20] Moreover, Zagarri has taken pains to demonstrate that Scottish notions of the equality of man and woman in marriage, and the importance of women's roles, were in wide circulation in the early American republic. Mark Spencer has exhaustively researched the circulation of Hume's works in eighteenth-century America and has uncovered not only wide dissemination of his books, but also numerous reprintings of his essays in more popular American and British magazines and newspapers. For example, although Hume's essay 'Of Love and Marriage' was dropped from the 1760 edition of *Essays and Treatises on Several Subjects*, this essay was reprinted in its entirety in a Boston magazine in 1785.[21] These writings were thus in general circulation.

Elaine Forman Crane has helpfully traced some of the influences on one well-known elite woman in early America, Abigail Adams, noting that Adams demonstrated familiarity with writings of Montaigne, Jonathan Swift, Madame de Sévigné, Pufendorf, Montesquieu, and Hume, among many others. In a well-known letter to her husband, a Revolutionary leader and future President of the United States, John Adams, Abigail used a phrase

---

[19] See e.g. Richard B. Sher and Jeffrey R. Smith (eds.), *Scotland and America in the Age of Enlightenment* (Edinburgh: Edinburgh University Press, 1990); Drew R. McCoy, *The Elusive Republic: Political Economy in Jeffersonian America* (Chapel Hill, NC: University of North Carolina Press for the Institute of Early American History and Culture, 1980); and Robert A. Ferguson, *American Enlightenment, 1750–1820* (Cambridge, Mass.: Harvard University Press, 1997).   [20] Zagarri, 'Morals, manners, and the republican mother', 203.

[21] Mark G. Spencer, 'The circulation of David Hume's works in eighteenth-century America', paper presented at the International Seminar on the History of the Atlantic World, 1500–1800, Harvard University, August 2000. Spencer traced the reprintings of the essay on love and marriage in British periodicals, many of which circulated in the colonies, noting that it was reprinted in *The Universal Magazine* in 1764, *The Sentimental Magazine* in 1777, and *The Lady's Magazine* in 1779 (p. 16). It also appeared in American periodicals, such as *The Boston Magazine* 1 (Nov. 1783): 15–18. Many thanks to Mark Spencer for this reference.

that sounds remarkably similar to writings of Hume, as Crane has noted, and as we shall see in what follows.[22] In this letter, Abigail asked that John 'remember the Ladies' when making the new laws for the new nation. In support of her petition, Adams informed her husband: 'That your Sex are Naturally Tyrannical is a Truth so thoroughly established as to admit of no dispute but such of you as wish to be happy willingly give up the harsh title of Master for the more tender and endearing one of friend.' Abigail Adams was not the only early American woman to quote this passage, as Crane has deftly shown. Nancy Shippen Livingston also echoed the notion, writing in her commonplace book in 1783: 'that men are generally tyrannical I will own, but such as know how to be happy, willingly give up the harsh title of master for the more tender & endearing one of friend.'[23] It is clear that shifting notions of ideal masculine behaviour, and the need for men to be friends rather than masters, were in general circulation among the élite of the North American colonies.

Margaret and James Parker, the couple upon whom I will focus much of this discussion, were not as thorough as Adams or Livingston in documenting their reading matter, at least not in their surviving papers.[24] None the less, they did leave some traces. Certainly, their letters convey that both were relatively well educated. Margaret, as an élite daughter of a Virginia family, would have received a standard immersion in the histories and writings of an eighteenth-century curriculum for girls. Her letters demonstrate a literate familiarity with conventions for polite letter writing. James was a Scot who had presumably been educated in Scotland in the mid-eighteenth century. It is therefore reasonable to assume that he might well have been exposed, in some form or other, to the writings of Hutcheson and Hume. His decision to inoculate his family against smallpox in 1769, a decision that horrified his less progressive neighbours in Virginia, clearly stemmed from a transatlantic knowledge of theories and practices of medicine, something that might, again, be expected of an educated eighteenth-century Scot.[25] Finally, later letters of his son seem to suggest that James was reading authors as varied as Voltaire, Rousseau, and Gibbon, as he was accused of irreligion in his reading matter by his evangelical son.[26] At any rate, it seems reasonable that

---

[22] Crane, 'Political dialogue'; the letter is reprinted on p. 770, and Crane discusses this passage on pp. 745–5.   [23] Nancy Shippen Livingston, as quoted at ibid. 758.

[24] The bulk of the Parker Papers are located at the Liverpool Record Office at the Liverpool City and County Libraries, Liverpool, England (now catalogued as 920 PAR I–IV, formerly as PA). Related documents are to be found in the American Loyalist Claims, Public Record Office, London; the Charles Steuart papers, National Library of Scotland, Edinburgh; and the Library of Virginia, Richmond.

[25] See Adele Hast, *Loyalism in Revolutionary Virginia: The Norfolk Area and the Eastern Shore* (Ann Arbor: UMI Research Press, 1982); Keith Mason, 'A loyalist's journey: James Parker's response to the revolutionary crisis', *Virginia Magazine of History and Biography*, 102 (1994): 139–66.

[26] James's son, Patrick, wrote to his father that, 'as for Voltaire Rousseau Gibbon & your Frederick the II King of Prussias opinion on Religion—it matters not to me, This far however I think (perhaps it may be presumption in me) that it by no matter of means, becomes Such

James at the least, and possibly Margaret as well, would have had familiarity with some of these theories, whether directly or from their reprintings or influences on more popular magazines and newspapers. Certainly, if they had not read Hume or Hutcheson, they could easily have encountered their theories in magazines and books of the day. Increasingly, the kind of languages brokered by the Scottish Enlightenment informed these marital negotiations, although the dynamics of marriage changed little.

This newer vocabulary infuses the marital letters of Margaret and James Parker. A native of Virginia, she married her Scottish-born husband, James, in the later 1750s, and they exchanged jesting, affectionate letters during short absences from each other. They resided in Virginia in relative peace and prosperity in the 1760s and 1770s. They had three surviving children: Patrick, Charles, and Susan. During the Revolutionary War, James was to become a Loyalist officer and exile who fled back to Britain at the end of the war. Margaret, meanwhile, stayed in Virginia with family throughout the war, in part relying on her sister and her sister's family. Margaret eventually joined her husband in England by 1784. Her letters begin in 1760 and continue, with numerous breaks, into the 1780s.[27] The language of marriage as friendship heavily informed all their letters. Margaret repeatedly ended her letters by calling James 'my Dearest friend'.[28] She also tended toward signatures such as: 'God grant you health & happiness, to make you some amends for your long sufferings, prays your ever affectionate Margaret'.[29] James also signed his letters with forms including 'your affectionate freind' and 'I ever remain Your Most Affect[ionate]'.[30] Despite its relative copiousness and richness, the

---

Reptiles as These must be in the Sight of God to Set up an opinion in Opposition to the Declard & Established Will of God handed Down To us by the prophets & Apostles but Let me alone on this head—I shall try & Get to Heaven my own Way, & in the Meantime I will attend to the measuring of my own business—with[ou]t troubling my self with the opinions of Messrs. Voltaire Gibbon & Frederick the IInd King of Prussia but when I do read their works just Look upon them as men of the Greatest Genius and talents who have in my Eyes unfortunately applyed them to turning into Ridicule what shall forever by me & people of my blind way of thinking be held Sacred' (Patrick Parker to James Parker, dated 'Norfolk Virginia Sep: 29th. 1789', PA 10.15, Parker Family Papers, Liverpool Library and Record Office (hereafter noted as LRO)). I have used the older microfilm references (PA), although new numberings were provided by the Record Office more recently, as 920 PAR I–III.

[27] This information can be found in the Parker Family Papers, LRO. Further secondary information is available in Mason, 'A Loyalist's journey', and Alan L. Karras, *Sojourners in the Sun: Scottish Migrants in Jamaica and the Chesapeake, 1740–1800* (Ithaca, NY: Cornell University Press, 1992), and Sarah M. S. Pearsall, ' "After all these revolutions": epistolary identities in an Atlantic world, 1765–1815' (Ph.D thesis, Harvard, 2001).

[28] See, e.g, Margaret Parker to James Parker, dated 'Eastwood October 21 1783', PA 8.29, and Margaret Parker to James Parker, undated but labelled 'recd 22nd July 1784 from Mrs Parker', PA 8.36, Parker Family Papers, LRO.

[29] Margaret Parker to James Parker, dated 'Eastwood October 4th 1783', PA 8.28, Parker Family Papers, LRO.

[30] James Parker to Margaret Parker, dated 'London 5th feby 1784', PA 8.30, and James Parker to Margaret Parker, dated 'London 23d August 1783', PA 8.27, Parker Family Papers, LRO.

correspondence between Margaret and James Parker has received only minimal attention from historians.[31]

In fact, Margaret and James engaged in an ongoing epistolary debate in the 1760s about her vow of obedience to him. Since James's letters for this period are missing, it is impossible to know exactly how this debate began, but Margaret pursued it with a vengeance. Margaret claimed that she would deny ever having agreed to 'obey' at their wedding, although she acknowledged that she intended to do so anyway: 'I shall follow your example & say that I promised to love & honour, but not a word of obey. I'll deny that I said it, altho I intend to do it.'[32] In another letter that ended the epistolary dispute over her obedience, she declared: 'As for the quarrel I'm quite done with it & will agree to acknowledge my obedience, or any thing else that you shall propose if that will be a means of bringing you back again tho I think that's saying a great deal too, when I think of that expression of yours that wives are easier got than Husbands.' Margaret apparently did not place much weight on her promise to obey, as she looked upon it merely as an expedient to bring her husband back.

Margaret continued sardonically:

You allways had Eloquence enough to perswade me to anything that you desire me to do, well now you see I am all submission as good Wives ought to be, & I intend to make one of thet number at least I'll do what I can to be one, & if I'm not perfection, & I know my self to be very far from it I have this consolation that I've one to please whose good sense can make large allowances for the frailltys of humane Nature.[33]

The 'good wife' was a character that both Margaret and James could recognize, and Margaret aligned herself to this ideal type. Both knew that submission perfectly suited the 'good wife', but there is a mocking tone in her pronouncement. Even as she avowed her submission, she also allowed

---

[31] The most extended treatment occurs in Carmeline V. Zimmer, 'Margaret Ellegood Parker: a loyalist merchant's wife', in R. A. Rutyna and P. C. Stewart (eds.), *Virginia in the American Revolution* (Norfolk, Va.: Old Dominion University, 1983), 60–79. Alan Karras, in his discussion of Scottish networks in Virginia, has conceded that: 'If James Parker stood at the center of the web, his wife merits her place immediately beside him' (*Sojourners*, 160). But Karras, interested in different subjects, quotes none of her letters and devotes little attention to her. Margaret's statements about the family slaves receive brief attention in Philip D. Morgan, *Slave Counterpoint: Black Culture in the Eighteenth-Century Chesapeake and Lowcountry* (Chapel Hill, NC: University of North Carolina Press for the Omohundro Institute of Early American History and Culture, 1998), 270. Keith Mason quotes from a few of Margaret's letters, including one lamenting her departure from Virginia and notes of James Parker: 'Given the obviously affectionate character of their relationship, Parker would have been unable to dismiss his wife's opinions about as vital a matter as their future residence' ('A loyalist's journey', 147). However, Mason suggests that economic reasons, not affectionate ones, would have been more important to James. Her letters are cited as an example of women's belief in their own inferiority by Daniel Blake Smith, *Inside the Great House: Planter Family Life in Eighteenth-Century Chesapeake Society* (Ithaca, NY: Cornell University Press, 1980), 161.

[32] Margaret Parker to James Parker, dated 'Norfolk 22d August 1760', PA 8.2, Parker Family Papers, LRO.

[33] Margaret Parker to James Parker, dated 'Norfolk 5th Sepbr 1760', PA 8.3, Parker Family Papers, LRO.

that in future she doubted she would entirely steer a course of compliance to James. She thus called upon James as the good husband to make allowances for his imperfect wife. She called upon his 'good sense' as a man of 'gallantry', as Hume might have phrased it. It is also clear that 'eloquence' and 'persuasion' formed part of the Parker relationship.

Such eloquence and persuasion would remain important for Margaret and James in the post-Revolutionary era. Even a young, newly married Margaret was conversant with conventions and was a clever letter-writer. These epistolary skills came to the fore after the war, when James Parker, exiled from Virginia and living in London, entreated his wife to join him there. Margaret, a native Virginian, was loath to quit what she termed her 'native Country'.[34] At the end of the war, and well into 1783, Margaret Parker hoped that her husband would return to Virginia, a plan James never approved (most of his letters to Margaret from this period are missing). In plain terms, Margaret and James had 'separate interests'. Writing to each other in 1782 and 1783, James and Margaret faced the problem that they both sought different ends. Although Margaret did not want to remain separated from her husband, she none the less did want to stay in Virginia, or at the very least to prolong her time there, before joining James in Britain. Margaret, knowing that she should be 'all submission as good Wives ought to be', never explicitly flouted James's 'Rule'; indeed, she constantly emphasized her affection and her willingness to follow any plan he wanted. Although she 'courteously yielded' to James's plans, she nevertheless stalled in her execution of them. She also tried to persuade James into doing what she wanted. She did so in several ways: she attempted to convince him of the safety and possibility for peace in Virginia; she claimed she was too weak to make the journey to England alone; and she played upon his sympathies at her pain at having to leave her family. In tracing out these various strategies, it is possible to comprehend better how women deployed the coercive language of affection.

Margaret must have felt that part of James's refusal to come to Virginia lay in his fears of the local, patriot population, as she repeatedly reassured him that he would not be so 'insulted' again. In a letter written in 1782–3, Margaret assured James: 'far be it from me [to] wish you to come for me if I thought it would subject you to a single insult I have not heard of any body being ill treated here for many months & by the articles of peace you have a right to come.'[35] In a letter from July 1783, Margaret maintained: 'the violence of our countrymen begins to subside and I dare say they will be quite cool some time hence I would not have had any friend of mine to have ventured here when the news of the peace first reached us, & for

---

[34] Margaret Parker to James Parker, dated 'Eastwood 27th July 1783', PA 8.26, Parker Family Papers, LRO.

[35] Margaret Parker to James Parker, undated (1782–3?), PA 5.12, Parker Family Papers, LRO.

sometime after for my own part I should be ungrateful if I did not confess that I have been treated with great respect by every body & friendship by many.'[36] In another letter from that same month, Margaret attempted to persuade James that the political climate was changing, appealing to his class prejudices: 'I would bear any mortification on earth better then seeing you insulted especially by a set not worthy to be your Serv[an]ts however I hope that will not be the case. We certainly have many clever & good men among us who I hope will get the power into their hands when things come to be a little more settled.'[37] Margaret was not especially successful in convincing her husband of the friendliness of Virginians. Her husband, faced with angry mobs, held as a prisoner of war for years, and soldier in the losing British cause, was deeply bitter about Virginians.[38] None the less, Margaret certainly tried to convey that he had nothing to fear from them.

Margaret's second strategy to woo James back to Virginia was to convey how arduous it would be for her to make the transatlantic journey to England: 'I do not know how I shall support my Self in such an undertaking without some new friend to comfort me you know how sick I have always been in the water & indeed except in the management of family affairs I am a very helpless creature.' While Margaret here sought to exploit her feminine 'helplessness', she could not quite bring herself to do so. After all, she had spent the last eight years on her own, living with her widowed sister, and taking care of herself and her children. She had demonstrated that she was far from helpless. Rather, she contended, in a Hutchesonian way, that she could manage 'family affairs'. Still, she relied on a fiction of feminine weakness in other areas. She carefully professed her affection for James: 'there is nothing on earth I so earnestly desire as to meet with you again I would be contented to settle in any part of the world with you, if I could have you to conduct me.' Margaret was fearful lest James accuse her of not being a 'good wife': 'I hope my Dear that you will not think me wanting in duty or affection that I have not yet determined whether I shall leave the Country till I hear from you again.' Knowing that her husband was against the idea of their son, Pate, accompanying her from Virginia to England, she declared: 'if I could have

[36] Margaret Parker to James Parker, dated 'Eastwood 9th July 1783', PA 8.25, Parker Family Papers, LRO.

[37] Margaret Parker to James Parker, dated 'Eastwood 27th July 1783', PA 8.26, Parker Family Papers, LRO.

[38] Even before the Revolutionary War had begun, furious mobs had confronted James when he had had the audacity to inoculate his family against smallpox. Mason argues that this moment of ethnic and class tension put James on the road to Loyalism. See Mason, 'A loyalist's journey', *passim*. Certainly, James's wartime experiences, serving in a Loyalist regiment, held as a prisoner of war, and separated from his family for years, embittered him against the new American order, and Virginians in particular. Given the tenor of James's later pronouncements, that Virginians were 'the most unprincipalled villains on earth', it seems unlikely that James would ever have returned to Virginia. James Parker to Patrick Parker (copy), dated 'Portglasgow 20 Octr. 1787', PA 11.162, Parker Family Papers, LRO.

my Dear Pate to go with me, I would go immediately but that I fear would be a disadvantage to him., he is much distress'd at the thoughts of my going without a friend.'[39] In this last statement, Margaret upheld her son Pate as a good family member, who was worried by the idea of her going alone. Margaret thus insinuated that James should also be 'much distress'd' by this notion. In 1784, she continued to prevaricate about the challenges of travel: 'I have determin'd to see you this summer if I can get a good ship . . . I do not think I shall ever get to you alive if I attempt to go by my self, you know how much I have always suffered on the water.'[40] Again Margaret crafted stories about her seasickness and her frailty.

Finally, Margaret's third strategy was to remind James of the anguish of parting from her family and her native land. Here Margaret hoped to use sympathetic sway to make James feel her agony, and so win him over to the idea of resettling in Virginia. As part of this project, Margaret reminded James of her unending sympathy for *him*: 'It is impossible my Dear for me to discribe [*sic*] what I have felt for your Situation these several years past. my affection for you (rather increas'd if possible by misfortunes) may have made me perhaps imagine your sufferings greater than they were in reality.'[41] Again, Margaret emphasized that she was not lacking in duty or affection and would agree to any plan James proposed. None the less, she continually reminded him of the pain of separating from her American family:

I am exceedingly anxious to know what plan you have thought off for geting settled with your family again, yet I dread to know it as I greatly fear it cannot be here, and the joy I shall have in meeting you again my beloved friend will be greatly damped if it must be at the expense of parting with all my Dear and valuable friends here . . . but I will hope for the best perhaps we may be so happy as to live together yet.[42]

Here Margaret, while deferring to her husband, nevertheless hinted strongly what her own preference was: that James return to Virginia and live with her and her family. While Margaret ostensibly left to James the power to make the 'plan' for their future, she still conveyed her own opinion. She also placed two different ties of friendship against each other. Of course a 'good wife' placed her dearest friend, her husband, above all other ties, and so Margaret noted that she did just that. But she wanted her dearest friend to know that other loyalties were also important to her and that other friends (by which she meant family primarily) had a claim on her presence.

[39] Margaret Parker to James Parker, undated (1782–3?), PA 5.12, Parker Family Papers, LRO.

[40] Margaret Parker to James Parker, undated but labelled 'recd 22nd July 1784 [*sic* 1783] from Mrs Parker', PA 8.36, Parker Family Papers, LRO.

[41] Margaret Parker to James Parker, dated 'Eastwood 9th July 1783', PA 8.25, Parker Family Papers, LRO.

[42] Margaret Parker to James Parker, dated 'Eastwood 9th July 1783', PA 8.25, Parker Family Papers, LRO.

Margaret pursued a similar theme in another 1783 letter, in which she again reminded James of the misery she would undergo on quitting her native land and her family:

I observe my Dear that you have given me a hint to prepare for leaving my native Country & friends, twas what I feard must be the case . . . tho I would not hesitate one moment to go with you my Dearest friend to any place on earth, yet I cannot think of parting forever with my Dear & valuable friends on this side the atlantick. without many a heartfelt sigh. they have all been so kind & attentive to me in my distress.[43]

She again stressed her submission and affection. Terming James her 'Dearest friend' in the best Hutchesonian tradition, she still continued by expressing her sorrow at being forced to leave Virginia. Again, she was willing to craft a narrative in which her loyalty to her 'Dearest friend' would surmount her loyalties to her 'Dear & valuable friends', even as she stalled in leaving her friends in Virginia. In a standard claim, Margaret asserted that she would willingly go anywhere on earth with her husband; this claim made her a good wife. But in fact she obviously felt pulled by other ties, to her family of birth and to her native land, and she made sure that James knew that she was conflicted. If James refused to come to Virginia, Margaret was not likely to let him forget the anguish his decision was causing her and her family. She reminded him of his duties as a good husband to sympathize with her emotions.

Indeed, James was not unsympathetic to Margaret's laments at leaving her family, but equally he was not blind to the fact that Margaret was coercive in her use of feeling. In a February 1784 letter, James responded to Margaret's woe: 'I cannot think of a longer seperation. what gives me the most sensible concern is to part with Mrs Aitchison [Margaret's sister in Virginia] living beside her would have been a comfort & satisfaction to me but we shall be deprived . . . However you'll always hold in remembrance that this is not any Act of mine, nor is it in My power to prevent it.'[44] James commiserated with Margaret, but he reminded her that war and loss had removed any 'power' he might have had to prevent it. James was not pleased to force his wife into a decision she abhorred, but equally he felt he had no other choice. In following his political loyalties, and losing, he had for-feited his usual powers as head of the household. Even as a Loyalist who lacked some power, though, as a husband he still retained authority over Margaret. In a later letter, James repeated his avowals of sympathy: 'I really sympathize with you on this trying scene of leaving your Country and all

[43] Margaret Parker to James Parker, dated 'Eastwood 27th July 1783', PA 8.26, Parker Family Papers, LRO.
[44] James Parker to Margaret Parker, dated 'London 5th Feb. 1784', PA 8.30, Parker Family Papers, LRO.

our friends some of whom stand the first in My esteem and affection and with whom I allways wished and hoped to finish my life. Providence has ordered it otherwise & we must submit.'[45] Such a claim was a bit disingenuous. While James had had to submit to Providence and to the new political regimes, Margaret had to submit to James and join him in what was to her a foreign land. Élite white men may not have had the powers they wanted, and certainly Loyalist men lost much by the war. But they retained powers of household authority, even when separated from their actual household.

The tension between coercion and love, between rule and gallantry, then, informed this transatlantic correspondence. This marriage was a loving one, not one ending in separation or divorce. Spouses were 'dearest friends', and the notion of marriage as friendship was fundamental. Yet it is possible here to discern what Hume feared: the husband and the wife 'driving some separate end or project'. Margaret deployed the language of sympathy to achieve ends that were at odds with those of her husband. In rendering herself a sentimental heroine, she played upon her husband's pity. Margaret was a mother, yet rarely did she mention the children. In fact, she invoked her position as a wife far more often than her position as a mother. She placed her love for her husband above all else, and so found a certain power in crafting herself as a good wife. In claiming that her whole happiness lay with her husband, she placed responsibility with James to act as a good husband. The idiom of romance and marital love gave her a way to call upon her husband and make demands, thus gaining a kind of sympathetic sway.

Such sway, however, was limited. Husbands, too, deployed these newer vocabularies, and ultimately retained final authority in these marriages. Like his wife, James invoked the coercive language of affection. Unwilling to accept that he himself had caused the suffering of his wife, he disavowed that responsibility. He defended his actions by averring that he had no choice, either. He called upon Margaret to feel for his plight, offering sympathy even as he demanded it in return. James privileged his affection and his feelings for Margaret. Husbands did sympathize with their wives, even as they presumed that wives ultimately could and should submit. Lessons of mastery were changing in the eighteenth century. Men were expected less to be masters and rulers of a 'little commonwealth' than to be 'friends, lovers, and patrons', demonstrating affection, generosity, and gallantry. In fact, according to Hutcheson, to beat a wife into submission was not only 'tyrannical' but actually 'unmanly', a shift from earlier understandings in which a good man corrected his subordinates as necessary

---

[45] James Parker to Margaret Parker, dated 'London 5th March 1784', PA 8.31, Parker Family Papers, LRO. James's statement here directly contradicts Alan Karras's claim that James Parker was a key 'sojourner', thus representing a group whose 'ultimate goal of returning home' was central to their identity (*Sojourners*, 5). James himself claimed he had wanted live out his life in Virginia.

(*System*, 165). The good husband relied on respect in his marital relations. James Parker had learned these new lessons. He sought to sympathize with his dear wife. But this move did not undermine his authority. Rather, in demonstrating their character as polite men and indeed patrons, such men's 'gallantry' revealed this authority.

If these newer vocabularies gave women greater leverage in their negotiations, it nevertheless also demanded that they achieve 'unity' with their husbands. Such a view reinforced the notion that women lacked separate understandings, and could safely be subsumed under their husband's identity and choices. To join in 'the greatest fondness and sympathy' was to become one person, and, as was traditional, that one was the husband. As we have seen, women did not always want to follow their husbands in every respect, and so they were left, as Margaret Parker was, to use a language of affection that might sway their husbands. However, it might not, and if it did not, they had little recourse. In fact, Margaret eventually capitulated and went to London in 1784, reunited with her husband but separated from her family and native land for the rest of her days. And hers was one of the happier stories. For couples with serious marital disagreement, Hume (and many others) would have never allowed divorce. It is difficult not to agree with Hume that husbands' sympathy and gallantry served only to 'discover' their authority in different ways. It certainly constrained the growth of a sense of women, and especially wives, as beings capable of independent thought and action, even as it allowed them other sorts of authority within household negotiations.

On the face of it, the languages exchanged between husbands and wives placed each spouse on equal footing, in a happy partnership and with perfect equality of sentiment. Similarly, thinkers like Hutcheson and Hume had stressed the amiable unity and perfect equality of ideal marriages. Yet in their formulation, as we have seen, and as Okin and Bloch have also stressed, continued assumptions about male superiority lurked behind the fictions of equality. So too here, these languages of love conceal the fact that husbands, for all their claims of powerlessness, still retained more authority than their wives to make decisions and lives for themselves. They borrowed languages from social theory that stressed sympathy, but these languages cloaked the machinations of authority, of a very real and significant legal and financial disparity between husbands and wives. In the end, equivalent claims of powerlessness did not carry equal weight. If husbands had to submit to Providence, wives still had to submit not only to Providence but also to their husbands. These newer ideals and languages could give women in certain situations some greater leverage, but it was a very limited leverage indeed.

The question then becomes a slightly different one: why were men so eager to revel in gallantry and to stress amiable equality over masculine authority? James Parker, like Hutcheson and Hume, stressed the vocabulary of sentiment even as assumptions about masculine authority continued. For James, citing his sympathy gave him a way to negotiate with his wife when she was stalling in the execution of his plans for them. But in following the story of James and Margaret, it is possible to discern more clearly the contradictions inherent in the philosophies. That is, equality sat uneasily with submission, and we have seen how James and Margaret coped. But having looked at the Parkers, we then have to return to the philosophers and ask: why were Hutcheson and Hume so eager to theorize equality and the end of tyranny when legal situations quite clearly left power in the hands of men? In part, these claims remind us that the men who spun the theories did not exist outside of the cultures that surrounded them. After all, while these theorists may have influenced others with their explicit musings on marriage, gender, and authority, musings that often stayed implicit in actual marriages, they were also themselves influenced by larger cultural norms. Shifting notions of politeness for both men and women were major features of post-Restoration élite British culture, and thus an emphasis on gallantry might be seen as an extension of this project.[46] In part, the increasing emphasis on the refining influences of mixed company and of women in particular might have served to shift notions of ideal masculinity.

At the same time, an emphasis on male gallantry was a wonderfully self-congratulatory notion, for individuals and for societies. James Parker could disavow responsibility for making political choices that ultimately took his wife away from her family and homeland by citing Providence and emphasizing his own sympathy. John Adams could reply to his wife's requests to 'remember the ladies' in the new American republic with self-satisfied jokes about the fact that men were really the true subjects who 'have only the Name of Masters'.[47] Okin notes of Jean Jacques Rousseau that this sentimental ideal allowed him to argue that 'women do not *need* equality either within or outside of their domestic havens'.[48] In much the same way, Britons (and British-Americans) could console themselves that their cultures were better than those in which polygamy flourished, or in which men treated women with 'tyranny'. These men were not 'Oriental despots' or 'lawless bashaws'.[49] Such an emphasis, on the contrast between what Hume termed 'barbarous nations' and 'a polite people', thus served to allow élite Britons and British-Americans to bask in their own refinement and superiority, one that distinguished them both from the 'lower orders' and from allegedly

---

[46] See Lawrence E. Klein, *Shaftesbury and the Culture of Politeness: Moral Discourse and Cultural Politics in Early Eighteenth-Century England* (Cambridge: Cambridge University Press, 1994); John Brewer, *The Pleasures of the Imagination: English Culture in the Eighteenth Century* (London: HarperCollins, 1997); and Philip Carter, *Men and the Emergence of Polite Society, Britain, 1660–1800* (Harlow, Essex: Longman, 2001).

[47] John Adams to Abigail Adams, as quoted in Crane, 'Political dialogue', 756.

[48] Okin, 'Women and the making of the sentimental family', 76.

[49] See Pearsall, ' "The late flagrant instance" ', 553.

inferior nations (*Essays*, 133). The 'bonds of love and friendship' were all that were required in a culture that did not confine women to chains.

Except, of course, that such a society did confine women to chains, most notably on the slave ships and the plantations that provided a solid foundation for the British Empire's spectacular eighteenth-century economic expansion. Separating themselves from the colonies in which slavery flourished allowed Hutcheson and Hume to offer reassurance to themselves and others that Britons, at least, were untouched by the contamination of the colonial and imperial project in which Britain was involved. James and Margaret, too, commended themselves as being good masters of slaves, and not 'cruel' ones who treated slaves with unkindness. Both of them referred to their slaves as 'poor creatures' and worried that in selling them off after the war, the slaves would end up in the hands of cruel masters who would act like 'Tyrants'.[50] They distinguished themselves from such masters, even as they forcibly moved some slaves overseas and sold others. These self-serving notions suggest the ways in which individuals, whether philosophers or not, crafted idealized visions of household relations even when evidence declared otherwise. Placing individual stories alongside philosophical theories makes abundantly clear what the limitations of those theories were. It also highlights the glaring contradictions between the theories and vocabularies of politeness and sympathy and the hard reality of eighteenth-century household relations. When 'the Human Heart is laid open', it is a richer, if more incoherent, process than the 'the dry Maxims of Philosophy' would have us believe.

REFERENCES

Manuscript Sources

Parker Family Papers: Liverpool Libraries and Record Office, 920 PAR I–IV (formerly PA).

Printed Primary Sources

The Complete Letter-Writer, 4th edn. (London: Stanley Crowder and Co. and Henry Woodgate, 1757).
Hume, David, *Enquiries Concerning Human Understanding and Concerning the Principles of Morals* (1777), ed. L. A. Selby-Bigge, 3rd edn., rev. P. H. Nidditch (Oxford: Clarendon Press, 1975).
—— 'Essay on love and marriage', *The Boston Magazine*, 1 (Nov. 1783): 15–18.

---

[50] Margaret Parker to James Parker, dated 'Eastwood 27th July 1783', PA 8.26, and James Parker to Margaret Parker, dated 'London 5th Feb. 1784', PA 8.30, Parker Family Papers, LRO.

—— *Essays Moral, Political, and Literary*, ed. Eugene F. Miller, rev. edn. (Indianapolis: Liberty Fund, 1987).

Hutcheson, Francis, *An Essay on the Nature and Conduct of the Passions and Affections with Illustrations on the Moral Sense* (1742), ed. Paul McReynolds, 3rd edn. (Gainesville, Fla.: Scholars' Facsimiles & Reprints, 1969).

—— *A System of Moral Philosophy* (1755), ed. Bernhard Fabian, facsimile edn. (Hildesheim: Georg Olms Verlag, 1990).

Locke, John, *Two Treatises of Government*, ed. Peter Laslett (Cambridge: Cambridge University Press, 1988).

Secondary Sources

Baier, Annette C., 'Hume on women's complexion', in Peter Jones (ed.), *The 'Science of Man' in the Scottish Enlightenment; Hume, Reid, and their Contemporaries* (Edinburgh: Edinburgh University Press, 1989), 33–53.

Bailey, Joanne, *Unquiet Lives: Marriage and Marriage Breakdown in England, 1660–1800* (Cambridge: Cambridge University Press, 2003).

Barker-Benfield, G. J., *The Culture of Sensibility: Sex and Society in Eighteenth-Century England* (Chicago: University of Chicago Press, 1992).

Basch, Norma, *Framing American Divorce: From the Revolutionary Generation to the Victorians* (Berkeley: University of California Press, 1999).

Bloch, Ruth H., 'Changing conceptions of sexuality and romance in eighteenth-century America', *William and Mary Quarterly*, 60 (2003): 13–42.

Brewer, John, *The Pleasures of the Imagination: English Culture in the Eighteenth Century* (London: HarperCollins, 1997).

Carter, Philip, *Men and the Emergence of Polite Society, Britain, 1660–1800* (Harlow, Essex: Longman, 2001).

Cott, Nancy F., *Public Vows: A History of Marriage and the Nation* (Cambridge, Mass.: Harvard University Press, 2000).

Crane, Elaine Forman, *Ebb Tide in New England: Women, Seaports, and Social Change, 1630–1800* (Boston: Northeastern University Press, 1998).

—— 'Political dialogue and the spring of Abigail's discontent', *William and Mary Quarterly*, 56 (1999): 745–74.

Dayton, Cornelia Hughes, *Women before the Bar: Gender, Law, & Society in Connecticut, 1639–1789* (Chapel Hill, NC: University of North Carolina Press, 1995).

Ferguson, Robert A., *American Enlightenment, 1750–1820* (Cambridge, Mass.: Harvard University Press, 1997).

Fliegelman, Jay, *Prodigals and Pilgrims: The American Revolution against Patriarchal Authority, 1750–1800* (Cambridge: Cambridge University Press, 1982).

Gillis, John R., *For Better, For Worse: British Marriages, 1600 to the Present* (Oxford: Oxford University Press, 1985).

Gobetti, Daniela, *Private and Public: Individuals, Households, and Body Politic in Locke and Hutcheson* (London: Routledge, 1992).

Hast, A., *Loyalism in Revolutionary Virginia: The Norfolk Area and the Eastern Shore* (Ann Arbor: UMI Research Press, 1982).

Jacobson, Anne Jaap, (ed.), *Feminist Interpretations of David Hume* (University Park, Pa.: Pennsylvania State University Press, 2000).

Karras, Alan L., *Sojourners in the Sun: Scottish Migrants in Jamaica and the Chesapeake, 1740–1800* (Ithaca, NY: Cornell University Press, 1992).

Klein, Lawrence E., *Shaftesbury and the Culture of Politeness: Moral Discourse and Cultural Politics in Early Eighteenth-Century England* (Cambridge: Cambridge University Press, 1994).

Knott, Sarah, 'A cultural history of sensibility in the era of the American Revolution' (D.Phil. thesis, Oxford, 1999).

Lewis, Jan, 'The republican wife: virtue and seduction in the early Republic', *William and Mary Quarterly*, 44 (1987): 689–721.

—— ' "Of every age sex & condition": the representation of women in the Constitution', *Journal of the Early Republic*, 15 (1995): 359–87.

Macfarlane, Alan, *Marriage and Love in England: Modes of Reproduction, 1300–1840* (Oxford: Oxford University Press, 1986).

Mason, Keith, 'A Loyalist's journey: James Parker's response to the revolutionary crisis', *Virginia Magazine of History and Biography*, 102 (1994): 139–66.

McCoy, Drew R., *The Elusive Republic: Political Economy in Jeffersonian America* (Chapel Hill, NC: University of North Carolina Press for the Institute of Early American History and Culture, 1980).

Morgan, Philip D., *Slave Counterpoint: Black Culture in the Eighteenth-Century Chesapeake and Lowcountry* (Chapel Hill, NC: University of North Carolina Press for the Omohundro Institute of Early American History and Culture, 1998).

Okin, Susan Moller, 'Women and the making of the sentimental family', *Philosophy and Public Affairs*, 11 (1982): 65–88.

Outhwaite, R. B. (ed.), *Marriage and Society: Studies in the Social History of Marriage* (New York: St Martin's Press, 1982).

Pearsall, Sarah M. S., ' "After all these revolutions": epistolary identities in an Atlantic world, 1760–1815', (Ph.D. thesis, Harvard, 2001).

—— ' "The late flagrant instance of depravity in my family": the story of an Anglo-Jamaican cuckold', *William and Mary Quarterly*, 60 (2003): 549–82.

Sapp, Vicki J., 'The philosopher's seduction: Hume and the fair sex', *Philosophy and Literature*, 19 (1995): 1–15.

Sher, Richard B., and Smith, Jeffrey R. (eds.), *Scotland and America in the Age of Enlightenment* (Edinburgh: Edinburgh University Press, 1990).

Smith, Daniel Blake, *Inside the Great House: Planter Family Life in Eighteenth-Century Chesapeake Society* (Ithaca, NY: Cornell University Press, 1980).

Smith, Merril D., *Breaking the Bonds: Marital Discord in Pennsylvania, 1730–1830* (New York: New York University Press, 1991).

Spencer, Mark G., 'The circulation of David Hume's works in eighteenth-century America', paper presented at the International Seminar on the History of the Atlantic World, 1500–1800, Harvard University, August 2000.

Stone, Lawrence, *The Family, Sex and Marriage in England, 1500–1800* (New York: Harper & Row, 1977).

—— *Road to Divorce: England, 1530–1987* (Oxford: Oxford University Press, 1990).

—— *Broken Lives: Separation and Divorce in England, 1660–1857* (Oxford: Oxford University Press, 1993).

Wilson, Lisa, *Ye Heart of a Man: The Domestic Life of Men in Colonial New England* (New Haven: Yale University Press, 1999).

Zagarri, Rosemarie, 'Morals, manners, and the republican mother', *American Quarterly*, 44 (1992): 192–215.

—— 'The rights of man and woman in post-revolutionary America', *William and Mary Quarterly*, 55 (1998): 203–30.

Zimmer, Carmeline V., 'Margaret Ellegood Parker: a loyalist merchant's wife', in R. A. Rutyna and P. C. Stewart (eds.), *Virginia in the American Revolution* (Norfolk, Va.: Old Dominion University, 1983), 60–79.

BIBLIOGRAPHY

Note: The following list includes those works contained in the Secondary Source lists of the individual articles that are of general relevance to Hume studies.

Anscombe, G. E. M., 'Hume and Julius Caesar', in *From Parmenides to Wittgenstein: Collected Philosophical Papers* (Oxford: Blackwell, 1981), i. 86–92.

Ashworth, E. J., ' "Do words signify ideas or things?": the scholastic sources of Locke's theory of language', *Journal of the History of Philosophy*, 19 (1981): 299–326.

Ayer, Alfred J., *Hume* (Oxford: Oxford University Press, 1980).

Ayers, Michael, 'Natures and laws from Descartes to Hume', in, G. A. J. Rogers and S. Tomaselli (eds.), *The Philosophical Canon in the 17th and 18th Centuries: Essays in Honour of John W. Yolton* (Rochester, NY: University of Rochester Press, 1996), 83–108.

Bahr, F. A., 'Pierre Bayle en los "Early Memoranda" de Hume', *Revista latinoamericana de filosofia*, 25 (1999): 7–38.

Baier, Annette C., 'Hume on women's complexion', in Peter Jones (ed.), *The 'Science of Man' in the Scottish Enlightenment; Hume, Reid, and their Contemporaries* (Edinburgh: Edinburgh University Press, 1989), 33–53.

—— *A Progress of Sentiments: Reflections on Hume's* Treatise (Cambridge, Mass., and London: Harvard University Press, 1991).

Barfoot, Michael, 'Hume and the culture of science in the early eighteenth century', in M. A. Stewart (ed.), *Studies in the Philosophy of the Scottish Enlightenment* (Oxford: Clarendon Press, 1990), 151–90.

Barker-Benfield, G. J., *The Culture of Sensibility: Sex and Society in Eighteenth-Century England* (Chicago: University of Chicago Press, 1992).

Baroncelli, Flavio, *Un inquietante filosofo perbene: saggio su David Hume* (Florence: La Nuova Italia, 1975).

Beck, Lewis White, 'A Prussian Hume and a Scottish Kant', in *Essays on Kant and Hume* (New Haven: Yale University Press, 1978), 111–29.

Bell, Martin, 'Sceptical doubts concerning Hume's causal realism', in K. Richman and R. Read (eds.), *The New Hume Debate* (London: Routledge, 2000), 122–37.

Berman, David, 'The repressive denials of atheism in Britain in the seventeenth and eighteenth centuries', *Proceedings of the Royal Irish Academy*, 82/9 (1982): 211–45.

—— 'Deism, immortality, and the art of theological lying', in J. A. Leo Lemay (ed.), *Deism, Masonry, and the Enlightenment* (Newark: University of Delaware Press, 1987), 61–78.

—— *A History of Atheism in Britain: From Hobbes to Russell* (London: Croom Helm, 1988).

Bongie, Laurence L., *David Hume: Prophet of the Counter-Revolution*, 2nd edn. (Indianapolis: Liberty Press, 2000).

Botterill, George, 'Hume on liberty and necessity', in P. Millican (ed.), *Reading Hume on Human Understanding* (Oxford: Oxford University Press, 2002), 277–300.

Box, M. A., *The Suasive Art of David Hume* (Princeton: Princeton University Press, 1990).

Brandt, Reinhard, 'The beginnings of Hume's philosophy', in George Morice (ed.), *David Hume: Bicentenary Papers* (Edinburgh: Edinburgh University Press, 1977), 117–27.

Brewer, John, *The Pleasures of the Imagination: English Culture in the Eighteenth Century* (London: HarperCollins, 1997).

Buckle, Stephen, *Hume's Enlightenment Tract: The Unity and Purpose of* An Enquiry Concerning Human Understanding (Oxford: Clarendon Press, 2001).

Burton, John H., *Life and Correspondence of David Hume*, 2 vols. (Edinburgh: William Tait, 1846).

Capaldi, Nicholas, *David Hume: The Newtonian Philosopher* (Boston: Twayne Publishers, 1975).

Carabelli, Giancarlo, *Hume e la retorica dell'ideologia: uno studio dei 'Dialoghi sulla religione naturale'* (Florence: La Nuova Italia, 1975).

Carlyle, Thomas, 'Diderot' (1833), in *Critical and Miscellaneous Essays*, 5 vols. (London: Chapman and Hall, 1899), iii. 177–248.

Carter, Philip, *Men and the Emergence of Polite Society, Britain, 1660–1800* (Harlow, Essex: Longman, 2001).

Clark, Ian D. L., 'The Leslie controversy, 1805', *Records of the Scottish Church History Society*, 14 (1963): 179–97.

—— 'From protest to reaction: the moderate regime in the church of Scotland', in N. T. Phillipson and R. Mitchison (eds.), *Scotland in the Age of Improvement* (Edinburgh: Edinburgh University Press, 1970), pp. 200–24.

Clarke, M. L., *Classical Education in Britain 1500–1900* (Cambridge: Cambridge University Press, 1959).

Connon, Robert W., 'Hume's theory of mental activity', in D. F. Norton, N. Capaldi, and W. L. Robison (eds.), *McGill Hume Studies* (San Diego: Austin Hill Press, 1979), 101–20.

—— and Pollard, M., 'On the authorship of "Hume's" *Abstract*', *Philosophical Quarterly*, 27 (1977): 60–6.

Craig, Cairns, 'T. S. Eliot, I. A. Richards and empiricism's art of memory', *Revue de metaphysique et de monde*, 1 (1998): 113–17.

Craig, Edward J., *The Mind of God and the Works of Man* (Oxford: Clarendon Press, 1987).

Daston, Lorraine, *Classical Probability in the Enlightenment* (Princeton: Princeton University Press, 1988).

Davie, George, *A Passion for Ideas: Essays on the Scottish Enlightenment* (Edinburgh: Polygon, 1994).

Deleuze, Gilles, *Empiricism and Subjectivity: An Essay on Hume's Theory of Human Nature* (1953), trans. C. V. Boundas (New York: Columbia University Press, 1991).

—— *Kant's Critical Philosophy: The Doctrine of the Faculties* (1963), trans. H. Tomlinson and B. Habberjam (London: Athlone, 1984).

—— *Essays Critical and Clinical*, trans. D. W. Smith and M. A. Greco (London and New York: Verso, 1998).

Eagleton, Terry, *The Ideology of Aesthetics* (Oxford: Blackwell, 1990).

Easton, Patricia, (ed.), *Logic and the Workings of the Mind: The Logic of Ideas and Faculty Psychology in Early Modern Philosophy*, North American Kant Society Studies in Philosophy, 5 (Atascadero, Calif.: Ridgeview, 1997).

Echelbarger, Charles, 'Hume and the logicians', in P. Easton (ed.), *Logic and the Workings of the Mind: The Logic of Ideas and Faculty Psychology in Early Modern Philosophy*, North American Kant Society Studies in Philosophy, 5 (Atascadero, Calif.: Ridgeview, 1997), 137–51.

Emerson, Roger, 'The "affair" at Edinburgh and the "project" at Glasgow', in M. A. Stewart and J. P. Wright (eds.), *Hume and Hume's Connexions* (Edinburgh: Edinburgh University Press, 1994), 1–22.

Ferguson, Robert A., *American Enlightenment, 1750–1820* (Cambridge, Mass.: Harvard University Press, 1997).

Fiering, Norman, *Moral Philosophy at Seventeenth-Century Harvard: A Discipline in Transition* (Chapel Hill, NC: University of North Carolina Press, 1981).

Fieser, James, 'Hume's concealed attack on religion and his early critics', *Journal of Philosophical Research*, 20 (1995): 431–49.

Finlay, C. J., 'Enlightenment and the university: philosophy, communication, and education in the early writings of David Hume', *History of Universities*, 16 (2000): 103–34.

Flew, Antony, *Hume's Philosophy of Belief* (London: Routledge, 1961).

Fogelin, Robert J., *Hume's Scepticism in the* Treatise of Human Nature (London: Routledge and Kegan Paul, 1985).

Frasca-Spada, Marina, *Space and Self in Hume's* Treatise (Cambridge: Cambridge University Press, 1998).

—— 'The science and conversation of human nature', W. Clark, J. Golinski and S. Schaffer (eds.), *The Sciences in Enlightened Europe* (Chicago: University of Chicago Press, 2000), 218–45.

—— 'Hume on sense impressions and objects', in M. Heidelberger and D. Stadler (ed.), *History of Philosophy of Science: New Trends and Perspectives*, Vienna Circle Institute Yearbook, 9/2001 (Dordrecht and London: Kluwer Academic Publishers, 2002), 13–24.

—— 'Belief and animal spirits in Hume's *Treatise*', *Eighteenth-Century Thought*, 1 (2003): 151–69.

Garrett, Don, *Cognition and Commitment in Hume's Philosophy* (Oxford: Oxford University Press, 1997).

Gaskin, J. C. A., *Hume's Philosophy of Religion*, 2nd edn. (London: Macmillan Press, 1993).

—— 'Hume on religion', in David F. Norton (ed.), *The Cambridge Companion to Hume* (Cambridge: Cambridge University Press, 1993), 313–44.

Gilardi, Roberto, *Il giovane Hume,* vol. i: *Il 'background' religioso e culturale* (Milan: Vita e Pensiero, 1990).

Gorman, Michael M., 'Hume's theory of belief', *Hume Studies*, 10/1 (1993): 89–101.

Graf, Arturo, *L'anglomania e l'influsso inglese in Italia nel secolo XVIII* (Turin: Ermanno Loescher, 1911).

Grant, Alexander, *The History of the University of Edinburgh*, 2 vols. (London: Longmans, Green, 1884).

Greig, J. Y. T., *David Hume* (London: Cape, 1931).

Grimsley, Ronald, 'D'Alembert and Hume', *Revue de Littérature Comparée*, 35/4 (1961): 583–95.

Hacking, Ian, *The Emergence of Probability* (Cambridge: Cambridge University Press, 1975).

Hearn, Thomas K. Jr., 'General rules in Hume's *Treatise*', *Journal of the History of Philosophy*, 8 (1970): 405–22.

Hilson, J. C., 'Hume: the historian as man of feeling', in J. C. Hilson, M. M. B. Jones, and J. R. Watson (eds.), *Augustan Worlds* (New York: Barnes and Noble, 1978), 205–22.

Huxley, Thomas Henry, *Hume* (London: Macmillan, 1879).

Jacobson, Anne Jaap, (ed.), *Feminist Interpretations of David Hume* (University Park, Pa.: Pennsylvania State University Press, 2000).

Jones, Peter, *Hume's Sentiments: Their Ciceronian and French Context* (Edinburgh: Edinburgh University Press, 1982).

—— (ed.), *The 'Science of Man' in the Scottish Enlightenment: Hume, Reid and their Contemporaries* (Edinburgh: Edinburgh University Press, 1989).

Kail, P. J. E., *Projection and Realism in Hume* (Oxford: Oxford University Press, forthcoming).

Klein, Lawrence E., *Shaftesbury and the Culture of Politeness: Moral Discourse and Cultural Politics in Early Eighteenth-Century England* (Cambridge: Cambridge University Press, 1994).

Kors, Alan Charles, *D'Holbach's Coterie: An Enlightenment in Paris* (Princeton: Princeton University Press, 1976).

Kozanecki, Tadeusz, 'Dawida Hume'a nieznane listy w Zbiorach Muzeum Czartoryskich (Polska)', *Archiwum Historii Filozofii i Mysli Spolcznej*, 9 (1963): 127–41.

Kreimandahl, Lothar, 'Humes frühe religionsphilosophische Interessen im Lichte seiner "Early Memoranda"' *Zeitschrift für philosophische Forschung*, 53 (1999): 553–68.

Laird, John, *Hume's Philosophy of Human Nature* (London: Methuen, 1932).

Law, Alexander, *Education in Edinburgh in the Eighteenth Century* (London: University of London Press, 1965).

Lawrence, Chris, 'The nervous system and society in the Scottish Enlightenment', in B. Barnes and S. Shapin (eds.), *Natural Order: Historical Studies of Scientific Culture* (London: Sage, 1979), 19–39.

Leroy, André-Louis, *David Hume* (Paris: Presses Universitaires de France, 1953).

Livingston, Donald W., 'Anscombe, Hume and Julius Caesar', *Analysis*, 35 (1974): 13–19.

—— *Hume's Philosophy of Common Life* (Chicago and London: University of Chicago Press, 1984).

—— *Philosophical Melancholy and Delirium: Hume's Pathology of Philosophy* (Chicago and London: University of Chicago Press, 1998).

—— and King, James T., (eds.), *Hume: A Re-Evaluation* (New York: Fordham University Press, 1976).

Loeb, Louis E., 'Hume on stability, justification, and unphilosophical probability', *Journal of the History of Philosophy*, 33 (1995): 101–32.

—— 'Causal inference, associationism, and scepticism in Part III of Book I of Hume's *Treatise*', in P. Easton, (ed.), *Logic and the Workings of the Mind: The Logic of Ideas and Faculty Psychology in Early Modern Philosophy*, North American Kant Society Studies in Philosophy, 5 (Atascadero, Calif.: Ridgeview, 1997), 283–306.

—— *Stability and Justification in Hume's* Treatise (Oxford: Oxford University Press, 2002).

LoLordo, Antonia, 'Probability and skepticism about reason in Hume's *Treatise*', *British Journal for the History of Philosophy*, 8 (2000): 419–46.

Mackie, John L., *The Miracle of Theism* (Oxford: Oxford University Press, 1982).

Maia Neto, J. R., 'Hume and Pascal: Pyrrhonism vs. nature', *Hume Studies*, 18 (1991): 41–9.

Manning, Susan, *The Puritan-Provincial Vision: Scottish and American Literature in the Nineteenth Century* (Cambridge: Cambridge University Press, 1990).

Martin, Marie, 'The rational warrant for Hume's general rules', *Journal of the History of Philosophy*, 31 (1993): 245–57.

Mazza, Emilio, 'La mamma di Hume: interpretazioni di un detto apocrifo', in *Il mestiere di studiare e insegnare filosofia: saggi in onore di Franco Alessio* (Milan: Wise, 2000), 143–52.

—— '"So easy and light": paganesimo e scetticismo nella *Natural History of Religion*', in L. Turco (ed.), *Filosofia, scienza e politica nel Settecento britannico* (Padua: Il Poligrafo, 2003), 189–209.

McCracken, Charles, *Malebranche and British Philosophy* (Oxford: Clarendon Press, 1983).

McIntyre, Jane, 'Hume's passions: direct and indirect', *Hume Studies*, 26/1 (2000): 77–86.

Metz, Rudolf, 'Les Amitiés françaises de Hume et le mouvement des idées', *Revue de littérature comparée*, 9/4 (1929): 644–713.

Michael, Emily, 'Frances Hutcheson's *Logicae compendium* and the Glasgow school of logic', in P. Easton (ed.), *Logic and the Workings of the Mind: The Logic of Ideas and Faculty Psychology in Early Modern Philosophy*, North American Kant Society Studies in Philosophy, 5 (Atascadero, Calif.: Ridgeview, 1997), 83–96.

Michael, Frederick S., 'Why logic became epistemology: Gassendi, Port Royal and the reformation in logic', in P. Easton (ed.), *Logic and the Workings of the Mind: The Logic of Ideas and Faculty Psychology in Early Modern Philosophy*, North American Kant Society Studies in Philosophy, 5 (Atascadero, Calif.: Ridgeview, 1997), 1–20.

Miller, Thomas, *The Formation of College English: Rhetoric and Belles Lettres in the British Cultural Provinces* (Pittsburgh: University of Pittsburgh Press, 1997.)

Milton, J. R., 'Induction before Hume', *British Journal for the Philosophy of Science*, 38 (1987): 49–74.

Moore, James, 'Hume and Hutcheson', in M. A. Stewart and John P. Wright (eds.), *Hume and Hume's Connexions*: (Edinburgh: Edinburgh University Press, 1994), 23–57.

Moore, James, 'Hutcheson's theodicy: the argument and the contexts of *A System of Moral Philosophy*', in P. Wood (ed.), *The Scottish Enlightenment: Essays in Reinterpretation* (Rochester, NY: University of Rochester Press, 2000), 239–66.

Mossner, Ernest C., 'The continental reception of Hume's *Treatise*, 1739–1741', *Mind*, 45 (1947): 31–43.

—— 'Hume's early memoranda, 1729–1740: the complete text', *Journal of the History of Ideas*, 9 (1948): 492–518.

—— 'The first answer to Hume's *Treatise*: an unnoticed item of 1740', *Journal of the History of Ideas*, 12 (1951): 291–4.

—— 'Hume and the French men of letters', *Revue Internationale de Philosophie*, 6 (1952): 221–35.

—— 'Hume at La Flèche, 1735: an unpublished letter', *University of Texas Studies in English*, 37 (1958): 30–3.

—— *The Life of David Hume* (Edinburgh: Nelson, 1954), 2nd edn., (Oxford: Clarendon Press, 1980).

Mounce, H. O., *Hume's Naturalism* (London and New York: Routledge, 1999).

Murphy, R. T., *Hume and Husserl: Towards Radical Subjectivism* (The Hague: Martinus Nijoff, 1980).

Norton, David Fate, *David Hume: Common-Sense Moralist, Sceptical Metaphysician* (Princeton: Princeton University Press, 1982).

—— 'An introduction to Hume's thought', in David Fate Norton (ed.), *The Cambridge Companion to Hume* (Cambridge: Cambridge University Press, 1993), 1–32.

—— and Norton, Mary, *The David Hume Library* (Edinburgh: Edinburgh Bibliographical Society, 1996).

Noxon, James, *Hume's Philosophical Development: A Study of his Methods* (Oxford: Clarendon Press, 1973).

Osler, Margaret J., 'John Locke and the changing ideal of scientific knowledge', *Journal of the History of Ideas*, 31 (1970): 3–16.

Owen, David, 'Hume's doubts about probable reasoning: was Locke the target?', in M. A. Stewart and J. P. Wright (eds.), *Hume and Hume's Connexions*, (Edinburgh: Edinburgh University Press, 1994), 140–59.

—— 'Philosophy and the good life: Hume's defence of probable reasoning', *Dialogue*, 35 (1996): 485–503.

—— *Hume's Reason* (Oxford: Oxford University Press, 1999).

Palter, Robert, 'Hume and prejudice', *Hume Studies*, 21 (1995): 3–23.

Parusnikova, Zuzana, 'Hume and post-modernism', *Hume Studies*, 19/2 (1993): 1–17.

Passmore, John A., *Hume's Intentions* (Cambridge: Cambridge University Press, 1952); rev. edn. (London: Duckworth, 1968).

—— 'Descartes, the British empiricists and formal logic', *Philosophical Review*, 62 (1953): 545–53.

Pears, David F., (ed.), *David Hume: A Symposium* (London: Macmillan, 1963).

Penelhum, Terence, *Hume* (London: Macmillan, 1975).

—— *David Hume: An Introduction to his Philosophical System* (West Lafayette, Ind.: Purdue University Press, 1992).

—— *Themes in Hume: The Self, the Will, Religion* (Oxford: Clarendon Press, 2000).

Phillipson, Nicholas, *Hume* (London: Weidenfeld and Nicolson, 1989).

Pompa, Leon, *Human Nature and Historical Knowledge* (Cambridge: Cambridge University Press, 1990).

Popkin, Richard H., 'So, Hume did read Berkeley', *Journal of Philosophy*, 61 (1964): 773–8.

—— *The High Road to Pyrrhonism*, ed. R. A. Watson and J. E. Force (San Diego: Austin Hill Press, 1980).

Rivers, Isabel, 'Shaftesburian enthusiasm and the evangelical revival', in J. Garnett and C. Matthew (eds.), *Revival and Religion since 1700: Essays for John Walsh*, (London: Hambledon, 1993), 21–39.

—— *Reason, Grace and Sentiment: A Study of the Language of Religion and Ethics in England 1660–1780*, 2 vols. (Cambridge: Cambridge University Press, 1991–2000).

Rousseau, G. S., 'Nerves, spirits, and fibres: towards defining the origins of sensibility', *Blue Guitar*, 2 (1976): 125–53.

Russell, Paul, 'Hume's *Treatise* and Hobbes's *The Elements of Law*', *Journal of the History of Ideas*, 46 (1993): 51–63.

Salmon, C. V., 'The central problem of David Hume's philosophy: an essay toward a phenomenological interpretation of the First Book of the *Treatise of Human Nature*', *Jahrbuch für Philosophie und phänomenologische Forschung*, 10 (1929): 299–449.

Sapp, Vicki J., 'The philosopher's seduction: Hume and the fair sex', *Philosophy and Literature*, 19 (1995): 1–15.

Schuurman, Paul, 'Locke's logic of ideas in context: content and structure', *British Journal for the History of Philosophy*, 9 (2001): 439–66.

—— 'The empiricist logic of ideas of Jean le Clerc', in Wiep van Bunge (ed.), *The Early Enlightenment in the Dutch Republic, 1650–1750* (Leiden: Brill, 2003), 137–53.

Scott, William Robert, *Francis Hutcheson: His Life, Teaching, and Position in the History of Philosophy* (Cambridge: Cambridge University Press, 1900).

Sher, Richard B., *Church and University in the Scottish Enlightenment: The Moderate Literati of Edinburgh* (Edinburgh: Edinburgh University Press, 1985).

—— 'Professors of virtue: the social history of the Edinburgh moral philosophy chair in the eighteenth century', in M. A. Stewart (ed.), *Studies in the Philosophy of the Scottish Enlightenment* (Oxford: Clarendon Press, 1990), 87–126.

—— and Smith, Jeffrey R., (eds.), *Scotland and America in the Age of Enlightenment* (Edinburgh: Edinburgh University Press, 1990).

Siebert, Donald T., *The Moral Animus of David Hume* (London and Toronto: Associated University Presses, 1990).

Smith, Norman Kemp, *The Philosophy of David Hume* (London: Macmillan, 1941).

Spencer, Mark G., 'The circulation of David Hume's works in eighteenth-century America', paper presented at the International Seminar on the History of the Atlantic World, 1500–1800, Harvard University, August 2000.

Stewart, M. A., 'The origins of the Scottish Greek chairs', in Elizabeth M. Craik (ed.), *'Owls to Athens': Essays on Classical Subjects Presented to Sir Kenneth Dover* (Oxford: Clarendon Press, 1990), 391–400.

Stewart, M. A., 'The Stoic legacy in the early Scottish Enlightenment', in Margaret J. Osler (ed.), *Atoms, 'Pneuma', and Tranquillity* (Cambridge: Cambridge University Press, 1991), 273–96.

—— 'An early fragment on evil', in M. A. Stewart and J. P. Wright (eds.), *Hume and Hume's Connexions* (Edinburgh: Edinburgh University Press, 1994), 160–70.

—— 'Hume's historical view of miracles', in M. A. Stewart and J. P. Wright (eds.), *Hume and Hume's Connexions*, (Edinburgh: Edinburgh University Press, 1994), 171–200.

—— *The Kirk and the Infidel* (Lancaster: Lancaster University, 1995).

—— 'The dating of Hume's manuscripts', in P. Wood (ed.), *The Scottish Enlightenment: Essays in Reinterpretation* (Rochester, NY: University of Rochester Press, 2000), 267–314.

—— 'Two species of philosophy: the historical significance of the first *Enquiry*', in P. Millican (ed.), *Reading Hume on Human Understanding* (Oxford: Clarendon Press, 2001), 67–95.

—— 'Religion and rational theology', in A. Broadie (ed.), *The Cambridge Companion to the Scottish Enlightenment* (Cambridge: Cambridge University Press, 2003), 31–59.

—— (ed.), *Studies in the Philosophy of the Scottish Enlightenment* (Oxford: Clarendon Press, 1990).

Strachey, Lytton, 'Hume', in *Portraits in Miniature and Other Essays* (London: Chatto and Windus, 1931), 141–53.

Walsh, W. H., 'Hume's concept of truth', in G. Vesey (ed.), *Reason and Reality*, Royal Institute of Philosophy Lectures, 5, 1970–1971 (London: Macmillan, 1972), 99–116.

Wright, John P., *The Sceptical Realism of David Hume* (Manchester: Manchester University Press, 1983).

—— 'Dr George Cheyne, Chevalier Ramsay, and Hume's letter to a physician', *Hume Studies*, 29/1 (2003): 125–41.

Yolton, John, *Perceptual Acquaintance from Descartes to Reid* (Oxford: Basil Blackwell, 1984).

Zabeeh, Farhang, *Hume, Precursor of Modern Empiricism: An Analysis of his Opinions on Meaning, Metaphysics, Logic and Mathematics*, 2nd edn. (The Hague: Martinus Nijoff, 1973).

INDEX OF NAMES